RESEARCH METHODOLOGY
Methods and Techniques

RESEARCH METHODOLOGY

METHODS AND TECHNIQUES

DR. D.R. KAPOOR
Ms. PUJA SAIGAL

Foreword by

PROF. B.K. PASSI
UNESCO Chair
Former NCTE Vice Chairperson

REGAL

REGAL PUBLICATIONS
New Delhi - 110 027

RESEARCH METHODOLOGY
Methods and Techniques

ISBN 978-81-8484-217-3

REPRINT : 2019

Typeset by
RAHUL COMPOSERS
New Highway Apartments, Lakshmi Niwas
760, Pocket-D, Lok Nayak Puram, New Delhi - 110 041

Printed in India at
MAYUR ENTERPRISES
WZ Plot No. 3, Gujjar Market, Tihar Village, New Delhi - 110 018

Published by
REGAL PUBLICATIONS
F-159, Rajouri Garden, New Delhi - 110 027 • Phone : 45546396
E-mail : regalbookspub@yahoo.com

Contents

UNIT III

METHODOLOGY

UNIT IV

METHODS

Foreword

Over last few decades, research in different disciplines of knowledge has undergone various processes and phases of change. This has led to the emergence of various research approaches which are shaped by different research paradigms. The various research paradigms have different criteria for epistemology, ontology and reality which have influenced research methods and methodology. Moreover, the introduction of technological innovations such as, microelectronics; computers and internet, websites, research engines, research-gate, and new soft-wares, has made possible for the researchers in India to collaborate globally and contribute more effectively towards research activities.

A scholar, who is well versed with research methods and techniques, could generate new knowledge, new theory, innovative practice, and new model for the benefit of learning communities. It behooves on scholar to be methodical and use appropriate methods and techniques in order to find answers to his questions or and confirm or disconfirm his hypothesis. He must have great concern for the validity of argument, and the soundness of evidence. Nonetheless, a scholar should acquire practical research skills and techniques through interaction with experts, peers and exploring other sources of knowledge.

Authors have made a sincere, exhaustive and intelligent attempt to elucidate the practical aspects of research. This book deals with basic research methods both quantitative and qualitative. Guidelines for the review of literature would equip scholars as how to analyze and synthesize research literature. Formulation of research proposal has been well explained. Various aspects of research methodology such as research design, sampling procedures, development and construction of research tools, analysis of data are well elaborated with practical examples. Inferential statistics covered parametric and non-parametric techniques which would help researchers to explore in-depth relationships between variables. It also expresses as how validity of argument and the soundness of evidence lead to generate testable and tested knowledge. How to design, write and communicate the results in a logical ways are well taken up in report writing.

It would be worthwhile to mention here that MIER P.G. College of Education and SAHYOG INDIA provided all support to Dr. D.R. Kapoor to take up this assignment in conjunction with others projects. This book provides a practical base for doing research in social sciences including education. The scholars, practitioners, professionals and researchers will find it useful, rewarding and enjoyable.

PROF. B.K. PASSI
UNESCO Chair
Former NCTE Vice Chairperson

Preface

Research is viewed as a professionally-oriented activity to improve practice, aspects of human experience and/or contribute to the sum total of human knowledge. Experts agree that it is a "critical and systematic enquiry" aimed at informing judgments and decisions in order to improve action. Every year new facts, new concepts, innovative practices, new methods, new models, new processes and new ways of doing things come into our lives due to ever-increasing significant research in the physical, the biological, as well as the social and psychological fields.

In this technological age, it is now possible and easy to help more people without hassles to gain access to research findings that can possibly make difference to institutions and professionals. It is now easier for the researchers to view and review a large array of research literature. Such a system could connect research studies not only to related work but also help to do meta-analysis for policy implications. Research is also recognized as the basis of our personal, social, cultural, economic and political development. Therefore, need for research is to re-design our programmes and evolve new strategies in order to get optimum results.

Quality of research depends on system, scholars, supervisors, and support. System calls for the best inputs, and the best processes to produce the best outputs and impact. The scholars and the supervisors have to conform to standards at par with international standards. Institutions are required to keep pace with the growing knowledge and strive hard ceaselessly to meet the international standards in educational research.

It is a fact that all phenomena and knowledge have both quantitative and qualitative dimensions. The distinction between objectivity and subjectivity, normally associated with quantitative and qualitative research, is neither accurate nor useful. Standards for quality research, whether primarily designed to gather quantitative or qualitative data, typically emphasize the traits of objectivity, internal validity, external validity, reliability, rigor, open-mindedness, and honest and thorough reporting.

Scientific investigation in social sciences calls for "a continuous process of rigorous reasoning supported by a dynamic interplay among methods, theories, and findings" (NRC, 2002). Scientific inquiry in social sciences including education is more descriptively-oriented, more dependent on context. It recognizes the importance of philosophical, historical, social and cultural and political and ethical requirements.

Selection of the problem is one of the most important phases in research process. Weak and ill conceived idea or problem will put a researcher in deep trouble. In such a situation, sometimes, researcher may resort to undesirable acts with stimulation to get degree. This may not be useful to the researcher (i.e. the pursuit of truth is compromised by disingenuousness or ineptitude on the part of the researcher) as well as to the society (i.e. wastage of resources). Neophytes need to be sensitized about the selection of topic for research.

Review of Literature is the fundamental of research preparation. The researchers get minimal formal training. Cut and paste method could not equip them as how to analyze and synthesize research literature. As a result, it is all alleged that most dissertation literature reviews are poorly conceptualized and written. Purposeful reading, recording, accessing and storing of literature are the necessary skills which researcher must possess and utilized.

In the formulation of research proposal, the researcher should understand what research is intended—it implies proper identification of topic, operational definition of terms to be used, review of literature, and formulation of hypotheses or research questions. How the research will be done—will include research design, method, sample, tools for the collection of data and selection of appropriate techniques for the analysis of data and why the proposed research is undertaken should focus on the need and importance of the proposed research. The formulation of a research problem is both expectation-laden and value—impregnated. Purpose is to achieve a particular end, either the advancement of some area of theory or a practical benefit. Therefore, the investigator should be clear about the purpose of research undertaken.

A researcher should continuously upgrade his or her research skill. Researcher should understand the validity of argument and the soundness of evidence. It also involves recourse to ideas which have been tested against empirical evidence. Moreover, researcher should not twist data to suit theory but use factual data to modify theory. The researcher has to decide which method is appropriate to his or her research study and should be used.

There is a general agreement among the experts and stakeholders that evaluation is a significant tool to assess the strengths and weaknesses in research. Insights and cues from the evaluation would provide substantial support to devise strategies to ensure quality in research. We all realize that the institutions of higher learning engaged in academic research should adopt more objective, more reliable and valid method of evaluation. Therefore, there is a need to evolve a more integrated and comprehensive model of evaluation based on clearly defined dimensions of quality.

Preparation and presentation of a research report is the most important part of research process. No matter how brilliant the hypotheses are formulated and how well a research study is designed, these are of little value unless communicated and addressed effectively to the audiences. If the report is confusing or poorly written, the time spent of gathering and analysis of data would be wasted. Therefore, it is essential to design, write and communicate the results in a logical, in a research report.

All stakeholders/shareholders namely, policy-makers, service providers, managers, community, faculty, parents and students—could be well served by the development of tested knowledge. Moreover, the purpose of research is to enable researchers to work out their path independently and determine the right things for themselves. They have, therefore, to pass through—virtue ethic, result ethic, universal ethic, public exposure ethic, and caring ethic. Without adequate training and supervision, the neophyte researcher will open the floodgate of Ghost writers and anything can be outsourced for price which is a dangerous signal to quality research.

We hope that the scholars, teachers, professionals, practitioners and policy planners, may find this book a useful and rewarding.

DR. D.R. KAPOOR
Ms. PUJA SAIGAL

UNIT I

MEANING, NATURE AND SCOPE OF RESEARCH

CHAPTER

1

Research and its Characteristics

Meaning, Nature and Scope

Research generally refers to a search for truth and knowledge. Redman and Mory (1923) define research as a "systematic effort to gain new knowledge". It is also a scientific inquiry for finding solution of problem. In other words, it is formal, systematic and scientific investigation either for (a) new discovery or development of new theory or modification the existing theory; or for (b) development of new methods, models techniques, innovation, improved practices for practical implications or to fill the gap between realized and expected outcomes.

Knowledge and practical aspects of research have been well explained by the eminent researchers. For example, research is considered to be "more formal, systematic, intensive process of carrying on the scientific methods of analysis" (Best & Kahn, 1992). "An endeavour to discover, develop and verify knowledge" (Rummel, 1973). It is an "objective, impartial, empirical and logical analysis and recording of controlled observations that may lead to the development of generalizations, principles or theories, resulting to some extent in prediction and control of events that may be consequences or causes of specific phenomena" (Koul, 2008). From practical point of view "Research is an honest, exhaustive, intelligent searching for facts and their meanings or implications with reference to given problems" (Cook, 2000). Research is simply a systematic and refined technique of thinking, employing specialized tools, instruments, and procedures in order to obtain a more adequate solution of a problem than would be possible under ordinary means (Swann, 2007).

Best and Kahn (1992) have summarized the main characteristics of research:

1. Research is directed towards the solution of a problem. It may attempt to answer a question or to determine the relation between two or more variables.
2. Research emphasizes the development of generalizations, principles, or theories that will be helpful in predicting future occurrences. Research usually goes beyond the specific objects, groups or situations investigated and infers characteristics of a target population form the sample observed. Research is more than information retrieval, the simple gathering of information. Although many school research departments gather and tabulate statistical information that may be useful in decision-making, these activities are not properly termed research.
3. Research is based upon observable or empirical evidence. Certain interesting questions do not lend themselves to research procedures because they cannot be observed. Research rejects revelation and dogma as methods of establishing knowledge and accepts only what can be verified by observation.
4. Research demands accurate observation and description. The researcher uses quantitative, numerical measuring devices, the most precise means of description. The researcher selects or devices valid data gathering instruments or procedures and employs appropriate mechanical, electronic, or psychometric devices to refine human observation, recording, computation, and analysis of data.
5. Research involves gathering new data from primary or first-hand sources or using existing data for a new purpose. Teachers frequently assign a so-called research project that involves writing a paper dealing with the life of a prominent person. The students are expected to read a number of encyclopaedias, books, or periodical references, and synthesize the information in a written report. This is not research, for the data are not new. Merely reorganizing or restating what is already known and has already been

written, valuable as it may be as a learning experience, is not research. It adds nothing to what is known.

6. Although research activity may at times be somewhat random and unsystematic, it is more often characterized by carefully designed procedures, always applying rigorous analysis. Although trial and error are often involved, research is rarely a blind, shotgun investigation-trying something to see what happens.
7. Research requires expertise. The researcher knows what is already known about the problem and how others have investigated it. He has searched the related literature carefully. He is also thoroughly grounded in the terminology, the concepts, and the technical skill necessary to understand and analyse the data that he has gathered.
8. Research strives to be objective and logical, applying every possible test to validate the procedures employed, the data collected, and the conclusions reached. The researcher attempts to eliminate personal bias. There is no attempt to persuade or to prove an emotionally held conviction. The emphasis is on testing rather than on proving the hypothesis. Although absolute objectivity is as elusive as pure righteousness, the researcher tries to suppress bias and emotion in his or her analysis.
9. Research involves the quest for answers to unsolved problems. Pushing back the frontiers of ignorance is its goal, and originality is frequently the quality of a good research project. However, previous important studies are deliberately repeated, using identical or similar procedures, with different subjects, different settings, and at a different time. This process is replication, a fusion confirm or to raise questions about the conclusions of previous study.
10. Research is characterized by patient and unhurried activity. It is rarely spectacular and the researcher must accept disappointment and discouragement as he pursues the answers to difficult questions.
11. Research is carefully recorded and reported. Each important term is defined, limiting factors are recognized, procedures are described in detail, references are carefully documented, results are objectively recorded, and conclusions are presented with scholarly cautions and restraint. The written report and accompanying data are made available to the scrutiny of associates or other

scholars. Any competent scholar will have the information necessary to analyze, evaluate, and even replicate the study.

12. Research sometimes requires courage. The history of science reveals that many important discoveries were made inspite of the opposition of political and religious authorities. The polish scientist Copernicus (1473-1543) was condemned by church authorities when he announced his conclusion concerning the nature of the solar system. His theory that the sun, not the earth was centre of the solar system in direct conflict with the older Ptolemaic theory, angered supporters of prevailing religious dogma, who viewed his theory as a denial of the story of creation as described in the book of Genesis. Modern researchers in such fields as genetics, sexual behaviour, and even business practices have aroused violent criticism from those whose personal convictions, experiences, or observations were in conflict with some of the research conclusions.

In brief, research is an activity which involves thorough study of research literature to find gaps or inconsistencies in theories or mismatch between realized and anticipated goals/results. Deductive and inductive reasonings are applied for the formulation of hypotheses or research questions. Appropriate research design, methodology and procedures are adopted, good data and techniques for the analysis are used to get substantial evidence which provide scope for replication/generalization or transfer of results obtained in a specific context to another context.

1.1 EDUCATIONAL RESEARCH : MEANING, NATURE AND SCOPE

Educational research draws extensively on the disciplines of philosophy, sociology and psychology. Educational research is, therefore, concerned not only with activities of teachers and students in schools, colleges, and universities but all life long learning from cradle to grave. Some see educational research as primarily for the benefit of the individual and other see it as the means of producing human resources necessary to maintain the economy. Some are concerned that research should be of benefit to society; some are attempting to improve classroom practice. Some are concerned with the policy context within which practice takes place. Others look to wider socio-political issues which underlie, influence or circumscribe the organization and conduct of education. Educational research has to work within and around these different conceptions.

Educational research refers to a systematic attempt to gain a better understanding of the educational process, generally with a view to improving its efficiency. It is an application of scientific method to the study of educational problems.(Travers, 1958).

Educational research is that activity which is directed towards *development of a science of behaviour in educational situations—to achieve most effective methods.* (John W. Best, 2008). It is also a *contextual analysis* of data *in a scientific way* to *understand* the behaviour, to *predict* the behaviour in order to *modify* the behaviour in educational setting.

It is the efforts carried out by the public or private bodies in order to *improve educational methods and educational activities in general.* (Lazarsfied & Sieber, 2003). Methodical processes to *add to one's body of knowledge.* (Howard & Sharpe, 1983) and *'the collection and analysis of information on the world of education so as to understand and explain it better' with significance for practicing teachers.*

It is viewed as a *critical*, *reflexive*, and *professionally oriented* activity—to improve practice, aspects of human experience and/or contribute to the sum of human knowledge. (Hitchcook and Huges, 1989). Educational research is meant to make our schools better places for both the children and adults who share their lives there (Eiser, 1993). Research in education is a "*critical and systematic enquiry* aimed

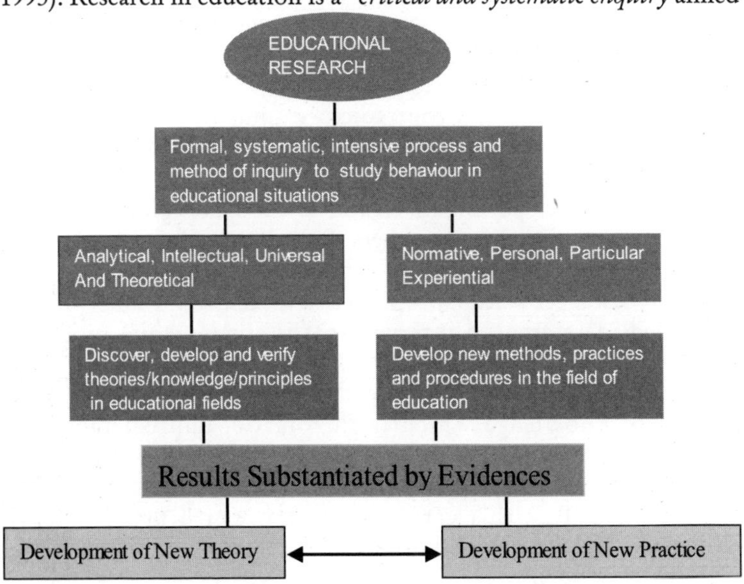

Figure 1.1 : Educational Research

at informing judgments and decisions in order to *improve action.*" (Bassey, 2001).

Educational research is analytical, intellectual, universal and theoretical on one hand. Such problems can usefully be divided into three categories: problems of value (what is good, what ought to be done, what is aesthetically pleasing), problems of fact(what is so in the world and why, what was so and why, what will be so), and problems of logic (what is valid and why). It is also normative, personal, experiential, particular and practical on the other. Both aspects of the research are supplementary as well as complementary. This has been shown in Figure 1.1.

1.2 NATURE OF EDUCATIONAL RESEARCH

1.2.1 Dynamic, and Multifaceted

Change is integral to educational research. Change, innovation, and experimentation are constantly occurring in education. In order to keep up with these changes, the practitioners and professional are always in search of evidences to improve upon their practices. Therefore, educational research is to challenge assumptions and expectations.

Unpredictability and uncertainty is recognized as crucial aspects of the research situation in education. Knowledge is partial, provisional, and contingent upon certain contexts and conditions. Meanings are 'endlessly deffered'—never fixed, always related to prior connotations and definitions. (Derrida, 1976). There is a possibility of recognizing multiple and contradictory findings as valid research outcomes. It is 'transgressive' forms of validity which acknowledge the contradictions and uncertainties. Educational Research questions established research paradigms, creates new and multiple identities for research, researched and researchers. Raised issues about knowledge, power and the dominance of linguistic, epistemotogical and methodological certainties, proposes a new view of learning. What is published in referenced international journals, while satisfying stringent criteria from university-based researchers may be of little help in the complex world of the classroom (Smith, 2000) and the growth of knowledge which is rhizomatic, unpredictable and multifaceted. It offers interpretations that are diverse, uncertain and polyvocal, and which do not necessarily lead to clear directions or sure answers. It is this very uncertainty which makes it both challenging and exciting (Atkinson, 2005).

1.2.2 Metadisciplines

Education is informed and cuts across a number of disciplines.

It constitutes a sort of metadisciplines. (Bates, 1999). For example, it is informed by social sciences such as anthropology, sociology, economics and psychology. The consequent complexity is also magnified by the variety of sub-areas within education (e.g. policy, administration, school education, higher education, teacher education. Therefore, diversity has made the development of common ground difficult. (Feuer *et al.*, 2002). The presence of numerous disciplinary perspectives focusing on different parts of the system means that there are many legitimate research frameworks, methods and norms of inquiry. (Howe & Eisenhart, 1990). The challenge for the field of education is to bring diverse communities—both scientific and otherwise to integrate theories and empirical findings across disciplines, domains, cultures, and methods.

1.2.3 Closed Generalization

In educational research, there is no need to try and provide results which can be generalized. The findings may have important implications, either for personal use or others working in the similar areas. Bassey (2003) draws a distinction between 'open' generalization where there is confidence that the findings can be extrapolated and 'closed' generalization which refers to a specific set of events.

1.2.4 Evidence-based

Educational research is methodical, using appropriate techniques and attending to details. It is also concerned for the validity of argument, and the soundness of evidence. Educational research is more than just telling stories or analyzing discourses; it is a means by which we can generate testable and tested knowledge about how students learn in classrooms, what promotes and what inhibits learning, the consequences of policy and so on. In educational research, we do not intend to minimize the significance of humanistic, historic, philosophical, and other non-scientific forms of study in education. Much of educational research seems to be nature of open questions. What is happening (description) ?; Is there a systematic effect (cause)?; and why or how is it happening (process or mechanism)? Therefore, question-answering is often used in education as a substitute for hypothesis-testing.

1.2.5 Quantitative as well as Qualitative

Educational research often does not follow well-defined patterns squarely into one approach (quantitative) or another (qualitative). The scientific study of the social world is impossible because all human activities, including learning and teaching, involve beliefs, values, intentions, and goals that give the activities meaning.

Therefore, interpretations of human actions are contextually bound. Educational research can only provide findings that are firmly embedded in social, cultural, economic, political, ethical contexts, in which case researchers would be restricted to using qualitative methods like narrative enquiry, or storytelling. No method is good or bad, scientific or unscientific in itself. Rather, it is the appropriate application of method to a particular problem that enables judgment about scientific enquiry

1.2.6 Ethical

Educational research addresses the question of value, such as questions of what we ought to do—ethics in education, and the ethic of education. It involves the formulation of a problem, the proposing of solutions, and testing of one or more of these solutions.. As in science, solutions are tested by means of critical discussion. The formulation of research problem in education is both expectation-laden and value-impregnated. Educational research is based on the principle of caring others, i.e. how to protect the subjects of research from the breach of confidence, undue pressure, and stress. The researcher is responsible for ensuring the integrity of the research. If we accept that education research should speak about those things where we can not pronounce with certainty and scientific detachment, we must accept that other intellectual virtues, specifically, practical wisdom—"a true and practical state involving reason, concerned with what is good and bad for a human being." (Aristotle, 2000).

1.2.7 Predictability

Educational research lacks predictability as is observed in pure sciences on account of little control over variables. Degree of predictability is contingent upon degree of control. Research on human subjects has numerous problems namely; no two persons are alike in feelings, drives or emotions. What may be reasonable prediction for one may be useless for another; no one person is completely consistent from one moment to another That is why it is difficult to predict; human beings are influenced by the research process itself, and behavioural sciences have been limited by a lack of adequate definition.

- No two persons are alike in feelings, drives or emotions. What may be a reasonable prediction for one may be useless for another.
- No person is completely consistent from one moment to another.
- Human beings are influenced by the research process itself.

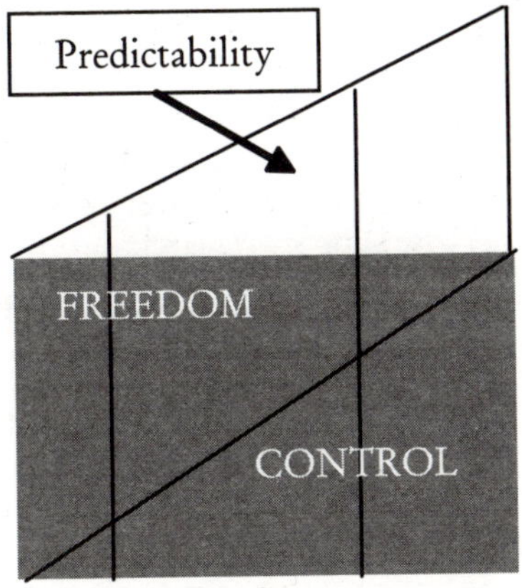

Figure 1.2 : Degree of Predictability

Education is centrally concerned with people: learners, teachers, parents, citizens and policy-makers. The volition or will, of these individuals decreases the level of control that researchers can have over the process. (NRC, 2002, p. 86). "People behave more erratically than protons do, education research, in comparison with physics research, has to cope with more sources of "noise" and larger "error limits". (NRC, 2002, p. 83).

1.2.8 Rigor

Educational reseach is based on scientic inquiry which calls for rigour. At one-technical level, rigour means being methodical, using appropriate techniques and attending to detail. At another logical-level, it is expressed as a concern for the validity of argument, and the soundness of evidence. Any teacher with common sense, intelligence and insight can undertake research for the solution of specific problem in education if he is committed to research that produces, and makes reference, to ideas which have been subjected to intensive critical scrutiny. It is a means by which one can generate testable and tested knowledge about how students learn in classrooms. Whether answering open questions or testing hypotheses, it is the discovery of unexpected that leads to learning. How data are collected and handled is central to ensuring rigour. Interviews need to be carefully conducted, questionnaires adequately piloted, and data accurately analysed. Conclusions are drawn on solid and substantial evidences.

1.2.9 Intricate Web of Relations

As in other applied fields—such as agriculture, health, crime, justice, and welfare-educational research relies critically on relationships between researchers and those engaged in professional practice: teachers, administrators, curriculum developers, university deans, school board members, and a host of others. The educational research enterprise could not function without these relationships, and its vitality depends in part on the willingness of practitioners to participate in or otherwise support research.

1.3 SCOPE OF EDUCATIONAL RESEARCH

1.3.1 Scope of Educational Research is Wide and Varied

It calls for :

- Identifying of gaps/inconsistencies in the existing theories
- revealing of a hitherto unrecognized mismatch between expectation and experience (actual or anticipated) that has far reaching practical or theoretical implications;
- formulation of a new and important problem;
- the production of a new and better solution to an existing problem; and
- development of a constructive way of challenging existing expectations.

1.3.2 The Scope of Research in Education in the Present Scenario

It can be examined in the following scenario:

- No amount of learning by trial and error, no amount of experience gathered through casual practice and no amount of wisdom collected in the form of casual observations, traditions can ever promise such rapid progress and improvement in education as is required all over world today.
- The present portal strategy dedicated to supporting interactive public access to research could enable users of its resources to move from research overviews and syntheses to the original studies and relevant meta-analysis, with an option of consulting the research instruments and perhaps the data as well. Such a system could connect research studies not only to related work but to the relevant field, practice, organization, and state policies
- All parties involved in education—as policy-makers, providers, managers, teachers, parents and students—could be well served by the development of tested knowledge about learning, teaching and the organization of education. Decisions based on research evidence would surely save time, money, and energy. Evolving best practices,

processes and input can ensure best products in the forms of best behaviour and learning outcomes. Figure 1.3 depicts the scope of educational research.

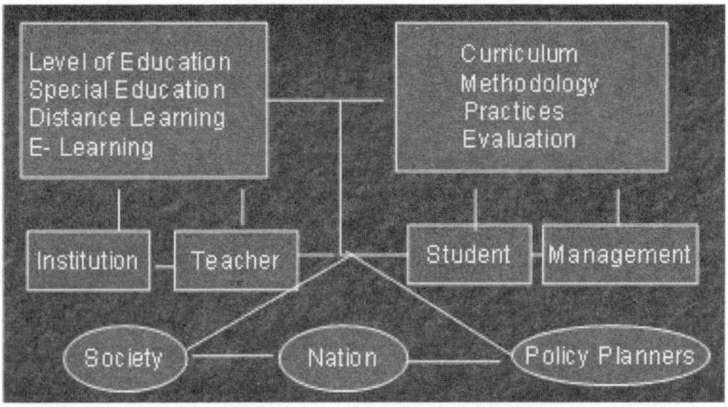

Figure 1.3 : Scope of Educational Research

Scope of Career-Path and Societal betterment: Research in education is intellectually stimulating and its outcomes may be good for one's career. The intellectual stimulation comes from experimenting with ideas, and, more importantly, because it is a means by which human experience may be improved. (Swann, 2005). Educational research is not purely motivated by self-interest. Nor it is motivated solely by the pursuit of knowledge for its own sake. Rather, it is concerned that research should be of benefit to society. Therefore, some researchers are attempting to improve classroom practice; some are concerned with the policy issues which underlie the conduct and effectiveness of education.

1.3.3 Professional Growth

Teacher as a researcher is also a practitioner, knower and doer, expert and executer. Acquaintance with the processes and products of research will enable a teacher to create knowledge on his own and at least to respect and welcome new knowledge. It provides him energy, edge, passion and excellence in execution of his job. It builds critical thinking and discipline. Research enables the teacher to discover the root causes of inconsistencies and to know what kind of information to gather and how to analyse for improving the quality of teacher education. It enables the researchers to become acquainted with the concern of teacher and also create a context within which teacher may begin to appreciate the benefits of such research studies. Research in the Teacher Education Institutions should identify and lay emphasis on such practices which promote, (a) the logical acts of teaching i.e., defining, demonstration, modeling, explaining, (b) the psychological acts of teaching i.e., caring, motivating, encouraging, rewarding, and punishing, (c) and moral acts of teaching i.e., showing honesty, courage, tolerance, compassion, respect and fairness. Fleming (1999) in his survey cites "more than half of the teachers agreed that educational research gave them practical suggestions for improving instructions."

Research in education may lead to professional growth. At work place, practice is enhanced by critically reflecting on the ways we understand and engage in through action research. Thrust should be to connect all our capabilities—from our most advanced skills that exist today in innovation, invention and research to solve our clients' problem. (Sam Palmisano, 2007) and future is about innovation and how nimble one is; the future is all about how open-minded one is to learn. (N.R. Murthy, 2007).

Figure 1.4 reflects the relationship between experience and research practices in professional growth.

Professional Growth

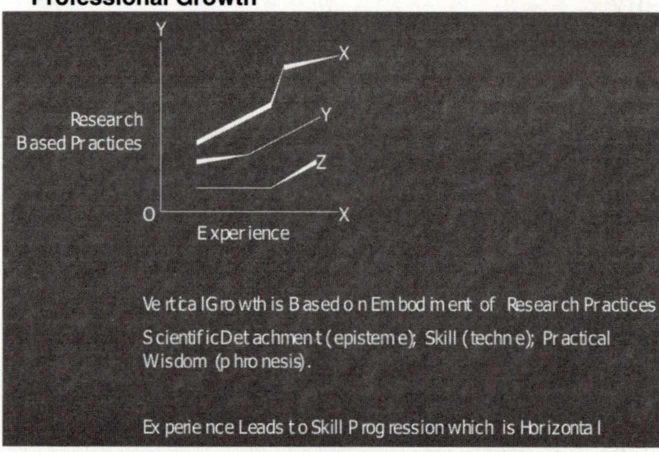

Figure 1.4 : Professional Growth

Figure 1.4 reveals that embodiment of research-based practice may lead to vertical profession growth. Experience may also lead to skill progression but in horizontal way.

1.3.4 Levels of Education

Elementary, secondary, higher, special education, distance and E-Learning are integral parts of educational system. Governments as well as private sectors in education also contribute significantly to our national development. Quality of higher education depends on the quality of primary and secondary education. Therefore, scope of educational research is spread over all these levels of education. There is ample of scope educational research in special education or inclusive education; enrichment of instructional materials, changes in the processes of curricular transaction, incorporation of innovative practices, use and size-effect of new technologies are to be taken up on the substantial evidence of research studies.

1.3.5 Problem-solving

Research involves reflexive imagination, creative and critical thinking. This helps researcher in solving problem. Problem may the problem of low performance, problem of how to deal with diverse population in the classroom, the problem of enhancing the learning outcome, problem of reduction of tension, anxiety, among the children, or may be the problem of special child. Problem may be of quality enhancement, institutional building, incorporation of innovative practices, teacher effectiveness and student participation in the process of learning, Virtually, there is ample scope for the researcher to be engaged and involved in addressing practical problems in teaching and learning. It enables the researcher to make judgments on the basis of evidence rather than whim, orthodoxy, fashion or expediency. When problem-solving involves learning, a greater degree of creativity is involved. It also enables researcher to encapsulate, criticize and develop new knowledge through his interaction with the world of knowledge.

1.3.6 Areas of Immediate Concern

Research areas of utmost concern are curriculum, methods, practice, and evaluation.

(a) Sociological Bases of Education

Rapid social change and the resulting diversification of life world are increasing confronting researchers with new social contexts and perspectives. Impact of ethnographic, phenomenological, grounded theories, case studies making use of inductive reasoning have been found significant in teaching and learning processes. Knowledge and practice are studied as local knowledge and practices (Harre, 1998). Ontology—the nature of social reality, epistemology—knowledge aspect, and human nature and agency provide ample scope for research in education.

(b) Educational Psychology

Cognitive and non-cognitive factors, such as, intelligence and multiple intelligences—liguisitics, logical-mathematical, visual-spatial, bodily-kinaesthetic, interpersonal and intrapersonal, aptitudes, creativity, attitudes, interests, motivation, personality traits, needs and adjustment of pupils provide promising scope of research in educational psychology. Such aspects which include various personality traits—interests, needs and values are important for determining success in certain educational and vocational fields such as medicine, social work, teaching, etc. demand for the development of some tools for measuring such attributes which would require ellaborate and carefully planned research work.

(c) Philosophical Bases of Education

Special features of Indian Philosophy in relation to education-Indian Philosophical Thoughts and their impact on Indian system of Education with reference to teacher, learner, discipline and processes for the transaction are the areas which can be investigated. Two of the highly topical issues that future researcher has to seriously consider are: *(i)* the knowledge aim in education; and (ii) the value orientation of education. The education system needs sound theoretical and ideological bases. In this context philosophical research contributes towards building a normative framework for educational priorities, curriculum, curricular practices and management of the education system through a cross-examination of ideas reflected by different philosophers in the field of education.

(d) Special Education

Another important area where a good deal of research can be undertaken is that among the *exceptional children.* It includes the study of all children who are either handicapped in some way or are gifted. The handicapped children may be physically handicapped, the mentally handicapped or the socially handicapped. The gifted children are fast learners and exceptionally bright and have very high general mental ability or special abilities. Shanker (1968) points out that study of all these types of children with a view to finding ways and means of their proper location, care, rehabilitation, education and guidance is essential both from the individual and the social points of view.

(e) Curriculum Development

In the backdrop of National Curriculum Framework (NCF, 2005) it is important that each curricular area is to be revisited by the researchers and probed in depth to find answers to problems related to teaching-learning of different subjects.

1.3.7 Institutional-Building Research

It requires an effectively interlinked network of research institutions, a base of useable information, method for rationally applying that information and effective feedback on the results application. Research knowledge base should be built and experiences are to be shared between teachers and teacher education institutions. The process is continuous and circular; feedback on the effect of application improves institutional capacity and database, and methods of teaching. Effective feedback requires familiarity with socio-economic-cultural settings, intensive field study, documentation and field pre-testing for appropriate design and implementation. It determines specific relationships between the investments of time, money, materials, equipments, services and the output in terms of number of teachers trained, curriculum materials produced and innovative practices initiated and incorporated.

1.3.8 Educational Management

Research and training in educational leadership should focus on, educational policy formation and implementation; resource allocation and budgeting; personal selection, development and evaluation; human resource management and collective negotiation; instructional strategies and curriculum; pupils evaluation; family and community involvement; organization decision-making; meditating disputes and taking action in a highly politicized and contested environment; and data driven decision-making. Each is complex and requires conceptual understanding as well as ability to put knowledge into action in educational setting. All decisions affecting the conduct and organization education and educational research are made on the basis of substantial evidence. (a) It is not being influened by power struggles between different educational factions, (b) regardless of gender, class and race, and (c) are taken largely out of self-interest. Decision-making in the field of education is based on a combination of experience, expert opinion and research results.

1.3.9 National Concerns

In this context, disadvantages in education arising due to inequalities of gender, case, language, culture, religion or disabilities need to be addressed. Research related to education of the disadvantaged groups, inclusive education, gender equity, education of rural children and functioning of rural schools provide ample scope for researchers to conduct studies in order to improve the system. Exchanging or sharing of good practices and research experiences across the universities can further improve the quality of education in India. It is imperative to identify financial, social and educational implications of right to education at state and national levels. Researches for improving system for preparing teachers should lay emphasis on both pre-service and in-service, system of producing textbooks and learning materials and the examination system. Integration of ICT in education as a pedagogic, administrative and monitoring tool and the related practices require extensive research for maximum efficiency within the boundaries of democracy, human dignity and freedom. Classroom processes and practices and management strategies are other useful areas of research in his context.

1.3.10 Research for Policy Planning

Policy is quintessentially concerned with practical problems, such as how best to teach children of different abilities, how to pay teachers to motivate them, how to deal with the disparities of opportunity arising from class, sex or race. The object of research into policy is to find out how to change things. All government policies, indeed all executive and administrative decisions, involve empirical predictions. At best, it identifies what works and what does not, and it can offer explanation and understanding of why things work. For instance, how can the use and application of ICT in educational institutions increase learning outcomes? To create policy or to change policy, we need to know how and why something work and why others do not, and to what extent they work under different circumstances. We need both explanatory and predictive knowledge. What kinds of evidence are needed to test if it is working or not? What is the best way of collecting that evidence?

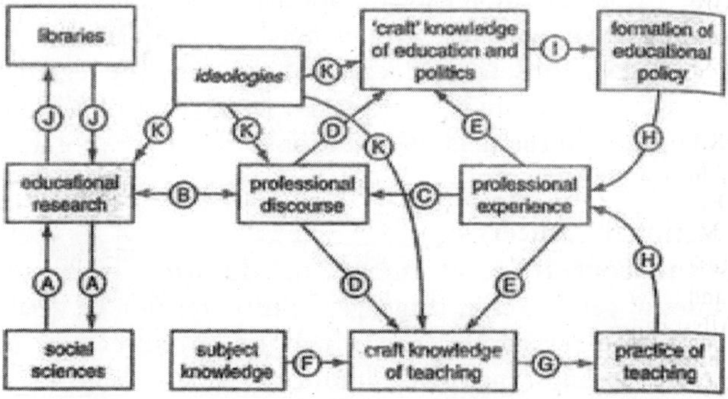

Figure 1.5 : Research for Policy Planning

(Educational Research in Practice (2003), edited by Joanna Swann and John Pratt. Conyinuum: New York).

Bassey (1998) suggested how educational research impinges on the craft knowledge of classroom practice and policy-making:

A. Educational research uses and contributes to methodologies of the other social sciences.
B. Reports of educational research contributes to professional discourse and *vice-versa.*
C. Reports of professional experience contribute to professional discourse.
D. Professional discourse provides ideas that add to craft knowledge.
E. Professional experience provides knowledge of what has worked.
F. Subject knowledge is transmited through craft knowledge into a teachable form.
G. Craft knowledge of teaching determines the practice of teaching.
H. Memories of practice and of policy formation are stored as professional experience.
I. Craft knowledge of management and politics determines policy formation.
J. Libraries store and inform educational research.

Policy planners are deeply concerned that research should be of benefit to society. Some are attempting to improve classroom practice; some are concerned with the policy context within which practice takes place. Others look to the wider socio-economic-political issues which underlie, influence or circumscribe the organization and conduct of education. Educational research, therefore, should be directed, in some way or other, towards the improvement of educational practice.

References

Bailey, K.D. (1987). *Methods of Social Research.* 3rd edn., New York: Free Press.

Bassey, M. (1998). Enhancing Teaching Through Research. *Professional Development Today*, 1(2), pp. 39-46..

Bassey, M. (2001). A Solution to the Problem of Generalisation in Educational Research: Fuzzy Prediction. *Oxford Review of Education*, 27(10), pp. 5-22.

Best, J. and Kahn, J. (2009). *Research in Education.* 10th edition, Needham Heights: Allyn and Bacon.

British Educational Research Association (2000). *Good Practice in Educational Research Writing,* Southwell, Notinghamshire,UK: British Educational Research Association.

Corey, S.M. (1962). *Research in Education.* NCERT, New Delhi.
Cozby, P. (2009). *Methods in Behavioural Research.* 10th edition, Bemont: Wadsworth.
Festinger, L. and Katz, D. (1976) (eds.). *Research Methods in the Behavioural Sciences.* New Delhi: Amerind Publishing Co.
Good, Carter V. (1966). *Essentials of Educational Research: Methodology and Design.* New York: Applleton-Century Crofts.
Goode, W.J., and Hatt, P.K. (1990). *Methods in Social Research.* New Delhi: McGraw-Hill.
Guthrie, G. (2010). *Basic Research Methods.* New Delhi: Sage.
Hillway, T. (1956). *Introduction to Research.* Houghton Miffin Co.
Hylla, E. (1956). The Nature and Functions of Educational Research. *Report of the First International Conference on Educational Research.* Educational Studies and Documents, No. XX, UNESCO.
Kerlinger, F. (1986). *Foundations of Behavioural Research.* 5rd edition, Orlando: Harcourt Brace.
Kothari, C.R. (2004). *Research Methodology: Methods & Techniques.* New Delhi: New Age International Publishers.
Koul, L. (2009). *Methodology of Educational Research.* Vikas Publishing House, New Delhi-14.
Laws, S. (2003). *Research for Development.* New Delhi: Vistaar Publications.
Leedy, P. and Ormrod, J. (2010). *Practical Research: Planning and Design.* 9th edition, Needham Heights: Allyn Bacon
Ozga, J. (2000). *Policy Research in Educational Settings.* Buckingham,UK: Open University Press.
Paneerselvam, R. (2004). *Research Methodology.* New Delhi: Prentice-Hall of India.
Punch, K.F. (2009). *Introduction to Research Methods in Education.* New Delhi: Sage.
Singh, J. (2008). *Methodology and Techniques of Social Research.* New Delhi: Kanishka Publishers.
Somekh, B., and Lewin, C. (2005). *Research Methods in the Social Sciences.* New Delhi. Vstaar Publications.
Sukhia, S.P., Mehrotra, P.V. and Mehrotra, R.N. (1974). *Elements of Educational Research.* New Delhi: Allied Publishers.
Swann, J. (2000). How can research lead to improvement in education. *Prospero,* 6(3/4), pp. 130-38.
Swann, J. and Pratt, J. (2003). (Eds.). *Educational Research in Practice.* London: Continuum.
William Wiersma (1986). *Research Methods in Education: An Introduction.* Allyn and Bacon, Inc. London.

CHAPTER

2

Research Paradigms

Research in different disciplines of knowledge has undergone various processes and phases of change. We proceeded from traditional approach to scientific and from scientific to modern, from modern to systemic. There are many approaches to educational research shaped by different research paradigms. The various research paradigms have different criteria for epistemology, ontology and reality which have influenced research methods and methodology. There are four main research paradigms in educational research:

- Positivism
- Post-Positivism (Interpretivism)
- Criticalism
- Post-Modernism

Each of these research paradigms has its own epistemological and ontological characteristics. According to Bryman (2001) epistemology refers to the ways knowledge is acquired. In other words, epistemology concerns what we know and how we can know the reality of the research subject (Wills, 2007). Ontological assumptions refer to the nature of the world and the human being in social contexts (Bryman, 2001; Wills, 2007).

2.1 POSITIVISM PARADIGM

The post/positivist paradigm contains two main themes; controlling the research condition such as human behavior and investigating those through scientific methods (Douglas, 1973 as cited in Cohen, Manion, and Morrison, 2000). Because it is controlled, the post/positivist paradigm tends to generalize findings with one truth. As it is very structured and clear, it is easy to be objective in this paradigm. However, an inherent weakness of the paradigm is that it cannot investigate all phenomena in education particularly regarding motivation, values and "intentions and feelings" (Anderson and Arsenault, 1998, p. 5). The post/positivist paradigm seeks to find the truth within controlled conditions that are scientifically observable. Even so, it is problematic to find the "one truth" in some specific social context such as education. For example, students' achievement is not strictly limited influence by one specific factor. It is difficult to isolate people and control the results in natural phenomena. Epistemological research in the post/positivist paradigm is how the special world can be investigated as natural science. Hypothesis have to be tested by empirical approaches. In post/positivism, the objective results through scientific method ontology which empahsise that social phenomenon are independent from other factors. In addition, data analysis uses logical reasoning (a thinking process) and provides explanations with certain generalizations. These generalizations have however become a challenge in educational research. Due to the sheer complexity of educational phenomena, and generalisation is often difficult to construct.

Broadly speaking, positivism denotes the idea that:

1. Scientific knowledge is derived from the accumulation of data obtained theory-free and value-free from observation.
2. Anything that cannot be observed, and thus in some way measured (that is, quantified) is of little or no importance, or even, in extreme versions, non-existent.
3. Science is the pursuit of foundational knowledge.
4. Scientific method is applicable not only to the study of natural phenomena but also to human and social affairs.

Since the focus of the post/positivist paradigm is to discover the 'truth' through empirical investigation, the quality standards under this paradigm are validity and reliability.

1. Validity

Anderson and Arsenault (1988, p. 257) write that "validity refers to the extent to which what we measure reflects what we expected to measure [which] has to forms: internal and external. Therefore, "an experiment is valid if results obtained are due only to the manipulated independent variable and if they are generalizable to individuals or contexts beyond the experimental setting" (Gay & Airasian, 2000, p. 371).

2. Reliability

Though statistical analysis reliability can be estimated by internal consistency based on the correlation among the variables by using Cronbach's alpha reliability coefficient (Brown, 2007; Newby & Fisher, 1997). The size of the data source is directly linked to quality standards. The larger the source of the data, the greater the reliability of the results (Babbie, 1990).

3. Objectivity

According to Guba and Lincoln, (1989, p. 235), "objectivity responds to the positivist demand for neutrality and requires a demonstration that a given inquiry is free of bias, values, and/or prejudice".

2.2 INTERPRETIVISM PARADIGM

Interpretivist paradigms study individuals with their many characteristics, different human behaviours, opinions, and attitudes (Cohen, Manion, & Morrison, 2011). The interpretive paradigm helps the researcher acquire knowledge by investigating the phenomena of the world and human in many ways. Therefore, its advantage is in finding a meaningful observation of objects. It gives opportunities to seek understanding and make sense of others' perspectives which are shaped by the philosophy of social constructions (Taylor, 2008). Through this paradigm, we can gain a fuller understanding of meanings, reasons, and insight human action (Bryman, 2011). It must be noted however that this subjectivity leads to results that are relatively complex to analyse and interpret objectively (Bryman, 2001). Nevertheless, it is generally acknowledged that it is more difficult to be objective in human research than in scientific settings. Therefore, subjectivity is an integral aspect of such research.

Through the interpretive paradigm, a researcher can observe a situation with different approaches to solving problems. Through this interpretive paradigm, a researcher can observe a situation with different approaches to solving problems. Through this, a multiple number of possible solutions and interpretations also emanate. Consequently, the function of epistemology in an interpretive paradigm is to acquire knowledge by investigating the phenomena in may ways, as the social context is different from natural science. The interpretive paradigm empahsises that the world in social phenomena has different meaning. A single factor influences the change in social context. As a result, different researches can reach different conclusion for the same observation.

The interpretivist paradigm seeks the understanding and meaning of people and situations which involves the subjectivity of the researchers. Therefore, the quality standards in this research paradigm are trust worthiness and authenticity.

1. Trustworthiness

The trustworthiness criteria comprise four quality standards: the credibility (via member checking), transferability (via thick description), dependability (via outside reviewer), and conformability (conformability data audit) (Guba & Lincoln, 1989).

(a) Credibility

Credibility is parallel to internal validity. In credibility, the idea of similarities between constructed realities of respondents and the reconstructions attributed to them are measured (Gurba & Lincoln, 1989, p. 237). In interpretive research, different methods are applied to assess the credibility of the findings. According to Merriam (1989) (as cited in Howitt, 2007) multiple methods and perspectives, and member checking are applied for improving credibility.

(b) Transferability

Guba and Lincoln (1989) describe transferability as a term that refers to the generalization of research findings which can be applicable in different contexts.

(c) Dependability

In interpretive research, data should be trackable and results should be consistent. Therefore, a detailed audit trail should be given (Guba & Lincoln, 1989; Howitt, 2007).

(d) Conformability

The process of assuring data, interpretation and outcomes are rooted from the contexts and persons (Guba & Lincoln, 1989). According to Howitt (2007), conformability can be established by giving the readers clear track of data and interpretations.

2. Authenticity

Various viewpoints for measuring authenticity criteria a mention by Bryman (2008) are: ontological authenticity which helps members to understand their social milieu. Educative authenticity helps members to appreciate others perspectives. Catalytic authenticity applies to provoke members to engage in action for circumstances change. Lastly, it is tactical authenticity which empowers members to take necessary steps for engaging in action. Natural personal and social setting will help to establish the authenticity.

2.3 CRITICALISM/CRITICAL THEORY PARADIGM

Critical theory paradigm is "explicitly prescriptive and post/positivist, entailing a view of what behaviour in a social democracy should entail" (Fay, 2000 as cited in Cohen, Manion, Morrison, 2001, p. 28). There are three independent forms of scientific inquiry: empirical-analytic, concerned with prediction and control; historical-hermeneutic, concerned with understanding; and critical theory, concerned with emancipation (freedom from domination). The critical theorist focuses on 'interpretive understanding of systems of belief and modes of communication using methods of historical-hermeneutic science; the critical of these; and the investigation of their causes by the methods of empirical-analytic science' (Blaikie, 1993).

The critical paradigm promotes the notion of social justice in order to create the world which is "fairer, more equitable, more inclusive and more harmonious" (Taylor, 2008). In addition, according to Kincheloe and McLaren (2002), critical theory is concerned with the power and justice of several issues in society such as economy, race, gender and education. It considers the power of social politics and ideology which influence educational research. This paradigm relates to "political agenda and that the task of the researchers is not to be dispassionate, disinterested, and objective" (Morisson, 1995 as cited in Cohen, Manion, Morrison, 2001, p. 28) which involves self-criticisms and McLauren, 2002, p. 100). Therefore, it considers the power of social politics and ideology, which influence educational research.

In critical theory, finding the issue is important and subjective. Its main objective is to improve existing situations which can be achieved through action research. The action can be continually changed to improve the quality of existing educational practices. This action shall then change and solve the problems. Therefore, the solutions are constructed by the reality. The predominant weakness of this paradigm is the difficulty surfaced when trying to conclude many interpretations. It also requires observational skills regarding the changes impacting subsequent actions. Furthermore, this approach relates to "political agenda and that the task of the researchers is not to be dispassionate, disinterested, and objective" (Morisson, 1995 as cited in Cohen, and Morrison, 2001, p. 28).

In critical theory, practical issues can construct knowledge. The theory tends to change certain conditions through criticizing practical, political and social issues. Therefore, the results are often subjective. The critical theory paradigm tends to see the world as something that has to change. It criticizes social phenomena and changes them based on the interrogations of the phenomena involving both social and individual interactions.

Critical theory lays emphasis on progressive educational reforms, supports corporate ideology and the current free-market discourse or globalization. Theory also advocates for effective policy formation, institutional restructuring, and other significant development that emerge alongside the imperatives of late capitalism. A critically informed in practice also calls for an interpretation of how social learning processes, institutional practices, and the role of teachers are being shaped.

Criticalism provides the opportunity to think critically and change the situations, especially issues in society; such as political, social, economic, education, etc. In the context of educational research, this paradigm puts emphasis on criticizing the problems and makes the changes. Therefore, the quality standard in this paradigm focuses on critical reflectivity, empowerment, and envisioning.

1. Praxis

According to Taylor and Wallace, (1996, p. 1) "Praxis concerns the way in which the researcher attempts to stimulate the reader to take deliberate action towards changing practice." The reflection on researchers' practices, not as merely a self-evaluation, can be a learning process for the readers. According to Bain, Ballantyne, Mills, and Lester (2002, p. 10), "reflection is an intrinsically good and desirable aspect of professional development." This paradigm employs writing as the process of inquiry for exploring individuals' own voices (Richardson, 2000). Therefore, it also can help researchers to understand and affect themselves emotionally and intellectually within their pedagogical practices.

(a) Pedagogical Thoughtfulness

Pedagogical Thoughtfulness is a quality of research writing that engages the reader (and also the writer) in thinking about educational issues, especially teaching and learning (Ellis & Bochner, 2000; Howitt, 2008). Through writing readers may be able to reflect on their own teaching practice and share with researchers working in the same context. Researchers may also reflect on their own pedagogical practices.

(b) Critical Reflexivity

Researchers' subjectivity could lead to overestimating their judgment on the phenomenon through the process of inquiry. The critical reflexivity helps the readers to judge researchers' subjectivity, awareness and self-exposure (Richardson, 2000). According to Johnson (as cited in Afonso, 2007), "reflexivity involves self-awareness and 'critical self-reflection' by the researcher on his or her potential biase and predispositions as these may affect the research process and conclusions" (p. 47). As a result, this criterion is powerful for envisioning the future and for empowering notion of educational process, not only to criticize, but also to act for the better future world.

(c) Re-envisioning

Re-envisioning is important paradigm, as the nature of the criticalism is creating the changes. Imaginative thinking and envisioning can help to solve problems in life and think critically. According to Robertson & Gerber (2001), it is important for constructing the positive image of the future which could affect the future of society. Therefore, the envisioning is one of quality standards in the criticalist paradigm.

2.4 POSTMODERNISM PARADIGM

The paradigm of postmodernism focuses on seeking subject understanding through textual "reconstruction, without trapping on the certainty of objectivity" (Polkinghorne, 1992). Moreover, according to Taylor (2008), "postmodernism elicits both fear and favour via its basic principle: be suspicious of all grand narratives (including that of postmodernism, respond its critics, not without irony)". Research under the postmodern paradigm focuses on the importance of self-reflections, envisioning, and lived experiences through impressionistic writing which stimulates researchers to express their emotionality in an engaging manner. Some of characteristic features of postmodernism are:

- Resistance towards certainty and resolution;
- Rejection of fixed notions of reality, knowledge, or method;
- Acceptance of complexity, lack of clarity, and multiplicity;

- Acknowledgement of subjectivity, contradiction and irony;
- Irreverence for traditions of philosophy or morality;
- Deliberate intent to unsettle assumptions and presuppositions in ways of thinking;
- Disruption of binaries which define things as either/or; and
- Refusal to accept boundaries or hierarchies. (Atkinsons, 2002a).

According to Denzin and Lincoln (2000), the postmodern paradigm allows individuals include their personal responsibility, emotionality, and ethics of care, multi-voiced texts, and dialogues to know something without claiming to know everything. Therefore, the postmodern paradigm will be powerful in facilitating research that is reflective, voicing and multi-perspective thinking.

Postmodernism employs the art based research to empower and engage the readers. Through its impressionistic writing it is "intuitive and subjective" which involve personal voice and emotions (LeCompte & Preissle, 1993, p. 354). It includes a process of self-monitoring, and disciplined subjectivity, that exposes all phases of the research activity to continual questioning and re-evaluation (Burns, 1996). According to Ellis and Bochner (2000), the idea of validity in the narrative research related to the researchers' work to engage the readers that the researcher experiences are lifelike and believable and help the readers to communicate with others different perspective and their personal experiences.

The postmodern process of deconstruction is one which seeks to interrogate these constructed 'texts'. The process might involve the deconstruction of language, drawing on linguistics and literary theory; of actions, drawing on anthropology and cultural studies; or of social patterns and constructs, drawing on sociology and social psychology. The effect of a deconstructive approach is to question the assumed educational, theoretical or moral superiority of particular world-views or dominant paradigms in educational research and practice. Some of the criteria or parameters of postmodernism are:

1. Representation

Taylor & Wallace (1996) state that, "representation concerns the challenge of representing others without reducing them to objects of researcher's gaze" This standard will judge representing of others voices during the inquiry process. Therefore, in this quality standard, how the researchers represent the reality and other voices become important.

The other concept which is important for representation criteria is crystallization. The crystallization recognizes the different views of interpretations. According to Denzin and Lincoln (2000), within crystallization process, the researchers could present the same tale in many different perspectives. The idea of crystallization not only gives the space to recognize the different views, but also contributes the powerful interpretation for the research. According to Richardson (2000, p. 934), within the postmodernism paradigm, "We do not triangulate; we crystallize. We recognize that there are a far more than "three sides" from which to approach the world". Therefore, this paradigm emphasizes the plurality of the truth.

(a) Polyvocality

Polyvocality employs different genres on writing to create meaning and emotion. It is because there are alternative options to deliver information and feeling between researcher and readers' consciousness (Richardson, 2000). Thus, readers can gain emotional appreciation from the writing.

(b) Verisimilitude

The verisimilitude is the standard to judge either the idea or writing is similar with the reality and truth. According to Ellis and Bochner (2000), verisimilitude is presentation feeling of truthlikeness upon the reader who reads the narrative inquiry writing. Therefore, through the standard, researchers need to represent their writing in an engaging manner. Although the writing can be fictitious, the important point is truthlikeness.

(c) Criteria of Writing/Literary Criteria (Orientation, Strength, Richness, and Depth)

Impressionistic writing becomes the way to represent the data in this paradigm. According to Richardson (2000), writing as a method of inquiry helps researchers to find out how the world, we, and others are constructing within our perspectives. Moreover, narrative inquiry engages the readers with the orientated, strong, rich, and deep textual representation. In addition, oriented text means, "the text should be oriented to answering the question of how the researcher as educator stands in relation of life" (Taylor, Gilmer, Tobin, 2002, p. 31). This can be represented through involving value and teaching experiences in relation to the pedagogical context into research. In educational research, writing should represent "strong pedagogical perspective"

TABLE 2.1

Characteristic of Research Paradigm in Educational Research (Lather, 2006 as cited in Howitt, 2008; Taylor, 2006)

Characteristics	*Post/Positivism*	*Interpretivism*	*Criticalism*	*Postmodernism*
(1)	*(2)*	*(3)*	*(4)*	*(5)*
Focus of Research	Discovery of truth	Creation of meaning	Emancipation (Power and agency)	Difference (self-other dialectic)
Reality	Objective	Subjective and constructive	Subjective (basis of issue of power)	Subjective (self and critical reflections)
Truth	One truth	Many truth	Many truth (socio-political power)	Many truth (sometimes no truth), challenges all grand narratives
Discourse	Structured, transparent, reflecting reality	Dialogic and creates the reality	Controlled by rhetorical and political purpose	Impressionistic writing, engaging, emotions
Objectives	Knowing the word, communication as transmission	Understanding the world Communication as transaction	Changing the World Communication as decision-making	Understanding and Empowering the World Communication as engagement.
Findings	Precise, numerical	Comprehensive, holistic, rich description	Critique of power, privilege	Critique all grand narratives, self-reflections, empowerment
Quality Standards	Validity Reliability Objectivity	Trustworthiness (credibility, dependability, confirmability, transferability, fairness) Authenticity (Ontological, educative, catalytic, and tactical)	Praxis (pedagogical thoughtfulness, critical reflexivity, and re-envisioning)	Representation (polivocality, verisimilitude, ambiguity, playfulness, paradox, literacy criteria)

(Taylor, Gilmer, Tobin, 2002, p. 32) to interpret the phenomenon. The varied and meaningful description of phenomenon should be applied to create the rich text. Finally, the rich text should shape the writing to encourage the readers to think reflectively within their pedagogical experiences.

Characteristic of Research Paradigm in Educational Research is shown in Table 2.1.

References

Anderson, G.L. (1989), Critical theory status and new directions. *Review of Educational Research*, 59: 240-70.

Atkinson, E. (2000a). What can postmodern thinking do for educational research?, Paper presented at the annual meeting of the American Educational Research Association, New Orleans, 24-28 April.

Bryman, A. (2001). *Social Research Methods*. London: Oxford University Press.

Bryman, A. (2008). *Social Research Method* (3rd Ed.), New York: Oxford University Press.

Cohen, L., Manion, L. and Morrison, K. (2000). *Research Methods in Education*. London and New York: Taylor & Prancis Group.

Cole, M. (2001). Educational postmodernism, social justice and social change. *International Journal of Theory and Research in Education*, 12 (1/2), pp. 69-85.

Creswell, J. (2005). Educational Research: Planning, Conducting, and Evaluation Quantitative and Qualitative Research. New Jersey: Pearson Prentice Hall.

Denzin, N.K. and Lincoln, Y. S. (2000). *Handbook of qualitative research*. London: SAGE.

Howitt, C. (2007). *Quality standards associated with the postpositivist and interpretive research paradigms (lecture notes)*. Perth: SMEC, Curtin University of Technology.

Somekh, B., and L. Lewin, C. (2005). *Research Methods in the Social Sciences*. New Delhi: Vistaar Publications.

Taylor, P.C. (2006). Major research paradigms for science and mathematics educators *(Lecture notes)*. Perth: SMCE, Curtin University of Technology.

Taylor, P.C. (2008). Multi-paradigmatic research design spaces for cultural studies researchers embodying postcolonial theorizing. *Culture Studies of Science Education (4)*, 1-8.

Taylor, P.C. and Wallace, J. (1996). *Doing Qualitative Research in Science and Mathematic Education*. London: Sage Publication.

Wiersma, W. (1991). *Research Methods in Education*. London: Allyn and Bacon.

Willis, J.W. (2007). World Views, Paradigms and the Practice of Social Science Research (pp. 1-26). *Foundations of qualitative research: Interpretive and Critical Approaches*. Thousand Oaks, CA: Sage.

CHAPTER

3

Fundamental, Applied and Action Research

3.0 FUNDAMENTAL RESEARCH

Fundamental or basic research is a research carried out to increase understanding of fundamental principles or, an investigation on basic principles and reasons for occurrence of a particular event of process. Fundamental research is primarily concerned with formulation of theory or testing of theory or making addition to the quantum of knowledge.

Collaborative International Dictionary of English explains fundamental research as:

(i) Diligent inquiry or examination in seeking facts or principles: laborious and continuous research after truth.
(ii) Systematic observation of phenomena for the purpose of learning or discovery of new facts or testing the application of theories to known facts.

Fundamental research is also called theoretical research as it is study or investigation of some natural phenomenon or relating to pure science. Sometimes, it may not lead to immediate use or application. Fundamental or basic research includes original investigation for the advancement of scientific knowledge. The primary aim of the investigation is achievement of fuller knowledge or understanding of the subject matter under study, rather than making practical application of new knowledge, i.e. knowledge for knowledge sake.

In pure research the investigator may attack any problem any where that appeals to his fancy. After he has selected his problem he need only apply scholarly methods to its solution and publish the results, with no concern about any practical social use of his findings. It involves:

- highly developed intellectual capacities for interpreting evidence, making arguments, and establishing valid grounds for action,
- the development of generalities that hold across cases. They usually aim to theorize,
- the act of transformation from the experiential to the theoretical, i.e. viewing them through the normalizing lens of theory, and
- use of a professional language. Such a language captures generalities and exists from theories.

Strokes (1997) suggests that two issues are crucial in the conduct of research: whether the research is conducted with a concern for how the results of the research will be used, and whether the research is conducted with a concern for fundamental understanding (Table 3.1).

TABLE 3.1

Quadrant Model of Scientific Research

Quest for fundamental understanding?	*Consideration of Use?*	
	No	*Yes*
Yes	Pure basic research (Bohr)	Use-inspired basic research (Pasteur)
No	Applied research unmotivated by applications (Brahe)	Pure applied research (Edison)

Where neither of these is a concern, the result is applied research unmotivated by applications, which Strokes suggests is exemplified by the Danish astronomer Tycho Brahe. Where use is a concern, but fundamental understanding is not, the result is pure applied research, exemplified by the work of Thomas Edison. Conversely, where fundamental understanding is a concern, but application is not, we have pure basic research, exemplified by the work of the Danish physicist Niels Bohr. Finally, where considerations of use and fundamental understanding both are important, we have "Pasteur's quadrant"-use-inspired basic research.

Piaget's theory of cognitive development is a good example of that has been developed with little or no concern for application. In fact, a large number of researchers and educationists have explicated the usefulness of his theory for teaching practices from pre-school to higher education. (Read, 1995; Karplus *et al.*, 1977; Harcharick, 1993). The theory also has been shown to have implications for teaching children with mental retardation (Kahn,1996) and with other disabilities (Wolinsky, 1970).

3.1 BASIC FEATURES OF FUNDAMENTAL RESEARCH

- Fundamental research is analytical, intellectual, universal and theoretical.
- Fundamental research is based upon high quality research design.
- It makes use of sophisticated techniques involving originality, imagination and inventiveness.
- Its methodology is rigorous involving highly structured, intensive and systematic scientific processes.
- It employs careful sampling techniques in order to extend the results or findings beyond the selected sampled groups and draws broad generalizations or principles leading to development of theories.
- It uses precise, most reliable and valid tools of measurements.
- Fundamental research is concerned with minor effect size. If it is to test an existing theory, even small differences can increase one's confidence that theory has some validity.
- Formulation of theories or testing of theories is the outcome of the scientists' perseverance, consistent, and continuous efforts spread over a pretty long period.

Hypotheses or research questions were searched out deductively, relevant data was collected and analyzed minutely, and significant statistical inferences were derived in order to build generalization.

3.2 APPLIED RESEARCH

Applied Research refers to scientific study and research that seeks to solve practical problems. It is directed toward practical application of scientific knowledge, i.e. the production of useful materials, devices, systems, methods, or improved processes,

Although it is impossible to generalize completely, applied research deals with practical problems and generally empirical. Because applied research resides in the messy real world, strict research protocol is not possible. For example, it may be impossible to use random sample. Thus, transparency in the methodology is critical. Testing is mostly useful that is directed towards decisions with some immediate practical consequences. (Mackeachie, 1997). Implications for interpretation of results brought about by relaxing a more or less cannon of methodology are also required to be developed.

A product of all research in behavioual sciences is a set of conclusions and recommendations or for policy implications. These conclusions may not be at a sophisticated level of theorizing or at a level of theorizing. Most psychologists would agree that it is wise to keep theorizing down to the level that involves a minimal use of abstract terms. In applied research, effect-size of Null Hypothesis Significance should be high for policy implications.

Research that has no obvious practical application is of little importance in education. Research in education is meant to increase the potential for practical improvement in the conduct and/or organization of learning and teaching. Broadly speaking, applied research exhibits one or more of the following characteristics:

- The revealing of a hitherto unrecognized mismatch between expectation and experience (actual or anticipated) that has far-reaching practical implication;
- The formulation of a new and important problem;
- The production of new and better solution to the existing problem;
- The development of a constructive way of challenging existing expectations; and
- Applied research does not provide results which can be generalized; the finding may have important implications, either for personal practice or others working in the similar areas. (Swann, 2007).

Characteristics of Applied Research are given in Table 3.2

In brief, applied research is normative, personal, particular and experiential. Applied research enables us to seek answer; it is not an exercise which merely contributes to knowledge archives. Its purpose is to contribute to our own well-being, to improve our conditions and our own lives. Educational research is more or less is an applied research. Purpose is to improve classroom practice, or look to the wider socio-political issues which underlie, influence or circumscribe

TABLE 3.2
Characteristics of Applied Research

1. Goals	It is directed toward practical application of scientific knowledge, i.e. the production of useful materials, devices, systems, methods, or improved processes.
2. Identifying the research problem	Review of past literature and Field experience: (1) Identifying unrecognized mismatch between expectation and experience (actual or anticipated) that has far-reaching practical implication; (2) The production of new and better solution to the existing problem.
3. Hypotheses	A specific statement of the problem usually serves as the research hypothesis.
4. Review of Literature	A review of available literature gives the teacher a general understanding of the area to be studied.
5. Sampling	Generally Non-Probability Sampling Techniques are used such as Incidental or Purposive Sampling
6. Experimental Design	Design is carefully planned in detail prior to start of the study. Major attention is given to maintaining comparable conditions and reducing error and bias. No scope for the manipulation of independent variable.
7. Measurement	An effort is made to obtain the most reliable and valid measures for collection of data.
8. Analysis of Data	In as much as generalizability of results is not a goal, statistical significance is usually emphasized. Big size-effect is required that has some validity in its application.
9. Application of Results	Conclusions and recommendations are made for policy implications. Decisions reached are applied for the solution of problem or improvement of practice.

the organization and conduct of education. Thus, research in education is both expectation-laden and value-impregnated.

Figure 3.1 shows difference between fundamental and applied research in educational research.

An example given by Turney and Robb (1971) would make the distinction between the basic and applied research more clear.

'If a researcher were to conduct a study using white rats to determine the effect of positive *vs.* negative reinforcement on learning

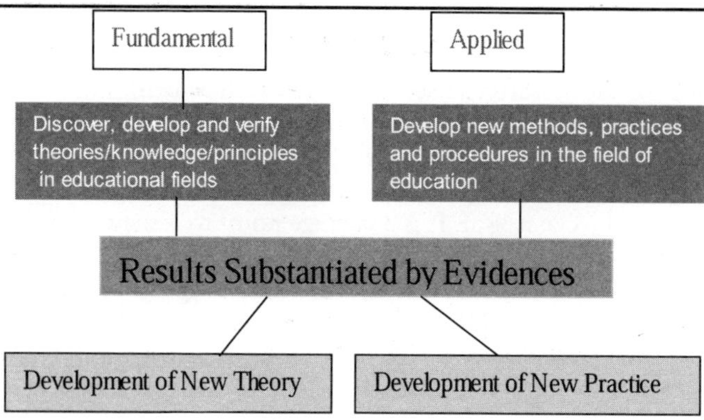

Figure 3.1 : Fundamental *v.* Applied Research

to run a maze successfully, he would be conducting basic research. If he rewarded one group of rats with food pellets for correct turn in maze but administered electric shocks to the group of rats making incorrect turn. He could, then, determine which group mastered the maze in a shorter period of time. Even though, this information has no immediate application to motivation, it may be useful for building a theory, concerning motivation and learning whereas food and electrical shocks might be impractical to use in the classroom, the researcher could conduct an experiment using praise and criticism as motivational factors in human beings. This type of experiment directed towards solution of problem practically would be classified as applied research.'

Piaget's theory of cognitive development is a good example of that has been developed with little or no concern for application. In fact, a large number of researchers and educationists have explicated the usefulness of his theory for teaching practices from pre-school to higher education. (Read, 1995; Karplus *et al.*, 1977; Harcharick, 1993). The theory also has been shown to have implications for teaching children with mental retardation (Kahn,1996) and with other disabilities (Wolinsky, 1970).

Both basic and applied research should be encouraged and supported. While basic research, at the time the particular investigation was made, may have been evaluated chiefly in terms of the satisfaction afforded the researcher, at a later date the same pure research may have practical and social value. The efforts of the extreme purist and of the extreme technologist are complimentary, contributing to a range of research and a diversity of attitude beneficial to society. (Good, 2008)

3.3 ACTION RESEARCH

Most of the researchers see action research as being carried out by practitioners—whether in a professional group or university—to understand and improve their own practice. Action research in education is to examine problem in the backdrop of the learner experience in the classroom. It is a vantage point to review their own understanding of the subject matter i.e. how to read situation and how to act on it. It is also meant to generate intellectual space for reflection and the sharing of ideas. Most of the researchers see it as: (1) seeking improvement in the action, (2) it is to be based on the child's experience in the classroom, and (3) it is reflective. In simple term, action research is a better understanding of what a teacher is doing in the classroom? How to act, reflect, revise and revitalize? How can a practicing teacher help his students improve the quality of their learning?

The practitioner feels that there is mismatch between anticipated and actual results in an existing situation. Therefore, need arises how to make the existing phenomenon more efficient and effective. It also becomes focal point to understand how to read situation and how to act on it to inform practice. It involves 'systematic process' overcoming 'commonsense knowing'. In this context action research is a viable option. Action research is "to plan, act, observe and reflect more carefully, more systematically, and more rigorously than one usually does in everyday life." (Kemmis *et al.*, 1992).

Action research, therefore, is any systematic inquiry conducted by teacher researchers to gather information about the particular circumstance or phenomena that affects their action, how they teach, and how well their students learn. The information is gathered with the goals of gaining insight, developing reflective practice, effecting positive changes in the school environment and on educational practices in general, and improving student outcomes. (Mills, 2003)

There is a wide range of different approaches to action research. Noffke (1997) groups these within three dimensions: the professional, the personal and the political. The first focus on improving what is offered to clients in professional settings, the second is concerned with factors such as developing 'greater self-knowledge' and 'a deeper understanding of one's own practice.' The third is concerned with social action and social change. Grundy's (1982) earlier categorization suggests a hierarchical : the 'technical', the 'practical' and the 'critical'. The technical focuses upon making a better product (for example, more efficient and effective practice), the practical focuses upon

TABLE 3.3

Difference between Fundamental Research, Action Research and Research

Area	*Fundamental Research*	*Action Research*	*Applied Research*
(1)	*(2)*	*(3)*	*(4)*
1. Training Required	Intensive and Extensive training in measurement, statistics, and research methods are needed. Much of the scientific research done in education is weak because of deficiencies of the researchers in these areas.	Only a limited training in statistics and research methods is needed because rigorous design and analysis are not usually necessary. More training in educational measurement is needed than most teachers possess. Even if teacher's research can be carried out with the aid of a consultant.	Trainings in statistics, research methods, and measurement and evaluation are needed.
2. Goals	Pursuit of truth and to obtain knowledge that will be generalizable to a board population and to develop and test educational theories.	To obtain knowledge that can be applied directly to the local classroom situation, and to give the participating teachers in-service training	It is directed toward practical application of scientific knowledge, i.e. the production of useful materials, devices, systems, methods, or improved processes. Although it is impossible to generalize completely:
3. Locating the research problem	(1) Theory provides a framework by serving as the point of departure for the pursuit of a research problem.	Problems identified in the school situation that are causing the research worker trouble or are interfering with the efficiency of his teaching.	(1) The revealing of a hitherto unrecognized mismatch between expectation and experience (actual or anticipated) that has far-reaching practical implication;

(*Contd.*)

TABLE 3.3 (*Contd.*)

(1)	*(2)*	*(3)*	*(4)*
	(2) Very well identify gaps, inconsistencies and weak points in theory help in locating the research problem. (3) Problems are identified by a wide range of Methods.		(2) The production of new and better solution to the existing problem;
4. Hypotheses	Highly specific hypotheses are developed that employ operational definitions and are testable.	A specific statement of the problem usually serves as the research hypothesis. Ideally, action research hypotheses should approach rigor of formal research.	A specific statement of the problem usually serves as the research hypothesis. Ideally, applied research hypotheses should approach rigor of formal research.
5. Nature of the Sourcing	An appropriate review of primary source of material is usually earned out, giving the research worker is thorough understanding of the current state of knowledge in the research area. This enables him to build upon the knowledge accumulated by others.	A review of available secondary sources gives the teacher a general understanding of the area to be studied. Exhaustive review of primary sources is almost never done.	A review of available literature gives the teacher a general understanding of the area to be studied.

6.	Sampling	Probability Sampling Techniques are used. Such as Random Sampling, Stratified Random Sampling, etc.	Pupils available in the class of the teacher or teachers doing the research are used as subjects.	Non-Probability Sampling Techniques are used such as Incidental or Purposive Sampling.
7.	Experimental design	Fundamental research is based upon high quality research design. Design is carefully planned in detail prior to start of the study and adhered to as closely as possible. Major attention is given to maintaining comparable conditions and reducing error & bias. Control of extraneous variables is important. Independent variable is manipulated to see the effect.	Procedures are planned in general terms prior to start of study. Changes are made during the study if they seem likely to improve the teaching situation. Little attention is paid to control of the experimental conditions or reduction of error. Because participating teachers are ego-involved in the research situation, bias is usually present.	Design is carefully planned in detail prior to start of the study. Major attention is given to maintaining comparable conditions and reducing error & bias. No scope for the manipulation of independent variable.
8.	Measurement	It uses most precise, accurate, most reliable and valid tools of measurements.	Less rigorous evaluation of measures than in scientific research. Participants often lack training in the use and evaluation of educational measures, but can do a satisfactory job with help of a consultant.	An effort is made to obtain the most valid measures available. A thorough evaluation of available measures and a trial of these measures usually precede their use in the research

(*Contd.*)

TABLE 3.3 (*Contd.*)

(1)	*(2)*	*(3)*	*(4)*
9. Analysis of Data	Complex analysis often called for. In as much as generalizability of results is a goal, statistical significance is usually emphasized. If it is to test an existing theory, even small differences can increase one's confidence that theory has some validity	Simple analysis procedures usually are sufficient. Practical significance rather than statistical significance is emphasized. Subjective opinion of participating teachers is often weighted heavily.	Analysis of data often called for. In as much as generalizability of results is not a goal, statistical significance is usually emphasized. Big size-effect is required that has some validity in its application.
10. Application of Results	Results are generalizable, but many useful findings are not applied in educational practice.	Findings are applied immediately to the classes of participating teachers and often lead to permanent improvement. Application of results beyond the participating teachers is usually slight	Conclusions and recommendations are made for policy implications. Decisions reached are applied for the solution of problem or improvement of practice.

developing the 'practical judgement'of the participant-researcher grounded in experience and self-reflection, crtical leads to 'emancipatory' action research, (i.e. compulsions of traditions, precedent, habit, coercion as well as from self-deception.)

Action research is a reflective cyclic process. This reflective cycle starts with:

(a) identifying the problem,
(b) understanding the situation,
(c) analysing the problem,
(d) form this analysis identification of a suitable, often small scale, systematic intervention aimed at achieving a more desirable outcome will be evolved, and
(e) at the end the finding will be analyzed, evaluated and reflected upon with the aim of providing further modification to, or redefinition of the original intervention.
(i.e. How to act, reflect, revise and revitalize?

References

Best, J. and Kahn, J. (2009). *Research in Education.* 10th edition, Needham Heights: Allyn and Bacon.

Corey, S.M. (1962). *Research in Education.* NCERT, New Delhi.

Cozby, P. (2009). *Methods in Behavioural Research.* 10th edition, Bemont: Wadsworth.

Festinger, L. and Katz, D. (1976) (eds.). *Research Methods in the Behavioural Sciences.* New Delhi: Amerind Publishing Co.

Good, Carter V. (1966). *Essentials of Educational Research: Methodology and Design.* New York: Applleton-Century Crofts.

Goode, W.J., and Hatt, P.K. (1990). *Methods in Social Research.* New Delhi: McGraw-Hill.

Guthrie, G. (2010). *Basic Research Methods.* New Delhi: Sage.

Hillway, T. (1956). *Introduction to Research.* Houghton Miffin Co.

CHAPTER

4

Essentials of Scientific Inquiry

4.1 SCIENTIFIC INQUIRY

Scientific inquiry implies "a continuous process of rigorous reasoning supported by a dynamic interplay among methods, theories, and findings" (NRC, 2002). Scientific inquiry in social sciences including education is more descriptively oriented, more dependent on context, less cumulative, and more intuitive than the idealized model of experimentation. It recognizes the importance of philosophical, historical, social and cultural context, participant involvement, political considerations, and ethical requirements as inherent features of the study of social and educational phenomenon. (Eisenhart and DeHaan, 2005). However, if educational research is in line with scientific principles and attends to the relevant contextual features of education, it could then be considered scientific.

The term "Scientific Inquiry" means the application of rigorous, systematic, and objective procedures to obtain reliable and valid knowledge relevant to education activities and programmes, and includes research that:

- Employs systematic, empirical methods that draw on observation or experiment;
- Involves rigorous data analyses that are adequate to test the stated hypotheses and justify the general conclusions drawn;

- Relies on measurements or observational methods that provide reliable and valid data across evaluators and observers, across multiple measurements and observations, and across studies by the same or different investigators;
- It is evaluated using experimental or quasi-experimental designs in which : (a) individuals, entities, programmes, or activities are assigned to different conditions, and (b) with appropriate controls to evaluate the effects of the conditions of interest, (c) with preference for random assignment experiments, or other designs to the extent that those designs contain within condition or across condition;
- Ensures that experimental studies are presented insufficient detail and clarity to allow for replication, or at a minimum, offer the opportunity to build systematically on their findings and approved by a panel of independent experts through a comparably rigorous, objective and scientific review. (NCR, 2002).

4.2 PRINCIPLES OF SCIENTIFIC INQUIRY

All sciences including the scientific study of education have to observe a set of epistemological or fundamental guiding principles. These are:

- Pose significant questions that can be investigated empirically,
- Link research to relevant theory,
- Use methods that permit direct investigation of the questions,
- Provide a coherent and explicit chain of reasoning,
- Yield findings that replicate and generalize across studies, and
- Disclose research data and methods to enable and encourage professional scrutiny and critique.

Johnson (2009) proposed a set of guidelines that is more inclusive and might better represent scientific enquiry in education. Guidelines are:

- Identify important problems and pose questions that can be investigated empirically or through potentially useful approaches,
- Continually generate, discover, describe, and construct new knowledge , and test/evaluate knowledge claims,
- Separately and inter-connectively explore, reflect upon,

describe, predict, and explain the natural world and meaningful social and personal "worlds" and experiences,

- Explicate researcher and research values, purposes, commitments and key background assumptions,
- Use methods and strategies that, separately or in combination, can produce warranted investigation of particular research question,
- Rely on multiple sources of evidence, Link explanatory research to relevant theory, through theory generation, theory testing, and ongoing theory modification,
- Describe the nomological (i.e. general law like) knowledge domain, but also describe ideographic, local and contextual knowledge domain, , and interconnect these to continually produce meaningful "practical theory",
- Replicate, document mediating and moderating processes, delineate conditions of generalization, and identify broad generalizations when possible, but also identify complex contextual interactions to aid in particular understanding and practical application of educational of social theory,
- Articulate, replicate, develop, and test "manualized models", practice-based model, middle-level theoretical models, transtheoretical and transdisciplinary models of educational phenomena, and interconnect these continually for scientific learning,
- Explicate creative and formal reasoning process (i.e inductive, deductive, abductive, critical theory) to help stimulate and warrant findings and valueschoices, and
- Fully disclose research process and findings to encourage professional and social scrutiny. Continually encourage self-examination and critique and ongoing improvement of the education scientific enterprise.

These principles need to be understood and internalized by all professional communities and scientific researchers.

Concerted efforts should be made to train social scientists in certain habits of mind:

- dedication to the primacy of evidence,
- to elucidation and reduction of biases that might affect the research process, and
- to disciplined, creative, and open-minded thinking.

The National Council of Research (2002) described several features in education that shape its scientific study. These are:

- the role of values and democratic ideals in the schools,
- the volition and diversity of people (teachers, students, administrators),
- the variability of curriculum, instruction, and governance across education settings.
- The presence of metadisciplines in educational research (i.e. anthropology, psychology, sociology, economics and neuroscience),
- The understanding of causal processes and mechanisms requires close attention to contextual factors and to capture these complexities typically involves qualitative modes of inquiry. Therefore, qualitative and quantitative research tools can both be employed rigorously and together often can support stronger scientific inferences, and
- The randomly assigning of units of analysis in various conditions in education is not always feasible

4.3 SCIENTIFIC INQUIRY PROCESSES

When we engage in scientific inquiry we usually think there is a set procedure which involves to—hypothesise, design an experiment, get data, analyse it, make conclusions. This process doesn't take into account a lot of the things that scientists do as they tackle a problem—follow hunches, use their imagination, discuss in corridors with colleagues. Not all scientists approach problems in the same way—many have preferred inquiry procedures which tie into their own preferred ways of learning and understanding. Different types of problems and contexts require different approaches.

No matter whether you are a physicist or a biologist, psychologist, educator as you inquire into something you are likely to cover different aspects. These are indicated in the chart on the next page—it is like a road map—there are many different ways of arriving at the objective.

The more aspects that you visit the sounder your whole inquiry will be. You may find that you only seem to be able to get started if you have a real concrete experience of what you are investigating, while someone else needs to sit back and read information that others have collected to get an overview. By recognizing that different people have different entry points into the inquiry process and particular skills it is possible to come together in collaborative inquiry which takes the group beyond each individual. Dialogue is the key.

Often many ideas get lost because people move from one thing to another randomly without being aware of the different parts of the

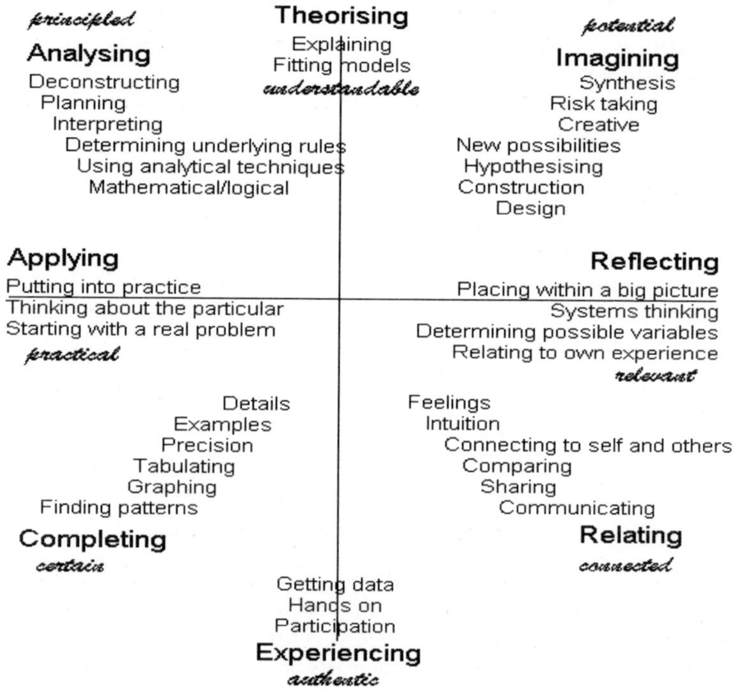

Figure 4.1 : Roadmap to Scientific Inquiry

process. By having this map of scientific inquiry upfront students can be explicitly aware of their process–what is going wrong, what is going right and what is missing. With practice students learn to ask questions coming from each perspective of the map that moves their inquiry onwards and gives it rigor, leading to enhanced understanding and insight.

This becomes very powerful when coupled with students being asked to critically think about ideas of science using questions of:

1. **Is it intelligible?**
2. **Is it plausible?**

How is it convincing, logical, relevant, authentic, trustworthy, connected, supported by evidence, practical, meaningful, humane or fit a bigger picture?

3. **Is it Useful?**

How does it have greater explanatory or predictive power compared to other models? How does it have more elegance, simplicity, order or symmetry? How does it fit into other ways of explaining the world? How does it uplift, inspire or advance the world? In what ways can it be ethically applied?

4. Is it Believable?

What are my underlying beliefs and values about the world and

Optimising Your Investigative Approach

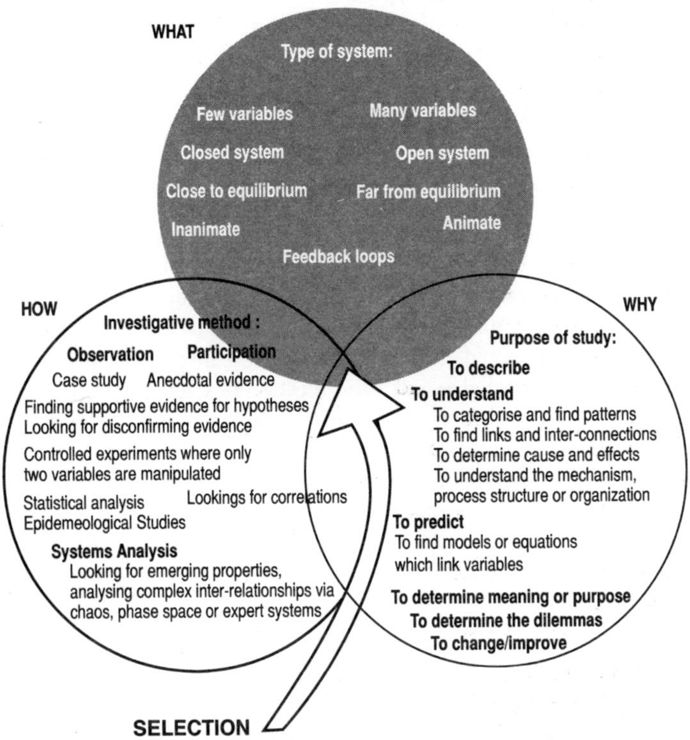

* Is your selection of method appropriate to the system studied?
* Will it be able to achieve your desired purpose?
* What are the limitations of such a method and what can you claim?
* In water way does your selection achieve appropriate rigor, reliability, internal consistency, ability to be generalised, trustworthiness, authenticity or objectivity?
* What preconceptions, values or biases are your bringing to this study and how do they affect the selection of method, purpose and system. To what degree do these values affect the way you interpret your findings?
* What do you intend to do with the results of the study and are there any ethical considerations?

(Holistic Education Network of Tasmania, 2003)

Figure 4.2 : Shows the Investigative Approach

how does this ide interact with these? How much of this idea am I willing to take on board and with what provisos? In what ways have I been convinced to accept this idea and am I happy that the type of validity claims are approapriate?

Students can explore the meaning of plausibility and realize that each perspective of the map has a plausibility dimension. For example, in the *Relating* aspect plausibility might mean how does this relate to other studies, is it connected or does it feel right?

The inquiry process is done in a context of understanding the appropriateness of the type of study for a particular purpose and type of problem or phenomena. So coupled with their inquiry process students need to be aware of the choices they make whenever they begin to inquire.

4.4 METHOD OF SCIENTIFIC INQUIRY

The inductive method alone did not provide a completely system for the solution of the problems. Random collection of individual observation without unifying concept or focus often obscured investigations and therefore rarely led to a generalization or theory. The method of inductive reasoning came to be used by the scientists as a most reliable and valid method of scientific inquiry. The controversy of inductive or deductive has been relegated to background on the integration of both methods to arrive at logical conclusion. This inductive-deductive method is now recognized as an example of a scientific approach. Moreover, no method is good or bad, scientific or unscientific. Rather, it is the appropriate application of method to a particular problem that enables judgment about scientific quality.

The Steps of the Scientific Inquiry:

1. Identification of the problem
2. Definition of the problem
3. Formulation of hypothesis or research question
4. Collection, organization, and analysis of data
5. Interpretation of results
6. Verification, rejection, or modification of the hypothesis/ research question by the test of its consequences in a specific situation
7. Formulation of conclusions
8. Policy implications

It is useful for thinking about the kinds of expertise that might be required of different roles in the educational enterprise. For this, the classification of different kinds of systems of inquiry proposed by Churchman (1971) provides a useful organizing principle :

- In the Leibnizian inquiry system, the most important form of evidence is rationality—whether the conclusions follow logically from the assumptions. When methods are appropriate, inquiries into educational phenomena require some sort of empirical data from the situation under study.
- In Lockean inquiry system, the main source of evidence is observation of the world. Empirical data are collected and the attempt is made to build a theory that acc outs for the data. Emphasis is, therefore laid on "scientific detachment" in observation.
- Within a Singerian inquiry system, one can never separate out the meanings of a piece of research from it consequences. Education research is a process of representing educational processes, and representation are never right or wrong, merely more or less appropriate for a particular purpose, and it is perfectly fair to expect the researcher to defend the appropriateness of the representations.

Hillway (1978) presents the role of the investigator as that of a detective. He points out that:

- The scientist must be alert and trained to seel clues that will develop into fruitful hypotheses;
- He must be familiar with the sources of information;
- He must be able to extract the desired information quickly and effectively;
- He must check hypotheses for validity;
- He must evaluate all the information he gathers before attempting to synthesize it with respect to his hypotheses; and
- Finally, the scientist must test their hypotheses against objective evidence, not mere plausibility.

References

Ackoff, R.L. (1962). *Scientific Method.* New York: John Wiley & Sons.

Best, J.W. and Kahn, J.V. (2008). *Research in Edcation.* Pearson, Prentice Hall, Inc. and Dorling Kindersley Publishing, Inc. (India).

Brodbeck, M. (1963). Logic and scientific method in research on teaching. In N.L. Gage (ed.), *Handbook of Research on Teaching* (pp. 44-93), Chicago: Rand McNally.

Englehart, Max D. (1972). *Methods of Educational Research.* Chicago: Rand McNally.

Festinger, L. and Katz, D. (1976) (eds.). *Research Methods in the Behavioural Sciences*. New Delhi: Amerind Publishing Co.
Freedman, P. (1960). *The Principles of Scientific Research.* 2nd ed., New York: Pergamon Press.
Good, Carter V. (1966). *Essentials of Educational Research: Methodology and Design.* New York: Applleton-Century Crofts.
Koul, L. (2009). *Methodology of Educational Research.* Vikas Publishing House, New Delhi-14.
Popper, K. (1959). *The Logic of Scientific Discovery*. New York; Harper.
Roy, B.N. (1978). *Text-Book of Deductive Logic*. Sarkar & Sons, Calcutta.
William Wiersma (1986). *Research Methods in Education: An Introduction*. Allyn and Bacon, Inc. London.

CHAPTER

5

The Role and Development of Theory

5.1 THEORY

The term theory is used often in educational research; for example, curriculum theory or learning theory. Kerlinger (1973) has defined theory as a "set of interrelated constructs (concepts), definitions and propositions that presents a systematic view of phenomena by specifying relations among variables with the purpose of explaining and predicting the phenomena".

This definition emphasizes three things:

1. A theory is a set of statements comprising of interrelated constructs, definitions and propositions;
2. A theory sets out the relations among the set of constructs, definitions or propositions in order to present a systematic view of phenomena; and
3. A theory explains a phenomena by specifying what variables are related to what variables and how they are related, thus enabling the scientist to predict from certain variables to certain other variables.

Some example of substantive theories from different areas of research relevant to education are attribution theory, reinforcement theory, various learning theories and personal construct theory (from psychology); reference group theory and social stratification theory (from sociology); the theory of vocational personalities and career anchor (from occupational sociology); various leadership theories (from management and administration); and theories of children's moral development and of teacher career cycles.

Brodbeck (1963) has mentioned that theory is a *deductively corrected set of laws* and that all statements in a theory, both explained and explaining, are generalizations. The laws explain the explaining are the axioms; those generalizations explain the theorems. Theories can range from a single, simple generalization to a complex formulation of laws.

5.2 THE ROLE OF THEORY

In theory verification—we start with a theory, deduce hypotheses from it and design a study to test these hypotheses, while in theory generation—we do not start with a theory, instead theory is generated systematically from the data we have collected. Quantitative or qualitative research can be used for theory generation as well as for verification (Hammersley, 1992; Brewer and Hunter, 1989).

There is a constant and intricate relationship between facts and theory. *Theories define, classify, and predict facts.* Theories possess significance when they are built upon, classified, tested by facts. Thus, the growth of science is dependent upon the accumulation of facts and the formulation of new or broader theories.(Van Dalen, 1973). Theory summarizes and puts in order the existing knowledge in a particular area. It permits deeper understanding of data and translates empirical findings into a more easily retainable and adaptable form. 'It is a capital mistake to theorize before one has data. Insensibly one begins to twist fact to suit theories instead of theories to suit facts'.

The use of theory is more commonly associated with basic *research as well as applied research.* Sometimes the term theory-testing research is used as a part of basic research. Those who engage in pure research devote their energies to the formulation and reformulation of theories and may not be concerned with their practical applications. Piaget's theory of cognitive development is a good example of that has been developed with little or no concern for application. In fact, a large number of researchers and educationists have explicated the usefulness of his theory for teaching practices from pre-school to higher education. (Read, 1995; Karplus *et al.*, 1977; Harcharick, 1993). The theory also has been shown to have implications for teaching children with mental retardation (Kahn, 1996) and with other disabilities (Wolinsky, 1970).

Theory testing research would enable us to test the theory with its primary and related hypotheses and, presumably, would either confirm or refute the theory, thus providing needed information for revising or extending the theory if necessary.

However, when a theory has been established, it may suggest many applications of practical value. John Dewey once said that there was nothing more practical than a good theory. Theory may not claim to be a good theory if it could not stand the test of field. (Varma, 1983). For example, theories about the relationship between the position of the earth and other moving celestial bodies were essential to the successful launching and return of space vehicles. Theories of the behaviour of gases were essential to the development of refrigeration and air conditioning.

Basically, theory helps provide *a framework by serving as the point of departure for the pursuit of a research problem.* The theory identifies the crucial factors. It provides a guide for systematizing and interrelating the various facets of the research. However, besides providing the systematic view of the factors under study, the theory also may very well identify gaps, weak points, and inconsistencies that indicate the need for additional research. Also, the development of the theory may light the way for continued research on the phenomena under study.

In educational research, *theory serves a synthesizing function*, combining ideas and individual bits of empirical information into a set of constructs that provides for deeper understanding, broader meaning, and wider applicability. In a sense, a theory attaches meaning to facts and places them in proper perspective. Through this process, the theory aids in defining the research problem; that is; it helps identify the proper questions to be asked in the context of the specific project. Another function of theory is to provide one or more generalizations that can be tested and then used in practical applications and further research. A theory of learning, for example, could explain the relationship between learning and variables of motivation, rewards and practice.

As indicated in Kerlingers's (1973) definition, a theory also serves the purpose of *explaining and predicting*. It suggests an explanation of observed phenomena, and it can also predict as yet unobserved or undiscovered factors by indicating their presence. Operating under the assumption that the theory is consistent, the researcher is then tipped-off in terms of what to look for. In other words, scientists were spurred on to look for other missing elements.

5.3 DEVELOPMENT OF THEORY

Good theories have not born in a day. Theories are the outcome of the scientists' perseverance, consistent, and continuous efforts spread over a pretty long period. Hypotheses or research questions were searched out deductively or inductively, relevant data was collected and analyzed, significant statistical inferences were derived in order to build generalization.

A product of all research in behavioural sciences is a set of conclusions that involves theoretical terms. These conclusions may be at a sophisticated level of theorizing or at a level of theorizing that is quite low. Most psychologists would agree that it is wise to keep theorizing down to the level that involves a minimal use of abstract terms. We may think of levels of theorizing namely:

Identification of research problem: This involves scrutiny of original source and deep knowledge. Gaps, weak points, and inconsistencies in the theory that indicate the need for additional research, are identified. Main goal is either to discover new theory, or modify or to create new knowledge base.

Formulation of Hypotheses: Searching hypothesis/research question is an intellectual, analytical, and theoretical exercise. On the basis certain premises, hypotheses are formulated. Hypotheses are based on professional language. Such language captures generalities and exists from theories. Here the purpose of the research is defined as the producing of arguments and ideas, generalities and theories. For testing hypothesis analytical approach is employed. Variables are separated and examined microscopically under a perfectly controlled condition to predict the results accurately.

Elementism: Examples of theories at this level are primitive form of classification in terms of some significant set of ideas or idea. In case of education, classification of abilities derived from factor analysis, or classification of teacher acts that may be the result of extensive classroom observation, would come under the level of elementism.

From the Experiential to the Theoretical: A transition from the experiential to the theoretical is considered to be necessary because it is assumed that outsiders, such as researchers, are in a better position to put the characteristics of a phenomena in right perspectives by : (a) comparing them with those of other settings, and actors, (b) by viewing them through the normalizing lens of theory. (Butlerman-Bos, 2008). Empirical data are collected and the attempt is made to build a theory that accounts for the data; or conversely, multiple theories are developed that generate testable hypotheses that can then form the basis of of a "crucial experiment," which will indicate the theories is correct. (Churchman, 1971).

Explaining and Predicting Results: Data obtained within and across study is incorporated into a meaningful whole; standing alone, they are not likely to mean much. As the facets of the research study, the data derive significance from the theory or theories into which they fit. Conversely, the theories become acceptable to the extent that they enhance the meaning of data. Through this process, more adequate theories and unobstructed facts are secured; theory stimulates research, and conversely, research stimulates theory development and theory testing.

The Process of Generalization: The process of testing of generalization is carried out to develop a good theory. The theory must be compatible with the observations made relative to it and with already existing knowledge. It must adequately explain the events or phenomena under study. The greater the generalizability of the theory, the more useful it will be because of its wider applicability.

Descriptive Theories and Taxonomies: Formulation of Descriptive Theories and Taxonomies occurs at a more complex level than mere classification. An example of theorizing at this level is the taxonomy of human learning provided by Gagne. Gagne classified learning into eight different categories, which vary from the most simple to the most complex. Bloom's Taxonomy of cognitive behaviour can also be placed under this level.

Postulates and theories: At the highest level, a theory consists of a set of basic statements called the axioms of theory, which tell us what the theory is all about. Such axiomatic statements or postulates as they are called include primitive terms. These are terms that are intuitively understood and can not be otherwise completely defined. The criterion by which a theory is judged is not its truth or falsity, but rather its usefulness. Theories sometimes decrease in usefulness in the light of new knowledge, and they are combined, replaced, and refined as more knowledgeable is made available.

5.4 CHARACTERISTICS OF SOUND THEORY

- A theory must be stated in simple and precise terms. It should conform to the Law of Parsimony.
- A theory must be in conformity both with observed and with the previously established body of knowledge, or validated theories.
- A theory must provide means for its own interpretation

and verification. In other words, it must provide deductions which can be tested empirically.

- A theory must guide new discoveries and identify areas which are in need of investigation. It can do so if it is based on empirical facts and relationships.

Theories often offer a crude and general explanation of phenomena. Unrecognized mismatch between expectation and experience (actual or anticipated) has far reaching theoretical implications. This poses a challenge of testing theory to bridge the gap between expectation and experience. Thus, theories are refined and modified on verified facts. For example, if the facts found do not substantiate the theory, a scientist must reject or reformulate the theory to fit the new facts.

References

Aristotle (2000). The Nicomachean ethics (R. Crips, Trans.) Cambridge. UK: Cambridge University Press.

Butlerman Bos, J.A. (2008). Will a clinical make education research more relevant for practice? *Educational Researcher*, 37(7), 412-20.

Dewey, J. (1938). *Logic: The theory of inquiry*. New York: Holt, Rinehart & Winston.

Doyle, A.C. (1891). A Scandal in Bohemia. *Sunday Magazine*, July.

Harcharich, K. (1993). Piaget and the university internship experience. *Journal of Cooperative Education*, 29, 24-32.

Kahn, J.V. (1996). Cognitive skills and sign language knowledge of children with severe and profound mental retardation. *Education and Training in Mental Retardation*, 31, 162-68.

Karplus, R. *et al.* (1977). *Science teaching and the development of reasoning.* Berkeley: Lawrence Hall of Science, University of California.

Mayer, R.E. (2000). What is the place of science in educational research? *Educational Researcher*, 29 (6), pp. 38-9.

Naish, M. and Hartnett, A. (1975). What theory cannot do for teachers. *Education for Teaching*, 96, pp. 12-1.

Tyrus Hillway (1956). *Introduction to Research.* Boston: Houghton-Mifflin.

Wolinsky, C.F. (1970). Piget's theory of perception: Insights for educational practices with children who have perceptual difficulties. In *I.J. Athey & D.O. Rubadeau (Eds.), Educational implications of Piaget's theory. Waltham, MA: Ginn-Blaisdell.*

CHAPTER

6

Action Research

WHAT IS AN ACTION RESEARCH?

Action research came into limelight as a result of Stenhouse's Humanities Project and Elliot's Ford Teaching Project during the 1970s. These projects were concerned with developing innovative ways of teaching moral issues and with reform in the teaching of science using 'discovery learning' methods. Since the mid-1980s there has been a resurgence of interest in action research in the U.S.A. with the center of focus on improving learning and teaching. (Zeichner, 2003)

Action Research: Action is outcome of stimulation. Stimulation comes from mismatch between expectation and experience (Anticipated and actual). Process of research involves identification of variables coming in the way of optimization of results (behavioural or practice) and introduction of intervening variable or variables to get the optimum results. Optimum implies substantial effect of intervening variable or variables on individual behaviour or existing practice. (Gupta & Kapoor, 2009).

Most of the researchers see action research as being carried out by practitioners—whether in a professional group or university—to understand and improve their own practice. Action research in education is to examine problem in the backdrop of the learner experience in the classroom. It is a vantage point to review their own understanding of the subject matter, i.e. how to read situation and how to act on it. It is also meant to generate intellectual space for reflection and the sharing of ideas. Most of the researchers see it as: (1) seeking improvement in the action, (2) it is to be based on the child's experience in the classroom, and (3) it is reflective. In simple term, action research is a better understanding of what a teacher is doing in the classroom? How to act, reflect, revise and revitalize? How can a practicing teacher help his students improve the quality of their learning?

The practitioner feels that there is mismatch between anticipated and actual results in an existing situation. Therefore, need arises how to make the existing phenomenon more efficient and effective. It also becomes focal point to understand how to read situation and how to act on it to inform practice. It involves 'systematic process' overcoming 'commonsense knowing'. In this context action research is a viable option. Action research is "to plan, act, observe and reflect more carefully, more systematically, and more rigorously than one usually does in everyday life." (Kemmis *et al.*, 1992).

Action research, therefore, is any systematic inquiry conducted by teacher researchers to gather information about the particular circumstance or phenomena that affects their action, how they teach, and how well their students learn. The information is gathered with the goals of gaining insight, developing reflective practice, effecting positive changes in the school environment and on educational practices in general, and improving student outcomes. (Mills, 2003)

There is a wide range of different approaches to action research. Noffke (1997) groups these within three dimensions: the professional, the personal and the political. The first focus on improving what is offered to clients in professional settings., the second is concerned with factors such as developing 'greater self-knowledge' and 'a deeper understanding of one's own practice.' The third is concerned with social action and social change. Grundy's (1982) earlier categorization suggests a hierarchical : the 'technical', the 'practical' and the 'critical'. The technical focuses upon making a better product (for example, more efficient and effective practice), the practical focuses upon developing the 'practical judgement'of the participant-researcher grounded in experience and self-reflection, critical leads to 'emancipatory' action research. (i.e. compulsions of traditions, precedent, habit, coercion as well as from self-deception.)

Action research is a reflective cyclic process. This reflective cycle starts with

(a) identifying the problem,
(b) understanding the situation,

(c) analysing the problem,
(d) form this analysis identification of a suitable, often small scale, systematic intervention aimed at achieving a more desirable outcome will be evolved, and
(e) at the end the finding will be analyzed, evaluated and reflected upon with the aim of providing further modification to, or redefinition of the original intervention.
(i.e. How to act, reflect, revise and revitalize?)

There are two essential aims of all action research, to improve and to involve. Action research aims at improvement in three areas, firstly, the improvement of practice, secondly, improvement of the understanding of the practice by its practitioners, and thirdly, the improvement of the situation in which the practice takes place. (Carr and Kemmis,1986). Some of the objectives of action research are:

6.1 OBJECTIVES OF ACTION RESEARCH

- To study problems scientifically to bring about improvement in practices;
- To guide, correct, evaluate and take action;
- To initiate, generate and incorporate new idea or innovation;
- To create intellectual space for reflective thinking and action;
- To improve the quality of decision-making;
- To study problems in view of student experience in the classroom setting;
- To build reflective practitioners;
- To build professional culture in the educational arena;
- To make progress on school wide priorities;
- To make the staff more capable in joint ventures, accepting mutual criticism and collaborating in the execution of innovative practices; and
- To develop scientific attitude through self-direction, self-control, and self-analysis for modification of individual action and practices.

6.2 FRAMEWORK FOR CONDUCTING OF ACTION RESEARCH

- Identify a problem or issue,
- Think of questions to be asked/information to be gathered,
- Collect data,

- Analyze data,
- Identify intervention aimed at achieving a more desirable outcome,
- Evaluate impact, and
- If need arises modify, or redefine the original intervention.

6.3 PROCESSES

A variety of procedural plans have been evolved by different scholars. All adopt methodical and iterative sequences of research. The methodology offers a systematic approach to introducing innovations in teaching and learning. Selection of action research processes are as follow:

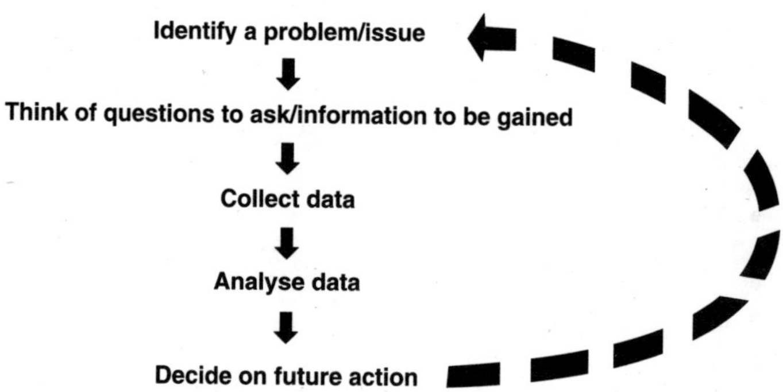

Figure 6.1 : Process of Action Research

(Harmer, 2002: 345)

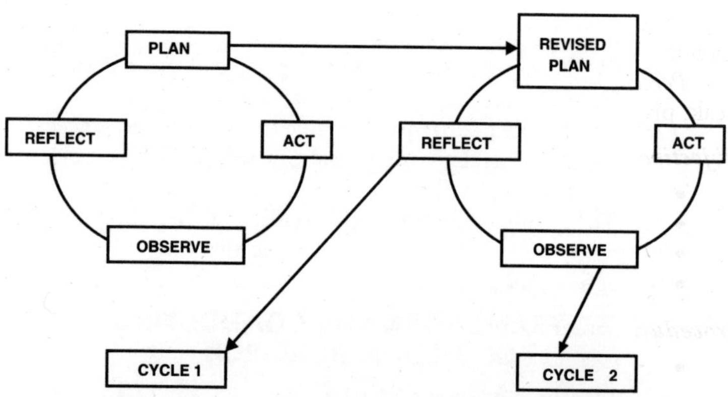

Figure 6.2 : Process of Action Research

It is thus an *emergent* process which takes shape as understanding increases; it is an *iterative* process which converges towards a better understanding of what happens. This process is based on the principles of reflective critique (i.e. reflective evidence is derived from authentic data); dialectical approach (i.e. dialogues between stakeholders); collaborative resource (i.e. sharing of resource and new ideas); risk (i.e. threat to taken for granted processes); plural structure (i.e. collaborative focus of enquiry); and theory, practice and transformation (interrelatedness)

6.4 PERSONAL POINTS TO CONSIDER

- Involve yourself in the action research
- Be organized
- Start small
- Ensure supportive work-in-progress discussions are planned for
- Be tolerant and supportive throughout the process
- Be persistent about monitoring
- Be prepared to work hard to ensure sharing of responsibility for the whole process
- Be open to changing how you think about things
- Register progress with all interested parties not just those involved directly
- Ensure time to write up your work
- Be explicit about what you have achieved
- Continually question yourself if your work is actually helping you.

(Kemmis and McTaggart, 1992)

6.5 PRACTICAL EXAMPLE

Topic: Study of "Low Achievement of Students of 8th Class" in Science .

Perception: "Low achievers in Science" were lazy, academically weak, problematic, awkward and troublesome.

Objectives of the Study

- To ascertain the causes of low achievement in science
- To identify intervention aimed at modifying teaching
- To ascertain the impact of intervention
- To develop further action plan

Procedure

- A semi-structured interview procedure was used for interviewing "Low Achievers" in Science.

Main Causes for them not doing well in Science were identified as such:

1. the module was too difficult;
2. there was too much materials to learn;
3. they had made insufficient personal effort;
4. the teacher's teaching was boring, unfriendly and impatient;
5. the teacher taught at a very fast pace;
6. they were not motivated; and
7. no one helped them when faced with problems.

Interpretation

- the students attributed their failure mainly to external factors (1, 2, 4, 5 & 6); and
- one controllable factor (3).

Intervention

- the students were motivated to increase the amount of effort;
- teacher helped them to overcome factors 1 & 2 by breaking the materials into smaller chunks before presenting them;
- teacher exercised control over the delivery pace (Factor 5); and
- teacher used pedagogical skills to overcome factors (4, 6 & 7).

Impact

- Desirable results were obtained

6.6 FORMAT FOR ACTION RESEARCH

Steps

1. Introduction
   (Need, Importance and Review of literature)
   Statement of Problem
2. Objectives/Research questions
3. Methodology
   (a) Sample, (b) Method, (c) Tools
4. Results/Findings
5. Intervention
6. Impact of intervention
7. Interpretation
8. Suggestions

6.7 CRITERIA FOR QUALITY IN ACTION RESEARCH

The action research paradigm requires its own criteria. Action research should not be judged by the criteria of positivist science, but rather than within the criteria of its own terms. Certain prerequisites which need to be fulfilled in order to ensure quality in action research are:

1. Is the action research explicit in developing praxis of relational participation?
2. Is action research guided by a reflexive concern for practical outcomes?
3. Is the action project governed by constant and iterative reflection as part of the process of organizational change or improvement?
4. Is action research is inclusive of practical, propositional, presentational and experiential knowledge on different levels?
5. Does action research engage in significant work? The significance of the project is an important quality in action research.
6. Does the action research result in sustainable change?

(1) Rigour

Rigour in action research ensures quality. It refers to how data are generated, gathered, explored and evaluated, how events are questioned and interpreted through multiple action research cycles. In other words, action researcher should develop requisite skills and techniques to assess quality in action research (Reasons and Bradbury (2001).

1. How are engaged in the steps of multiple and repetitions action research cycles (how diagnosing, planning, taking action and evaluating were done), and how those were recorded to reflect that they are a true representation of what was studied.
2. How are challenged and tested your own assumptions and interpretations of what was happening continuously through the project, by means of content, process and premise reflection, so that your familiarity with and closeness to the issues are exposed to critique.
3. How you accessed different views of what was happening which probably produced both confirming and contradictory interpretations.
4. How your interpretations and diagnoses are grounded in scholarly theory; rigorously applied, and how projects outcomes are challenged, supported or disconfirmed in terms of the theories underpinning those interpretations and diagnoses.

The value in action research is not whether the challenge process was successful or not, but rather that the exploration of the data-that is how a particular change was managed-provided useful and interesting theory which may contribute to learning on the subject of change management. What does a good action research project look like? Eden and Huxham (1996) provide an extensive list of the fifteen characteristics of good action research. The foundation characteristics reflect the intentionality of the researcher to change an organization, that the project has some implications beyond those involved directly in it and that the project has an explicit aim to elaborate or develop theory as well as be useful to the organization. Theory must inform the design and development of the actions. Eden and Huxham place great emphasis on the enactment of the action research cycles, in which systematic method and orderliness is required in reflecting on the outcomes of each cycle and the design of the subsequent cycles.

A good action research project contains three main elements, a good story, rigorous reflection on that story; and an extrapolation of usable knowledge or theory from the reflection on the story.

(2) A Good Story

As action research is about real time change, its core is the story of what takes place. The action research cycle of the general objective pre-step and the three main steps of planning, action and fact finding describe how the project is conceived, what is intended, the cycles of action and the outcome, both intended and unintended. The story must be presented in a factual and neutral manner, that is to say, as if it had been recorded on camera, and so that all the actors (teacher, students, parents and administrators) could agree on what had taken place. In short, the story is based on directly observable behaviour. Therefore, you need to be able to present evidence to support your narrative. Recorded data in journals and organizational documents are important supporting evidence.

Accordingly, it is critical that fact be clearly distinguished from value, that the basic story does not contain the author's inferences or interpretations, or at least, not without such inferences or interpretations being explicitly identified as such. For instance, if an action research story contains an assertion that a certain group was out to wreck the project, the narrative would need to be clear that there was evidence that group was trying to wreck the project, rather than it being an inference of the researcher or any party who saw itself as victim of that group's action.

(3) Rigorous Reflection

The critical process for making tacit knowledge explicit involves not only providing an analysis of what you think is going on in the story, but also of how you are making sense of it as the story unfolds (Weick, 1995). The rigorous of your inquiry is demonstrated by how you expose these activities to critique and how your conclusions are supported by your development of theory of usable knowledge.

(4) Linked to Knowledge-base

The third issue in action research is how the action research project is linked to theory and usable knowledge. It needs to have some interest and relevance to the uninvolved reader, the third person readership.

References

Altrichter, H., Posh, P. and Somekh, B. (1993). *Teachers Investigate Their Word an Introducation to the Methods or Action Research*. London : Routledge.

Burgess, J. (2006) 'Participatory Action Research: First Person Perspectives of a Graduate Student', *Action Research*, 4(4): 419-37.

Clive Opie (2004). *Doing Educational Research*. Vistaar Publications, New Delhi.

Elliott, J. (1991). *Action Research for Educational Change*. Buckingham, U.K. & Bristo, PA: Open University Press.

Elliott, J. (1994). Research on Teacher Knowledge and Action Research, *Education as Action Research*, 2(1), 133-7.

Grundy, S. (1982). 'Three Modes of Action Research' *Curriculum Perspectives*, 2(3): 23-24.

Holly, M.L. Arhar, J. and Kasten, W. (2004). *Action Research for Teachers : Travelling the Yellow Brick Road*, 2nd Education, N.J. Prentice-Hall.

McMiff, J. (1988). *Action Research : Principles and Practice*, London: Macmillan Education.

Reason, P. and Bradbury, H. (eds.) (2001). *Handbook of Action Research: Participating Inquiry & Practice*. London & Thousand Oaks, CA : Sage.

Zeichner, Kenneth M. (2003). 'Teacher Research as Professional Development for Educators in the USA, *Educational Action Research*, 11(2) 301-26.

CHAPTER

7

Research Approaches

Quantitative and Qualitative

7.1 QUANTITATIVE RESEARCH APPROACH

Quantitative Research describes and interprets what is. It is concerned with conditions or relationships that exist, opinions that are held, processes that are going, effects that are evident, or trends that are developing. It is primarily concerned with the present, although it often considers past events as they relate to current conditions. Quantitative research is based on the logical-positive paradigm, which utilizes experimental research methodologies. Quantitative research is truly scientific form of education research—"a continuous process of rigorous reasoning supported by a dynamic interplay among methods, theories, and findings" (NRC, 2002, p. 2).

7.1.1 Characteristics of Quantitative Research

- It is a scientific endeavour that needs to follow set rules and procedures. The variables and procedures are described as accurately and completely as possible so that the study can be replicated by other researchers.
- It is empirical—involves exploration of those things that can be seen, felt, heard, tasted, and smelled as the ground for all scientific knowledge. It is based on logical positive paradigm which utilizes experimental methods and quantitative measures to test specific hypothetical generalization with narrow-angle lens.

- It is often reductionist—involves the study of discrete parts of a system.
- It is objective—a researcher's personal biases have no part in the research endeavour. The researchers treat their subjects of study as having an existence independent of themselves and without any intrinsic meaning.
- It is usually deductive—researchers test a theory and look for confirmation through observations. It involves hypothesis formulation and testing.
- It often employs methods of randomization so that error may be estimated when population characteristics are inferred from observations of samples. Closed-ended structured questionnaires, tests, attitudes scales, rating scales, etc. are used to collect quantitative data based on precise measurement.
- Quantitative social scientists tend to analyze large sample of allegedly representative cases drawn from broader population of interest. Qualitative social scientists tend to study small samples of purposively chosen cases of a given event or process. Since the letter "n" is generally used to represent the size of a scholar's sample, therefore, as a standard practice, quantitative research is referred as "large-n" research and qualitative research as "small-n" research.
- Quantitative research aims at description, explanation and prediction of social phenomenon. The emphasis is not on in-depth contextual analysis of data or deep understanding of phenomenon.
- Behaviour of the subjects under study is assumed to be regular and predictable.
- The form of final report is statistical with details about the use of various types of statistics, e.g., correlations, comparison means, percentages, etc. and their statistical significance.

7.1.2 Various Approaches

(a) collection of data through questionnaire or tests or observations, etc., (b) analyzing of data, and (c) interpretation of data to arrive at logical conclusions or generalizations. It can further be classified into:

(1) *Inferential approach:* This means to form a database to infer, i.e., to understand features of relationships of the population. Large-n researchers typically use a variant of

regression analysis. They collect data on a representative sample of a well-defined population. Regress the dependent variable on a vector of independent and control variables, and assess the absolute size and relative magnitude of the estimated regression coefficient. In this process, the variables are measured correctly. The model is properly specified. The individual regression coefficients are twice the size of their respective standard errors. Derived sample value (statistics) approximates population value (parameter).

(2) *Experimental approach:* This approach attempts to establish cause and effect relationship among groups of subjects that make up the research study. It is characterized by a greater control over the research environment where some variables are operated to scrutinize their effect on other variables. For instance effect of ICT on learning outcomes.

(3) *Simulation approach:* This entails the creation of artificial environment within which relevant information and data can be produced. It is useful in building models for understanding future conditions.

As its proponents have shown (Erichson, 1986; Howe, 1990), qualitative research is well suited to the task of making sense of the socially complex, variable rich, and context-specific character of education. Quantitative work has a harder feel to it, which helps it produce results that come across as clearer, more definitive,, and more conducive to causal inference.

7.1.3 Essentials of Quantitative Research

(1) *The World:* Knowable and Predictable.

(2) *Aim or Objective:* Pursuit of Single truth.

(3) *The Nature of Research:* Empirical and Reductionist.

(4) *The Researcher:* Objective and Expert.

(5) *Methodology:* Deductive, Hypothesis-driven, randomized sample, large sample. *Tools*: Tests, Questionnaires, Scales.

(6) *Criteria:* Quantitative research represents the world with observed truth and objectivity through empirical investigation.

- *Validity:* The quality standards under this paradigm are validity (i.e. internal validity—to what extent the findings meet expected results; external validity- the ability of findings to be generalized to other situations and contexts.

- *Reliability*: is an important indicator for the consistency of research findings which can then be replicated.
- *Objectivity*: responds to the positivist demand for neutrality and requires a demonstration that a given inquiry is free of bias, values, and/or prejudice (Guba & Lincoln, 1989).

(7) *Analysis of Data:* Quantitative, Statistically significant.

(8) *Results and Findings:* Confirmation or disconfirmation of hypotheses. Thus, the systematic and objective analysis and recording of controlled observations should lead to the development of generalizations, principles, or theories, resulting in prediction and possibly ultimate control of events. (Best, 2008, p. 25).

7.1.4 Merits of Quantitative Research

- Quantitative research mostly uses statistical method in drawing comparison between concepts, ideas, products or packages, etc. Therefore, results are more reliable. Quantitative research involves quantifications based on numbers. Thus it is easier to identify, classify the variables to predict the results. The internal and external validity can be easily established.
- It is objective—a researcher's personal biases have no part in the research endeavour.
- The results of quantitative research can be generalized. The findings can be extrapolated to other situations and contexts.
- The use of multivariate methods and analysis is helpful in measuring and controlling the variable or variables which intervene between the independent and dependent variables.
- Quantitative research represents the world with observed truth and objectivity through empirical investigation

7.1.5 Limitations

- The researchers treat their subjects of study as having an existence independent of themselves and without any intrinsic meaning. The emphasis is not on in-depth contextual analysis of data or deep understanding of phenomenon.
- In educational research, there is no need to try and provide results which can be generalized. The finding may have

important implications, either for personal use or others working in the similar areas.

- Post-modernism questions established research paradigms: creates new and multiple identities for research, researched and researcher; raises ethical issues; the growth of knowledge is rhizomatic, unpredictable and multifaceted. Disentangling facts from values offers a distorted view of reality.
- Quantitative research can not uncover textual silences beneath the noise and splendour of social, political and educational rhetoric.
- Quantitative research can not offer interpretation that are diverse, uncertain and polyvocal. Moreover, it is difficult to quantify the action or thinking of people.
- Positivism—as exemplified in the applied sciences and social science research, which apes the methodology of the natural sciences—disavows the role reflection (Habermas, 1971). The result was the absolutizing of 'facts' and the reification of the existing order' (Jay, 1973).
- The selection and use of large samples for drawing reliable statistics also involve lot of efforts in terms of money and manpower.

7.2 QUALITATIVE RESEARCH METHOD

Qualitative research is viewed as reflexive, intuitive, creative and professionally oriented exploratory scientific inquiry. It is scientific research which is more descriptively oriented, more dependent on context, less cumulative, and more intuitive—in other words, more qualitative.

Qualitative research is based on the phenomenological paradigm, which uses a variety of interpretive methodologies. Qualitative research uses systematic procedures to discover non-quantifiable relationships between existing variables. The aim of qualitative research is to conduct in-depth study of research question. Thus, qualitative research is exploratory or explanatory or descriptive.

Three cardinal principles of qualitative research are:

(1) Each research question is uniquely defined by a specific set of circumstances.

(2) There can be no attempt to answer a question without deep knowledge of the specific contextual parameters defining those circumstances.

(3) Such deep knowledge comes only to those who have paid their dues (Denzin and Lincoln, 2000).

7.2.1 Characteristics of Qualitative Research

(1) It is intuitive–it involves deep knowledge to explore the real world;
(2) It is holistic–research needs to explore systems because the whole is often seen as more than the sum total of the parts;
(3) It is subjective–researchers acknowledge being value-bound;
(4) Methods are often inductive–the process moves from specific observations;
(5) It dependable–uses systematic and rigorous approaches to research in stead of method of reliability;
(6) It is auditable–verifiable through full and transparent explication of method; and
(7) Its findings are idiographic–may not be able to generalize, yet have their own intrinsic worth.

7.2.2 Qualitative Research Approach

In *biographical studies* the investigator begins with an objective set of experiences in the subject's life, noting life course, stages and experiences.

Ethnographical: This is concerned with studying an entire culture of the group of people or known as cultural anthropology or more recently a naturalistic inquiry. It is a method of field study that became popular in the later part of the nineteenth century. It is a method for carrying out qualitative observational research. It has continued to show significant development, suggesting promising techniques for the study of behaviour in educational situation.

Phenomenological: It is concerned with study of the structures and essence of experience of particular phenomenon for people. It is personal experience of a phenomenon and the essential experience of others who have also experienced this phenomenon intensely. How X ideological perspective is manifested in this phenomenon. This focuses on the subjective experiences of people over a long period of time.

Case-based Research: This is concerned with case study. Case may be individual or institution. The case study is an intensive examination of "single case of a particular phenomenon". Andrew Bennett expanded the term to "include both within case analysis of single cases and comparisons between or among a small number of cases. In case-based research a wide array of different data sources and a number of different analytic strategies are utilized. The case study examines units of analysis that are not drawn from a well-demarcated population.

Grounded Theory: Grounded theory is a research strategy whose purpose is to generate theory from data. The focus of grounded theory approach is on the development of inductive, "bottom-up" theory that is "grounded" directly in the empirical data. Analytical and interpretive procedures are used for analyzing and conceptualizing data through coding (open coding, axial coding and selection coding), non-statistical sampling, writing of memos, diagramming of conceptual relationships, written and verbal reports. The findings of grounded theory are not arrive at by means of statistical procedures or other means of quantification, but are derived from data gathered by a variety of means including 'observation' interview, documents, and videotapes.

After all, modern social science's most enduring contributions have been concepts rather than causal inferences, and the most fecund concepts have originated incase-based rather. Instead of proceeding with a preconceived theory and set of hypotheses, *grounded theory* tries to study a phenomenon and a set of data in context through which the theory emerges. The phrase "grounded theory" refers to theory that is developed inductively from a corpus of data. If done well, this means that the resulting theory at least fits one dataset perfectly. In grounding theory building there are various phases, namely, open coding, axial coding and selective coding. Open coding is the part of the analysis concerning with identifying, naming, categorizing and describing phenomena found in the text. Essentially, the text is read in search of the answer to the repeated question "what is this about? What is being referenced here? Axial coding is the process of relating codes (categories and properties) to each other, via a combination of inductive and deductive thinking. Grounded theorists emphasize causal relationships, and fit things into a basic frame of generic relationships. The frame consists of elements, such as, phenomenon, causal conditions, context, intervening conditions, action strategies and consequences. In contrast selective coding is the process of choosing one category to be the core category.

7.2.3 Research Design

"In a qualitative study, the activities of collecting and analyzing data, developing and modifying theory, elaborating or refocusing research questions, identifying and dealing with validity threats are usually going on more or less simultaneously, each influencing all of others. In addition, the researcher may need to reconsider or modify any design decision during the study in response to new developments" (Maxwell, 1998).

7.2.4 Essentials of Qualitative Research

1. The World

Ambiguous: Unpredictability and uncertainty is recognized as crucial aspects of the research situation. It reflects real world situations as they unfold naturally without any manipulation and pre-determined constraints or outcomes.

2. The Nature of Research

Thinking, seeing and messing about ideas in order to change the world. Truth is to be understood in systemic circular relations. Aim is to question the assumed educational, theoretical or moral superiority of particular world-views or dominant paradigms in educational research and practice. It involves deconstruction and reconstruction of ideas. Deconstruction is one which seeks to interrogate these constructed 'texts'. The process might involve the deconstruction of language, drawing on linguistics and literary theory, of actions, drawing on anthropology and cultural studies, drawing on sociology and social psychology. It recognizes multiple views and multiple voices and turns its attention to the 'margins' rather than 'centre' in order to the 'vicious binaries' by which society is constructed and defined. It is more like a prism which refracts multiple images of 'realities'

3. The Researcher

Subjective: Challenge the existing paradigms, i.e., the areas of certainty, objectivity, validity and truth. Involve himself in the in-depth understanding and active participation of the subjects. Scholar who 'produce data' are complex creatures whose perceptions and communications are shaped at every turn by the context in which they find themselves;

4. Methodology

Research Designs

Research designs may be formulated to achieve the goals of the research. They link theoretical frameworks, research questions, presentation goals, methods, and generalization. Their realization is the result of evidence obtained in the research process

Method

Inductive—Research questions are formulated and modified in the process of observations in the field. Hypotheses are more likely to emerge from the data than to be formulated prior to the research.

Sampling

In qualitative research:purposive sampling method is generally used in qualitative research. Purpose is to get insight about phenomenon, not empirical generalization from a sample to a population. Qualitative research cannot be conducted through *a-priori* samples only. Sampling goes on throughout research, through various sampling techniques, such as, typical case sampling, intensity sampling, critical case sampling, sensitive case sampling, convenience sampling, primary selection and secondary selection.

Tools and Techniques of Qualitative Research

Tools and techniques of qualitative research are innumerous, such as, observation, interview, triangulation, Focus Group Discussion, Reflective Dialogue.

Qualitative Research cannot be conducted through static tools and techniques, because very often the researcher employing qualitative research methodology does not have a sound theoretical base related to the reality. Theory in fact is the product of enquiry. Data are created by human efforts; put more prosaically, the way in which information is collected affects the content of the data themselves; scholar who 'produce data' are complex creatures whose perceptions and communications are shaped at every turn by the context in which they find themselves; and both the content and the quality of data are prime concerns

It is in-depth analysis of contextually-bound data. It involves the subjectivity of the researcher. All qualitative research methods adhere to certain themes such as *qualitative data, content sensitivity, emphatic neutrality, inductive analysis and naturalistic inquiry.*

Interpretation of results: The whole phenomenon under study is understood as a complex system that is more than sum of its parts; focus on complex interdependencies and system dynamics that can not meaningfully be reduced to a few discrete and linear, cause-effect relationships.

Findings: Qualitative, Valuable and Idiographic or transferable

7.2.5 Merits of Qualitative Research

- Qualitative research is reflexive, intuitive, creative and professionally oriented exploratory scientific inquiry.
- Social and cultural context, participant involvement, political considerations, and ethical requirements are the

inherent features of the study of social and educational phenomena. (Dehaan, 2005).

- Qualitative methods can "illuminate important nuances, identify potential counterhypotheses, and provide additional sources of evidence for supporting causal claims in complex educational settings" (NRC, 2002, pp. 125-26).
- Research questions are uniquely defined by a specific set of circumstances, and answered adequately on the basis of deep knowledge of the specific contextual parameters defining those circumstances.
- The whole phenomenon under study is understood as a complex system that is more than sum of its parts; focus on complex interdependencies and system dynamics that can not meaningfully be reduced to a few discrete and linear, cause-effect relationships.
- Separately and interconnectively explore, reflect upon, describe, predict, and explain the natural world and meaningful social and personal 'worlds' and experiences.
- Describe nomological (i.e., general law like) knowledge domain, but also describe ideographic, local and contextual knowledge domains, and interconnect these to continually produce meaningful "practical theory".
- Data are not gathered like grapes on a vine but also created by human efforts; put more prosaically, the way in which information is collected affects the content of the data themselves.
- Skimpy methods produce skimpy data. Conversely, the more time you take to get to know the people whose lives you are trying to understand, the more likely it is that they will take the time to share their honest reflections with you.
- Qualitative research produces spectacular results in terms of depth. It allows the reader to gain deeper understanding, empathy life lived and values held in a very different fashion from one's own eyes (Lareau and Shultz, 1996).

7.2.6 Limitations

- Quantitative research mostly uses subjective techniques, etc. Therefore, results are not more reliable and valid. Thus, it is not easier to identify, classify the variables to predict the results. The internal and external validity cannot be easily established.

- It is subjective—a researcher's personal biases affect the outcomes of the research endeavour.
- The results of qualitative research cannot be generalized. Therefore, findings cannot be extrapolated to other situations and contexts.
- Controlling the variable or variables which intervene between the independent and dependent variables is not possible.

Table 7.1 reflects difference between Quantitative and Qualitative Methods of Investigation.

TABLE 7.1
Quantitative versus Qualitative Methods of Investigation

	The World	
Knowable	⇐——⇒	Ambiguous
Predictable	⇐——⇒	Variable
Single truth	⇐——⇒	Multiple realities
	The Nature of Research	
Empirical	⇐——⇒	Intuitive
Reductionist	⇐——⇒	Holistic
	The Researcher	
Objective	⇐——⇒	Subjective
Expert	⇐——⇒	Participatory and collaborative
	Methodology	
Deductive	⇐——⇒	Inductive
Hypothesis-driven	⇐——⇒	Exploratory
Reliable	⇐——⇒	Dependable
Reproducible	⇐——⇒	Auditable
	Findings	
Quantitative	⇐——⇒	Qualitative
Statistically significant	⇐——⇒	Valuable
Generalizable	⇐——⇒	Idiographic or transferable

These two orientations—reductionism and holism—are obviously opposites. The former explains a whole by its parts, the later the parts by a whole (James,1963). Both strategies can be useful, but both can also become hasty and dogmatic. In other words, each orientation becomes rigid and dogmatic when it is believed to be only true approach. For instance, reductionists tend to accuse holists of making unverifiable (meaningless) statements, where holists tend to accuse reductionists making invalid statements. Quantitative methods produce breadth but sacrifice depth; qualitative methods produce depth, revealing a complexity that quantitative methods miss, but they sacrifice breadth. Therefore, the best quantitative studies should be built on at least some level of depth, and the best qualitative studies also should offer at least some level of breadth. (Gottlieb, 2006). No method is good or bad, scientific or unscientific in itself. Rather, it is the appropriate application of method to a particular problem that enables judgment about scientific enquiry.

Bryman (1992) identified 11 ways of integrating quantitative and qualitative research—

1. The logic of triangulation means for him checking for examples of qualitative against quantitative results
2. Qualitative research can support quantitative research and *vice-versa*
3. Both are combined in or provide a more general picture of the issue under study
4. Structural features are analyzed with quantitative methods and processual aspects with qualitative approaches
5. The perspective of the researchers drives quantitative approaches
6. While qualitative research emphasizes the viewpoints of the subjective
7. The problem of generality can be solved for qualitative research by adding quantitative findings
8. Whereas qualitative findings may facilitate the interpretation of relationships between variables in quantitative data sets
9. The relationship between micro and macro-levels in a substantial area can be clarified by combining qualitative and quantitative research
10. There is mixed form of research
11. There is a use of qualitative research in quasi-experimental designs

Kadriye Erickan and Wolff-Michael Roth (2008) have given an integrative framework for evaluating research in education.

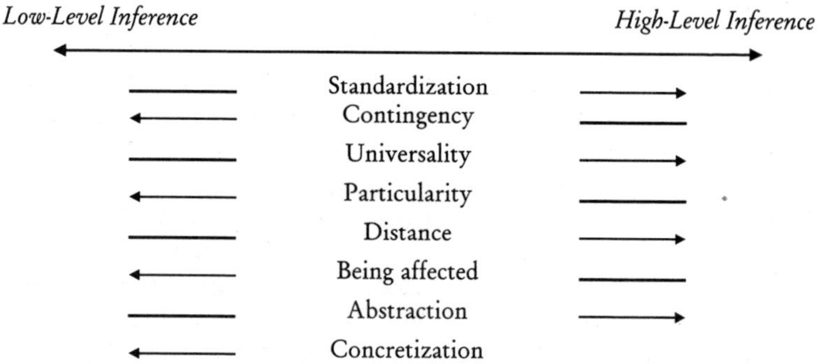

Figure 7.1 : Integrative Framework of Research

The aim of evaluation in this approach is to assess research results that are characterized simultaneously by high and low inference levels. Instead of dichotomizing research as quantitative or qualitative, we need integrative approaches that provide appropriate forms of knowledge needed by decision-makers.

Johnson (2009) proposed a set of guidelines that is more inclusive and might better represent research in education. These guidelines are:

- Identify important problems and pose questions that can be investigated empirically or through other potentially useful approaches. Continuously generate, discover, describe, and construct new knowledge, and test knowledge claims.
- Separately and interconnectively explore, reflect upon, describe, predict, and explain the natural world and meaningful social and personal 'worlds' and experiences.
- Explicate researcher and research values, purposes, commitments, and key background assumptions.
- Use method and strategies that, separately or in combination, can produce warranted investigation of particular research questions.
- Rely on sources of evidences.
- Link exploratory research to relevant theory through theory generation, theory testing, and ongoing theory modification.
- Describe nomological (i.e., general law like) knowledge domain, but also describe ideographic, local and contextual knowledge domains, and interconnect these to continually produce meaningful "practical theory".

- Replicate, document mediating and moderating processes, delineate conditions of generalization, and identify broad generalizations when possible, but also identify complex contextual interactions to aid in particular understanding and practical application of education/social theory.
- Articulate, explicate, develop, and test manualized models, practice-based models, middle-level theoretical models, met-models (i.e., models of models) and trastheoretical and transdisciplinary models of educational phenomena, and interconnect these continually for scientific learning.
- Explicate creative and formal reasoning processes (i.e., deductive, inductive, abductive, critical-theory) to help situate and warrant findings and value choices.
- Fully disclose research processes and findings to encourage professional and societal scrutiny.
- Continually encourage self-examination and critique and ongoing improvement of the education scientific enterprise.

References

Anfara and Mertz (2006). *Theoretical Frameworks in Qualitative Research.* Thousand Oaks, C A: Sage.

Bailey, K.D. (1987). *Methods of Social Research.* 3rd. edn. New York: Free Press.

Bassey, M. (2001). A solution to the problem of generalisation in educational research: Fuzzy prediction. *Oxford Review of Education*, 27(10), pp. 5-22.

Best, J. and Kahn, J. (1995). Research in Education. 10th edition, Needham Heights: Allyn and Bacon

Cozby, P. (2009). Methods in Behavioural Research. 10th edition, Bemont: Wadsworth.

Denzin, N.K. and Lincoln,Y.S. (2000). *Handbook of Qualitative Research*, London: Sage

Flick, U. (2007c). *Designing Qualitative Research* .Thousand Oaks, CA: SAGE

Goode, W.J. and Hatt, P.K. (1990). Methods in Social Research. McGraw-Hill, New Delhi.

Guthrie, G. (2010). Basic Research Methods. New Delhi: Sage.

Marshall, C. and Rossman, G.B. (2006). Designing Qualitative Research. 4th edn., New Delhi: Sage.

Maxwell, J.A. (1996). Qualitative Research Design: An Interaction Approach. Thousand Oaks, CA: Sage.

Neuman, W.L. (1994). Social Research Methods: Qualitative and Quantitative Aproaches. 2nd, Edn. Boston: Allyn and Bacon.

Punch, K.F. (2009). Introduction to Research Methods in Education. New Delhi: Sage.

Singh, J. (2008). Methodology and Techniques of Social Research. New Delhi: Kanishka Publishers.

Somekh, B. and Lewin, C. (2005). Research Methods in the Social Sciences. New Delhi. Vstaar Publications.

Wallen, N.E. and Fraenkel, J.R. (1991). Educational Research: A Guide to the Process. New York: McGraw-Hill.

Zeller, R.A. (1996). 'Validity', in J.P. Keeves (ed.), Educational Research, Methodology and Measurement: An International Handbook. 2nd edn. Oxford: Elsevier. pp. 822-9.

CHAPTER

8

Areas of Research in Education

Research in education has been perceived in diverse ways, sometimes in a manner consistent with current ideas in the social sciences and at sometimes in ways that make it more utility-oriented. As an applied discipline, education presents a highly challenging task for different kinds of research (Kumar, 2006). Education is also metadisciplines that cuts across a number of disciplines. For example, it is informed by social sciences such as anthropology, sociology, economics and psychology and open to explore these areas in light of educational implications.

Knowledge is expanding rapidly in all the disciplines including education. Firstly, in the knowledge society, the researcher has to identify mismatchs between actual and anticipated outcomes on the basis of his experiences or knowledge or contacts with mentor/expert which provide ample opportunities for research to devise new methods, new tools, new models, new techniques, and strategies for enhancing learning and teaching. Secondly, there are inconsistencies and gaps in the existing theories. Researcher can pick theme to fillup those gaps or to rectify inconsistencies. Considering this point of view, the fields of educational research can be classified in terms of the following content areas:

1. Psychology of Education,
2. Philosophy of Education,
3. Sociology of Education,
4. Curriculum

5. Educational Planning, Management and Administration,
6. Science Education,
7. Economics of Education,
8. Educational Technology,
9. Inclusive Education,
10. Teacher Education, and
11. Priority Areas of Educational Research in India.

8.1 PSYCHOLOGY OF EDUCATION

Research in educational psychology in India is of fairly recent origin. Research in educational psychology has great significance for a teacher. He has to understand the child he is teaching, understand the teaching-learning process, and constantly strive to improve his method of teaching. Almost all issues in education in general and teaching in particular have a psychological dimension—even aims and objectives in their interpretation and their bearing on the development and functioning of individuals, at one end, and administration, rather management, in respect of the style of functioning of personal and human relations involved, at the other (Nayer, 1997). There are numerous psychological situations and tendencecies which have siginificant impact on the performance of the teacher, i.e. stress, anxiety, attrition, depression, delinquency, adiction, and phobia, etc.

An analysis of the material presented in the Directory of Behavioural Science Research in India (Pareek, 1967), and Six Surveys of Research in Education (Buch, 1973, 1979, 1987, 1991; NCERT, 1997, 2006) show that a bulk of work had been in the areas of intelligence and aptitudes, personality and social dynamics including attitudes, interests. Buch (1987, 1991) had pointed out that a majority of the researchers seem to be concerned with conducting either descriptive or correlational surveys of learner characteristics and environmental variables. The studies dealing with motivation had mostly been ignored its role in learning process; they only referred to achievement motive and affiliation motive. If one judges the value of all such research efforts, one is bound to conclude that the work done in different areas of educational psychology is very meagre both quantitatively and qualitatively. Trend report revealed that objectives and/or hypotheses had been not often stated with clarity, proper wording, correct focus, appropriateness and adequacy. (Fifth Survey of Educational Research, 1997)

Substantial experimental studies in realistic settings in the field of educational psychology were found few, partly because of their inherent difficulty and partly because the field's general reluctance to appreciate and accommodate such efforts. It is, therefore, essential to indicate some of the areas in which a good deal of work may be done to improve upon the present situation. (Nayer, 1997)

8.1.1 Usefulness of various theories of learning for designing conditions that produce effective learning in schools have been the central theme of researches in the recent years. There are learning theories namely, behaviourist theories, constructivist theories, neruoscience theories, learning-analytical and holistic theories, Kolb's learning styles (accommodative, divergent, convergent and assimilative) which have direct bearing on learning outcomes can be undertaken for their application in the classroom situation. Although much of learning theories have emerged from laboratory research where variables were controlled and meanipulated to predict the behavioural changes. Hence, clinical or laboratory experiments in the field of education can be undertaken for understanding, modification and prediction of behaviour.

8.1.2. Cognitive and non-cognitive factors, such as, intelligence and multiple intelligences-liguisitics, logical-mathematical, visual-spatial, bodily-kinaesthetic, aptitudes, creativity, attitudes, interests, motivation, personality traits, needs and adjustment of pupils provide promising fields of research in educational psychology.

8.1.3. One of the most urgent tasks is to *study problems, arising within and outside the school environment,* which affect the effectiveness of the teacher in his task of improving the learning of students. The fundamental processes of perception, processes of learning and teaching, environment within and outside the school and their impacts on students' achievements can be investigated. Research studies on technology-rich learning environment which will have substantial bearing on teacher performance and students' achievements may be undertaken. Nayar (1997) suggests that learning as a process has to be studied, understood, and undertaken in relation to the products (intended and/or actual) as well as the different kinds of internal and external variables that affect both. Causal-comparative studies with selected variables and employing multivariate analysis can be undertaken. In order to establish and understand these relationships better, experimental studies are also needed.

8.1.4. Another important area where a good deal of research can be undertaken is that among the *exceptional children.* It includes the study of all children who are either handicapped in some way or are gifted. The differently abled may be physically handicapped, the intellectually challenged or the socially handicapped. The gifted children are fast learners and exceptionally bright and have very high general mental ability or special abilities. Study of all these types of children with a view to finding ways and means of their proper location, care, rehabilitation, education and guidance is essential both from the individual and the social points of view.

With regard to the intellectually challenged children also, there is need to determine the number of children of various degrees of retardation in the various states. There is also need to ascertain the possible causes of mental retardation in children, whether it is caused by poor diet, unhealthy climatic conditions, ill-health of parents, or any other factors. After ascertaining the causes, we need to develop specific methods and techniques for handling the various categories of mentally retarded children so that proper educational programmes through concrete and practical media can be planned and organized. Similarly, there is need to study the problems of socially handicapped or the delinquent children.

8.1.5. Creativity : A country like India cannot afford to lose creative genius. Thus research in the area of creativity needs immediate attention of Indian researchers. Developing tests for identifying creative children deserve top priority. While discussing new directions for educational research in India, Buch (1991) has suggested that there is need to devise programmes and methods which would promote creativity and divergent thinking. He is of the opinion that unless research-based programmes and methods of teaching are tried, tested and used, the formal school system may not be in a position to develop and nurture creativity. Thus, there is need for undertaking studies to investigate the efficacy of various curricular strategies in the development of creative thinking. Studies on problem-solving and logical operations using cognitive development theory of Piaget and his methodology may be of immense use to classroom teachers.

8.1.6. Studies relating to redesigning and reconstuction of *curriculum* according to the needs of individuals at various stages of development and its impact on teaching and learning can be undertaken. Pedagogical practice, methods, techniques, strategies for the effective transaction of curriculum can be investigated to see their impact on individual's learning outcomes. The problem of addressing to diverse population in the classroom is closely related to development and adjustment of individuals.

8.1.7. Psychological tests are developed and are used primarily for the determination and analysis of individual differences in general intelligence, aptitudes, educational achievement and non-intellectual personality characteristics. Therefore, there is a great need for developing these tests for educational classification, assessessment, evaluation, selection and planning.

The available intelligence and aptitude tests are mostly of foreign origin which need to adapted to the conditions of this country. Besides these specific aptitude tests, different test batteries should be developed for assessing suitability for specific courses of study or jobs.

Such aspects which include various personality traits—interests, needs and values are important for determining success in certain educational and vocational fields such as medicine, social work, teaching, etc. demand for the development of some tools for measuring such attributes.

8.1.8. Cross-cultural researches should also get due attention by the researchers. Classroom management researches with due emphasis on classroom climate, leadership styles, student activism and unrest and stress may also be undertaken.

8.1.9. Qualitative research approach involving case studies, ethnographic studies and other situation-related studies, attempting comprehensive and deep probes, needs priority so as to yield clear pictures of the effects of a multiplicity of unique socio-psychological and educational factors in active interplay.

8.1.10. Normative surveys in the field of educational psychology would yield-better results if they focus on developmental components. Studies in personality should put focus more on developing desirable traits and utilizing them for improving behaviour and performance and for inculcation of desirable human values. Intervention studies employing different treatments and techniques need encouragement not only for problem cases, but for all for promoting balanced, healthy, harmonious and well integrated personality development.

8.1.11. Guidance and Counselling : Trends inferred from earlier surveys revealed that studies in guidance and counseling could be classified into five areas namely, developmental aspects, interest and vocational choice, tests of evaluation of exceptional children, descriptive and correlational. Five more areas reported in the 2nd Survey of Research in Education were—needs and problems of children, vocational preferences and vocational maturity, student appraisal, study habits, appraisal of counseling, follow-up and school climate. Three more areas namely, selection of students, mental health, and evaluation of guidance services were added (Joshi & Gakhar, 1987). Thereafter, studies which have implications for personal, social, educational, vocational development and adjustment of students were included.

- Guidance and counselling has ample scope for futhrer research. Developmental, correlational, descriptive studies can be ubdertaken in relation to demographic and familial variables like sex, age, parental attitudes and personal traita of intelligence, self-concept, problems of students with academic achievement, mental health, decision-making, and othetr adjustment variables.
- In view of mass communication and globalization, individual life style and adjustment has undergone trmenduous change. What role do the factors like family, community, and other socio-political and economic factors play in the personal, educational and career development of individuals in their success in career and personal life planning and adjustment needs to be studied further.
- Problems relating stress, anxiety, depression, obsession, and suicidal tendency among students which require clinical investigation can be undertaken to find out tangible solutions.
- Longitudinal and cross-sectional studies with wider samples of populations which may be more representative of the school age popultion can be investigated to arrive at conclusive findings.
- New research areas in the Indian context need to be focused on evaluative and follow-up studies assessing the effectiveness of different kinds of training strategies for improving training programmes for teachers and counsellors.
- Emerging issues of child abuse, sex abuse, gender inequalities, drug abuse, prvention and rehabilitation of people with HIV/AIDS, children of diverced/single parents, coping with stress, anger, violence, rape, terrorism, natural disater, etc. are significant topics for a researcher.
- There is need for development of indigenous tools and tests suited to various age and maturity levels and local needs to accommodate cultural variations.

- Supportive role of the community in providing formal/ informal counseling to youngsters in their process of growing up and making decisions and adjustment to life situations is a major area for a researcher.

Priority areas of research in educational psychology include processess of development such as family processes, parenting, scaffolding, peers, the development of agression, violence, emotional and academic self-regulation, metacognition, creativity, adolecent deviancy and risk behaviour. Priority areas may also include children with special needs, education of deprieved and marganized section of the society, and new technology rich environment and their impacts on learning outcomes.

8.2 PHILOSOPHY OF EDUCATION

Education has been called the dynamic side of philosophy or an active aspect of philosophic belief. Theory and practice can never attain perfection unless it is based on the sound footing of a systematic philosophy. Philosophy has various dimensions which provide ample scope for exploration.

Logical dimensions reveal various significant roles which logic can perform in the formation of educational concepts, generalizations and analogies, and in drawing out of educational inferences. Logic can also help in curriculum framing and it can provide the very basis of the teaching-learning process. It is, therefore, needed to find out as to how many possible logical operations are involved in teaching-learning process.

Ethical dimension helps in formulating the theory of education in its most general phases. In examining the aims of education, the motivation of learning, or the measurement of its results, we are dealing with ethical problems, the problems of values. Ethical considerations also come up unavoidably in examining the social or political setting of the educative process. Values are also important considerations in selecting which courses should be included in the curriculum. Ethics has been the major concern of our national policy of education. Value aim of education also raises some fundamental questions which needed to be answered through philosophical research. What exactly does value education mean? What are its objectives? What values are to be inculcated in education and in what manner? What role has the teacher to play in the process of value inculcation? The philosophical examination of all such issues would lead to proper conceptualisation and articulation of a rationale for policies and programmes in this crucial national concern.

A philosophical analysis of the problems of indiscipline, unrest, strikes, disobedience of authority and the like in the context of the prevalent circumstances and conditions would be highly significant and fruitful.

One of the tasks of philosophy of education is to identify, anlayse and clarify the different concetual and logical issues underlying the debate research studies would provide rationale for policies and programmes of national concern.

Through curriculum knowledge is trans media. The nature of knowledge not only have an influence on the way in which the curriculum is organized and taught, but it also helps to determine the shape of teaching-learning strategy. In view of the demand for a philosophical foundation of education; there is an imperative need for undertaking research into the various problems pertaining to its different dimensions. With reference to the emerging context, some of the questions that may be raised are:

1. What does the knowledge society and the new information order mean for school and teacher education?
2. How important is knowledge as an aim of education in the new context?
3. What is knowledge and how is it related to 'education', 'information', 'understanding' or 'deep knowledge'?
4. To what extent shall educational goals and objectives subject themseves to demands of technology?
5. How shall one deal with value conflicts arising from the ethos of the IT society-efficiency, utility, economy—and pursuit of knowledge as an intrinsic end?
6. What shall 'liberal education' mean in the new information order?

Philosophical discussion of knowledge in the present context could cover the conceptual, logical and normative issues outlined above and pave the way for the articulation of a new philosophy of education as would appropriately respond to the demands and challenges of the knowledge society. (The Sixth Survey of Research in Education, 2006, p. 9).

In India, there is need for the development of a philosophy of education from the Indian stand-point. The aims and means of education are to be deduced from the *Indian* conception of life. A study of the utterances of Vyasa and Valmiki, Buddha, Sankaracharya, Swami Vivekananda, Sri Aurobindo, Tagore, J. Krishnamurthi, Annie Besant, and Mahatma Gandhi would help us in formulating our own system of education. Special features of Indian Philosophy in relation to education; Indian Philosophical Thoughts and their impact on Indian system of Education with reference to teacher, learner, discipline and processes for the transaction are the areas which can be investigated.

Every aspect of education, its meaning, aims, content and process-holds out exciting possibilities for logical and conceptual examination. There are also philosophical insights to be gained about the relationship of education itself with other spheres of human activity, social, political, economic and religious classification of concepts; analysis and appraisal of arguments, statements and theories; synthesis and integration of such understanding with substantive issues of curriculum, systems of schooling, the process of learning and teaching, school management and educational institutions; and issuing normative guidelines on aims, curriculum, methods, institutions and teachers—can all be legitimate functions of philosophical inquiry in education.

8.2.1 Areas of Philosophical Research in Education

Contributions of educationists/philosophers and their impact and relevance in the present provide ample scope for research.

Impact of philosophy on education from the viewpoint of identifying aims and objectives, relevant contents, disciplines, methods, and evaluation processes provide rich areas for exploration. An educational researcher may be interested in making an analytical and critical appraisal of the educational philosophy of a thinker or a group of thinkers and present their ideas on education in a consolidated, formal, and systematized form. The researcher can undertake studies to analyse educational philosophy, contributions of individual thinkers, philosophical schools, scriptures, historical/ cultural periods, thereby, drawing their implications for the present day education system.

8.2.2 School of Thoughts

Philosophy can be classified under different schools of thought like idealism, naturalism, realism, existentialism, pragmatism, socialism or communism i.e., dialectical materialism. Every school of thought projects its educational philosophy based on its own ideology regarding the attainment of the basic goals of education. Abstractions and forma1 statements governing principles and ideas of a school of thought on educational systems can also be considered as one of the areas of philosophical inquiry.

8.2.3 The Philosophical bases of Curriculum

The nature of knowledge not only have an influence on the way in which the curriculum is organized and taught, but it also helps to determine the shape of teaching-learning strategy. In view of the demand for a philosophical foundation of education; there is an imperative need for undertaking research into the various problems pertaining to its different dimensions, for instance, reconstruction of curricula in the light of emerging knowledge-base, the ethos of the IT society—efficiency, utility, economy and pursuit of knowledge as an intrinsic end, and privatization and globalization.

8.2.4 The Philosophical bases of Instructional Processes

Many questions are being raised about the meaning of terminologies, concepts, and activities concerned with instructional processes. For instance, how does the term "imparting" different from "instruction"?, Is there any need for "punishment" in education? or what must be the grounds for punishing learners? A number of such philosophical questions related to the instructional processes need to be answered through analytical exercises. Through such exercises clear-cut ideas are generated about the activities carried out in educational settings and appropriate norms are suggested from time to time for educational practices.

8.2.5 Study of the Philosophically-based Issues which Influence Education

There can he several issues of education related to imbibing certain social ideals into the system. The issues like 'freedom of the classroom set-up, autonomy of the higher education institution, democratic values in education,' 'equality of educational opportunities', 'policies and practices of educational opportunities' require philosophical analysis from time to time in order to accommodate the changes in societies. This helps us in examining appropriate social aims and norms existing in a given educational set-up. The norms for further development can be established.

8.2.6 Analytical Study of Certain Themes

Philosophical inquiries are made on analysis of certain themes, their ontological and epistemological aspects, taking into account the assumptions of the representative schools of philosophy, and to synthesize viewpoints to provide premises for education. For instance, 'Experience as a Major Premise in Education', "Conception and Perception of Environmental Education", 'Phenomenology in Relation to Education', "Dialecticism in Indian Education", etc. These studies help us to evaluate the significance of certain themes or ideas in the context of education.

Two of the highly topical issues that future researcher has to seriously consider are: (i) the knowledge aim in education; and (ii) the value orientation of education. The education system needs sound theoretical and ideological bases. In this context philosophical research contributes towards building a normative framework for educational priorities, curriculum, curricular practices and management of the education system through a cross-examination of ideas reflected by different philosophers in the field of education.

8.3 SOCIOLOGY OF EDUCATION

Education does not operate in vacuum. It operates in a society. In fact, both interact with and affect each other. Sachchidananda (1997) has rightly remarked that the educational system is a sub-system of the social system and is not autonomous. Socialisation is part of the educational process at an informal level. Sociological factors have a great impact on the educational thought and practice. One of the main objectives of research in sociology of education is to explain social realities. The study of all such realities and factors is of great practical significance. According to Travers (1969), although the central topic of educational research is the development of a science of behaviour in educational situations, peripheral studies pertaining to sociological and anthropological problems are of considerable importance.

Research in sociology of education examines education in its social context, including the relation between education and political and economic systems, the role of education in social and cultural reproduction, and the production of learning and other outcomes in schools. In addition, priorty areas of research in Sociology of Education include the micro-macro relationship in sociology of education, the complementary use of qualitative and quantitative methods, the multilevel analysis of the effects of schools, policy analysis in education, the sociology of teaching, and race differences in educational achievement, the role of education in stratification, the sociology of classrooms and school organization, as well as school desegregation, and curriculum.

In India, very few researches have been conducted in the field of sociology of education. The problems like the teacher's role as an agent of social change and modernization, teacher's morale, the impact of population explosion on children's admissions and academic achievement in schools, social determinants of educability of school children, the role of education in family planning, sociology of different tribes, and social obstacles in the inculcation of democratic and secular values among school children need to be investigated on a priority basis.

Shah (1987, p. 100) in the Third Survey of Research in Education has revealed several research gaps in sociology of education. Some sub areas are impact of education on the advancement of knowledge and technology, the relation of education with religion, economy and polity, the influence of peer group and religion on educational motivation, the aspirations and achievements of pupils of various social groups and the classroom as a social system which have drawn very meagre attention.

8.3.1 Some important problems of research related to sociology of education are the study of population explosion and changes, demographic trends and the impact of political and social pressures on an educational system. Subjects like educational aims, curriculum contents, methods and techniques in teaching-learning process conducive to socio-economic and politico-cultural situations prevailing in the country from time to time deserve attention by researchers.

The role and function of the school should be determined in the light of the needs of the specific community background. In the problem of delinquency, the study of social factors and cultural background of the community are also important. Problems relating to tribal cultures, rural community, community development, industrialization, urbanisation, crime and family need to be investigated thoroughly.

There is need to conduct researches on the problems and issues of education for equality, life-long education, Navodaya Schools, socially useful productive work and vocationalisation-of-education, secular education, value education, reservations in the institutions of higher learning, merit-based admissions, education for equity and excellence, common school system, liberal education, and peace education.

8.3.2 Educational Issues with Social Implications: The teacher's role in education deserves attention by the researchers. While studying job satisfaction among teachers, it is also important to study their job commitment in the context of social needs and social realities. Community support to educational effort through the school; and community control and supervision over school activities need to be studied. Such studies have social ramifications in the context of commercialisation of school "education; access, equity, relevance and excellence as indicators of quality school education; and decline in attendance of children of disadvantaged groups in primary schools. For understanding complex social situations and role of education, multi-disciplinary perspective need to be strengthened to make researches in educational sociology more socially relevant and policy oriented.

8.3.3 Gender-based Researches: The research on gender-based inequality due to which women in India have suffered, all along, is also the concern of research in educational sociology and population education. Kanitkar (2006) has suggested studies on unequal treatment given to women, declining sex-ratio, higher death rates among women and girls in certain age-groups, domestic violence, dowry deaths, burning, battering, neglect and humiliation of women, preference for male child, lower literacy among the girls, drug abuse, HIV/AIDS should also be undertaken in light of its implication in education.

8.3.4 Priority areas of research in sociology of education may include:

Education, Society and Sustainability

- *Social justice, social sustainability*: social factors affecting school success; social structures and differential participation and outcomes; alternative education and educational dis/re-engagement; impact of housing, geographical and school mobility; education in and for rural communities; impact of globalisation; partnerships. Conversation analysis-education and social justice, sociology of knowledge and science, critical pedagogies, right to education, universalization of education, education and quality of life, and education of marginalized section of the society are the priority areas.
- *Environmental and social sustainability*: teaching and learning in tropical environments; environmental education in the community.
- *Social and educational policy*: regarding gender, indigenous education, teaching and teacher education; partnerships; community capacity building; issues of policy implementation; human rights and education.
- *Culture and Lifestyles*: Youth Culture, self-perception, gender age; health/well-being, violence, risk, digital and media culture; recreation and leisure: social relationships; history of sport and physical education; sport in society; Olympic studies; sport as public diplomacy; sport and physical activity are the specific areas.

Social and Cultural Constructions of difference:

- *Gender*: discourses of gender; gendered and gendering practices; differential social access and participation; gendered subjectivities; neo-liberalism and gender; gender and cultural geography; gender and aspirations; gender and literacy
- *Age*: conceptualisations and practices of childhood, adolescence, adulthood and ageing; their impact on policy and practice.
- *Indigeneity*: social, political and cultural constructions of 'cultural' difference; language and literacy.
- *Community contexts and education*: rural contexts; indigenous communities; school-community relations; parents and schools.

Psychological and Social Development of Children

- Social factors, and development and learning—parenting and academic effects; suspensions and academic outcomes; pre-school care and developmental effects.

8.4 CURRICULUM

Some of the important aspects of curriculum research mentioned in a bulletin of UNESCO (1951) are: general principles of curriculum building, analysis of curriculum in various subjects, organization and development of curriculum, its transaction and evaluation, adaptation of curriculum to local needs, effects of examinationon curriculum organization, adaptation of curriculum to children's mental abilities and physical development, analysis of text books, concept development in various subjects, effectiveness of various teaching methods, human relation in curriculum development, study habits, duration of school work, revision and modernization of of curriculum.

Curriculum ideology and planning, innovative enrichment, teachers' role in effective transaction of curriculum in specific actual classroom situations, and methodological studies in comparative perspective deserve careful consideration by the researchers. The relevance, suitability, and transaction of the latest National Curriculum Framework for School Education (2005) may also be investigated.

8.5 EDUCATIONAL PLANNING, MANAGEMENT AND ADMINISTRATION

Studies which will have implications for developing policies in respect of recruitment of teachers; job analysis of headmasters, teachers, and administrative officers of education department; attrition among teachers; decentralization, and monitoring of different levels educational in the Indian context would be fruitful studies in the areas of educational administration and supervision.

Whereas, the quality education, accountability, manpower planning, appraisal of faculty members, institutional environment or climate, institutional effectiveness, professional development, and pedagogic leadership are the emerging areas in planning, administration and management of education.

Valecha and Abraham (1987) have pinpointed that a critical analysis of educational Acts, factors influencing the universalization of education, development and trying out of leadership programmes, institutional viability in terms of size and curriculum offering, evolution of management practices adopted by different educational agencies and effective functioning and management of colleges need to be explored.

Studies on the various techniques of plan formulation (perspective and annual), implementation, monitoring and evluation of plan schemes in education sector can be undertaken. The modalities of decentralized planning, institutional planning, role of NGOs in the process of plan farmulation and implementation should be given priority by the researchers. Assessment and benchmarking of institution on the parameters of quality can also be undertaken as research study.

Management of resources focusing on infrastructure (library, labs and technologies) and support (emotional, social, instructional and reinforcement) has larger implications in improving the learning outcomes can be undertaken for investigation.

8.6 SCIENCE EDUCATION

Environmental studies; curriculum, syllabus and textbook; learning science and models of teaching; teaching strategies; outcomes of science education; correlates of achievements in science; and educational technology had generally been undertaken during 1988 to 1992. Few more areas in science education were added such as students attitudes towards science, cognitive studies of science, teaching' materials, creativity, and gender issues in science teaching. A few interdisciplinary studies, i.e. status of science teaching in Indian schools for the visually impaired, teaching aptitude of science and non-science student teachers in relation to their level of anxiety, reform of science education in the context of education for all and cross-cultural hurdles in learning science.

Vaidya in his review has clarified that the research frontiers that needed to be traversed are:

1. History and philosophy of science and policy studies in science.
2. Science education in context of multi-cultural and international perspectives.
3. The fields of history of science, philosophy of science and sociology of science are deeply intertwined. The need is to develop curricula, teaching materials with these perspectives in mind. Evaluation of curricula and learning materials in relation to other cognitive and attitudinal aspects can be undertaken for research.

8.7 ECONOMICS OF EDUCATION

The major objectives of research endeavour in this area of economics of education are:

1. to apply effectively the relevant economic analysis to the field of education with a view to raise the efficiency of educational system at different levels;
2. to identify the variables of cost effectiveness and strategies for optimum use of finanacial resources, and
3. to identify the role of education in social and economic development of the country.

Areas of research in economics of education include:

(1) Problems of optimum size of an educational institution and resource allocation pose severe challenges because of the formidable obstacles in measuring educational inputs and outputs,

(2) Application of marginal and mathematical (linear programming) analysis for the determination of optimum size of our educational institutions and least cost combinations amongst different costed techniques of a given institutional unit are some of the problems available for investigation,

(3) Construction of *efficiency indices* of school units would also be helpful,

(4) In view of the market complexities, the determination of *shadow prices* at conceptual level in respect of teachers'

salaries and other inputs of the system may provide valuable information.

(5) Analysis of cost behaviour of educational institutions is also an important area of research. In this connection, identification of cost determinants at various levels will be of special importance while planning for facilities for education. Studies aiming to determine the pattern of educational expenditure at various levels, grant-in-aid, capital outlays, unit costs and opportunity costs may also be conducted, and

(6) There is a need for economic evaluation of various educational programmes undertaken by the central and state governments. These include agricultural education, vocational education, workers' education, adult education and extension education. The problems of wastage and stagnation at elementary, secondary and higher education levels need more attention of researchers. For the purpose of efficient use of resources, wastage and stagnation problems at this level need to be investigated on a systematic basis for different regions and community groups and for male and female categories.

8.8 EDUCATIONAL TECHNOLOGY

Research studies in educational technology show variety in design and thrust. The larger part of the cake has gone to Mass Media and ETV programmes. However, there has been studies on other areas like effectiveness of advance organisers, branching programmes, and use of information technology in library sciences. Most of the studies have been done on comparison of methods. New trust areas in research are: the effectiveness of Internet, virtual classroom, virtual teaching, video conferencing.

Assessment and optimun utilization of ICT resources (including human resources) which are available in learning institutions. Impacts of ICT application in classroom teaching and in other professional aspects of teachers. What is the levels of learners' competency in ICT skills? How ICT is embedded within the curriculun? What are ICT policy provisions in college or school in terms of student access and teacher expertise/use ? Does the use of ICT offer affordances to the intended learning or could the outcomes have been achieved more effectively through simpler, more conventional methods? Creation of framework for enhancing learning opportunities that computer-based material and accessible resources offer.

Research studies can be undertaken for the development of computer course ware materials for enrichment of learning process at secondary and higher secondary levels as well as for the development of technological aids such as audio-video cassetes, CD ROMs, interactive multimedia, internet as integral part of curriculun package. Developing strategies for optimizing the use of ICT in school and teacher education institutions.

Eight thrust areas in educational technology have been identified as given below:

- Techno-Logical—Literacy-studies may include phenomenological strategy, primary hermeneutics (textual analysis), use and impact of technological devices and processes, development of instruments for measurement of technological literacy for different age group.
- Conception of Technological Phenomena—do the conceptions held by students conform to normative expectations?
- Perception of technology—how do students view particular aspects of technology? Do they view technology as being good and its contribution to learning outcomes?
- Technology and creativity—how does technology stimulate creativity? How does a student devise creative ways of finding solution through the use of technology?
- Gender in technological classroom—what prevents girls from being attracted to the use of technology in the learning process? What are the historical reasons for gender bias in this field?
- Technology and curriculum change—is there need to restructure curriculum in the light of new technologies?
- Integration of technology and other school subjects—what is the role of technology in the transaction of curriculum of subjects namely, science, mathematics, languages, social studies, etc.? One key area of research is relationship between technology and vocational education.
- Technology and teacher—does teacher make use of teachnology in the classroom and what is its impact on student learning? Does teacher make use of latest technology for enhancing his or her professional growth and what is impact on his or her teaching effectiveness?

8.9 INCLUSIVE EDUCATION

Areas under inclusive research include : (i) developing appropriate supplementary instruction material for learners with special needs; (ii) making appropriate modification in the course content, its presentation and transaction strategies to facilitate conceptual clarity among learners with different learning needs; (iii) developing and using appropriate learning friendly evaluation procedures for learners with special needs; (iv) evolving new models, techniques, strategies and capacity-building programmes and their impact on teacher's effectiveness in special education; and (v) research in the field redesigning of infrastructure for chidren with special needs.

In this context, the following research questions were suggested by Wang, Reynolds and Walberg (1990) in the field of inclusive education:

(1) Important variables such as classroom climate, pedagogic leadership, teacher expectations, teacher-student interactions, and time-on-task, the classroom instructional-learning processes that affect student learning performance.
(2) Rationale for handicap classifications, academic achievement, and placement of students with special needs.
(3) Indentification of the effective intervention strategies that foster increasing 'expertise' in students who are considered to be academically 'handicapped'.
(4) Evaluation of various programmes to study development of competency and skills among differently abled children.
(5) Study of teacher styles and instructional approaches for enhancing the capability of children with special needs.
(6) Study of institutional interventions in raising the capability of differently abled children.

Swarup (2006, p. 208) further suggests that more specific, precise and scientific researches are needed to make inclusive education a reality in practice on a much larger scale. More teacher training modules need to be developed so that not only pre-service but in-service teachers also could be trained in inclusive practices. Study in the area of curriculum development could be conducted to make it more need-based. These also include studies on the development of multi-instructional approaches and evaluation techniques and strategies. The administrative and management aspects of inclusive education need to be studied at the micro and macro-levels in rural and urban settings so that models thus developed could be replicated in varied situations. Experimental and logitudinal studies and the role of multimedia could be undertaken.

Kapoor and Parveen (2009) in their study have reported that there are many gaps in the researches in the field of inclusive education which have to be filled. Most of the areas of research in special education are still unexplored. There is very little work on development of tools for identification and assessment, intervention strategies, development of instructional materials, effectiveness of technologies in improving access of disabled persons to curriculum and personnel, and transfer of training effects and management of special education. Research in special education is more of a practical nature. Most of the researches in special education provide ample scope for action research. There is need for coordinated effort to identify areas, prioritize them in light of the perceived demands of the stakeholders.

8.10 TEACHER EDUCATION

'*A Survey of Research in Education* (Buch, 1974), classified teacher education research into six areas, namely, selection criteria; abilities and qualities of the teacher; pre-service and in-service training of teachers; workload, job satisfaction and difficulties experienced by the teachers; procedures and practices of teacher education in India; and personality variables of teachers.

In the Second Survey of Research in Education, (Mehrotra, 1979), the variables were clustered under contextual, input, process and output categories. In the third Survey of Research in Education, Jangira (1986) adopted a systems model of classifying variables under context-presage-process-product categories. A large number of researches have been undertaken in institutional context, institutional environment, curriculum, and innovative teacher training practices with purpose to improve the quality of teacher education at national, regional and state levels. Passi *et. al.* (1986) studied the effects of various models of teaching on the competence of student-teachers and their willingness to use the same in the classrooms.

In the Fourth Survey of Research in Education (1983-88), the studies have been viewed from three points of view i.e., their nature, methodology of research and systems approach to teacher education. (Singh and Malhotra, 1991). In the 5th Survey of Educational Research, Singh and Nirupma Jaimin (2000) classified various research studies on the basis of their approach: (a) Model-based Teaching Strategies, (b) Other Teaching Strategies such as objective-based, mastery learning, innovative and meta-cognitive strategies. The research studies on teaching strategies have been found by and large based upon experimental design. Most of the experiments of teaching strategies have been carried out in actual classroom situations and are quasi-experimental. Designing such studies in the classroom situation has an advantage of assessing the effectiveness of a teaching strategy in real conditions. Cohen and *et. al.* (2000) advocated the use of experimental and quasi-experimental research designs under varied resource constraints to examine how teacher use resources to affect students' learning. A large number of researches (42) were conducted and adopted in the country on micro-teaching. These studies were analysed and were found favourable and quite feasible in teacher education programmes (Singh and Joshi, 1990). The Concept Attainment Model, Information Processing Model, Synectics Model, and Inquiry Training Model were adopted, modified and used to identify their effectiveness. Joshi (2000) classified research studies by adopting the system model involving context-process-output components. A survey of Internship in Teaching with view to develop strategies for improving the total system of teacher education was conducted by Srivastava (1998).

In the Sixth Survey of Educational Research (NCERT, 2006), 98 studies were grouped under Teacher Education. Mehrotra (2000) observed "Although, it may appear that the studies have covered all aspects-context, pre-stage, process, product of teacher education—very vital areas have not been touched. Much research has been highly pedantic, limited in scope, tentative and jargon dominated. The concept of excellence and quality with regards to teachers, teaching and teacher education needs attention of excellent, reflective scholars.

Areas of research, which call for attention of practitioners, scholars and teacher educators and on priority, are identification of significant indicators of quality profile of teachers; comprehensive, timely database on quality profile of prospective teachers, and unemployed pool of teachers; impact of course work and field work on outcomes beyond beliefs and attitudes, e.g. practices and knowledge growth; evolving better tools for studying outcomes of teacher education; technology and its impact on learning environments; socio-economic and cultural variables and their impact on teacher education institutions; evaluation of programmes preparing graduates to foster learning for students with disabilities, and research on teacher tests and on concurrent, predictive, and consequential validity of the wide range of teacher tests.

Center of Advance Studies in Education has identified four thrust areas namely: (a) teaching, teaching behaviour, teacher education, (b) educational management, including innovations and change, leadership behaviour of heads, organizational climate of institutions, teachers morale, (c) educational technology including programmed learning, and (d) higher education for improving the quality of research in education.

Most of the teacher education institutions have never gone through any of *the "value-added" analyses* of the differences that individual teacher makes. This reflects omission of the wide availability of research in this field and its central role in much of the current thinking about educational improvement. "The research base is currently insufficient to support the use of value-added methodologies (VAM) for high-stakes decisions" (McCaffrey and *et. al.*, 2004). Areas of pedagogic leadership and critical pedagogy can also be explored.

8.11 PRIORITY AREAS OF EDUCATIONAL RESEARCH IN INDIA

The problem of determining priorities in educational research is complex and a subjective issue. Each researcher may have his own priorities common or uncommon to others. These priorities may be assigned in terms of individual needs and capacities, social targets, finances, value patterns, consideration of time and funds, and utility of a research problem. In this context, the Education Commission (1966) has noted that:

The priorities in educational research at the national level, from the point of view of the educational planners or administrators, may be very different from similar priorities at state or regional level. The Commission, therefore, did not favour any rigid framework of priorities. It has suggested that the decisions about the priorities should be taken by the Education Research Council in the Ministry of Education at the national level, by the State Department of Education at the state level and by the universities, teacher training colleges or institutes and teachers interested in the research work.

Educational Research and Innovations Committee (ERIC) of the National Council of Educational Research and Training have suggested some priority areas in educational research keeping in view the National Policy of Education-1986: Programme of Action, (1992) and the role of education in total programme of national development.

1. Research and policy-making in education affect each other. This relationship suggests that research in the development of policy concerns; policy studies in science and technology education; effectiveness of policy issues and dissemination of findings related to such issues; use of qualitative and participatory approaches involving triangulation of methodologies in resolving policy issues and concerns should be given priority.
2. Another priority area in the field of education is the fulfilment of the Constitutional Directive of Article 45 and Fundamental Right to Education (21-A) relating to the provision of free and compulsory elementary education for all children up to the age 14. Studies which will help to extend the educational programmes, formal and non-formal, to all children, especially belonging to scheduled castes and scheduled tribes including nomadic, semi-nomadic and denotified communities; hill areas and slums; and economically weaker sections of the society may be conducted.
3. Researches on elementary school children, may also be undertaken in the conceptualisation of life skills, identification and incorporation of life skills to curriculum, instructional materials, teaching-learning processes and educational evaluation; promotion of self directed learning; development and transaction of curriculum relevant to local needs; strategies to reduce gap between home language and school language; efficacy of mother tongue medium schooling *vis-a-vis* English medium and dominant language medium schooling; effectiveness of non-detention policy; community participation in the improvement of school practice; development of teaching-learning methodology in the context of multi-grade and multi-level teaching-learning in different subjects in primary schools/alternative schools; and culture specific pedagogy.
4. The dropout rate in school education is very high for various reasons and it is not likely to decrease very much in the near future. While every attempt should be made to increase the holding power of the school, we should also think of non-formal education as a possible alternative. Studies should be conducted to evolve organization and methods of self-learning so that children in school learn

better and those who drop out from school are not left out of the country's educational effort.

5. In spite of the best efforts of central and state-governments, the scheme of vocationalisation of education has not-yet picked up the desired momentum. There have been many factors responsible for the slow progress. Research relating to the study of such factors, namely, causes for failure of vocational education programme in the states and remedial measures, models of linkage between vocational education and industries in organised/unorganised sectors, absence of a well co-ordinated management system, unemployability of vocational pass-outs, mis-match between demand and supply, reluctance in accepting the concept of vocationalisation by the society, absence or proper provisions for professional growth and career advancement for the vocational pass-outs, etc. should be undertaken on priority basis.
6. The system of education in the country should make significant contribution towards developing suitable educational opportunities for the physically, mentally and socially challenged children with reference to inclusive education. This needs special research efforts for designing suitable training and orientation programmes for teachers and developing suitable instructional aids and materials for teaching such type of children.
7. At the higher education level, there is need for conducting evaluative studies to assess the impact of autonomous colleges and autonomous teaching departments, rural institutes/universities and academic staff colleges in providing quality education to college and university students.
8. Open and distance education is also an important priority area of research. The impact of open schools and universities at the national and state levels in achieving the goal of *Education for All* need to be explored with the help of comprehensive surveys, longitudinal, experimental and evaluative studies.

Educational Research and Innovations Committee (ERIC) of NCERT (2007) has identified priority areas of research.

Curricular Areas: In the backdrop of National Curriculum Framework (NCF-2005) it is important that each curricular area is to be revisited by the researchers and probed in-depth to find answers to problems related to teaching-learning of different subjects.

National Concerns: In this context, disadvantages in education arising due to inequalities of gender, case, language, culture, religion or disabilities need to be addressed. Research related to education of the disadvantaged groups, inclusive education, gender equity, education of rural children and functioning of rural schools should be on the agenda of priority.

Systemic Concerns: Researches for improving system for preparing teachers should lay emphasis on both pre-service and in-service, system of producing textbooks and learning materials and the examination system. Integration of ICT in education as a pedagogic, administrative and monitoring tool and the related practices require extensive research for maximum efficiency within the boundaries of democracy, human dignity and freedom. Classroom processes and practices and management strategies are other useful areas of research in his context.

Pedagogic Practices and Learning Processes: Within the ambit of child centered pedagogic, research in areas like thinking and learning processes of children, pedagogic approaches of training teachers, text-analysis and text-learning dynamics become crucial.

Research in educational leadership is an area of concern. Research and training in educational leadership should focus on, educational policy formation and implementation; resource allocation and budgeting; personal selection, development and evaluation; human resource management and collective negotiation; instructional strategies and curriculum; pupils evaluation; family and community involvement; organization decision-making; meditating disputes and taking action in a highly politicized and contested environment; and data driven decision-making. Each is complex and requires conceptual understanding as well as ability to put knowledge into action in educational setting.

Assessment and accreditation should be based on evidences objectively examined. Institution and delivery systems need to be assessed and accredited to have a detail view of the quality in teacher education. Assessment of institution may include infrastructure, organizational set-up, resources (financial and manpower) and management of faculty. Delivery system involves processes, procedures and use of resources to get optimum returns in terms of gains in students.

CONCLUSION

Current areas of interest in the school for research enquiry have included right to education (access, availability and affordability), gender discrimination in education, critical pedagogies, subject knowledge for teaching, the professional knowledge of beginning teachers, the management and leadership of schools, inter-professional working, widening participation in higher education, international education and the contribution of higher educational institutions to teacher education.

More widely a wide range of researches have been undertaken in recent years for enhancing the learning experience through mobile technologies, geographical enquiry in diverse places, policy and practice in literacy education, cross-curriculum links in mathematics and music, developing children's spirituality and equality and diversity in higher education. Work is also being undertaken on e-learning, self-study methodologies. Number of projects are being undertaken in the arena of reflective practice in early childhood education, primary and secondary education. Researches on quality of education at different levels are also being explored. Impact of partnerships between government and private sector in higher education can be undertaken as a subject matter of research.

REFERENCES

Best, J. and Kahn, J. (2009). *Research in Education.* 10th edition, Needham Heights: Allyn and Bacon

Cozby, P. (2009). *Methods in Behavioural Research.* 10th edition, Bemont: Wadsworth.

Goode, W.J., and Hatt, P.K. (1990). *Methods in Social Research.* New Delhi: McGraw-Hill,

Guthrie, G. (2010). *Basic Research Methods.* New Delhi: Sage.

Kothari, C.R. (2004). *Research Methodology: Methods & Techniques.* New Delhi: New Age International Publishers.

Koul, L. (2009). *Methodology of Educational Research.* Vikas Publishing House, New Delhi-14.

Laws, S. (2003). *Research for Development.* New Delhi: Vistaar Publications.

Leedy, P., Ormrod, J. (2010). *Practical Research: Planning and Design.* 9th edition, Needham Heights: Allyn Bacon.

Ozga, J. (2000). *Policy Research in Educational Settings.* Buckingham,UK: Open University Press.

Paneerselvam, R. (2004). *Research Methodology.* New Delhi: Prentice-Hall of India

Punch, K.F. (2009). *Introduction to Research Methods in Education.* New Delhi: Sage.

Singh, J. (2008). *Methodology and Techniques of Social Research.* New Delhi: Kanishka Publishers.

Somekh, B., and Lewin, C. (2005). *Research Methods in the Social Sciences.* New Delhi. Vistaar Publications.

Sukhia, S.P., Mehrotra, P.V. and Mehrotra, R.N. (1974). *Elements of Educational Research.* New Delhi: Allied Publishers.

Swann, J. (2000). How can research lead to improvement in education. *Prospero,* 6(3/4), pp. 130-38.

Swann, J. and Pratt, J. (2003). (Eds.). *Educational Research in Practice.* London: Continuum.

describe, predict, and explain the natural world and meaningful social and personal "worlds" and experiences.

- Explicate researcher and research values, purposes, commitments and key background assumptions.
- Use methods and strategies that, separately or in combination, can produce warranted investigation of particular research questions.
- Rely on multiple sources of evidence. Link explanatory research to relevant theory, through theory generation, theory testing, and ongoing theory modification.
- Describe the nomological [illegible] domain, but [illegible] produce meaningful research questions.
- [illegible]

These principles [illegible] professional communities [illegible]

[illegible]

UNIT II

RESEARCH PROBLEM, REVIEW OF RELATED LITERATURE AND EVALUATION HYPOTHESIS

CHAPTER

9

Selection of Problem and its Sources

9.1 Selection of the problem is one of the most important phases in research process. Weak and ill conceived idea or problem will put a researcher in deep trouble. In such a situation, sometimes, researcher may resort to undesirable acts with stimulation to get a degree. This may not be useful to the researcher (i.e. the pursuit of truth is compromised by disingenuousness or ineptitude on the part of the researcher) as well as to the society (i.e. wastage of resources). Beginners are likely to select a problem that is too board in scope to manage or too narrow to get reliable results. The difficulty for many beginners in research lies in an insensitivity to the problems or "problem blindness" (Good, 2008). Reasons of inappropriate selection of the problem are: lack of understanding of the nature of the research and systematic problem-solving activity; impatience and hurry in selection; hesitation in consulting experts or peers in the field of research; poor reading habit; overconfidence; and picking up of an area with no background knowledge.

Those who are more experienced know that research is often tedious, painfully slow, and rarely spectacular. They realize that the search for new knowledge and the solution of important problems take a great deal of time and energy and the intensive application of logical as well as divergent thinking. Researcher has to take it seriously because time consumed in the selection of appropriate and researchable topic will clear the path to conduct the research in a smooth way so as to achieve the objectives of research. The researcher should have some of the characteristics of the ant, which brings its single grain of sand to the anthill.

A researcher should clarify the following questions based on the personal and social considerations.

9.1.1 Personal Considerations

- Is the problem in line with my goal expectations and expectations of others?
- Am I genuinely interested in this problem but free from strong biases?
- Do I possess, or can I acquire the necessary skills, abilities and background knowledge to study this problem?
- Do I have access to the tools, equipments, laboratories, and subject necessary to conduct the investigation?
- Do I have the time and money to complete?
- Can I have adequate data?
- Does the problem meet the scope, significance, and topical requirements of the institution?
- Can I obtain administrative support, guidance, and cooperation for the conduct of the study?

9.1.2 Social Considerations

- Will the solution of this problem advance knowledge in the field?
- Will the findings be of practical value to the educators, the parents, the social workers or others?
- What will be the breadth of the application of the findings in terms of range of individuals, and the areas of coverage?
- If the topic has been covered, does it need to be extended beyond its present limits?
- Is the topic sufficiently delimited to permit an exhaustive treatment yet sufficiently significant to warrant investigating it?
- Will the study lead to the development of other investigations?

9.1.3 Selection Criteria

(1) Its relevance to the formulation of a general theory or its contribution to the body of knowledge. This involves scrutiny of original source and deep knowledge. Gaps,

weak points, and inconsistencies in the theory that indicate the need for further research are to be identified. Main goal is either to discover new theory, or modify or to create new knowledge. Such problems can usefully be divided into three categories: problems of value (what is good, what ought to be done, what is aesthetically pleasing), problems of fact (what is so in the world, and why, what was so and why, what will be so and why), problems of logic (what is valid and why). Researches in theoretical investigations involve philosophical, historical, and ethical studies, and empirical enquiries of various kinds. (Swann, 2003).

(2) Its contribution to the solution of practical problem to bridge mismatch between expectation and experience or its potential for practical improvement in the conduct and/or organization of learning and teaching. Identify important problems and pose questions that can be investigated empirically or through potentially useful approaches.

Key Points for the Researcher as Learner

- Seek mismatches (actual or anticipated) between your expectation and experience; turn (selected) mismatches into problems;
- When selecting a problem, be clear about what type of problem it is, and what type of solution will be required: practical (how can I/we——?) or theoretical (What——?, Why——? And so on);
- Put into an accessible form, the practical ideas so that they can be criticized by you and others and replaced with potentially better ideas;
- Weak and ill-conceived ideas can subsequently be eliminated through critical discussion;
- Don't be afraid to be dogmatic in the early stages of developing an idea, and don't abandon ideas in the face of premature criticism but subject the idea to severe criticism in order that the idea may need to modified or even abandoned;
- Work with other people, and draw on the world of public knowledge, but bear in mind the fallibility of all sources of ideas;
- Make judgments on the basis of arguments and evidence rather than whim, orthodoxy, fashion of expediency;

- The research should outline the basic assumptions, and
- Find ways to defend and maintain your confidence in explaining your topic of research before the experts.

Summary of selection of topic, areas and sources is given in Figure 9.1.

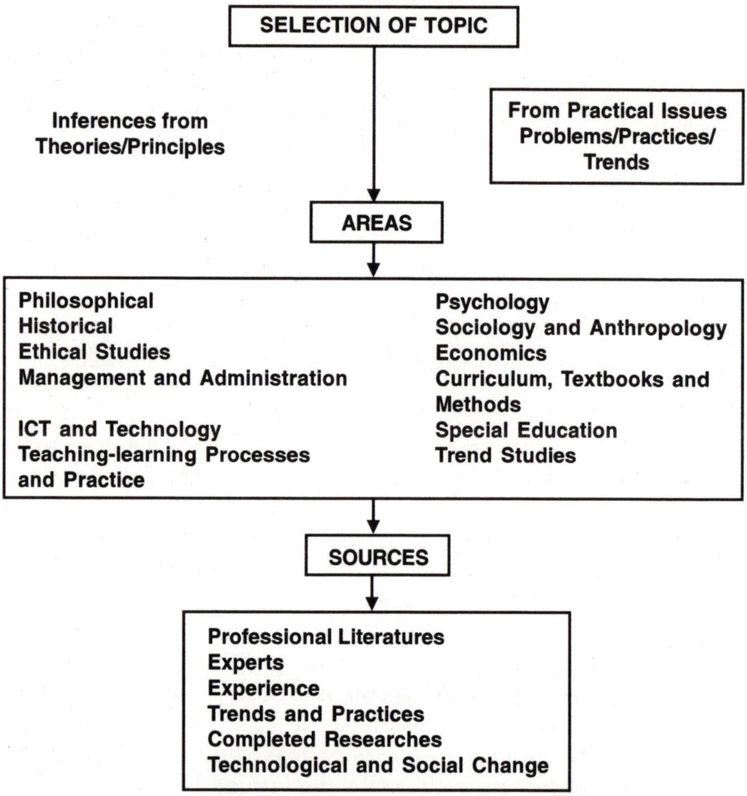

Figure 9.1 : Selection, Areas and Sources

9.2 SOURCES

9.2.1 Field of Study

- The researcher has acquired some basic knowledge of field in the academic course at graduate or post-graduate level. A few of them may have even specialization in a specific field at post-graduate level. Fields may be education, sociology, psychology, or/and philosophy, etc. This background scholarship would help him to identify both the available evidence and the unsolved problems.

- It has been typical of the scholar to select a thesis problem in his major field of concentration. The researcher may feel comfortable and get stimulated in his own field of inquiry. Therefore, he can make use of his imaginative, creative and original thinking in the conduct of inquiry.
- The researcher should go through priority areas in research as suggested by the centers of higher learning.

9.2.2 Professional Literature

- A researcher has to access the researches conducted in the area of his interest. The study of professional literature will expose a researcher to pressing research problems.
- The research reports, bibliographies of books and articles, periodicals, research abstracts, year books, dictionaries, and research guides suggest areas that need research. Some specialized sources as the Encyclopedia of Educational Research, Dissertation Abstracts, and the Hand Book of Research on Teaching, Psychological Abstracts and the Surveys of Research in Education provide rich sources of identifying appropriate problems for investigation.
- All published research reports generally conclude by making suggestions about further research.
- Dewey (1887) in his book on psychology refers to seventy-eight resources in chapter "Elements of Knowledge" and "Processes of Knowledge".
- *Honing Research Skills*-critical Reading, recording, accessing and storing of literature are the necessary skills which a researcher must possess and utilized in identifying problems of research. Critical thinking demands intensive and extensive reading. "To be perfectly original one should think much and read little, and this is impossible, for one must have read before one has learnt to think". (Byron, 1935)
- This also involves purposeful : (a) reviewing of the literature, (b) recording and storing of material related to the subject of study, (c) meta-analysis of researches, and (d) discussion of the results of various research studies to arrive at a logical conclusion in finding appropriate topic for research.
- Use of 'Internet' or 'search engines', 'websites' are essential for exploring the new areas or unsolved problems. 'There

can be no knowledge without knower. Knowledge does not exist in an abstract sense' (Shera, 1970).

9.2.3 Experts and Senior Scholars as Source

- Stimulating contacts between a professor and a student inside and outside the classroom or seminar, or conference or between a senior scholar and a younger worker, frequently have been profitable in the selection and development of problem for investigation. Well known examples are the influence of William James on Dewey, Thorndike, and Woodworth; Wundt on Cattle, Stanley Hall, Judd, and Titchener. Similarly in India, M. Varma, C.S. Kothari, Paneerselvam, M.B. Buch, D.B. Desai, B.K. Passi influenced many educational and psychological investigators.
- In all scientific endeavour, the interdependence of research workers is recognized in the identification and solution of problems. The relationship between Binet and Simon is a striking example of the influence of a senior scholar on a younger associate. Therefore, consultation with supervisor, senior researcher, practitioner and professional librarian would show you the way to the treasure of new research problems to explore.

9.2.4 Professional Experience

- One of the most fruitful sources of problems for the research is his own experience as a professional educator. In his interaction with peers, students, management, and other stakeholders, he has to encounter number of problems. Many of the problems confronted in the classroom, the school, or the community lend themselves to investigation, and they are perhaps more appropriate for the beginning researcher than are the problems more remote from his or her own teaching experience.
- A mismatch between his expectation and experience (actual and anticipated) stimulates him to explore and investigate the problem. Sometimes, teacher may come across students having behavioural problems. These problems hinder the performance of an individual and put a challenge before a teacher to diagnose the causes and find out tangible solution through scientific investigation.
- His professional experience prompts him to inquire or investigate into the emerging problems, "How to address

the diverse population in the classroom?"; "How to transact curriculum in an effective way?"; "How can we enhance the quality of teaching and learning?"; "How can we validate the examination results or external evaluation?"; "How can we design our curriculum to address the needs an individual as well as society?"; "How can we improve the system of evaluation involving peer, and stakeholders?"; "To what extent does one method yield more effective results than another?", etc.

9.2.5 Analysis of Evidence, Practices, Trends or Needs in a particular Area

- Meta-analysis of evidence would provide us insights into our weaknesses and strengths in our system, gaps and inconsistencies in our curriculum design, mismatch between what we have realized and what is the potential in learning and teaching, which can help the researchers in identifying problems.
- Impact of existing practices, methods, models, techniques of learning can be investigated to achieve the optimum results. There is also scope for conducting research on developing new innovative practices.
- It is alleged by the experts that there is a trend in deteriorating quality of education on account of its expansion so as to make it accessible and affordable to all sections of the society especially to the marginalized. There is a trend of burgeoning unemployment among educated youth challenging the validity of degrees. Government schools have not yet introduced new methods, curriculum, innovative practices, that is why the trend of low learning outcomes is reported. There trends provide us enough cues to take up research studies to break the vicious circle to bring about substantial improvement in the system so as to achieve the goals. We need new techniques of evaluation. We need to know the effects of various methods of evaluation upon the learning process.
- There are particular areas which need urgent attention of the researchers. For example, designing of instruction materials, infrastructure, and preparation of teachers in the areas of special education are in urgent need so as to raise the capacity of differently able children.

9.2.6 Inference from Theory

Theories such as learning theories, personality theories, theories of intelligence, and theories of motivation, sociological theories and many others provide rich sources of topic for research in classroom situations. Theoretical problems are those for which solution is theory or a set of theories. Such problems can usefully be divided into three categories:

- Problems of value—what is good?, what ought to be done?, what is aesthetically pleasing?.
- Problems of facts—what is so in the world and why?, what was so and why?, what will be so and why?.
- Problems of logic—what is valid and why?.

Logical reasoning, common sense and argument suggest that some practices may be better than others, and we can develop programmes of empirical research—specifically, a science of education—which challenge existing expectations about what works and why, and produce new theories which conjecturally are better. (Swann, 2000).

- The application of general principles involved in various theories to specific classroom situation makes an excellent starting point for research. The application of the existing theory in the classroom can be undertaken as topic of research.
- There are certain gaps and inconsistencies in the existing theories. These require further refinement and modification. Therefore, research studies can be identified in this context to fill the gaps or to clear the inconsistencies to get better results.
- It is only through the application of scientific method that we can appropriately test the validity, scope and practicability of various theories in educational situations.

9.2.7 Completed Researches

Repetition of researches already completed is generally not welcomed. Sometimes, replication or extension of completed research studies can be a profitable and worthwhile activity. For example:

- The study can be conducted at different times on different groups, in different contexts and places. The findings of the research can be used for the purpose of generalization and will provide additional evidence of the validity of the findings.
- The study can be undertaken in case there are gaps, inconsistencies or weaknesses in design, tools, treatment

and analysis of data. The purpose is cleansing of contradicting and refinement or modification or generation of viable and effective theory or practice.

9.2.8 Technological and Social Changes

- Socio-economic and technological changes have brought about tremendous improvement in our educational field. It has given rise to market-led; computer mediated world, a world where time and distance are compressed, a world where cross cultural interaction has expanded the boundaries of knowledge, a world which is more modern than modern and has given new challenges and opportunities in research.
- The paradigm of producing different knowledge is replaced by producing knowledge differently, is 'opening up new imaginaries' in research and interpretation. (St Pierre, 1997).
- Validity of fixed curriculum, learning models, methods and practices, are being challenged. Technology Rich Learning Environment has taken the place of conventional environment; this has given rise to new areas of research.
- The policies are being redesigned and reframed in the light of new emerging priorities. The question is, "how can the governmental programmes and schemes be made more effective on the evidence of researches"? The Government policy and commitment under 'Right to Education Act', that 'No Child is Left Uneducated' has attracted the attention of researchers as how to make it successful through the participation of stakeholders.

The following points are to be kept in mind when selecting a topic for research:

- What is known about the subject?
- Are there any gaps in the knowledge of the subject?
- Have areas of further study been identified by other researchers that you may want to consider?
- Who are the significant research personalities in this area?
- Is there consensus about the topic?
- What aspects have generated significant debate on the topic?
- What methods or problems were identified by others studying in the field and how might they impact your research?

- How does the study move beyond them?
- What is the most productive methodology for your research based on the literature you have reviewed?
- Is it intentionally chosen and justified strategy for searching, selecting, evaluating, and synthesizing the literature?
- What is the current status of research in this area?
- What sources of information or data were identified that might be useful to you?

REFERENCES

Best, J. and Kahn, J. (2009). *Research in Education*. 10th edition, Needham Heights: Allyn and Bacon.

Corey, S.M. (1962). *Research in Education*. NCERT, New Delhi.

Cozby, P. (2009). *Methods in Behavioural Research*. 10th edition, Bemont: Wadsworth.

Goode, W.J., and Hatt, P.K. (1990). *Methods in Social Research*. McGraw-Hill, New Delhi.

Guthrie, G. (2010). *Basic Research Methods*. New Delhi: Sage.

Hillway, T. (1956). *Introduction to Research*. Houghton Miffin Co.

Punch, K. (2006). *Developing Effective Research Proposals*. 2nd edition, London: Sage.

Rummel, J.F. (1958). *An Introduction to Research Procedures in Education*. New York: Harper Brothers.

CHAPTER

10

Formulation of Research Proposal

10.1. WHAT RESEARCH IS INTENDED

10.1.1 Identification of the Research Problem requires a lot of efforts and an extensive reading on the part of a researcher. Familiarity with the area and the sub-areas of the field is prerequisite. Researcher's inquisitiveness would help him to identify the gaps between the realized and the anticipated results in the selection of a research topic. He can make use of his personal experience, opinion of experts in the area of his interest, interacting with resource persons in National or International Conferences, Seminars, and Workshops in the identification of a research problem of his or her choice. Researcher can take premise from a theory. Identification of gaps/ deficiencies in the theory or its application in the classroom situation would stimulate him or her to pick up the new topic of research.

10.1.2 When a topic of research is identified, need arises to explain and justify, why do you like to undertake this research study? What are the expected outcomes of the proposed research study? What are its practical implications?

10.1.3 A review of Literature is the fundamental task of dissertation and research preparation. The researchers get minimal formal training. A little guidance from faculty or published sources, could not equip them as how to analyze and synthesize research literature. As a result, it is also alleged that most dissertation literature reviews are poorly conceptualized and written. Researchers may not be learning what it means to make and justify educational claims.

Literature reviewing should be a central focus of pre-dissertation coursework, integrated throughout the programme. 'Comprehensiveness' and 'Broadness' are two of the criteria assessing the 'Coverage'. First, a standard for evaluating the literature review, and Second, the discussion part of the dissertation, 'the writer task is to employ the research literature artfully to support and explain the choices made for this study, not to educate the reader concerning the state of science in the problem area' (Locke, Spirduso, and Silveraman, 1999).

10.1.4 Statement of problem should one or two sentences. Statement of the Problem should be specific, clear and researchable. A research worthy problem statement is the description of an active challenge faced by researchers and/or practitioners that does not have adequate solution. The research worthy problem statement should address all six questions, what, how, where, when, why and who. Usually, a problem requires some reworking to get it into a suitable form for the study to proceed effectively.

Example: a statement such as "The high school curriculum" is far too broad to serve as a problem statement. A good statement might be "A study of the effects of high school curriculum practices on 9th class reading achievement in Jammu City."

A good statement of the problem should provide the researcher with direction in pursuing the project. The statement should identify key factors in the research project.

Example: "effects" is confined to reading achievement. "9th class and Jammu city" limit and define the population under study; "high school curriculum practices is certainly more specific than word "curriculum".

10.1.5 Key factors in the statement of the problem should be elaborated, i.e. made more specific and measurable. Therefore, considerable definition of terms (key-factors) would be necessary. An operational definition assigns meaning to a construct or a variable by specifying the activities or "operations" necessary to measure it. Alternatively, an operational definition is a specification of the activities of the researcher in measuring a variable or in manipulating it. An operational definition is a sort of manual of instructions to the investigator. It gives meaning to a variable by spelling out what the investigator must do to measure it. Scientific investigators must sooner or later face the necessity of measuring the variables of the relations they are studying. Sometimes measurement is easy, sometimes difficult. To measure sex or social class is easy; to measure creativity, anxiety, or organizational effectiveness is difficult. The importance of operational definitions cannot be overemphasized. They are indispensable ingredients of scientific research because they enable researchers to measure variables. They are bridges between the theory hypotheses construct level and the level of observation. There can be no scientific research without observations, and observations are impossible without clear and specific instructions on what and how to observe. Operational definitions are such instructions. An operational definition is a good which passes the test of validity and actually provides evidence related to the conceptual definition.

10.1.6 Objectives of the study provide clear direction to research. They reflect the basic purpose of the study, i.e. what we want to achieve. Objectives of the study provide necessary safeguards in collection of requisite information. Quantitative or qualitative data thus collected are analyzed and interpreted *vis-à-vis* earmarked objectives or outcomes of the research project. After selecting the topic and defining the research problem, the researcher should mention the objectives of the research. This means that he should explain what he aims to achieve through the research. His objectives should also explain the extent to which the research work is related to the specific field.

10.1.7 Research questions or hypotheses are more operational than statement of the problem, as such, lend more specific structure to the study. If a topic defines the general area, then the research question defines what aspects of that topic one plans to investigate.

Researchable questions can be generated or developed through following sources:

- Personal experiences—sometimes our personal experiences of a particular phenomenon, or event can give 'insights' worth exploring;
- Theory—theoretical inspiration is most likely to happen when you find yourself relating theory to a real-world situation;
- An observation—viewing the world through fresh eyes can provide powerful research angles;
- Contemporary issues—sometimes an old topic can take on fresh life. A topic might suddenly become an agenda or focus of global attention;
- Gaps in literature—one can explore whether an important aspect of an issue has been ignored, whether there are assumptions underpinning a body of work that need to be re-examined.

Hypotheses vs. *Research questions*: The hypothesis is the cornerstone of scientific method and that is necessary component of the research process. Hypothesis is logical conjecture, hunch or educated guess about the nature of relationships between two or more variables expressed in the form of a testable statement. Not all research questions can be easily 'converted' into a hypothesis, nor should they.

A hypothesis may not be appropriate if:

- You do not have a hunch or educated guess about a particular situation;
- You do not have defined variables;
- Your question centers on phenomenological descriptions; and
- Your question centers on ethnographic study of a cultural group.

Researcher should check

- Is the question right for the researcher?
- Is the question right for the field?
- Is the question well articulated?
- Is the question doable?
- Does he get the tick of approval from those in the know?

10.2. HOW THE RESEARCH WILL BE DONE

Methodology or Procedures

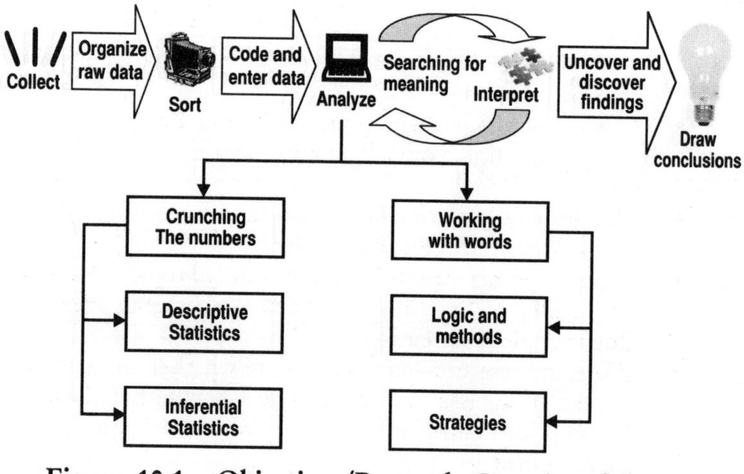

Figure 10.1 : Objectives/Research Questions/Theory

10.2.1 Method and Research Design

A well-defined problem points to a method of investigation. There is no one best method of research for all situations. Rather, there are a wide variety of methods for the researcher to choose from. There are three basic methods of research namely : (1) survey (i.e. descriptive or causal descriptive), (2) observation; and (3) experiment (McDaniel and Gates, 1991). The researcher should explain the method he is going to use. Research design gives the outlines of the research work. Research design is the plan, structure and strategy of the investigation conceived to obtain answers to research questions and to control variance. A research design is a framework for the collection, measurement and analysis of data.

10.2.2 Sample

The researcher should keep three things in mind in the selection of sample namely; (1) defining the population by specifying elements, sampling units, and extent; (2) method of selection, and (3) size of the sample.

The researcher should also observe while selecting the sample : (1) goal orientation, (2) measurability, (3) practicality, and (4) economy.

Methods: He may use probability techniques (simple random sampling or stratified sampling or cluster sampling or systematic sampling techniques. In case of non-probability techniques one can use convenience sampling, or quota sampling or purposive sampling.

Sample Size: Researcher can actually calculate the required size using the following formula:

$$N= ((KxS)/E)^2$$

where K is desired confidence level, S is sample standard deviation, and E is the required level of precision. In case the researcher is not interested in using the above formula, he can, however, use a 'sample size calculator' where the only things you need to know are: the population size; the confidence interval—what range you will accept above and below the mean, i.e. 0.05 or 0.01 confidence level.

10.2.3 Tools

A large variety of measurement devices are used in research, e.g. tests, questionnaires, inventories, scales, observation and interview schedules. In some researches, the researcher can use existing standardized instruments. For others, developing adequate measurement procedures may involve a substantial portion of the research effort. Their reliability and validity should be established

TABLE 10.1
Required Sample Size

Population	*Confidence Levels*		
	95% C.L ±5% C.L.	*99% C.L ±5% C.L*	*99% C.L ±1% C.L*
30	28	29	Insufficient
100	80	87	99
500	217	286	485
1,000	278	400	943
5,000	357	588	3845
10,000	370	624	6247
50,000	381	657	12486
100,000	383	661	14267
1,000,000	384	665	16369

before going for data collection. Sub-dimensions of the instrument of measurement need to be specified.

10.2.4 Data Collection

1. Outline the general plan for collecting the data. This may include survey administration procedures, interview or observation procedures. Include an explicit statement covering the field controls to be employed. If appropriate, discuss how you obtained *entré*.
2. Provide a general outline of the time schedule you expect to follow.

10.2.5 Data Analysis

1. Specify the procedures you will use, and label them accurately (e.g., ANOVA, MANCOVA, HLM, ethnography, case study, grounded theory). If coding procedures are to be used, describe in reasonable detail. If you triangulate, carefully explain how you went about it. Communicate your precise intentions and reasons for these intentions to the reader. This helps you and the reader evaluate the choices you made and procedures you followed.
2. Indicate briefly any analytic tools you will have available and expect to use (e.g., Ethnograph, NUDIST, AQUAD, SAS, SPSS, SYSTAT).

3. Provide a well thought-out rationale for your decision to use the design, methodology, and analyses you have selected.

10.3 LIMITATIONS AND DELIMITATIONS

A *limitation* identifies potential weaknesses of the study. Think about your analysis, the nature of self-report, your instruments, the sample. Think about threats to internal validity that may have been impossible to avoid or minimize—explain.

A *delimitation* addresses how a study will be narrowed in scope, that is, how it is bounded. This is the place to explain the things that you are not doing and why you have chosen not to do them—the literature you will not review (and why not), the population you are not studying (and why not), the methodological procedures you will not use (and why you will not use them). Limit your delimitations to the things that a reader might reasonably expect you to do but that you, for clearly explained reasons, have decided not to do.

10.4 SIGNIFICANCE OF THE STUDY

Indicate how your research will refine, revise, or extend existing knowledge in the area under investigation. Note that such refinements, revisions, or extensions may have either substantive, theoretical, or methodological significance. Think pragmatically (i.e., cash value).

How does the study address the audiences?

10.5 IMPLICATIONS

This can be a difficult section to write. Think about *implications*—how results of the study may affect scholarly research, theory, practice, educational interventions, curricula, counseling, policy.

When thinking about the significance of your study, ask yourself the following questions:

What will results mean to the theoretical framework that framed the study?

What suggestions for subsequent research arise from the findings?

What will the results mean to the practicing educator?

Will results influence programs, methods, and/or interventions?

Will results contribute to the solution of educational problems?

Will results influence educational policy decisions?

What will be improved or changed as a result of the proposed research?

How will results of the study be implemented, and what innovations will come about?

TABLE 10.2
Format of the Research Proposal

Step-1 Introduction
Step-2 Review of Literature
Step-3 Statement of Problem
Step-4 Operational Definition
Step-5 Objectives of the Study
Step-6 Hypotheses/Research Questions
Step-7 Methodology
- (a) Method
- (b) Sample
- (c) Tools/Instruments
- (d) Data Analysis

Step-8 Procedures
Step-9 Delimitations
Step-10 Implications
Step-11 Abstract

Common Mistakes in Proposal Writing

Failure to provide the proper context to frame the research question.
Failure to delimit the boundary conditions for your research.
Failure to cite landmark studies.
Failure to accurately present the theoretical and empirical contributions by other researchers.
Failure to stay focused on the research question.
Failure to develop a coherent and persuasive argument for the proposed research.
Too much detail on minor issues, but not enough detail on major issues.
Too much rambling–going "all over the map" without a clear sense of direction. (The best proposals move forward with ease and grace like a seamless river.)
Too many citation lapses and incorrect references.
Too long or too short.
Failing to follow the APA style.
Slopping writing.

References

Best, J. and Kahn, J. (2009). *Research in Education*. 10th edition, Needham Heights: Allyn and Bacon.

Corey, S.M. (1962). *Research in Education*. NCERT, New Delhi.

Cozby, P. (2009). *Methods in Behavioural Research*. 10th edition, Bemont: Wadsworth.

Goode, W.J., and Hatt, P.K. (1990). *Methods in Social Research*. McGraw-Hill, New Delhi.

Guthrie, G. (2010). *Basic Research Methods*. New Delhi: Sage.

Hillway, T. (1956). *Introduction to Research*. Houghton Miffin Co.

Punch, K. (2006). *Developing Effective Research Proposals*. 2nd edition, London: Sage.

Rummel, J.F. (1958). *An Introduction to Research Procedures in Education*. New York: Harper Brothers.

CHAPTER

11

Review of Literature

11.1 The literature review is the fundamental task of dissertation and research preparation. The researchers get minimal formal training. A little guidance from faculty or published sources, could not equip them as how to analyze and synthesize research literature. As a result, it is all alleged that most dissertation literature reviews are poorly conceptualized and written. Researchers may not be learning what it means to make and justify educational claims. Literature reviewing should be a central focus of pre-dissertation coursework, integrated throughout the programme. (Boote and Beile, 2005). A research literature review is a systematic, explicit and reproducible method for identifying, evaluating and synthesizing the existing body of completed and recorded work produced by researchers, scholars and practitioners. (Fink, 2005). Researcher should find appropriate answer to the following questions:

- What previous empirical evidence is there about the question?
- What does the empirical evidence tell us about the answer to the question?
- What is known and what is unknown about the question?
- Are there any gaps in the knowledge of the subject?
- Have areas of further study been identified by other researchers that you may want to consider?
- Who are the significant research personalities in this area?
- Is there consensus about the topic?

- What aspects have generated significant debate on the topic?
- What methods or problems were identified by others studying in the field and how might they impact your research?
- How does the study move beyond them?
- What is the most productive methodology for your research based on the literature you have reviewed?
- Is it intentionally chosen and justified strategy for searching, selecting, evaluating, and synthesizing the literatre?
- What is the current status of research in this area?
- What sources of information or data were identified that might be useful to you?

11.2 GOALS OF THE REVIEW OF LITERATURE

- The ability to develop and defend epistemic warrants about the literature enables candidate to develop intellectual independence.
- Enable researcher to make a reasonable range of intellectual decisions. Making such decisions, in turn requires candidate to find, evaluate, and synthesize that literature purposefully.
- 'Productive insight' can be developed into an integrated set of concepts, theories, and empirical and normative claims gleaned from the literature.

Read it, discuss it, and continually re-evaluate to understand it. 'There can be no knowledge without knower. Knowledge does not exist in an abstract sense' (Shera, 1970).

11.3 TASKS

Krathwohl and Smith (2005) describe the essential tasks of a literature review for a research proposal as follow :

- Survey a select group of studies that provide a foundation for the proposed project,
- Discuss these studies in detail sufficient to provide an understanding of their relevance,
- Describe how they contribute to the study, and
- Indicate how the study moves beyond them.

11.4 CRITERIA

'Comprehensiveness' and 'Broadness' are two of the criteria assessing the 'Coverage'.

- First, a standard for evaluating the literature review.
- Second, the discussion part of the dissertation'; the writer task is to employ the research literature artfully to support and explain the choices made for this study , not to educate the reader concerning the state of science in the problem area. (Locke, Spirduso, and Silveraman, 1999).
- The centrality of relevance also applies to literature review. The primary purpose is not only to synthesize and summarize but also to inform and support some decisions.

11.5 STRATEGY FOR REVIEW OF LITERATURE

11.5.1 Finding the Literature

First step in reviewing the related literature is finding out the primary and secondary sources of research studies.

Second, the researchers should be aware about the various types of literature which they can consult to widen their sphere of knowledge in the related field of their interest. The university library is obviously a central location for finding the literature needed for review. Today, university libraries typically have three main research domains—the main library catalogue, the journal catalogue and the electronic resources index. Library performs many services for those who are sufficiently sophisticated to use them. For example, the shelf-list is a record of the university library holdings by call numbers, regardless of a physical location. The serial record is the list of our holding of periodicals or journals. Contents file are many numbered series of publications.

11.5.2 Types of Literature

(1) Discipline-based Reference Materials

If you are relatively new to a particular discipline or paradigm, subject-specific dictionaries and encyclopedias can help you navigate the discipline's central terms, constructs and theories. For example, Education Abstracts, Social Science Abstracts, Psychological Abstracts, and Sociological Abstracts.

(2) Subject-specific books

Introductory and advanced texts, anthologies, research reports, fiction and even non-fiction works can provide background and context

(3) Journal articles

These generally form the heart of a formal literature review because they are specific, focused on the content, and benchmark for credibility. For example, Review of Educational Research, American Educational Research Journal, Educational Researcher, Australian Research Journal, British Journal of Educational Research, All India Association for Educational Research, etc.

(4) Grey Literature

This refers to published and unpublished materials that do not have an international standard book number (ISBN) or an International Standard Serial Number (ISSN).

(5) Official publications, statistics and activities

Such materials can be useful source of background and contextual information and considered authentic documents.

(6) Writing Aids

This includes bibliographic reference works, dictionaries, encyclopedias, and thesauruses, almanacs, yearbooks. These resources can offer significant support during the writing-up process.

(7) Education Index

It covers more than 400 educational periodicals. It is a cumulative author-subject index to educational material. It is published monthly except July and August.

(8) Theses and Dissertations

Dissertation Abstracts International (DAI) is a reference tool that provides a monthly compilation of abstracts of doctoral dissertations to University Microfilms International by more than 450 universities and educational institutions. Theses Canada, Education Research Theses (Australia).

(9) Educational Resources Information Center (ERIC)

The ERIC mandate is to screen, organize, and provide access to educational reports and documents by continual monitoring of the pertinent literature. ERIC publishes two useful sources of information, Resources in Education (RIE) and Current Index to Journals in Education (CIJE).

(10) The most common is the Online Computer Library Center (OCLC)

The most common is the Online Computer Library Center (OCLC) with the holding of over 3,000 libraries. The list of books and periodicals available and the libraries holding these materials can be accesses on-line.

11.5.3 Using Resources

Resource persons are librarians, supervisors and experts and should be approached for finding the literature. Consultation with supervisors, researchers, practitioners and librarians would show you the way to the treasure of research literature.

11.5.4 Honing Research Skills

Reading, recording, accessing and storing of literature are the necessary skills which a researcher must possess and utilized. This also involves purposeful : (a) reviewing of the literature, (b) recording and storing of material related to the subject of study, (c) meta-analysis of researches, and (d) discussion of the results of various research studies to arrive at logical conclusion. Use of 'Internet' or 'search engines', 'websites' are essential for the review of vast array of available literature on the subject. Honing involves two types of screening, substantive screening and methodological screening. Substantive screening is content screening, i.e. relevant to your topic and question. Methodological screening—deals specifically with design, sample, data collection, and data analysis. Both contribute to your demonstration of mastery of the relevant literature.

11.6 MANAGING THE LITERATURE

11.6.1 Efficient reading requires sorting grains from the chafe, i.e. pick up what is relevant to your topic. Researcher should have focused and concentrated reading. It is to review the literature critically showing strengths, weaknesses and implications, as well as how various perspectives relate to one another and where they diverge.

11.6.2 Keep track of references so that in case of re-examination or need it can be accessed easily without the loss of time. Name all your sources and any point you like to make. If it is relevant include it in the text of your work, if it is not, leave it out. Keep details of every reference and make sure they include name, initials, date, title, publisher and page number. Keep references also on a separate word-processing file, which will enable to build these up alphabetically and simply paste into your work when you finish.

11.6.3 Writing relevant annotating: Use quotes only when they make a point strongly and clearly—too many can ruin the flow. And beware the temptation to use quotations out of context, particularly where a quote seems to fit your work perfectly but you are aware that your point of argument is different from that of the writer you are quoting.

11.7 RECORDING AND USE OF LITERATURE

The most suitable method of recording notes is the card system. The recording system involves use of two sets of cards namely Source Card (3′×5′) used for noting bibliographic information and Note Card (5′×7′) used for actual note taking.

11.7.1 Choosing Research Topic

Review of research is undertaken to have deep knowledge of the specific area. It helps an individual to identify the priority areas in choosing the specific topic of research. It makes us aware to avoid repetition. It develops curiosity to demystify the conventional areas of research and explore new potential areas.

11.7.2 Developing Research Questions

Gaps in literature—one can explore whether an important aspect of an issue has been ignored, whether there are assumptions underpinning a body of work those needs to be re-examined arguing rationale.

11.7.3 Informing your Study with Theory

Lies in the inferences that can be drawn from the various educational and psychological theories. Purpose is to determine whether a particular theory can be translated into actual practice. People's views and positions are frequently not as clear-cut and researcher should bear this *caveat* in mind. Therefore, research has a great deal to do with: ontological assumptions concerning the nature of social reality; epistemological assumptions concerning the bases of knowledge; and assumptions concerning human nature and agency. Figure 11.1 reveals the use of literature in research.

Review of Literature

Identification of Topic ———— Research Hypotheses

↓

Methodology
(Design/Method/Sample/Tools/Data Analysis)

↓

Discussion/Meta-Analysis

↓

Results/Evidence

Figure 11.1 : Use of Literature in Research

11.8 REVIEWING OF LITERATURE

11.8.1 Purpose

This involves purposeful : (a) reviewing of the literature, (b) recording and storing of material related to the subject of study, (c) meta-analysis of researches, and (d) discussion of the results of various research studies to arrive at a logical conclusion in finding appropriate topic for research.

11.8.2 Coverage

'Comprehensiveness' and 'Broadness' are two of the criteria assessing the 'Coverage'. 'Comprehensiveness' involves continuity, up-to-date information and reliable standard for evaluating the literature review, and 'Broadness' takes into account the discussion part of the dissertation'. The writer's task is to employ the research literature artfully to support and explain the choices made for this study, not to educate the reader concerning the state of science in the problem area'. (Locke, Spirduso, and Silveraman, 1999).

11.8.3 Writing Purposefully

The primary purpose is not only to summarize, organize, analyze and synthesize but also to inform and support some decisions.

11.9 In reviewing literature, the researcher should keep following points in mind:

- Restrict the use of quotations to those with particular impact
- Do not rely too much on secondary sources
- Do not neglect practitioner-oriented literature
- Do not give into the temptation to include and report everything you know or you have read
- Do not rely on 'old' literature. The age of classic piece of literature or research is not important. For example, Piaget's work (1950) and the Coleman report (1966) remain important today.

11.10 COMMON ERRORS IN REVIEWING THE LITERATURE

1. Carries out a hurried review of the literature in order to get started on the research project. This usually results in overlooking previous studies containing ideas that would have improved the student's project.
2. Relies too heavily upon secondary sources.

3. Concentrates on research findings when reading articles, thus overlooking valuable information on methods, measures, and so forth.
4. Overlooks sources other than education journals, such as newspaper and popular magazines which often contain articles on educational topics.
5. Fails to define satisfactorily the topic limits of his review of the literature. Searching too broad an area often leads to the students becoming discouraged or doing a slipshod job. Searching too narrow an area causes him to overlook many articles that are peripheral to his research topic but contain information that would help him design a better study.
6. Copies bibliographic data incorrectly and is then unable to locate the reference needed.
7. Copies far too much material onto note cards. This often indicates that the student does not have a clear understanding of his project and thus cannot separate important from a unimportant information.

11.11 INTERNET AS A SOURCE OF INFORMATION

Introduction of technological innovations such as, the use of computers, e-mail, networks, teleconferencing and new softwares made possible for the researchers in India to collaborate globally and contribute more effectively towards research. Now it is possible to make the entire world's knowledge, or even just a big chunk of it, available to anyone and everyone, anytime, anywhere to compare his or her research findings with others to arrive at logical conclusion. It is now easier for the researchers to view and review a large array of research literature. Such a system could connect research studies not only to related work but to the relevant curriculum materials, state policies, teacher reflections, media reports and support organizations.

The range of electronic databases available today is widespread. There are databases that focus on research. They cover a wide spectrum or materials across disciplines. For example, Academic Search Premier (EBSCO) contains both full-text journal articles and abstracts, covering nearly every academic field of study. EDGE (Informit) is a bibliographic database that indexes and abstracts articles that provide international coverage on various themes. PsycINFO (OVID) is indexing and abstracting device produced by the American Psychological Association. Sources indexed include scholarly books, peer-reviewed journals, and dissertations (theses) all in the field of psychology and the psychological aspects of related disciplines, medicine, psychiatry, sociology, education, linguistics, and anthropology. Google Scholar contains academic journals, conference papers, books, professional magazines, reports, and abstracts of doctoral dissertations. Researchgate members can exchange their research experiences and literature with scholars.

DELNET is a useful tool for researchers. Networked Digital Library of Theses and Dissertations, Directory of Open Access Journals provide free on-line service to the researchers. There are number of search engines through which one can access, and download the requisite information.

The internet provides extremely useful information. Searching materials relevant to research topic is complex. A specific skill is required for searching the creditable and appropriate materials. Therefore, number of books have been written to give practical guidance for how to use this source. However, it cannot be denied that Internet as a source is set with number of limitations. Therefore, it is essential that the scholar should make judicious use of Internet in conjunction with other sources of information.

There are several problems associated with the use of Internet. These are mentioned below :

- There is overload of information. In the mirage of information, researcher sometimes gets confused and cannot sort out what is relevant and what is not relevant.
- There is a question of accuracy or credibility of information gathered from Internet. Sometimes, information gathered does not reveal the original source from which the given information is acquired.
- It has been observed that the information on the web often changes quickly. For example, a very useful information once available may not be on the website or cannot be accessed. This causes unique referencing problems.
- Information gathered from Internet is sometimes misused. For example, information available on the Internet even though not relevant is twisted by the scholar to suit his or her theme under investigation. This is not permissible under research ethics.

References

Boyanov, M.I., S.D. Kelly, K.M. Kemner, B.A. Bunker, J.B. Fein and D.A. Fowle (2003). Adsorption of cadmium to *Bacillus subtilis* bacterial cell walls: a pH-dependent X-ray absorption fine structure spectroscopy study. *Geochimica et Cosmochimica Act,* pp. 67, 18: 3299-3536.

Chan, Steve (1997). In Search of Democratic Peace: Problems and Promise. Mershon *International Studies Review.* 41,1:59-92.

Constance M. Winchell (Eds.) (1967,1950). *A guide to Reference Books.* Chicago, American Library Association.

Fink, A. (2005). *Conducting Research Literature Reviews: From the Internet to Paper.* 2nd edn. London: Sage.

Goeser, C. (2003). On The Cross of The South: The Scottsboro Boys as Vernacular Christs in Harlem Renaissance Illustration. *International Review of African American Art.* 19,1: 19-27.

Good, Carter V. (2008). *Introduction to Educational Research.* Second Edition. Surjeet Publications. New Delhi.

Hart, C. (1980). *Doing a Literature Review.* London: Sage.

Hart, C. (2001). *Doing a Literature Search.* London: Sage.

Holt, Robert R. (2003). Some history of a methodological rediscovery. *American Psychologist.* 58,5: 406-407.

Keith, F.P. (2009). Introduction to Research Methods in Education. SAGE Publications India Pvt. Ltd., New Delhi.

CHAPTER

12

Delineating Variables and Operational Definitions

12.1 VARIABLES

Scientists somewhat loosely call the construct or properties they study "variables". Examples of important variables in sociology, psychology, and education are: sex, income, education, social class, organizational productivity, and occupational mobility, level of aspiration, aptitude, anxiety, religious affiliation, political preference, ego strength, task orientation, authoritarianism, conformity, intelligence, and achievement. It can be said that a variable is a property that takes on different values.

A variable is a symbol to which numerals or values are assigned. For instance, x is a variable: it is a symbol to which we assign numerical values. The variable x may take on any justifiable set of values—for examples, scores on an intelligence test or an attitude scale. In the case of intelligence we assign to x a set of numerical values yielded by the procedure designated in a specified test of intelligence. This set of values, often called IQ's ranges from low to high, from, say, 50 to 150.

A variable, x, however, may have only two values. If sex is the construct under study, then x can be assigned 1 and 0, 1 standing for one of the sexes and 0 standing for the other. It is still a variable. Other examples of two valued variables are: alive-dead, citizennoncitizen, teacher-nonteacher, republican-democrat, and so on. Such variables are often called dichotomies or dichotomous variables.

Most variables, however, are theoretically capable of taking on continuous values. It has been common practice in behavioural research to convert continuous variables into fractional scores. For example, scores on intelligence test could be broken down into high and low intelligence, or into high, medium, and low intelligence. Variables such as anxiety, introversion, and authoritarianism have been treated similarly. However, it is not possible to convert a truly dichotomous variable such as sex to a continuous variable, it is always possible to convert a continuous variable to a dichotomy or a polytomy. Such conversion can serve a useful conceptual purpose.

12.2 TYPES OF VARIABLES

12.2.1 Independent and Dependent Variables

The most important and useful way to categorize variables is—independent variable and dependent variable. This categorization is highly useful because of its general applicability, simplicity, and special importance in conceptualizing and designing research and communicating its results. An independent variable is the presumed cause of the dependent variable, the presumed effect. The independent variable is the antecedent; the dependent is the consequent. When we say: if A, then B, we have the conditional conjunction of an independent variable (A) and a dependent variable (B).

In experiment the independent variable is the variable manipulated by the experimenter. When, for example, an educational investigator studies the effect of different teaching methods, he may manipulate method, the independent variable, by using different methods. In non-experimental research, where there is no possibility of manipulation, the independent variable is the variable that has presumably been "manipulated" before he got it. He may, for instance, study the presumed effects on achievement of a ready-made teaching situation in which different methods have already been used. Methods, here, is also the independent variable, or he may study the effect on school achievement of parental attitudes. Here a parental attitude is the independent variable.

The dependent variable, of course, is the variable predicted to, whereas the independent variable is predicted from. The dependent variable, Y, is the presumed effect, which varies concomitantly with changes or variation in the independent variable, X. It is the variable that is not manipulated. Rather, it is observed for variation as a presumed result of variation in the independent variable. In predicting from X to Y, we can take any value of X we wish, whereas the value of Y we predict to be "dependent on" the value of X we have selected. The dependent variable is ordinarily the condition we are trying to explain. The most common dependent variable in education, for instance, is achievement or "learning". We want to account for or explain achievement. In doing so, we have a large number of possible X's or independent variables to choose from.

When the relation between intelligence and school achievement is studied, intelligence is the independent and achievement the dependent variable. Other independent variables that can be studied in relation to the dependent variable, achievement, are social class, methods of teaching, personality types, types of motivation (reward and punishment), attitudes towards school, class atmosphere, and so on. When the presumed determinants of delinquency are studied, such determinants as slum conditions, broken homes, lack of parental love, and the like, are independent variables and, naturally, delinquency (more accurately, delinquent behaviour) is the dependent variable. In the frustration-aggression hypothesis mentioned earlier, frustration is the independent variable and aggression the dependent variable. Sometimes a phenomenon is studied by itself, and either an independent or a dependent variable is implied. This is the case when teacher behaviours and characteristics are studied. The usual implied dependent variable is achievement or child behaviour in general. Teacher behaviour can, of course, be a dependent variable.

The relation between an independent variable and a dependent variable can perhaps be more clearly understood if we lay out two axes at right angles to each other, one axis representing the independent variable and the other axis the dependent variable. (When two axes are at right angles to each other, they are called orthogonal axes). Following mathematical custom, X, the independent variable, is the horizontal axis and Y, the dependent variable, the vertical axis. (X is called the abscissa and Y the ordinate.) X values are laid out on the X axis and Y values on the Y axis. A very common and useful way to "see" and interpret a relation is to plot the pairs of XY values, using the X and Y axes as a frame of reference. Let us suppose, in a study of child development, that we have two sets of measures: the X measures IQ the Y measures reading scores.

The relation between IQ scores and reading scores (RA) can now be "seen" and roughly approximated. There is a pronounced tendency, as might be expected, for more advanced IQ to be associated with higher RS, medium IQ with RS, and less advanced IQ with lower RS. In other words, the relation between the independent

TABLE 12.1
Relationship between IQ and Reading Scores

X: IQ Scores	*Y: Reading Scores*
72	48
84	62
96	69
108	71
120	100
132	112

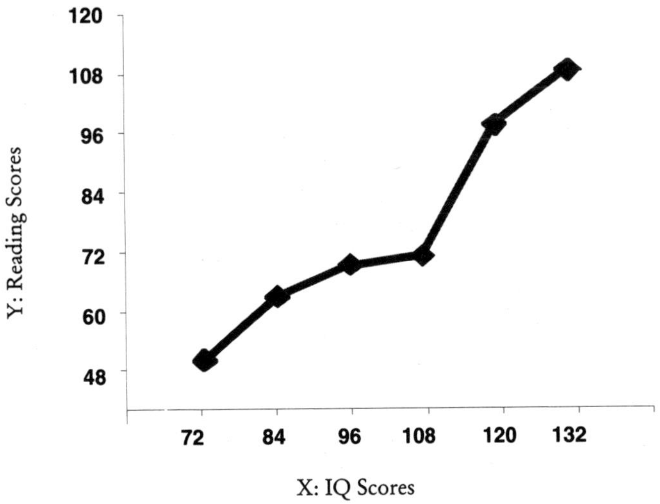

Figure 12.1 : Relationship between IQ Scores and Reading Scores

and dependent variables, in this case between IQ and RS, can be seen from a graph such as this. A straight line has been drawn into "show" the relation. It is a rough average of all the points of the plot. Note that if one has knowledge of independent variable measures and a relation such as that shown in Figure 1 one can predict with considerable accuracy the dependent variable measures. Plots like this can, of course, be used with any independent and dependent variable measures.

The researcher should be alert to the possibility of a variable being an independent variable in one study and a dependent variable in another. A good example is the variable "group cohesiveness". It is possible to study the determinants of cohesiveness and equally possible to study the presumed results of cohesiveness. In the former case cohesiveness is the dependent variable; in the later it is the independent variable.

It is quite possible to consider school achievement as an independent variable, even though it is usually treated as a dependent variable. In studies of success in college, for in stance, achievement in high school is often used as a predictor, or an independent variable. Here we have the interesting case of achievement being now the independent and now the dependent variable-achievement in different educational situations, naturally. Anxiety has been studied as an independent variable affecting the dependent variable achievement. But anxiety can readily be conceived and used as a dependent variable—for example, if we wished to study the effectiveness of types of teaching or types of teacher supportive behaviour, or types of tests, in reducing anxiety. It is also possible—but too rarely done—to treat a variable as an independent in one study and dependent in another study. We can even give a variable this dual role in the same study. In other words, the independent and dependent variables classification really a classification of uses of variables rather than a distinction between different kinds of variables.

In brief:

The dependent variable, of course, is the variable predicted to, whereas the independent variable is predicted from.

An independent variable is the presumed cause of the dependent variable, the presumed effect.

The terms "independent variable" and "dependent variable" come from mathematics, where x is the independent and y the dependent variable.

In multivariate analysis we deal with several independent and several dependent variables.

In experiments the independent variable is the variable manipulated by the experimenter.

12.3 ACTIVE AND ATTRIBUTE VARIABLES

It is important when planning and executing research to distinguish between these two types of variables. Manipulated variables will be called active variables; measured variables will be called attribute variables.

Any variable that is manipulated, then, is an active variable. Any variable that cannot be manipulated is an attribute variable. When one uses different methods of teaching, rewarding the children of one group and punishing those of another, creating anxiety through worrisome instructions, one is actively manipulating the variable methods, reinforcement, and anxiety.

On the other hand, it is impossible, or at least difficult, to manipulate many variables. All variables that are human characteristics—intelligence, aptitude, sex, socio-economic status, field dependence, education, need for achievement, and attitudes, for example—are attribute variables. Subjects come to our studies with these variables (attributes) ready-made. They are, so to speak, already manipulated. Early environment, heredity, and other circumstances have made individuals what they are. The word "attribute", moreover, is accurate enough when used with inanimate objects or referents. Organizations, institutions, groups, populations, homes, and geographical areas have attributes. Organizations are variably productive; institutions become outmoded; groups differ in cohesiveness; geographical areas vary widely in resources.

This active—attribute distinction is general, flexible, and useful. We will see that some variables are by their very nature always attributes, but other variables that are attributes can also be active. This latter characteristic makes it possible to investigate the "same" relations in different ways. A good example is the variable anxiety. We can measure the anxiety of subjects. Anxiety is in this case obviously an attribute variable. But we can manipulate anxiety, too. We can instance different degrees of anxiety, by telling the subjects of one experimental group that the task they are about to do is difficult, that their intelligence is being measured, and that their futures depend on the scores they get. The subjects of another experimental group are told to do their best but to relax; the outcome is not too important and will have no influence on their futures. Actually, we cannot assume that the measured, (attribute) and the manipulated (active) "anxieties" are the same. We may assume that both are "anxiety" in a broad sense, but they are certainly not the same.

12.3.1 Categorical and Continuous Variables

A distinction especially of categorical and continuous variables is useful in the planning of research and the analysis of data.

A continuous variable is capable of taking on an ordered set of values within a certain range. This definition means, first, that the values of a continuous variable reflect at least a rank order, a larger value of the variable meaning more of the property in question than a smaller value. The values yielded by a scale to measure self-image, for instance, express differing amounts of self-image from high through medium to low. Second, continuous measures in actual use are contained in a range, and each individual obtains a "score" within the range. A scale to measure dogmatism may have the range 1 through 7. Most scales in use in the behavioural sciences also have a third characteristic: there are a theoretically infinite set of values within the range. That is, a particular individual's score may be 4.72 rather than simply 4 to 5.

Categorical variables, belong to a kind of measurement called nominal. In nominal measurement, there are two or more subsets of the set of objects being measured. Individuals are categorized by their possession of the characteristic that defines any subset. "To recognize" means to assign an object to a sub-class or subset of a class or set on the basis of the objects having the characteristic that defines the subset. The individual being categorized either has the defining property or does not have it; it is an all-or-none kind of thing. The simplest examples are dichotomous categorical variables: sex, Republican-Democrat, white-black. Polytomies, variables with more than two subsets or partitions, are fairly common, especially in sociology and economics: religious preference, education (usually), nationality, occupational choice, and so on.

Categorical variables—and nominal measurement—have simple requirements: all the members of a subset are considered the same and all are assigned the same name (nominal) and the same numeral. If the variable is religious preference, for instance, all Protestants are the same, all Catholics are the same, and all "others" are the same. If an individual is a Catholic—operationally defined in a suitable way—he is assigned to the category "Catholic" and also assigned a "1" in that category. In brief, he is counted as a "Catholic." Categorical variables are "democratic": there is no rank order or greater than and less than among the categories, and all members of a category have the same value: 1 or 0.

The expression "qualitative variables" has sometimes been applied to categorical variables, especially to dichotomies, probably in contrast to "quantitative variables" (our continuous variables). Such usage reflects a somewhat distorted notion of what variables are. They are always quantifiable, or they are not variables. If x has only two subsets and can take on only two values, 1 and 0, these are still values, and the variable varies. If x is a polytomy, like religious preference, we quantify again by assigning 1's and 0's to individuals. If an individual, say, is a Catholic, then put him in the Catholic subset and assign him a 1. It is extremely important to understand this because, for one thing, it is the basis of quantifying many variables even experimental treatments for complex analysis. Earlier, the example of sex was given, 1 being assigned to one sex and 0 to the other. We can set-up a column of 1's and 0's just as we would set-up a column of IQ's or dogmatism scores. The column of 1's and 0's is the quantification of the variable sex. There is no mystery here. The method is easily extended to polytomies.

12.3.2 Extraneous Variables

Independent variables that are not related to the purpose of the study, but may affect the dependent variables are termed as 'extraneous' variables. For example, a researcher wants to study the relationship between children achievement in mathematics and methods of teaching. In this case, methods of teaching are independent variables and achievement in mathematics is dependent variable. It can be assumed that intelligence may affect the achievement in mathematics but it is not related to the purpose of the study, it will, therefore be termed as 'extraneous' variable. Therefore, study must be so designed to neutralize the effect of extraneous variables.

Control of Extraneous Variables can be ensured through

1. Holding an extraneous variable *constant* for instance I.Q.
2. *Randomization* which controls extraneous variables.
3. Building the extraneous variable right into the design as if they are independent variables.
4. *Matching* the subjects on one or more variables.
5. *Using statistical* method of control which is inherent in all research design.

12.3.3 Intervening Variables

There is a sharp difference between constructs and or observable variables. In fact, constructs are non-observables, and variables, when operationally defined, are observables. The distinction is important. If we are not always keenly aware of the level of discourse we are on when talking about variables, we can hardly be clear about what we are doing.

Constructs have been called intervening variables. Intervening variable is a term invented to account for internal and directly unobservable psychological processes that in turn account for behaviour. An intervening variable is an "in the head" variable. It cannot be seen, heard, or felt. It is inferred from behaviour. "Hostility" is inferred from presumably hostile or aggressive acts. "Learning" is inferred from, among other things, increases in test scores. "Anxiety" is inferred from test scores, i.e., from skin responses, from heart beat, and so on. If he wants to study the effects of different kinds of motivation, he must know that "motivation" is an intervening variable, a construct invented by man to account for presumably "motivated" behaviour. He must know that its "reality" is only a postulated reality. He can only judge that a youngster is motivated or not motivated by observing the youngster's behaviour. Still, in order to study motivation, he must measure it. But he cannot measure it directly because it is an in the head variable, an intervening variable, an unobservable entity. Other men have inverted the construct to stand for "something" presumed to be inside the individual, "something" prompting him to behave in such and such manner. This means that he must always measure presumed in decants of motivation and not motivation itself. He must, in other words, always measure some kind of behaviour, be it marks on paper, spoken words, or meaningful gestures, and then make inferences about presumed characteristics.

Intervening variable provides a causal link between other variables. Intervening variable is also called 'mediating variable' or 'intermediate variable'. For example, statistical association between income and longevity needs to be explained because just having money does not make one live longer. Other variables intervene between money and long life. People with high incomes tend to have better medical care than those with low incomes. Medical care is intervening variable. It mediates the relationship between income and longevity.

12.4 INTERACTION BETWEEN VARIABLES

12.4.1 Patterns of Interaction

The current emphasis in behavioural research is upon interactions between variables. For example, what method works best? or what factor is most important? has given way to questions specifying, what variables? In what combinations and amounts? Under what conditions? With what subjects? and to meet what objectives?

12.4.2 Interaction-proneness

Some factors are more interaction-prone than others. It is important to look for the interaction between variables, combining them to optimize outcomes.

12.4.3 Main Effects versus Interactions

In cases of learning, however, a main effect of one variable is to be judged more likely than the interaction of two other variables.

More generally, main effects are more likely than interactions. If every highest order interaction is significant, if every effect is specific to certain values on all other potential treatment dimensions, then a science is not possible. If generalizations are ever possible, it is because the great bulk of potential determining factors can be discarded.

12.4.4 Use of Inappropriate Independent Variables

It is useful to select independent variables such that they are relevant and arranged in realistic combinations with each other to take into account the interaction relationships.

Examples: Class size is an important independent variable only in relationship with different teaching methods; to consider it separately is to miss its relevance to teaching.

12.4.5 Flexible Treatment

Instead of predicting whether type A does better than type B in a given treatment, look for ways to change the treatment to fit individuals of different kinds. It is important to ask: What teaching methods work best for what kinds of students under what conditions?

12.5 OPERATIONAL DEFINITIONS OF VARIABLES

First, we can define a word by using other words, which is what a dictionary usually does. We can define "intelligence" by saying it is "operating intellect," Second, we can define a word by telling what actions or behaviours it expresses or implies. Defining "intelligence" this way requires that we specify what behaviours of children are "intelligent" and what behaviours are "not intelligent". We may say that a child of seven who successfully reads a story we give him to read is "intelligent". If the child cannot read story, we may say he is "not intelligent". In other words, this kind of definition can be called a behavioural or observational definition.

An operational definition assigns meaning to a construct or a variable by specifying the activities or "operations" necessary to measure it. Alternatively, an operational definition is a specification of the activities of the researcher in measuring a variable or in a manipulating it. An operational definition is a sort of manual of instructions to the investigator. It gives meaning to a variable by spelling out what the investigator must do to measure it.

Example of an operational definition is: Intelligence (anxiety, achievement, and so forth) is scores on X intelligence test, or intelligence is what X intelligence test measures. Notice that this definition tells us what to do to measure intelligence. It says nothing about how well intelligence is measured by the specified instrument.

(Presumably the adequacy of the test was ascertained prior to the investigator's use of it.) In this usage, an operational definition is an equation where we say, "Let intelligence equal the scores on X test of intelligence". "The meaning of intelligence (in this research) is expressed by the scores on X intelligence test".

There are, in general, two kinds of operational definitions: (1) measured, and (2) experimental. The definition given above is more closely tied to measure than to experimental definitions. A measured operational definition describes how a variable will be measured. For example, achievement may be defined by a standardized achievement test, by a teacher-made achievement test, or by grades.

An experimental operational defining spells out the details (operations) of the investigator's manipulations of a variable. Reinforcement can be operationally defined by giving the details of how subjects are to be reinforced (rewarded) and not reinforced (non-rewarded) for specified behaviours. In the Hurlock study, for example, some children were praised, some blamed, and some ignored. Dollard *et al.* (2000) define frustration as prevention from reaching a goal, or "... interference with the occurrence of an instigated goal response at its proper time in the behaviours sequence..." This definition contains clear implications for experimental manipulations. Barker, Dembo, and Lewin, apparently influenced by the definition of Dollard *et al.*, (2003) operationally defined frustration by describing children put into a playroom with "a number of highly attractive, but inaccessible, toys" (The toys were put behind a wire-net partition; the children could see them but not touch them).

Scientific investigators must sooner or later face the necessity of measuring the variables of the relations they are studying. Sometimes measurement is easy, sometimes difficult. To measure sex or social class is easy; to measure creativity, anxiety, or organizational effectiveness is difficult. The importance of operational definitions cannot be overemphasized. They are indispensable ingredients of scientific research because they enable researchers to measure variables and because they are bridge between the theory hypotheses construct level and the level of observation. There can be no scientific research without observations, and observations are impossible without clear and specific instructions on what and how to observe. Operational definitions are such instructions.

Though indispensable, operational definitions yield only limited meanings of constructs. No operational definition can ever express all of a variable. No operational definition of intelligence can ever express the rich and diverse meaning of human intelligence. This means that the variables measured by scientists are always limited and specific in meaning.

Example 1

Problem Statement

A Study of the Effects of Types of Material, Age, Sex, and Problem Complexity on Performance on a Concept Attainment Task.

Operational Definitions

A concept attainment task is very specific and is a part of the research study.

Types of Material

1. *Figural*: pictorial 3 by 3 cards in which the concepts are embeded.
2. *Verbal*: 3 by 3 cards with verbal statements corresponding to pictorial cards.

Relevant dimension

A characeristic common to all cards that examplify a concept.

Performance : The time in minutes required to the concept.

Problem Complexity : The number of relevant dimensions in the concept, the greater the number, the more complex the problem.

Example 2

Problem Statement

A Study of Slow Learners and Impact of Institutional Interventions on their Academic Achievements at Elementary stage.

Operational Definitions

(1) *Slow learners are students whose I.Q. ranges between* 76-89. Student identified by teachers as slow learners and on the basis of low academic achievements shall also be considered for the purpose of study.

(2) *Institutional Interventions*

(a) *Schools:* Interventions by school at the elementary stage for improving the performance of slow learners will include: (a) Identification of slow learners, (b) Special programmes for slow learners, (c) Feedback from slow learners, (d) Teacher training in this specific area, (e) Remedial measures taken by school, (f) Extra classes for slow learners, (g) Simplification of learning materials for the slow learners, (h) Continuous and regular interaction with parents, (i) Use of ICT in learning, and (j) Continuous and regular evaluation of slow learners.

(b) *Family*: Interventions taken by family for improving the performance of slow learners will include : (a) Understanding the special needs of the child, (b) Providing healthy learning environment and support at home, (c) Evaluating feedback from the schools, and (d) Interaction with teachers.

(3) *Academic Achievements*: (a) Performance in reading, writing and mathematics, and (b) participation in co-curricular activities. (Kapoor and Parveen, 2011)

In brief:

1. A research variable is often invisible (or at least partially invisible) to the researcher trying to observe it. Learning and emotions, for example, occur within a person's brain or neurological system; and educators or researchers cannot directly observe such learning and emotions. Rather, these internal outcomes have to be inferred from observable evidence. An operational definition is the observable evidence which the researcher is willing to accept as an indication that a variable exists or is occurring.
2. The essential characteristic of an operational definition is that it must focus on observable behaviour. There are other sorts of definitions which are useful in their own right, but which do not focus on observable behaviours. These other definitions—no matter how excellent and useful they might be—are not operational definitions.
3. Unless you have an operational definition of a research variable, it is impossible to collect data on the extent to which it exists or is occurring. In other words, you cannot do even Level I research without operational definitions. And since Level I research is the basis of all other empirical research, it is difficult to do most forms of empirical research without operational definitions.
4. When instructors lecture to students in Educational Research courses, they try to get them to understand important concepts. In the previous sentence, the instructor's outcome variable is "understanding important

concepts." Instructors cannot directly look into their students' minds and ascertain whether or not they understand what the instructors have been saying. Therefore, they need an operational definition, if they wish to determine their students' degree of comprehension. Examine each of the following definitions of "understanding important concepts," and determine which ones are operationally stated.

5. But to be useful in empirical research, a conceptual definition must always be backed up by at least one operational definition. Usually, when researchers think of a research variable, they first think of it in terms of a conceptual definition and then derive useful operational definitions based on this initial conceptual definition. Only after the operational definition has been derived can the researcher measure the extent to which the conceptual outcome is present or absent.
6. An operational definition is a good which passes the test of validity and actually provides evidence related to the conceptual definition. Several diverse pieces of evidence buttress our inferences much more effectively than isolated pieces of evidence.
7. Operational definitions can be extremely useful at both the purely practical and the highly theoretical levels of research. By understanding the researcher's operational definitions of these terms, we can make much better use of the results.

References

Cozby, P. (2009*). Methods in Behavioural Research.* 10th edition, Bemont: Wadsworth.

Festinger, L. and Katz, D. (1976) (eds.). *Research Methods in the Behavioural Sciences.* New Delhi: Amerind Publishing Co.

Good, Carter V. (1966). *Essentials of Educational Research: Methodology and Design.* New York: Applleton-Century Crofts.

Goode, W.J., and Hatt, P.K. (1990). *Methods in Social Research.* McGraw-Hill, New Delhi.

Guthrie, G. (2010). *Basic Research Methods.* New Delhi: Sage.

Hillway, T. (1956). *Introduction to Research.* Houghton Miffin Co.

Isaac, S., and Michael, W.B. (1972). Handbook in Research and Evaluation. San Diego, California: Robert R. Knapp, Publisher.

Punch, K. (2006). *Developing Effective Research Proposals.* 2nd edition, London: Sage.

Rummel, J.F. (1958). *An Introduction to Research Procedures in Education.* New York: Harper Brothers.

CHAPTER

13

Hypothesis

Meaning, Types and Formulation

13.1 HYPOTHESIS

The hypothesis is derived from the ancient Greek term, 'hypotithenai' which means "to put under" or "to suppose".

Hypothesis is, however, a combination of two words: Hypo: means less and Thesis: means statement. 'It is a proposition which can be put to a test to determine its validity' (Goode and Hatt, 1952). 'It is shrewd guess or influence that is formulated and provisionally adopted to explain observed facts or conditions' (John W. Best, 2005).

A hypothesis is an informed or shrewd guess or inference, with a reasonable chance of being right, formulated and tentatively adopted to explain observed facts or conditions and to guide in further investigation, in other words, to serve as the investigator's "eyes" in seeking answers to questions. (Good, 2008).

Hypothesis is a tentative explanation that accounts for facts and can be tested by further investigation. A hypothesis may be precisely defined as a tentative proposition suggested as a solution to a problem or an explanation of some phenomenon (Ary, Jacobs and Razavich, 1984). Hypothesis relates theory to observation and observation to theory. A hypothesis is a conjectural statement of the relation between two or more variables. (Kerlinger, 1956). Hypothesis is a formal statement that present the expected relationship between an independent and dependent variable. (Creswell, 1994).

13.2 CHARACTERISTICS OF HYPOTHESIS

- *Clear and accurate*: Hypothesis should be clear accurate so as to draw a consistent conclusion.
- *Statement of relationship between variables:* If hypothesis is relational, it should state the relationship between different variables. It must state the expected relationship between variables.
- *Testability:* A hypothesis should be open to testing, so that other deductions can be made from it and can be confirmed or disapproved by observation. The researcher should do some prior study to make the hypothesis testable.
- *Specific with limited scope:* A hypothesis, which is specific, with limited scope, is easily testable than a hypothesis with limitless scope.
- *Simplicity:* A hypothesis should be stated in the most simple and clear terms to make it understandable.
- *Consistency:* A hypothesis should be reliable and consistent with established and known facts. It should be consistent with the existing body of knowledge
- *Time-Limit:* A hypothesis should be capable of being tested within a reasonable time. In other words, the excellence of a hypothesis is judged by the time taken to collect the data needed for the test.
- *Empirical reference:* A hypothesis should explain or support all the sufficient facts needed to understand what the problem is about. It must have explanatory power.

13.3 DIFFERENCE BETWEEN HYPOTHESIS, ASSUMPTION AND POSTULATES

Hypotheses	*Assumptions*	*Postulates*
(1)	*(2)*	*(3)*
Hypotheses are tentative statements or a proposed explanation of any observable phenomenon.	Assumptions are statements of what the researcher believes to be facts but can not verify.	Postulates are propositions that are accepted as true. Postulates are fundamental propositions used to prove other statements.
The experiment will either prove the	Assumptions are basically hunches or	Postulates are not proven, they are

(*Contd.*)

(1)	*(2)*	*(3)*
hypothesis right or wrong.	feelings is anything that is taken for granted	simply accepted at their face values. Hull's Theory of Reinforcement is based on eight postulates of behaviour of an organism.
Hypothesis provides enough evidence, to be regarded a valid theory	Assumption can be used as premise of a particular argument but may not be otherwise accepted.	Postulate provides basis for logical reasoning. A mathematician begins by postulating a system of numbers which range from 0 to 9 and can permute and combine only thereafter.
Parametric and non-parametric tests are used to identify the significance of difference between two or more variables	Assumption has no evidence or not enough behind it, to be regarded a valid theory.	Postulates are used to for the discovery of other facts of nature.
Hypothesis is goal post to find answer to research questions	Formulae of statistics and measurement are based on number of assumptions	(a) Essential to development of any intellectual discipline; (b) Assumptions that do not lend themselves to direct verification;
A hypothesis is : (a) A very useful aid to organizing the research effort. (b) It specifically limits the enquiry to the interaction of certain variables. (c) It suggests the methods appropriate for collection, analyzing and interpreting the data e (d) resultant confirmation or rejection of the	Assumption is used to simplify the situation for logical procedure. How researchers approach research has a great deal to do with: (a) Ontological assumptions concerning the nature of social reality. (A person see social reality—as external, independent, given and objectively real, or, instead, as socially constructed;	(c) A basis for reference; (d) A foundation for erection of any theoretical structure; provides the framework for developing and testing theory. (e) Susceptible to challenge in the light of later advancement of

hypothesis through empirical or experimental testing; and (e) it gives a clear indication of the extent of knowledge gained. (Walliman, 2001).	subjectively experienced and the result of human thoughts as expressed through language; (b) Assumptions concerning epistemological bases of knowledge. (knowledge is real, objective and out there in the world to be captured, researcher can observe, measure and quantify it); and (c) Assumptions concerning human nature and agency. (do people respond in mechanistic way to their environment and the things that happen to them or do they initiate action and make choices? Is their behaviour determined by innate instinctual forces or by external conditions and forces, or do they act voluntarily and out of their free will?).	knowledge. (Robert K. Mautz)

13.4 TYPES OF HYPOTHESES

In a broad sense, researchers use two types of hypotheses: Research Hypothesis (Alternate Hypothesis). 2. Null Hypothesis (A Statistical Hypothesis).

13.4.1 A Research hypothesis (Alternate Hypothesis) is usually a conjecture, or a tentative statement about the solution to a problem or relationship of two variables, or nature of some phenomenon. While comparing two different methods, regarding their superiority, wherein, stating a particular method to be good or bad as compared to other one is called research hypothesis. Research hypothesis can be stated in different situations, for example:

1. When hypothesized mean (µHa) is not equal to population mean (µHo). (µHa ? µHo).
2. When hypothesized mean (µ) is more than population mean (μ_{Ho}), (µHa > µHo).
3. When hypothesized mean (µ) is less than population mean (μ_{Ho}), (µHa < µHo).

Example: The mean reading achievement of 3rd grade students taught by Method A is not equal the mean reading achievement of 3rd grade students taught by Method B.

Some times, we distinguish between directional hypothesis and non-directional hypothesis.

13.4.2 Directional hypothesis is where a direction of results is specified.

Example: The mathematical achievement of high ability students exceeds that of average ability students. Or

There is a positive relationship between intelligence scores and student's scores on mathematics achievement.

13.4.3 Non-Directional hypothesis is where no direction is specified.

Example: The mathematics achievement of high ability students equals that of average ability students. Or

There is no difference between mathematics achievement of high and average ability students.

13.4.4 A Statistical Hypothesis is given in statistical terms. Technically, in context of inferential statistics, it is a statement about one or more parameters that are measures of the populations under study. Where hypothesized mean (μ) is equal to population mean (μ_{Ho}).

Example: The mean reading achievement of 3rd grade students taught by Method A equals the mean reading achievement of 3rd grade the students taught by Method B.

13.4.5 The null hypothesis is the hypothesis of "no difference or no relationship". It is the one actually tested statistically. Any relation or difference in the findings is due to chance or sampling error and puts this supposition to a probability test. Let us assume that you want to compare a hypothesized mean (μ) with population mean (μ_{Ho}), then null hypothesis will be marked as:

$Ho{:}\mu = \mu_{HO} = 100$, where hypothesized mean is equal to population mean.

Example: There is no difference between 9th class boys and girls on the scores of emotional intelligence, or

There is no relationship between academic achievement scores and scores on a social adjustment inventory.

Stating the Null hypothesis—four alternatives, using the example of the difference two sample means are:

1. There is no difference between the means of two populations from which the two samples were drawn at random.
2. The two means in the two populations from which the samples were respectively drawn at random are equal.
3. The mean of sampling distribution of differences between an infinite number of pairs of means of randomly drawn samples equal to zero.
4. Any difference between two sample means drawn randomly from their respective populations is due to sampling error—that is, such difference can readily be attributed to chance

13.5 HYPOTHESIS AND RESEARCH QUESTION

Research question states what we are trying to find out. The hypothesis predicts, *a priori*, the answer to that question. Hypothesis is used when we do have an explanation (a theory) in mind behind our hypothesis. If this is the case, we should by all means formulate hypothesis as predicted answer to research questions and test them. If we can not predict with any confidence, we need go no further into the matter of hypotheses. Figure 13.1 explains difference between research Question and Hypothesis.

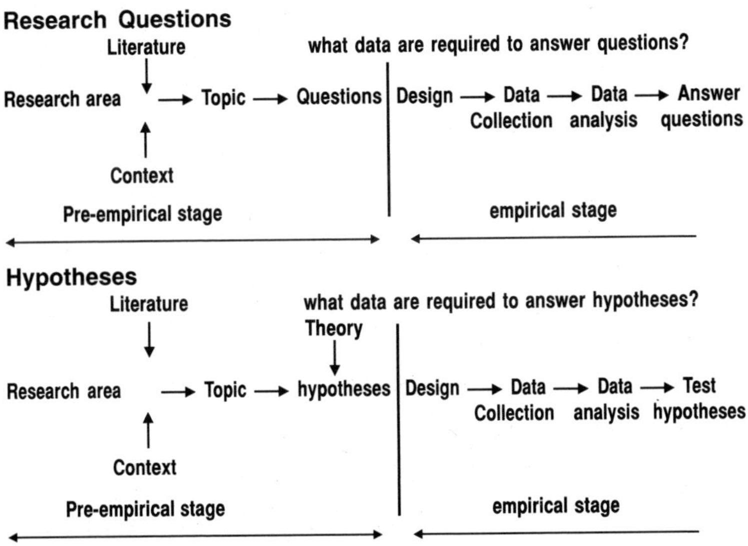

Figure 13.1 : Research Question and Hypothesis

13.6 IMPORTANCE OF HYPOTHESIS

- It has become an important tool for working out the plan of action to achieve the objectives of the study. With increasing use, the strengths of hypothesis have become more apparent. A well thought out set of hypotheses place clear and specific goals before the researcher. Researcher can not build his research thesis on a weak foundation of hypotheses.
- Hypothesis activates or stimulates exploration. Karl Popper (1992) argued, "We have inborn expectations; we have latent inborn knowledge, in the form of latent expectations, to be activated by the stimuli to which we react as a rule while engaged in active exploration".
- Hypotheses provide direction to research. A hypothesis serves as powerful beacon those lights the way for the research work. It provides the roadmap that expedites the exploration of the phenomena under consideration.
- Hypotheses sensitize the investigation to certain aspects, i.e. what is fruitful? What is fruitless? A hypothesis, therefore, provides criteria for evaluating research techniques, and organizing principles.
- Hypotheses are means by which investigator can understand with greater clarity his problem, and its ramifications. It provides him sources of research methodology and procedures to meet the goals.
- Hypothesis enables the researcher to relate logically known facts to intelligent guesses about unknown conditions. It explains what is needed to be done? How is to be done? and what are expected outcomes of research study?
- Hypotheses are framework for the conclusions of the study. Hypotheses, thus, formulated before the conduct of study are tested one by one on the bases of data evidences (quantitative or qualitative) to arrive at logical conclusions.

13.7 SOURCES OF HYPOTHESIS

Collection of factual information may be useful but alone does not lead to successful formulation of hypothesis. Deep knowledge of the area of investigation is essential for the formulation of hypothesis. Hypotheses are the products of considerable speculation, imagination, creative and divergent thinking. The research has to explore the various sources of knowledge and resort to extensive and intensive study of specific area before formulation of hypotheses for study. If a scholar is interested in theoretical research or testing of theory he should go for deductive reasoning for the formulation of hypothesis. On the other hand if a scholar is interested in field study or developing theory in the field, he should employ inductive reasoning for the formulation of research questions.

13.7.1 Richness of background knowledge of the specific area of investigation which is to be undertaken by the researcher is essential for the formulation of hypothesis. One finds limitless knowledge in almost any area of human pursuit which has accumulated in the form of literature as a result of painstaking efforts of past generations. Treasure of past researches, thus, needs to be explored to get knowledge of the specific area. The researcher should encapsulate, modify and develop hypothesis through interaction with the world of knowledge in area of his or her study. It would help the researcher to get insight into the matrix of relationships already established and what other relational variables are needed to be explored. For example:

Read and understand the literature on the issue of interest. Let's call the issue Y.

What facts do we have about Y?
What are the alternative theories that have been proposed to explain Y?
What are the alternative ways that Y has been measured?
What factors have been demonstrated to be related to Y?
What factors does the literature suggest might be related to Y, but which have not been tested as yet?

13.7.2 Interaction with Experts: We may find that there are specialists or experts who have already conducted researches on the specific areas of your choice. They have rich and varied experience. The researcher may approach the experts to seek their advice for the formulation of specific and researchable hypotheses. Researchers try out different ideas and linguistic formulations—all entailing a question and discuss them with experts as a means of clarifying their thoughts and identifying weaknesses in their formulations. A well designed specific hypothesis can be carved out in consultation with expert that may be helpful in the conduct of study. For example:

Who are the experts on the phenomenon Y?
What are the organizations specializing in the study of Y?
Do they organize conferences about Y?
Do they have publications on Y?

Who are people knowledgeable about Y worth conversing with?
What do they think are important questions about Y?
What problems and success have they had in studying Y?

13.7.3 Personal Field Experience: Formulation of hypothesis is experiential and a creative process. Rich and varied experience enables researcher to formulate adequate and researchable hypothesis. The researcher has to invent new ideas, arguments, and conjectures. Weak and ill-conceived hypotheses can be subsequently reframed through critical and creative thinking to suit the purpose of the study. Research seeks to challenge expectation through the formulation and testing of hypothesis. Being critical about ideas in which we have a vested interest is not always easy. But, in wider sense, researchers have the responsibility to search for error, to find out where theories are false, where arguments are invalid, and in what respects policies and practices have undesirable consequences. This would provide rich materials for the formulation of good and testable hypothesis. For example, a classroom teacher observes unrecognized mismatch between expectation and experience (actual or anticipated) that has far reaching practical or theoretical implications. On the basis of his experience and his knowledge, the researcher may inductively formulate hypotheses that attempt to explore the field for improving the learning outcomes. For example:

What have you observed something specific about Y in the classroom which can be explored for improving practice?
Can you identify unrecognized mismatch between expectation and experience in light of Y?
Do you hypothesize that exploration of factor Y may lead to improvement in practice?

13.7.4 Versatility of intellect: Hypotheses are also derived through deductive reasoning from a theory. A researcher may begin a study by selecting one of the theories in his own area of interest. After selecting the particular theory, the researcher proceeds to deduce a hypothesis from the theory through symbolic logic or mathematics. This is possible only when the researcher has a versatile intellect and can make use of it for restructuring his experiences. Considerable time and efforts are needed in formulation and refining of hypothesis. In addition to a versatile intellect, researcher should also be analytical so as to formulate adequate hypothesis.

One should summarize and understand what is known about Y and what is not known,

Identify a question the answer to which would inform the body of knowledge about Y in a meaningful way,

Then test hypothesis that would answer such a question, and

This process of inquiry is much more likely to produce an informed answer to the question.

13.7.5 Analogy and other practices: Reasoning by analogy generally is considered unacceptable as a source of proof, but it is a very fertile source of hypothesis. The premise is that if two situations are alike in certain aspects, relevant from the standpoint of the problem under consideration, they are probably similar in other relevant aspects. It is assumed that the existence of similarities between two situations is not accidental, that it is the result of the operation of some law common to the two situations. The insights that analogy provide are useful as much as they lead to their own refinement and verification through the acquisition of relevant data and the formulation of more adequate hypothesis.

13.8 FORMULATION OF HYPOTHESES

Nature of a hypothesis should be clearly stated, i.e. either null hypothesis or alternate hypothesis. Statement of hypotheses should be done with proper care, keeping in mind the object and nature of the problem. For Example:

13.8.1 Problem Statement

A Study of the effects of type of material, age, sex, and problem on performance on a concept attainment task in geometry.

13.8.2 Hypotheses

1. There is no difference in the mean performance of individuals using figural materials and those using verbal materials.
2. There is no difference in the mean performance of individuals in the age range 20-25 years and those of 26-30 years.
3. There is no difference in the mean performance of males and females.
4. Concept attainment problems in geometry.

13.9 CRITERIA FOR GOOD HYPOTHESIS

A good hypothesis is a very useful aid to organizing the research effort. It specifically limits the enquiry to the interaction of certain variables. It suggests the methods appropriate for collection, analyzing and interpreting the data, and the resultant confirmation or rejection of the hypothesis through empirical or experimental testing gives a clear indication of the extent of knowledge gained. (Walliman, 2001).

13.9.1 Informed

It must fit into the framework of excising theories and transform them into more perfect explanatory schemes. It should be based on sound knowledge and reliable information. Hypothesis should have relevant and logical explanation about the relationships of variables included in it. For example, What factors does the literature suggest might be related to Y, but which have not been tested as yet? Moreover,

- It should provide tentative answer to the proposed problem. This can be in the form of a declaration statement or in the form of directional statement or in a null-form; and
- It should be operational, that is, there should be a method of recording and measuring the variables involved in the hypothesis.

13.9.2 A Hypothesis as a Direct and Adequate Statement of Relationship

The formulation of a hypothesis is the first step in solving a specific theoretical or applied problem. Therefore, the test of the hypothesis should provide a single answer to the stated problem, not multiple ones. Since various hypotheses can be generated to address the same issue. The one that is the most clear-cut and direct statement of relationship is preferred.

A hypothesis formulated in such a way that it might provide answers to more than one issue is undesirable: Such compound hypotheses lead to complicated research studies, the results of which can be difficult to interpret.

13.9.3 A Hypothesis as a Parsimonious Statement of Relationship

A good hypothesis focuses on parsimonious statement of relationship.

From another perspective the relative parsimony of a hypothesis is dictated by the parsimony of the constructs and the interrelationships among them as presented in the theory.

13.9.4 A Hypothesis as a Refutable Statement of Relationship

If the hypothesis is stated and tested in such a way that the results are a forgone conclusion then why conduct the study. The result is a *fait accompli* before the fact, a "done deal."

"All men are mortal." Based upon all collective experience, this is not a refutable hypothesis.

"Dead men tell no lies." Since to lie, one must be alive, be able to think, recognize the difference between "A" and "not A", the hypothesis is irrefutable.

13.9.5 A Hypothesis as an Operational Statement of Relationship

A hypothesis cannot be tested unless the two variables x and y have been operationally defined. To operationally define a variable is to describe the procedures used to measure it.

13.9.6 A Hypothesis as a Reliable Statement of Relationship

There are two concerns in the measurement of any variable:

Is the measure reliable? Reliability refers to the accuracy of the measure, regardless of what it measures.

Is the measurement valid? In measurement theory, validity concerns whether and the extent to which the measuring instrument in fact measures what it is intended to measure.

Walliman (2001) posits that a good hypothesis is a very useful aid to organizing the research effort:

- It specifically limits the enquiry to the interaction of certain variables;
- It suggests the methods appropriate for collecting, analyzing and interpreting the data; and
- The resultant confirmation or rejection of the hypothesis through empirical or experimental testing gives a clear indication of the extent of knowledge gained.

REFERENES

Campbell, J.P., Daft, R.L. and Hulin, C.L. (1982). *What to Study: Generating and Developing Research Questions.* Beverly Hills, CA: Sage.

Chaters, W.M. (1997). Hypothesis in scientific research. Unpublished paper. University of Oregon, Eugene, OR.

Good, Carter V. (2008). *Introduction to Educational Research.* Second Edition. Surjeet Publications, Delhi.

Goethals, George W. (1958). A Framework for Educational Research. *Harvard Educational Review,* 28, 29-43.

Kothari, C.R. (2011). *Research Methodology: Methods and Techniques.* New Delhi: New Age International Publishers.

Koul, L. (2009). *Methodology of Educational Research.* New Delhi: Vikas Publications.

Travers, R.M.W. (1958). *An Introduction to Educational Research.* New York: The Mcmillan Co.

Van Dalen, Deobold B. (1962). *Understanding Educational Research.* An Introduction. New York: McGraw-Hill Book Co.

CHAPTER 14

Tests of Hypotheses

Johan Arbuthnot (1710) introduced Null Hypotheses Significance Testing. It has become an important tool for working scientists during the early 20th century. The founders of modern statistics (Fisher, Neyman, and Pearson) showed how to apply this tool in widely varying circumstances. With increasing use, both the strengths and limitations of Null Hypotheses Significance Testing became more important.

However, statisticians have developed several tests of hypotheses (also known as the tests of significance) for the purpose of testing hypotheses which can be classified as; (a) parametric or standard tests of hypotheses; and (b) non-parametric tests or distribution free tests of hypotheses.

14.1 PARAMETRIC TESTS OF HYPOTHESES

Parametric tests of hypotheses are based upon certain assumptions as given below:

- Observations must come from normal population
- Sample size is large
- Population parameters like mean, variance etc., must hold good before parametric tests can be used
- Parametric tests use interval and ratio data

14.2 NON-PARAMETRIC TESTS OF HYPOTHESES

There are situations when the researchers cannot, or do not

want to make such assumptions. In such situations, non-parametric tests are used.

- These tests are distribution free tests of hypotheses
- Non-parametric tests use nominal and cardinal data
- When our measurements are not as accurate as is necessary for standard tests of significance, then non-parametric methods come to our rescue which can be used fairly satisfactorily
- The parametric tests of difference like "t" or "F" make assumption about the homogeneity of the variances whereas this is not necessary for non-parametric tests of difference.

ACCEPTING OR REJECTING THE NULL HYPOTHESIS JOHAN ARBUTHNOT (1710) INTRODUCED NULL HYPOTHESIS SIGNIFICANCE TESTING

Testing the null hypothesis results in one of two outcomes:

Accepting (failing to reject) the null hypothesis as true, in which case it is concluded that any differences in the results are:

(1) Not statistically significant, therefore are probably
(2) Due to sampling error or chance.

Rejecting the null hypothesis as false, in which case it is concluded that the differences in the results are:

(1) Statistically significant, therefore are probably
(2) Due to some determining factor or condition, other than chance.

Accepting the null hypothesis also means that the corresponding research hypothesis is not supported or disconfirmed. Rejecting the null hypothesis also means the corresponding research hypothesis has survived a test of disconfirmation and, in that sense, is supported. More precisely, the differences in the data reasonably cannot be attributed to chance and the causal factors stated in the research hypothesis may possibly explain the difference, but not necessarily so as long as there are *plausible rival hypotheses* also to account for the data. Obviously, the more tests of disconfirmation a given research hypothesis can survive; the stronger is the evidence in its support.

14.3 TYPES OF ERROR

It is a well known fact that the inference through sampling may have certain amount of error. The error can be classified into Type-I error and Type-II error.

Type I (Alpha) Error—to reject the null hypothesis of no differences when it is true. In other words, to conclude falsely that a difference exists in the data when in fact it does not. Since such an error is particularly embarrassing to the scientist (saying something exists when it does not), he tends to avoid risking this error and chooses a conservative level of significance which minimizes it. It is the probability of rejecting the null hypothesis when it is true. It is denoted by α. In quality control, it is termed as producer's risk, because it is the probability of rejecting the good lot.

Type II (Beta) Error—to accept the null hypothesis of no differences when it is false. In other words, to conclude falsely that a difference does not exist in the data when in fact it does. It is denoted by ß. In quality control, it is termed as consumer's risk, because it is the probability of accepting a bad lot

The decision between risks—Whether to run the risk of a Type I or Type II error, since the probability of one increases as the other decreases, is a question of utility. Which is preferable in a given situation: (1) a Type I *fine screen* designed to eliminate chance differences at the expense of throwing away some genuine differences in the process? or (2) a Type II *coarse screen* that lets through some of the unwanted chance differences to insure that most of the genuine differences are kept? In order to avoid the probability of either error, it is essential to increase the sample size, N.

14.4 ONE-TAILED AND TWO-TAILED TESTS OF THE NULL HYPOTHESES

When a particular research hypothesis simply predicts that a *difference* will exist in the data and allows this difference to be in *either direction* (larger or smaller), it is a two-tailed test of its null hypothesis. In one-tailed test the difference can fall in either tail of this sampling distribution. If, on the other hand, the research hypothesis predicts the direction of the difference *(either* larger *or* smaller), it is a one-tailed test of the corresponding null hypothesis.

A two-tailed test will test both if the mean is significantly greater than *x* and if the mean significantly less than *x*. The mean is considered significantly different from *x* if the test statistic is in the top 2.5% or bottom 2.5% of its probability distribution, resulting in a p-value less than 0.05.

When using a one-tailed test, testing for the possibility of the relationship is in one direction and completely disregarding the possibility of a relationship in the other direction. A one-tailed test will test either if the mean is significantly greater than *x* or if the mean is significantly less than *x*, but not both. Then, depending on the chosen tail, the mean is significantly greater than or less than *x* if the

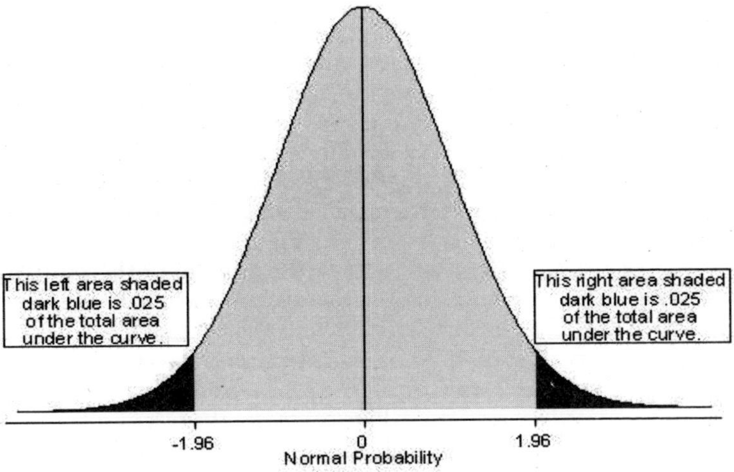

Figure 14.1 : Two-tailed Test of Hypothesis

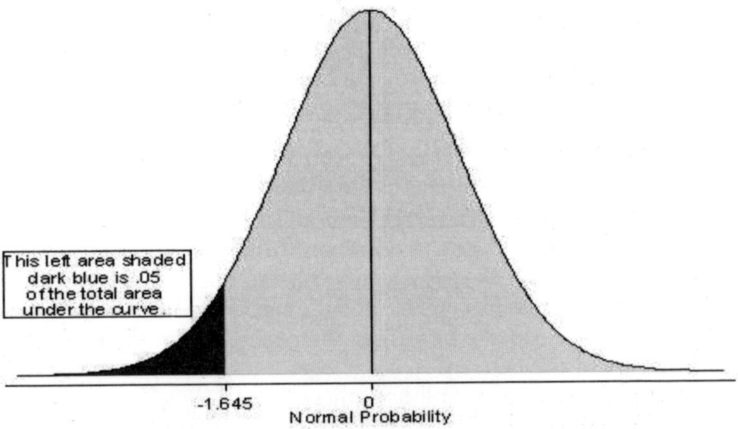

Figure 14.2 : One-tailed Test of Hypothesis

test statistic is in the top 5% of its probability distribution or bottom 5% of its probability distribution, resulting in a p-value less than 0.05. The one-tailed test provides more power to detect an effect in one direction by not testing the effect in the other direction.

14.5 THE POWER OF A STATISTICAL TEST

The power of a statistical test is defined as the probability of rejecting the null hypothesis of no differences when it is actually false.

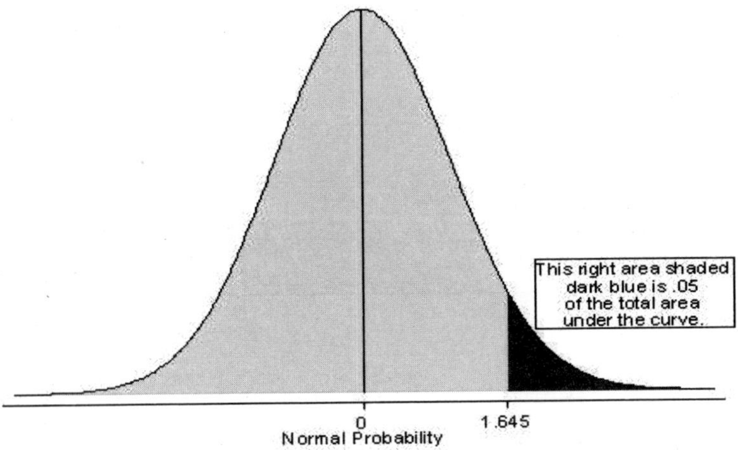

Figure 14.2A : One-tailed Test of Hypothesis

In other words, differences really do exist, and the null hypothesis ought to be rejected:

Power of a statistical test = I—probability of Type II error

The power of a statistical test is a function of:

- The underlying assumptions of the test: parametric tests make stronger assumptions than non-parametric tests.
- Whether the test is one-tailed (often more powerful in a certain region of admissable alternative hypotheses of interest) or two-tailed (less powerful in that same region).
- Sample size *N:* as *N* increases, power usually increases. Power efficiency refers to the increase in sample size necessary to make test *X* as powerful as a second test Y.

The Figure 14.3 shows what alpha, beta and power look like in a graph and illustrates some of the relationships between them. Alpha and beta represent the probabilities of Type I and Type II Errors, respectively.

Since power is 1-beta, the area to the right of 107.5 under the right curve represents your power in this experiment. It should be apparent from the graph that alpha, beta and power are closely related. In particular, you can see that reducing alpha is equivalent to moving the vertical line between the two sample means to the right. When you do this, alpha decreases, power (1—beta) decreases, and beta increases. On the other hand, moving that same vertical line to the left increases alpha, increases power, and decreases beta. To put it

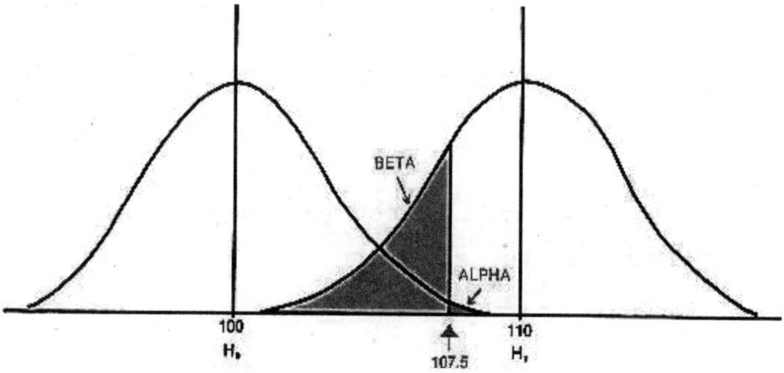

Figure 14.3: Alpha and Beta Errors

another way, increases in alpha increase power and decreases in alpha decrease power.

14.6 LEVEL OF SIGNIFICANCE AND REPLICATION

While the conventional level for rejecting the null hypothesis is $p = .05$ or .01 (5 percent and 1 percent, respectively), significance levels of 10 to 20 percent are tolerable in preliminary investigations, with replication. If two successive findings are each significant at the 10 percent level, this is roughly equivalent to a single finding at the 10 percent level since the two kinds of outcomes are about equally probable. Moreover, replication provides empirically stronger evidence than a single occurrence and justifies the more liberal test of the null hypothesis, avoiding the Type II error.

14.7 STATISTICAL SIGNIFICANCE *VERSUS* PRACTICAL SIGNIFICANCE

In the researcher's zeal to obtain statistically significant findings, he often overlooks the more relevant question: Is it educationally significant? Is the difference large enough to be practical? Are the gains important enough to be worth the cost and effort to obtain them? This question gets at the trade-off factor in educational decision-making and involves the problem of accountability in cost effectiveness economics. Even when these practical matters are settled or in the background, there are valuable considerations of social and psychological nature that frequently override a choice based solely on statistical significance.

Most of the criticism of Null Hypothesis Significance Testing (NHST) focuses on its misuse by researchers and misinterpretation by research consumers rather than on inherent weaknesses. For example, person interpreting statistically significant results as being equivalent to scientifically significant results. (Morrison & Henkel, 1970; Selvin, 1957).

Researchers also badly misuse Null Hypothesis Significance Testing (NHST) when they incorrectly conclude that the null hypothesis of no difference or relationship is true when their results fail to reject it.

Null Hypothesis Significance Testing (NHST) has been criticized for using arbitrary cut-off levels on the same time. American Psychological Association Task Force on Statistical Inference (1999) recommended that authors should report confidence intervals. The practice of basing scientific conclusions on single studies using arbitrary criteria, could give NHST a bad name that could be avoided.

Many of the null hypotheses tested in the research literature are false only in the *Statistically sense* of the word, but as a practical matter could be treated as if they were true with little likelihood of any negative consequences.

Most of the experts agree that it is the size and direction of observed differences that ought to be reported not only p-values (level of significance).

McKeachie (1997) reported that effect sizes are mostly useful that is directed toward decisions with some immediate practical consequences. If it is to test an existing theory, even small difference should increase one's confidence that theory has some validity.

Nickerson (2000) mentioned the "arbitrariness of the decision criterion". The researcher should not be bound by the clain of $\alpha = .05$. The investigator can report "$p = .06$" and leave it to the reader to decide how significant it is.

Rather than concluding that "there was no difference among the treatments ($p = .07$) or "two variables were not correlated. ($p = .06$)" authors should instead state that "the direction of the differences among the treatments was undetermined" or that "the sign of the correlation among the two variables was undetermined". This suggests rather that more data are needed before a determination can be made.

14.8 PARAMETRIC TESTS OF HYPOTHESES

14.8.1 Hypothesis Testing for Differences between Means

There are situations where the significance of difference between two means is examined. Such situations are stated as under along with their respective formulas:

- Population variances are known or the samples happen to be large. Formula used under this situation is as follows:

$$= \frac{\overline{X_1} - \overline{X_2}}{\sqrt{\frac{\sigma_{p1}^2}{n_1} + \frac{\sigma_{p2}^2}{n_2}}}$$

Example

We have

Variance of performance index of the trainees from college-1, $\sigma_1 = 4$

Variance of performance index of the trainees from college-2, $\sigma_2 = 9$

Number of trainees from the college-1, $n_1 = 64$

Number of trainees from the college-2, $n_2 = 49$

Mean performance trainees of college-1, $\overline{X_1} = 7$

Mean performance trainees of college-2, $\overline{X_2} = 6$

$$Z = \frac{7-6}{\sqrt{4/64+9/49}} = 2.02$$

The standard normal statistic for the given significance level of 0.05 level (Za) is 1.64

H_1 : calculated value (2.02) > table value (1.64). Hence, H_0 should be rejected.This is shown in Figure below.

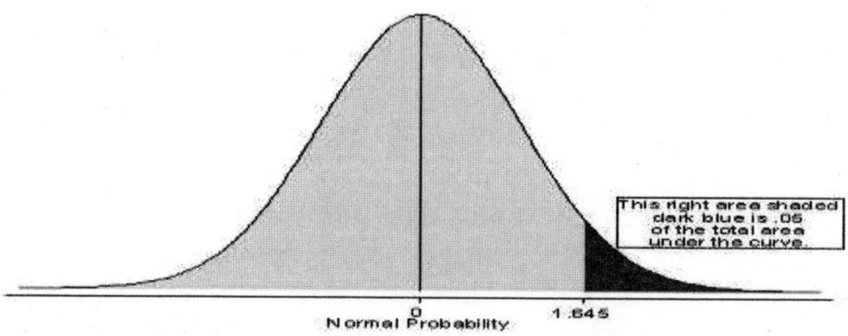

Example

We have

Variance of group one, σ_1	= 4
Variance of group two, σ_2	= 9
Sample size of students, n_1	= 64
Sample size of students, n_2	= 81
Mean of sample one, X_1	= 61
Mean of sample one, X_2	= 60
Level to be observed	= .0.01

$$Z = \frac{60-60}{\sqrt{4/64+9/81}} = 1.59$$

Since the calculated Z value (1.59) is in between –2.57 and + 2.57, the calculated value falls in the acceptance region. Hence, H_0 should be accepted.

In case, σ_{p2} are not known, σ_{s1} and σ_{s2} are used in the same formula, which can be rewritten as under:

$$\sigma_{s1} = \sqrt{\frac{\sum(X_{1i}-\overline{X_1})^2}{n_1-1}} \text{ and}$$

$$\sigma_{s2} = \sqrt{\frac{\sum(X_{1i}-X_1)^2}{n_2-1}}$$

- Samples happen to be large but are presumed to have been drawn from the same population whose variance is known.

The formula used under this situation is as follows:

$$Z = \frac{\overline{X}_1-\overline{X}_2}{\sqrt{\sigma_p^2\left\{\frac{1}{n_1}+\frac{1}{n_2}\right\}}}$$

In case σ_p is not known $\sigma_{s1.2}$(combined standard deviation of both the samples) is used. The formula thus obtained after replacing it is as follows:

$$\sqrt{\frac{n_1(\sigma_{s_1^2} D_1^2)+n_2(\sigma_{s_1^2}+D_1^2)}{n_1+n_2}}$$

where $D_1 = \overline{X}_1 - \overline{X}_{1.2}$, $D_2 = \overline{X}_1 - \overline{X}_{1.2}$ and

$$X_{1.2} = \frac{n_1\overline{X}_1+n_2\overline{X}_2}{n_1+n_2}$$

Example

Size of sample 1, n_1 = 100, Size of sample 2, n_2 = 150

X_1 = 200, X_2 = 220, $\sigma_{s1} = 10$, $\sigma_{s2} = 12$, σ_p = 11

$$Z = \frac{200-220}{\sqrt{(11)^2(1/100+1/150)}} = -14.08$$

Test is two-tailed at 0.05 level, therefore:

Test 1: H_0: I z I ≤ 1.96
Test 2: Ha: I z I > 1.96

The observed z value (–14.08) falls in the rejection region. So reject H_0.

- Samples happen to be small and population variances are not known but assumed to be equal.

The formula for this situation is as under :

$$t = \frac{\overline{X}_1 - \overline{X}_2}{\sqrt{\frac{\sum(X_{1i} - X_1)^2 - \sum(X_{2i} - X_2)^2}{n_1 + n_2 - 2} \times \sqrt{\frac{1}{n_1} + \frac{1}{n}}}} \text{ or}$$

$$\frac{\overline{X}_1 - \overline{X}_2}{\sqrt{\frac{\sum(n_1 - 1)\sigma_{s1}{}^2 - (n_2 - 1)\sigma_{s2}^2}{n_1 + n_2 - 2} \times \sqrt{\frac{1}{n_1} + \frac{1}{n_2}}}}$$

Example
When we have
Variance of group one , σ_1 = 4
Variance of group two, σ_2 = 16
Sample size of students, n_1 = 16
Sample size of students, n_2 = 25
Mean of sample one, X_1 = 60
Mean of sample one, X_2 = 58
Level to be observed =.0.01

$$\sigma_p = \sqrt{\frac{(n_1 - 1)\sigma_1 + (n_2 - 1)\sigma_2}{n_1 + n_2 - 2}} = \sqrt{\frac{(16 - 1)4 + (25 - 1)16}{16 + 25 - 2}} = 3.374$$

$$\sigma_{X_1 - X_2} = \sigma_p \sqrt{1/n_1 + 1/n_2} = 3.374\sqrt{1/16 + 1/25} = 1.08$$

$$t = \frac{60 - 58}{1.08} = 1.85$$

Degree of freedom (df) = (n_1 + n_2 – 2) = (16+25–2) = 39
The calculated value (1.85) is less than table value (t_a = 2.326) at 0.01 level with df 39 Hence, accept H_0.

14.8.2 Hypothesis Testing for Comparing Two Related Terms

The method for comparing two method samples in hypothesis testing is paired t-test. For this test, it is necessary that the observation in the two samples should be collected in the form of matched pairs. Its means that each observation in one sample must be paired with an observation in the other sample in such a way that, they are matched excluding the other factors which do not fall within the area of this test. The formula for calculating this is:

$$D = \frac{\sum D_i}{N}$$

And the formula for calculating the variances of the differences is:

$$(\sigma_{diff.})^2 = \frac{\sum D_i^2 - (D)^2 n}{n-1}$$

$$t = \frac{\overline{D} - 0}{\sigma_{diff} / \overline{n}}$$ with (n – 1) degree of freedom.

where, $\overline{D}$ = Mean of differences

Example

When we have

$\Sigma D_i = -7, \ \Sigma D_i^2 = 29, n = 9$

Mean differences, $\overline{D} = \Sigma D_i / n = -7/9 = -0.778$

$$\sigma_{diff.} \sqrt{\frac{29 - (-0.778)^2 9}{9-1}} = 1.715$$

$$\text{Hence, } t = \frac{-.0778 - 0}{1.715\sqrt{9}} = -1.361$$

Critical value of t-distribution with df 8 is =1.860

The calculated t-value (–1.361) is in the acceptance region. Hence, H_0 is accepted.

14.8.3 Hypothesis Testing of Proportions

You can test proportions by using the hypothesis testing point. Formula for hypothesis testing of proportions is as follows:

Standard deviation of the proportion of successes $= \sqrt{\dfrac{p \times q}{n}}$

If 'n' is large binomial distribution tends to become normal distribution. For proportion testing, use statistic 'z' as under.

$$Z = \frac{p - p}{\sqrt{\dfrac{p \times q}{n}}}$$

where p is the sample proportion.

Example

One-tailed single proportion

When we have

Sample size n = 50

Proportion (p) = 0.85

Sample proportion = 44/50 = 0.88

Level of significance = 0.05

$$\sigma_{\bar{p}} = \sqrt{\frac{p(p-1)}{n}} = \sqrt{\frac{0.85(1-0.85)}{50}} = 0.05$$

Significance level = 0.05, then the null and alternate hypotheses are:

H_0: $p \le 0.85$

H_1: $p \ge 0.85$

$$Z_{\bar{p}} = \frac{p-p}{\sigma_p} = \frac{0.88-0.85}{0.05} = 0.6$$

Since the calculated value (0.6) is less than $Z\alpha$ (1.64), the calculated value falls in the acceptance region. Hence, H_0 should be accepted. This is shown in Figure.

Acceptance Region

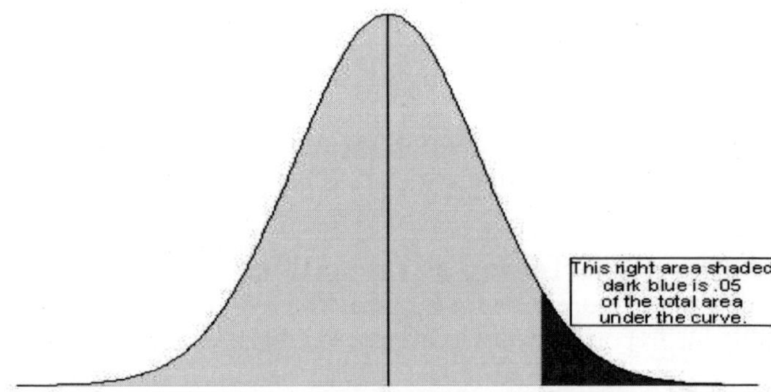

Figure : Acceptance and Rejection Region

Hypothesis Testing for Difference between Proportions

If two samples are drawn from different populations, one may be interested in knowing whether the difference between the proportion is significant or not point.

The formula for testing significance of difference is as under:

$$Z = \sqrt{\frac{p_1 - p_2}{\frac{p_1 \times q_1}{n_1} + \frac{p_1 \times q_1}{n_2}}}$$

where, p_1 = the proportion of success in sample one
p_2 = the proportion of success in sample two
q_1 = $1-p_1$
q_2 = $1-p_2$
n_1 = size of sample one
n_2 = size of sample two

Example

One-tailed test concerning two proportions
When we have
Size of sample of college – 1, n_1 = 100
Size of sample of college – 2, n_2 = 80
Number of failure in the college – 1 = 15
Number of failure in the college – 2 = 10
Significance level, α = 0.05

Solution : Let p_1 and p_2 be the proportion with respect to college–1 and college – 2 respectively. Then,

$$p_1 = 15/100 = 0\ .15;\ p_2 = 10/80 = 0.125$$

$$\sigma\bar{p}_1 - \bar{p}_2 = \sqrt{p_1(1-p_1)/n_1 + p_2(1-P_2)/n_2}$$

$$= \sqrt{0.15 \times 0.85/100 + 0.125 \times 0.875/80} = 0.05$$

$$Z\bar{p}_1 - \bar{p}_2 = \frac{\bar{p}_1 - \bar{p}_2}{\sigma\bar{p}_1 - \bar{p}_2} = 0.15 - 0.125/0.05 = 0.5$$

Since the calculated Z value (0.5) is less than $Z\alpha$ (1.64), it falls in the acceptance region. Hence, H_0 should be accepted.

This is shown in Figure.

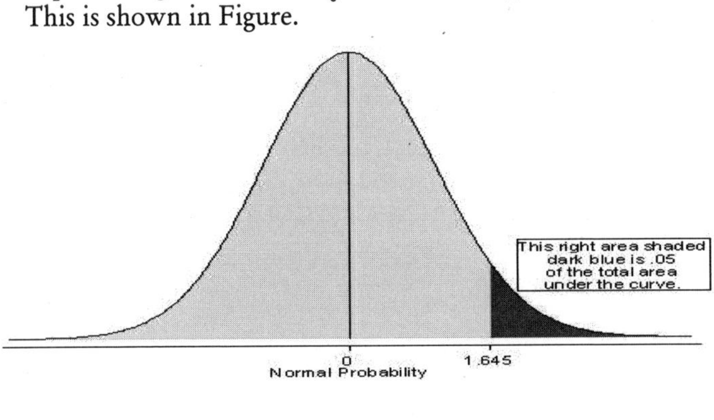

14.8.4 Hypothesis Testing for Comparing a Variance to a Hypothesized Population Variance

This test is used to compare a sample variance to some theoretical or hypothesized variance of population. It is different from z-test and t-test. The test used for this purpose is known as the chi-square test. It is used to test the null hypothesis.

The formula for this is as follows:

$$\chi^2 = \frac{\sigma_s^2}{\sigma_p^2}(n-1)$$

where n= number of items in the sample, or

$$\frac{\text{variance of the sample} \times \text{degree of freedom}}{\text{variance of population}}$$

Example

χ^2 Tests of hypotheses concerning variances

$$\chi^2 = \frac{\sigma_s^2}{\sigma_p^2}(n-1)$$

When we have

Variance of population, $\sigma^2 = 2$

Size of sample, n = 12

Variance of sample, $\sigma_s^2 = 3$

Significance level = 0.05

$$\chi^2 = \frac{(12-1)\times 3}{2} = 16.5$$

Degree of freedom (df) = (n–1)= (12–1) = 11.

The calculated value of chi-square (16.5) is less than the table chi-square value (19.675). The calculated value falls in the acceptance region. Hence, H_0 is to be accepted at 0.05 level.

14.8.5 Testing the Equality of Variances of Two Normal Populations

To test the equality of variances of two normal populations F-Test is used which is based on F-distribution.

The formula for this hypothesis testing is as follows:

$$F = \frac{\sigma_{s1}^2}{\sigma_{s2}^2}$$

where, $\sigma^2_{s1} = \dfrac{\sum(X_{1i} - \overline{X}_1)^2}{(n_1 - 1)}$

$$\sigma^2_{s1} = \frac{\sum (X_{2i} - \overline{X}_2)^2}{(n_2 - 1)}$$

The following presumptions are made while using this F-Test:

- The populations are normal
- Samples have been drawn randomly
- Observations are independent
- There is no measurement error

F-test is used to test the hypothesis, whether the two samples are from the same normal population with equal variance or from two normal populations with equal variance. It is also used to verify the hypothesis of equality between two variances.

Example

F-tests concerning two population variances

Let σ_1^2 and σ_2^2 be the variances of two population which follow normal distribution. The possible hypotheses are:

Test 1: H_0: $\sigma_1^2 \leq \sigma_2^2$ and H_1: $\sigma_1^2 > \sigma_2^2$ (right region of acceptance (white) and rejection region (shaded) in the normal curve).

Test 1: H_0: $\sigma_1^2 \geq \sigma_2^2$ and H_1: $\sigma_1^2 < \sigma_2^2$ (left region of acceptance and rejection in the normal curve).

Example

When we have (one-tailed test)

Size of sample from college-1, n_1 = 9

Size of sample from college-2, n_2 = 12

Variance of the sample from college-1, S_2^1 = 49

Variance of the sample from college-2, S_2^2 = 36

Significance level, α = 0.05

Then

$$F = S_2^1 / S_2^2 = \frac{49}{36} = 1.36$$

Degree of freedom (df) = (n_1-1) = (9–1) = 8; (n_2-1)=(12–1)=11

Table F value with 8 and 11 degree of freedom (df) = 2.90

Calculated F value (1.36) is less than table value (2.90) with 8 and 11 df. The calculated value falls in the acceptance region. Hence, H_0 should be accepted.

In case of

Test 1: H_0: $\sigma_1^2 \geq \sigma_2^2$ and H_1: $\sigma_1^2 < \sigma_2^2$ (left region of acceptance and rejection in the normal curve).

We have

Size of sample from college-1, n_1 = 10
Size of sample from college-2, n_2 = 14
Variance of the sample from college-1, S_2^1 = 49
Variance of the sample from college-2, S_2^2 = 81
Significance level, α = 0.05
Then

$$F = S_2^1 / S_2^2 = \frac{49}{81} = 0.605$$

Degree of freedom (df) = $(n_1-1)=(10-1)$ = 9; $(n_2-1)=(14-1)$ = 13
Table F value with 9 and 13 degree of freedom (df) = 2.71

The F distribution is not a symmetrical distribution. Hence, the F value (C_1) for left tail can be obtained by the equation as given below:

F-Value =

$$P\,(S_2^2 / S_2^1 \geq 1/C) = 0.01$$

Table F value with 13 and 9 degree of freedom (df) = 4.3

C_1 = 1/4.3 = .233

Since the calculated F value (0.605) is more than the cut off value, C_1 (0.233). It falls in the accepted region. So, accept H_0.

14.8.6 Hypothesis Testing of Correlation Coefficients

To calculate the significance of correlation coefficient based on sample data, following formulae are applied:

For simple correlation coefficient: $t = r_{yx}\sqrt{\dfrac{n-2}{1-r_{yx}^2}}$

The null hypothesis is either accepted or rejected based on the value of t.

For partial correlation coefficient: $t = r_p\sqrt{\dfrac{n-k}{1-r_p^2}}$

The null hypothesis is either accepted or rejected based on the value of t.

For multiple correlation coefficient: $F = \dfrac{R^2/(k-1)}{(1-R^2)(n-k)}$

14.9 NON-PARAMETRIC TESTS OF HYPOTHESES

Non-parametric tests of hypotheses are as follow:

Sign Test

Test 1: $H_o : p = ½$ and $H_1 : p > ½$
Test 2: $H_1 : p = ½$ and $H_1 : p < ½$

Example

When we have

Size of sample, n = 36

Number of plus (+) who scored above 60, X = 24

Number of minus (–) who scored below 60 = 11

Number of students who scored zero = 1

Significance level = 0.05

Since n is more than 30, the binominal distribution of this situation can be approximated to a normal distribution with following mean and variance

Mean = np = 36 × 0.5 = 18

Variance = np(1 – p) = 18 × 0.5 = 9

Then

$$Z = \frac{X - np}{\sqrt{np(1-p)}} = \frac{24-18}{\sqrt{9}} = 2$$

Since the calculated value (2) more than the table value of $Z\alpha$ (1.64). H_0 should be rejected. Hence, there is a significance of difference between two groups at 0.05 level.

Chi-square Test

$$X = \frac{\Sigma(\text{observed frequency} - \text{expected frequency})^2}{(\text{expected frequency})} \text{ or}$$

The value of the test-statistic is

$$X^2 = \sum_{i=1}^{n} \frac{(O_i - E_i)^2}{E_i}$$

Test 1: H_o: χ^2 (Calculated value) < Table value at .05 or .01 level with given df

Test 2: H_1: χ^2 (Calculated value) > Table value at .05 or .01 level with given df

Example

Use of ICT

Rate of return	*Low*	*High*	*Total*
0 – 8%	$30_{(o)}$, 20(e)	$10_{(o)}$, 20(e)	40
+ 8% to 15%	$20_{(o)}$, $30_{(e)}$	$40_{(o)}$, $30_{(e)}$	60
Total	50	50	100

χ^2 = (30–20)²/20 + (10–20)²/20 + (20–30)²/30 + (40–30)²/30 = 16.6

Degree of freedom (c–1)(r–1)= (2–1)(2–1) =1

The calculated χ^2 value (16.8) is more than table χ^2 (6.635). It does not fall in acceptance region. Hence,H_0 is rejected.

Goodness of Fit Test

The goodness of fit of a given set of data is performed using chi-square test. The combination of hypotheses for this situation is:

H_0: The given data follow an assumed distribution

H_1: the given data do not follow the assumed distribution

The observed chi-square statistic,

$$X^2 = \sum_{i=1}^{n} \frac{(O_i - E_i)^2}{E_i}$$

If the calculated chi-square value is less thanthe table chi-square value, it falls the acceptance region. Hence accept H_0; otherwise, reject H_0.

Example

Kolmogorov-Smirnov Test

The two-sample Kolmogorov-Smirnov test uses the maximal distance between cumulative frequency distributions of these two samples as the statistic.

Test 1: H_0: Value derived from KS Test < Table value at .05 or .01 level with given df

Test 2: H_1: Value derived from KS Test > Table value at .05 or .01 level with given df

In case of large sample, critical value of D at 0.05 level is:

$$1.36\sqrt{\frac{N_1 + N_2}{N_1 N_2}}$$

Critical value at 0.01 level

$$1.63\sqrt{\frac{N_1 + N_2}{N_1 N_2}}$$

Test 1: H_0: Value derived from KS Test < $1.36\sqrt{\frac{N_1 + N_2}{N_1 N_2}}$ value at 0.05 level. Null Hypothesis is accepted.

Example

Test 2: H_1: Value derived from KS Test > $1.36\sqrt{\frac{N_1 + N_2}{N_1 N_2}}$ value at 0.05 level. Null Hypothesis is rejected.

Example

When we have

D = 0.13 (the maximal distance between cumulative frequency distributions of these two samples)

N_1 = 50, N_2 = 60

Then critical value at 0.05 level = $1.36\sqrt{\frac{50+60}{50\times60}} = 0.260$

Calculated K-S value (0.13) is less critical value (0.260) at 0.05. It falls in the acceptance region. So H_0 is accepted.

Similarly we can find significance of difference at 0.01 level by using above mentioned formula.

Median test

Many times data are available that do not permit mathematical operations involved calculating the mean and standard deviation. Typically, such data either are markedly skewed or represent ordinal scale of measurement. In place of either a Z-test or t-test for a significance of the difference between two sample means, there is a significance difference between the median of two samples. Median test is based on chi-square for a 2×2 table. Formula for median test is as given below:

$$\chi^2 = \frac{N\,[(AD - BC) - N/2]^2}{(A+B)\ (C+D)(A+C)(B+D)}$$

Test 1: H_o: Value derived from median test < table value of chi-square at .05 or .01level with given df=1. Null Hypothesis is accepted

Test 2: H_1: Value derived from median test > Table value of chi-square at .05 or .01level with given df=1. H_0 is rejected.

Example

We have

	Sample-1	*Sample-2*	
No. of scores above combined median	4 B	10A	A+B= 14
No. of scores above combined median	9 D	5 C	C+D =14
	B+D =13	A+C=15	N=28

$$\chi^2 = \frac{28(90\text{-}20\ \text{-}28/2)^2}{(14)(14)(13)(15)} = 2.297$$

Degree of freedom = (c–1)(r–1) = (2–1)(2–1) = 1

The calculated χ^2 value (2.297)is less than χ^2 table value (3.84) with df=1 at 0.05 level. The calculated value falls in the acceptance region. So H_0 is accepted.

Fisher-Irwin Test

Fisher Irwin test is a distribution free test used in testing a hypothesis concerning no difference among two sets of data. It is employed to determine whether one can reasonably assume, for example, that two supposedly different treatments are in fact different in terms of the result they produce. Example:

	No. passed	*No. failed*	*Total*
New Training (A)	5	1	6
Old Training (B)	3	3	6
Total	8	4	12

Probability of Group A doing as well or better

= Pr. (5 passing and 1 failing) + Pr. (6 passing and 0 failing)

$$= \frac{8_{c5} \times 4_{c1}}{12_{c6}} + \frac{8_{c6} \times 4_{co}}{12_{c6}}$$

$$= \frac{224}{924} + \frac{28}{924} = 0.24 + 0.03 = 0.27$$

Alternatively, we can work out as under:

Probability of Group B doing as well or worse

= Pr. (3 passing and 3 failing) + Pr. (2 passing and 4 failing)

$$= \frac{8_{c3} \times 4_{c3}}{12_{c6}} + \frac{8_{c2} \times 4_{c4}}{12_{c6}}$$

$$= \frac{224}{924} + \frac{28}{924} = 0.24 + 0.03 = 0.27$$

Now we have to compare this calculated probability with the significance level of 5% or 0.05 already specified by the management. If we do so, we notice that the calculated value is greater than 0.05 and hence, we must accept the null hypothesis. This means that at a significance level of 5% the result obtained in the above table is not significant. Hence, we can infer that both training programmes are equally good.

McNemer Test

McNemar Test is non-parametric test to identify the effects of a particular treatment on a selected group of subjects by organizing the collected data into a 'before' and 'after' method in which subject has its own control. The subjects are randomly drawn from a population. Assumptions such as normality, continuity, equality, and variances required in parametric test regarding distribution are not met. Formula for calculation of critical value is as shown below:

$$\chi^2 = \frac{(|A-D|-1)^2}{(A+D)} \text{ with d.f. } = 1$$

H_0 : calculated value < table value of chi-square at 0.05 level. Null Hypothesis is accepted.

H_1: calculated value > table vale of chi-square at 0.05 level. Null Hypothesis is rejected.

Example

	Before	*After*
Method-1	50 B	55A
Method-2	45 D	C 65
		A+D =100

$$\chi^2 = (I\ 55 - 45\ I - 1)^2/100 = 0.81$$

Calculated χ^2 value (0.81) is less than χ^2 table value (3.84)with df=1 at 0.05 level. Hence H_0 is accepted.

Mann-Whitney U Test (Rank-sum test)

Mann-Whitney U Test is an alternative to the two sample t-test. For example, there are two independent samples namely n_1 and $n_{2,}$ and $N = n_1 + n_{2.}$ Combined positional ranks are obtained from the lowest (1) to the highest (N). In case of tie, average is taken.

If the size of second sample(n_2) is more than 8, one can have normal approximation to the given data with following random variable:

$$U = n_1n_2 + \frac{n_1(n_1+1)}{2} - R_1$$

The formulas for mean (μ_u) and variance (σ^2_μ) of U are:

$\mu_u = n_1n_2/2$

$\sigma^2_\mu = n_1n_2(n_1 + n_{2.}+1)/12$

$$Z_u = \frac{u-\mu u}{\sigma\mu}$$

Therefore, possible hypotheses are:

H_0: Two samples are drawn from identical populations.

H_1: Two samples are not drawn from identical populations.

Example

The sum of the ranks of sample-1:
(5, 6, 7, 10, 10, 15, 16,18, 19, 22, 22, 22, 25, 26, 29, 30, 32, 33, 35, 36) =418

The sum of the ranks of sample-2:
(1, 2, 3, 4, 8, 10, 12, 13, 14, 17, 20, 24, 27, 28, 31, 34, 37, 38) =323

Then

$$U = n_1n_2 + \frac{n_1(n_1+1)}{2} - R_1 = 20 \times 18 + 20 \times 21/2 - 418 = 152$$

$$\mu_u = n_1n_2/2 = 20 \times 18/2 = 180$$

$$\sigma^2_\mu = n_1n_2(n_1 + n_2 + 1)/12 = 20 \times 18 \times (20+18+1)/12 = 1170$$

$$\sigma\mu = 34.21$$

$$Z_u = \frac{u - \mu u}{\sigma\mu} = \frac{152-180}{34.21} = -0.819$$

Since the computed Zu (is less than Zá (1.64) at 0.05. Accept the null hypothesis. Thus two sample drawn from populations having identical distributions.

Run Test of Randomness (large sample)

One sample runs test is a test to used to judge the randomness of a sample on the basis of the order in which the observations are taken. We shall use the following symbols

n_1 = number of occurances of type 1 (say *H* in the given case)
n_2 = number of occurances of type 2 (say *D* in the given case)

the sampling distribution of 'r' statistic, the number of runs, is to be used and this distribution has its mean

$$\mu_r = \frac{2n_1n_2 + 1}{n_1 + n_2}$$

and the standard deviation $\sigma_r = \sqrt{2n_1n_2 \frac{(2n_1n_2 - n_1 - n_2)}{(n_1+n_2)^2\ (n_1+n_2-1)}}$

The formula for the standard normal statistic to test the significance of r is as given below:

$$Z = \frac{r-\mu}{\sigma}$$

It is a two tailed test. Hence, the values of table $-Z_{al2}$ and Z_{al2} define the left critical value and right critical value of r. If the calculated Z value is between $-Z_{al2}$ and $Z_{al2,}$ then accept the null hypothesis; otherwise reject the null hypothesis.

By using the table of area under normal curve, we find the appropriate z value. Using this we now calculate the limits of the acceptance region:

Example

We have

Frequency of winners, n_1 = 24

Frequency of losers, n_2 = 16

Number of runs, r = 17

Significance level, α = 0.05

Half of the significance level = 0.025

Since n_1 is more than 20, the sample of the problem is large. Hypotheses are: μ

H_0 : the occurrence of the runs of winners and losers is random

H_1: the occurrence of the runs of winners and losers is not random

$$\text{Then mean of r, } \mu^2 = \frac{2n_1n_2}{n_1+n_2}+1=\frac{2\times24\times16}{24+16}+1=20.2$$

$$\text{Variance of r, } \sigma^2 = \frac{2n_1\times n_2(2n_1\times n_2-n_1-n_2)}{(n_1+n_2)^2\ (n_1+n_2-1)}$$

$$= \frac{2\times24\times16\ (2\times24\times16-24-16)}{(24+16)^2\ (24+16-1)}=8.96$$

Standard Deviation $\sqrt{8.96}$ = 2.993

$$\text{Then } Z=\frac{r-\mu}{\sigma}=\frac{17-20.2}{2.993}=-1.069$$

Since the calculated Z value (–1.069) of r falls in the acceptance region between ($\pm$1.96) Zα. H_0 should be accepted. Thus the occurrences of the winners and losers are random.

The Kruskal-Wallis Test

This test is used to test the null hypothesis that 'k' independent random samples come from identical universes against the alternative hypothesis that the means of these universes are not equal. The test statistic is *H* for this test which is worked out as under :

$$H=\frac{12}{n(n+1)}\sum_{i=1}^{k}\frac{R_i^2-3(n+1)}{n_i}$$

where n= n_1 + n_2 +...........n_k and R_i being the sum of the ranks assigned to n_i observations in the ith sample.

Test 1: H_o: K-test (Calculated value) < table value χ^2 of at .05 or .01 level with given df).

Test 2: H_1: **K-test (Calculated value)** > Table value χ^2 at .05 or .01 level with given df).

Example

We have

Sum of the ranks of sample-1 = (3, 6, 11, 13, 15, 15, 17) = 80
Sum of the ranks of sample-2 = (2, 4, 5, 7, 12, 15) = 45
Sum of the ranks of sample-3 = (1, 8, 9, 10, 18) = 46

Formula for the calculation of H is

$$H = \frac{SSbg(R)}{N(N+1)/12}$$

$$SSbg(R) = \frac{80^2}{6} + \frac{45^2}{6} + \frac{46^2}{6} - \frac{171^2}{6} = 132.32$$

$$N(N+1)/12 = 28.5$$

$$H = \frac{132.32}{28.5} = 4.64$$

Degree of freedom= (n–1) = (3–1). Table value of chi-square with df=2 is 5.99 at 0.05 level.

The calculated χ^2 value (4.64) is less than table chi-square value (5.99). It falls in acceptance region. So H_0 is accepted.

References

Best, J. and Khan, J. (2009). *Research in Education.* 10th edition, Needham Heights: Allyn and Bacon.

Campbell, J.P., Daft, R.L. and Hulin, C.L. (1982). *What to Study: Generating and Developing Research Questions.* Beverly Hills, CA: Sage.

Charters, W.W. Jr. (1967). Hypothesis in scientific research. Unpublished paper. University of Oregon, Eugene.

Chaters, W.M. (1997). Hypothesis in scientific research. Unpublished paper. University of Oregon.

Goethals, George W. (1958). A Framework for Educational Research. *Harvard Educational Review,* 28, 29-43.

Kothari, C.R. (2011). *Research Methodology: Methods and Techniques.* New Delhi: New Age International Publishers.

Mangal, S.K. (2003). *Statistics in Psychology and Education.* New Delhi: Prentice-Hall of India.

Panneerselvam, R. (2004). *Research Methodology.* New Delhi: Prentice-Hall of India.

CHAPTER

15

Evaluation

No consensus is available on single model/criteria for evaluating educational research so as to ensure reasonable quality in research. There is a general agreement among the experts and the stakeholders that evaluation is a significant tool to assess the strengths and weaknesses in educational research. Insights and cues from the evaluation would provide substantial support to devise strategies to ensure quality in research. We all realize that the institutions of higher learning engaged in educational research should adopt more objective, more reliable and valid method of evaluation. Therefore, there is a need to evolve a more integrated and comprehensive model of evaluation based on clearly defined dimensions of quality.

15.1 EVALUATION STRATEGY

Evaluation strategies signify a broad, overarching and encompassing perspective on evaluation. Evaluation strategies/studies can be further classified on the basis of methods/models adopted for evaluation or on the basis of the purpose of evaluation. Evaluation strategies can be further classified into three major groups described next.

15.1.1 Scientific Method

Scientific methods are based on ethics and values laid out in the social sciences. They prioritize and evaluate the accuracy, objectivity, reliability and validity of the information generated. The scientific method includes experimental methods such as experimental and quasi-experimental designs; econometric-oriented designs, cost-effectiveness and cost-benefit analysis.

15.1.2 Project Management-Oriented Method

Project management-oriented methods are widely used nowadays in operations research, social research and even in development planning and management. The Programme Evaluation and Review Technique (PERT) and Critical Path Method (CPM), as part of network analysis, are probably the best-known management-oriented models. Some researchers also consider 'logframe analysis' as a management-oriented evaluation method.

15.1.3 Qualitative Method

Qualitative research method focuses on the importance of observation and the need to reveal the hidden areas and the value of subjective human interpretation.

15.2 FORMATIVE AND SUMMATIVE EVALUATION

15.2.1 Formative Evaluation

Formative evaluation provides the initial feedback needed to strengthen the intervention or policy formulation. It examines the programme's delivery process, quality of implementation and the impact of organizational inputs on the desired outcomes. Formative evaluations are performed to assess whether a programme is working well or not and if the programme is not working well then what modifications are required.

Formative evaluation usually requires the same data as summative evaluation, though the research design and methodology adopted for formative evaluation may differ. The main difference is in the case of data analysis procedures. In the case of formative evaluation, usually complex analysis procedures are used to explore the impact of interventions but causal relationship is not performed. This is because the purpose of formative evaluation is to ensure that the programme is moving in the right direction in a timely manner and that there are no gaps between strategies devised and outcome sought and if there are gaps, it helps programme managers in addressing the gap through formulation of strategies.

Formative evaluation can be sub-divided into the following categories:

(a) *Needs assessment:* This determines the programme's needs from the perspective of all stakeholders.

(b) *Feasibility assessment:* It assesses the feasibility of a programme, policy or a concept for implantation. It analyses both the technical and financial viability of an intervention.

(c) *Process evaluation:* Process evaluation evaluates the impact of an intervention on process indicators. For example, whether an intervention targeted to increase family-planning awareness has any impact on group meetings between eligible couples is studied through process evaluation. It investigates the process of delivering the output.

15.2.2 Summative Evaluation

Summative evaluations are more specific than formative evaluations. They try to identify the impact of a programme's activities and tasks in achieving its objectives. It tries to examine the effects or outcomes of a programme/intervention by ascertaining whether the outcomes are in consonance with the desired objectives. It determines the overall impact of the programme beyond the immediate target outcomes.

Summative evaluation can also be sub-divided into:

(a) *Outcome evaluations*: These try to analyse the impact of a programme's service delivery and organizational input on desired outcome.

(b) *Impact evaluation*: Impact evaluation ascertains the project impact by analysing whether the project's activities and tasks have been successful in achieving the desired objectives. It, therefore, assesses the overall effects of the programme as a whole.

(c) *Cost-effectiveness and cost-benefit analysis*: This assesses the benefit that is going to accrue from the project *vis-a-vis* the cost that is going to be involved in the project.

(d) *Meta-analysis*: Meta-analysis integrates the outcome estimates from multiple studies to arrive at an overall or summary judgement on an evaluation question.

15.3 GUIDING PRINCIPLES

The American Evaluation Association (2004) has created a set of Guiding Principles for evaluators. The order of these principles does not imply priority among them; priority will vary by situation and evaluator role. The principles run as follows:

- *Systematic Inquiry*: Evaluators conduct systematic, data-based inquiries about whatever is being evaluated. This requires quality data collection, including a defensible choice of indicators, which lends credibility to findings. Findings are credible when they are demonstrably evidence-based, reliable and valid. This also pertains to the choice of methodology employed, such that it is consistent with the aims of the evaluation and provides dependable data. Furthermore, utility of findings is critical such that the information obtained by evaluation is comprehensive and timely, and thus serves to provide maximal benefit and use to stakeholders.
- *Competence*: Evaluators provide competent performance to stakeholders. This requires that evaluation teams comprise an appropriate combination of competencies, such that varied and appropriate expertise is available for the evaluation process, and that evaluators work within their scope of capability.
- *Integrity/Honesty* : Evaluators ensure the honesty and integrity of the entire evaluation process. A key element of this principle is freedom from bias in evaluation and this is underscored by three principles: impartiality, independence and transparency.
- *Respect for people*: Evaluators respect the security, dignity and self-worth of the respondents, program participants, clients, and other stakeholders with whom they interact. This is particularly pertinent with regards to those who will be impacted upon by the evaluation findings. Protection of people includes ensuring informed consent from those involved in the evaluation, upholding confidentiality, and ensuring that the identity of those who may provide sensitive information towards the program evaluation is protected. Evaluators are ethically required to respect the customs and beliefs of those who are impacted upon by the evaluation or program activities. Examples of how such respect is demonstrated is through respecting local customs, e.g. dress codes, respecting people privacy, and minimizing demands on others' time. Where stakeholders wish to place objections to evaluation findings, such a process should be facilitated through the

local office of the evaluation organization, and procedures for lodging complaints or queries should be accessible and clear.

- *Responsibilities for General and Public Welfare*: Evaluators articulate and take into account the diversity of interests and values that may be related to the general and public welfare. Access to evaluation documents by the wider public should be facilitated such that discussion and feedback is enabled.

15.4 THE NATIONAL RESEARCH COUNCIL (USA)

The National Research Council (USA) (2002) has given a *scientifically-based* criteria for evaluating research which include:

(1) Pose a significant, important question that can be investigated empirically and that contributes to the knowledge-base
(2) Test questions that are linked to relevant theory
(3) Apply methods that best address the research questions of interest
(4) Base research on clear chains of inferential reasoning supported and justified by a complete coverage of the relevant literature
(5) Provide the necessary information to reproduce or replicate the study
(6) Ensure the study design, methods, and procedures are sufficiently transparent and ensure an independent, balanced, and objective approach to the research
(7) Provide sufficient description of the sample, the intervention, and any comparison groups
(8) Use appropriate and reliable conceptualization and measurement of variables
(9) Evaluate alternative explanations for any findings
(10) Assess the possible impact of systematic bias
(11) Submit research to a peer-review process
(12) Adhere to quality standards for reporting (i.e., clarity, cogence, completeness)

15.5 Dimensions. Berliner (2007) earmarked the dimensions and sub-dimensions for evaluating research in education, which are summarized as follows:

TABLE 15.1
Dimensions and Sub-dimensions of Evaluating Quality in Research

Dimensions of Quality			
Epistemic: Methodological and Theoretical robustness	*Technological*	*Capacity development and value for people*	*Economic*
Trustworthiness	Purposivity	Plausibility	Marketability and Competitiveness
Builds on what is Know + contribution to Knowledge	Salience/ timeliness	Partnership, collaboration and Engagement	Cost-effectiveness
Explicitness	Specificity and Accessibility	Reflexivity, deliberation and criticism	Auditability
Propriety	Concern for enabling Impact	Receptiveness	Feasibility
Paradigm-dependent Criteria	Flexibility and Operationali-sability	Transformation and personal growth	Originality
Scientific robustness		Social and economic robustness	

Evaluation is a systematic, rigorous, and meticulous application of scientific methods to assess the design, implementation, improvement or outcomes of a programme. It is a resource-intensive process, frequently requiring resources, such as, evaluator expertise, labour, time and a sizeable budget. (Rossi, Lipsey and Freeman (2004).

Evaluation system calls for the best inputs, and the best processes to produce the best outputs and impact (Kapoor, 2009). The scholars and the supervisors have to conform to standards at par with international standards. Institutions are required to keep pace with the growing knowledge and strive hard ceaselessly, to meet the international standards in educational research. The researcher is supposed to examine his or her research proposal on certain given criteria of evaluation before its submission. When a student submits a proposal for research, it is usually reviewed by a professor or a committee of professors. The usual criteria of a relevant problem, evidence of knowledge in the area, appropriate methodology, and good continuity in the proposal apply when a proposal is reviewed.

15.6 SELF-EVALUATION

Evaluation strategy demands that researcher should evaluate his or her proposal by clarifying the following questions:

15.6.1 Personal

- Is the problem in line with my goal expectations and expectations of others?
- Am I genuinely interested in this problem but free from strong biases?
- Do I possess, or can I acquire the necessary skills, abilities and background knowledge to study this problem?
- Do I have access to the tools, equipment, laboratories, and subject necessary to conduct the investigation?
- Do I have the time and money to complete?
- Can I have adequate data?
- Does the problem meet the scope, significance, and topical requirements of the institution?
- Can I obtain administrative support, guidance, and cooperation for the conduct of the study?

15.6.2 Social

- Will the solution of this problem advance knowledge in the field?
- Will the findings be of practical value to educators, parents, social workers or others?
- What will be the breadth of the application of the findings in terms of range of individuals, and areas of coverage?
- If the topic has been covered, does it need to be extended beyond its present limits?
- Is the topic sufficiently delimited to permit exhaustive treatment yet sufficiently significant to warrant investigating it?
- Will the study lead to the development of other investigations?

Criticality is a key factor in the assessment or evaluation of research work. Composition, reflection, context, transparency, enquiry, healthy skepticism, positiveness, and evolution in process are the basic elements of criticality. Research scholar should develop skills of critical thinking in order to develop a good thesis.

15.7 EVALUATION OF RESEARCH PROPOSAL/STUDY

A research proposal should explicitly explain,

(1) What research is intended?

1. Is it clear what position the research is 'coming from'?
2. Are the area and topic clearly identified?
3. Are the research questions appropriate?
4. Is the research appropriately set in context?

(2) How will the research be done?

1. Clarity about use of Method (experimental or descriptive or exploratory) and approach (qualitative or quantitative or mixed)
2. Size of the sample for the proposed research
3. Techniques used in the selection of sample
4. Tools/Instruments for collection of data
5. Are procedures in the collection of data followed?
6. Are technical aspects of the quality of data namely, the reliability, validity and established reactivity?
7. Analysis of data: Inferential or qualitative analysis.

(3) Why is the research intended?

1. Does it contribute to basic knowledge or to educational theory?
2. Does it lead to the solution of educational problems, either long range or short range?
3. What are its implications?

(4) Reporting

1. Have the research questions been answered?
2. How much confidence can we have in the answers put forward? (i.e. in assessing the way evidence has been used to answer questions and draw conclusions)
3. What can be concluded from the research on the basis of what was found? (i.e. assessing the generality and applicability of the findings and conclusions-internal and external validity)

(5) Presentation

1. Is report well designed, written and communicated effectively to others in the form of research?
2. Is each part of report logically connected and described?

3. Are figures, tables and diagrams presented clearly and as per given format?
4. Are the rules for typing the research report followed?
5. Are the reference citations as per the standard norms?

15.8 CRITERIA FOR EVALUATION OF A RESEARCH REPORT, ARTICLE, OR THESIS

I. Title of Proposal/Report

1. Precise identification of problem area, often including specification of independent and dependent variables and identification of target population.
2. Sufficient clarity and conciseness for indexing of title.
3. Effective arrangement of words in title.

II. The Problem

A. Description and Statement of the Problem

1. Statement of basic (felt) difficulty or problem situation—significance and importance of the problem area in either basic or applied research.
2. Careful analysis of known and suspected facts and explanation of existing information and knowledge that may have some bearing on problem—the spelling out of specific factors giving rise to the basic difficulty, of their interrelationships, and of their relevance to the problem area.
3. Soundness of the logic underlying selection of variables or factors to be studied and expression of their relationship to the problem area.
4. Systematic and orderly presentation of the interrelationships of relevant facts and concepts underlying the problem.
5. Clear identification of the problem statement through the use of an appropriate heading or paragraph caption (the same requirement holding for other major categories of the research).
6. Succinct, precise, and unambiguous statement of the research problem (including the delineation of independent, dependent, and classificatory variables), of the major questions to be resolved, or of the objectives to be investigated.

7. Distinction (if required) between problems or questions that are either factually-oriented or value-oriented.
8. Distinction in the instance of theoretically-oriented research or of basic research between the purpose, which is often goal-oriented or instrumental in relation to certain pragmatic objectives, and the research problem which is primarily directed toward the finding of relationships, the making of comparisons, or the noting of changes (possible cause and effect relationships) relative to operationally formulated research hypotheses.

B. *Delimitations*

Sufficient delimitations of the problem in order to make it more feasible and fruitful.

C. *Review and Evaluation of the Literature Pertinent to Problem Areas*

1. Adequacy and relevance of the previous investigation cited with reference to the basic difficulty posed, design of the current investigation, procedures followed, and projected analysis of data.
2. Appropriate development of a rationale or theoretical framework from the research studies cited with reference to the current problem under investigation.

D. Clear-cut statement of the conceptions, assumptions, or postulates underlying the problem being investigated.

E. Precise statement of (1) hypotheses or (2) deduced consequences of theories or (3) the objectives of a study (objectives being most common in survey and descriptive research).

1. Hypotheses involving relationships and comparisons.
2. Presentation of deducible consequences or predictions (if any) that are logically consistent with an hypothesis (i.e., antecedent-consequent statement: If *A* exists, then *B* follows).

F. *Definitions of terms*

1. Clarity in the definitions of key terms and variables (especially constructs).
2. Use of operational definitions whenever possible.

III. Methodology and Procedures

A. *Logic, structure, and strategy of study carefully delineated*

1. Distinction made between whether the research involves

variables manipulated and controlled by the investigator (usually found in experimental research) or whether an *ex post facto* situation exists involving the analysis of data already available or collected as in most field studies and correlational investigations.

2. Appropriate use of paradigms, flow charts, or schematic models.
3. Specification of threats to external and internal validity of the design employed.

B. ***Clear description of samples studied***

1. Mode of selection of subject cited (e.g., random assignment, matching, voluntary participation, or convenience by being available).
2. Data regarding how representative a sample is relative to a population.

C. ***Adequate information pertaining to the reliability, validity, and standardization*** properties of instrumentation: psychometric characteristic of scales or tests used.

D. ***Sufficient description of operational or field procedures*** followed in the collection of data—where, when, and how data were obtained.

E. ***Coordination of the specification of the relationship*** between the null (statistical) hypotheses and the research (problem) hypotheses.

F. ***Appropriateness of the statistical treatment and data processing procedures.***

G. ***Evidence of a preparatory pilot study having been conducted.***

H. ***Procedure clearly enough described*** so that other investigators can replicate (repeat) the study performed under essentially comparable conditions in the future.

I. ***Statement of methodological*** assumption such as adequacy of reliability and validity of measures, representativeness of samples, fulfilment of appropriate requirements for carrying out statistical tests.

IV. Presentation and Analysis of Data

A. ***Logical and orderly exposition*** in terms of the framework of the hypotheses, deductions, objectives, or questions asked in conjunction with the statement of the problem.

1. Objective rather than subjective or speculative presentation.
2. Analysis consistent with and supported by the facts obtained.
3. Absence of overgeneralizations or sweeping statements that go beyond the data.
4. Relationships of the findings to previously cited research explicitly shown.
5. Negative findings relative to the hypotheses as well as positive findings presented with minimal distortion or bias.
6. Uncontrolled factors influencing data outcomes appropriately cited and discussed.
7. Weaknesses in the data honestly conceded and discussed with appropriate emphasis.
8. Lack of confusion between facts and inferences clearly shown-separation of analysis of findings from interpretation and discussion of findings.
9. Resolution of contradictions, inconsistencies, or misleading elements in the findings.

B. Appropriate and clear use of charts, tables, figures, and graphs.

V. Summary and Conclusion

1. Precise and accurate statement of (1) the problem, (2) the methodology followed, and (3) the findings without the introduction of new or irrelevant information.
2. Conclusions at a scope and level of generality justified by the data presented.
3. Appropriate caution exercised and necessary qualifications made in drawing conclusions.
4. Conclusions in a form that other investigators can understand and subsequently verify.
5. Conclusions coordinated with the tentative acceptance or rejection of the research hypotheses presented or with the objectives or questions posed.
6. New questions set forth for possible investigation-recommendations for additional research in the problem area study.
7. Recommendations concerning implementation of the research findings when appropriate relative to the

objectives stated in the purpose of the investigation (most frequently encountered in survey studies and action research).

15.9 EVALUATION FEEDBACK

Supervisor feedback is a central element of the teaching and research. It is essential for the supervisor to evaluate and provide feedback what has been written by the scholar. Students should not be afraid to follow-up on any point that is unclear or confusing. It would help the researcher to inform his or her writing. The purpose of evaluation and feedback is to develop good academic and social relationship between supervisor and the researcher.

- The job of the supervisor is to evaluate the write up, i.e. what has been written and make specific suggestions for further improvement and to encourage researcher in future work.
- The supervisor offers alternatives, suggestions and recommendations in place of what the student has written.
- The supervisor points out omissions in the student's work.
- Student is provided additional academic insight into the topic under consideration.

15.9.1 Organization of the Assignment

- This may include introduction, literature review, objectives, analysis, results and conclusion. How each of these constituent sections may be put together to give a structure an over all coherence.
- The organization of individual sentences, in terms of length, relation to other sentences.
- Punctuation, lexis, syntax/word order, grammar, proofreading, citation, quotation, bibliography, presentation: page numbering, subtitling, figures, tables, acronyms, etc. are examined.

15.9.2 Content evaluation involves:

- Strengths of the assignment such as synthesis of literature, theory and practice, appropriate synthesis of personal experience; clear argumentation and reflection are noted .
- Weaknesses of the assignments as mentioned above are also identified and noted.

15.9.3 Methodology

In this process of evaluation, various aspects of research design and analysis are considered.

- *Research Design*—Roadmap of Project/Research Study Undertaken
- *Approach*—The philosophical and epistemology positions of the research are considered.
- *Methods*—Comments are made on the practical aspects of the research design, the sample, collection and analysis of data, and the researcher's criticality.
- *Process*—Comments are made on the process, timeframe and practicality of the conduct of the research.

Table 15.2 shows items for evaluating proposal or research study on five point scale.

TABLE 15.2

Rating Scale for the Evaluation of a Research Proposal/Study

Characteristics	*Completely Incompetent*	*Poor*	*Mediocre*	*Good*	*Excellent*
1. Problem is clearly stated					
2. Hypotheses are clearly stated					
3. Problem is significant					
4. Assumptions are clearly stated					
5. Limitations of the study are stated					
6. Important terms are defined					
7. Relationship of the problem to previous research is made clear					
8. Research design is described fully					
9. Research design is appropriate for the solution of the problem					
10. Research design is free of specific weaknesses					
11. Population and sample are described					
12. Method of sampling is appropriate					
13. Data-gathering methods or procedures are described					
14. Data-gathering methods or procedures are appropriate to the solution of the problem					
15. Data-gathering methods or procedures are utilized correctly					
16. Validity and reliability of the evidence gathered are established					
17. Appropriate methods are selected to analyze the data					

18. Methods utilized in analyzing the data are applied correctly
19. Results of the analysis are presented clearly
20. Conclusions are clearly stated
21. Conclusions are substantiated by the evidence presented
22. Generalizations are confined to the population from which the sample was drawn
23. Report is clearly written
24. Report is logically organized
25. Tone of the report displays an unbiased, impartial scientific attitude
26. References or Bibliography as per APA's norms

REFERENCES

Best, J. and Kahn, J. (2009). *Research in Education.* 10th edition, Needham Heights: Allyn and Bacon.

Cozby, P. (2009). *Methods in Behavioural Research.* 10th edition, Bemont: Wadsworth.

Goode, W.J., and Hatt, P.K. (1990). *Methods in Social Research.* New Delhi: McGraw-Hill.

Guthrie, G. (2010). *Basic Research Methods.* New Delhi: Sage.

Koul, L. (2009). *Methodology of Educational Research.* Vikas Publishing House, New Delhi.

Laws, S. (2003). *Research for Development.* New Delhi: Vistaar Publications.

Leedy, P., Ormrod, J. (2010). *Practical Research: Planning and Design.* 9th edition, Needham Heights: Allyn Bacon.

Ozga, J. (2000). *Policy Research in Educational Settings.* Buckingham,UK: Open University Press.

Potter, C. (2006). "Psychology and the Art of Program Evaluation". *South African Journal of Psychology,* 36 (1): 82–102.

Punch, K.F. (2009). *Introduction to Research Methods in Education.* New Delhi: Sage.

Rossi, P.H., Lipsey, M.W. and Freeman, H.E. (2004). *Evaluation: A Systematic Approach* (7th ed.). Thousand Oaks: Sage.

Singh, J. (2008). *Methodology and Techniques of Social Research.* New Delhi: Kanishka Publishers.

Swann, J. (2000). How can research lead to improvement in education. *Prospero,* 6(3/4), pp. 130-138.

Wooding, S., and Grant, J. (2003). *Assessing Research: The Researchers' View.* Cambridge, England: RAND Europe.

UNIT III

METHODOLOGY

CHAPTER

16

Research Design

16.1 RESEARCH DESIGN

Once the research project is identified clearly and defined, the next stage is to design the research. The research design provides complete guidelines or roadmap to (i) What does present study intend? (ii) How will the research be done? (ii) Why is the research intended? The research design is the conceptual structure within which research is conducted. It constitutes the blueprint for the collection, measurement and analysis of data. It also contains time-frame work and financial aspect for the conduct of research. As such the design includes an outline of what the researcher will do from writing the hypothesis and its operational implications to the final analysis of data.

A research design contains :

- Selection of research approach—qualitative or quantitative.
- Design of sampling plan—probability or non-probability sampling plan.
- Design of experiment—pure experimental or quasi-experimental.
- Design of questionnaire—Structured (reliability and validity), semi or unstructured (authencity).
- Data Collection—Administration of test/questionnaire/ scale or conduct of in-depth interview/case study/ observation.

- Data analysis—Statistical or in-depth analysis of contextually-bound data.
- Interpretation of results—inferences or interpretive.

Research design stands for advance planning of methods to be adopted for collection of relevant data and the techniques to be used in their analysis, keeping in view the objectives of the research and the availability of time and money.

16.2 SELECTION OF RESEARCH APPROACH

If the research study happens to be an exploratory or a formulative one, wherein the major emphasis is on discovery of ideas and insights, the research design must be flexible enough to permit the consideration of many different aspects of phenomenon. But when the purpose of a study is accurate description of a situation or of an association between variables (or in what are called the descriptive studies), accuracy becomes a major consideration. A research design which maximizes the reliability of the evidence collected is considered a good design. Studies involving the testing of a hypothesis of a casual relationship between variables require a design which will permit inferences about causality in addition to the minimization of bias and maximization of reliability. But in practice it is the most difficult task to put a particular study in a particular group, for a given research may have in it elements of two or more of the functions of different studies. It is only on the basis of its primary function that a study can be categorized either as an exploratory or descriptive or hypothesis-testing study. Accordingly the choice of a research design may be made in case of a particular study.

16.2.1 Qualitative Approach

All qualitative research methods adhere to certain themes such as *qualitative data, content sensitivity, emphatic neutrality, inductive analysis and naturalistic inquiry.* Figure 16.1 summarizes the research designs.

16.2.2 Quantitative Approach

Quantitative approach is based on the logical-positive paradigm, which utilizes experimental research methodologies. It involves either inferential or experimental or simulation processes.

Figure 16.2 reflects 'Research Design' in case of quantitative research.

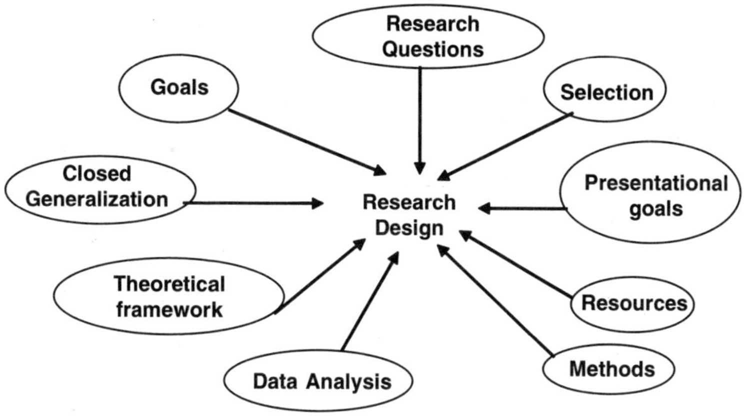

Figure 16.1 : Research Designs in Qualitative Research Approach

Comparing Groups	*Relating Variables*
Designs	
Experimental and quasi-experimental designs/Correlational surveys (non- experiments)	
Logic	
What are the 'effects' of this 'cause'?	What are the 'causes' of this 'effect'?
Conceptual frameworks	
Independent variable	
Independent variables	variable
Comparison groups ↓	X_1, X_2, X_3, X_4 → Y
Dependent variable	
Statistics	
t-test (two groups)	simple correlation and regression
ANOVA (more than two groups)	multiple correlation
ANCOVA	multiple regression (MLR)
MANOVA	
MANCOVA	

The two different strands of statistics can be brought together using the General Linear Model

Figure 16.2 : Research Design in Quantitative Research

Figure 16.3 given below shows type of study and research design.

Research Design	*Type of study*	
	Exploratory or Formulative	*Descriptive/ Diagnostics*
Overall Design	Flexible design (design must provide opportunity for considering different aspects of the problem)	Rigid design (design must make enough provision for protection against bias and must maximize reliability)
(i) Sampling design	Non-probability sampling design (purposive or judgement sampling)	Probability sampling design (random sampling)
(ii) Statistical design	No pre-planned design for analysis	Pre-planned design for analysis
(iii) Observational design	Unconstructed instruments for collection of data	Structured or well thought out Instruments for collection of data
(iv) Operational design	No fixed decisions about the Operational procedures	Advance decisions about operational decisions

Figure 16.3 : Type of Study and Research Design

16.3 DESIGN OF SAMPLING PLAN

A sampling plan is a mechanism by which the sampling units of a study are selected from the sampling frame of the population. The selection of sampling plan in a study in turn affects the cost and time to conduct the study, and the reliability of inferences of the study. Hence, it should be selected with utmost care. The sampling plan can be classified into probability sampling plans and non-probability sampling plans. Different sampling plans in each of these categories are listed as follow:

Probability Sampling Plans

1. Simple random sampling
2. Systematic sampling
3. Stratified random sampling
4. Cluster sampling
5. Multi-stage sampling

Non-probability Sampling Plans

1. Convenience/incidental sampling
2. Purposive sampling
3. Judgment sampling
4. Quota sampling
5. Snow ball sampling

16.4 DESIGN OF EXPERIMENT

There are three basic principles of experimental designs: (1) the Principle of Replication; (2) the Principle of Randomization; (3) Principle of Local Control. (Fisher, 1954).

Different models of experimental designs are:

(a) Informal experimental designs:
 (i) Before-and-after without control design.
 (ii) After-only control design.
 (iii) Before-and-after with control design.

(b) Formal experimental designs:
 (i) Completely randomized design (C.R. Design).
 (ii) Randomised block design (R.B. Design).
 (iii) Latin square design (L.S. Design).
 (iv) Factorial Design.

16.5 DESIGN OF INSTRUMENT OF MEASUREMENT

The questionnaire/test/scale/interview schedule/observation/case study must contains provisions to collect all the data items which are required for testing different hypotheses or finding answers to research questions.

16.6 DATA COLLECTION

Research Design must contain procedures for administration of test/questionnaire/scale or conduct of in-depth interview/case study/observation.

16.7 DATA ANALYSIS

Design of Research should specify the nature of data and techniques for its analysis. The analysis of data involves one or more of the following tasks:

- Computation of statistics, viz., mean, median, mode, standard deviation, coefficient of variation, coefficient of skewness

- Designing regression equation estimating response variable as a function of set of independent variable
- Performing correlation analysis
- Testing different hypotheses relating to various issues of the research
- Factor analysis
- Discriminant analysis
- Conjoint analysis

or

It involves incident-by-incident coding such as :

- In-vivo coding, Focused Coding, Axial coding, Theoretical Coding,
- Comparative Methods (i.e., comparisons at each level of analytic work)
- Writing memos.
- Sorting out memo to find the Theoretical Code(s).

16.8 INTERPRETATION OF RESULTS

The following steps are involved:

- Defining the real world problem
- Formulating a model of the real world problem
- Deducing model conclusions
- Interpretation of real world conclusions
- Validating of results.

16.9 PROCEDURES

Procedures for the conduct of study should be streamlined keeping in view the time constraints and cost of the project. Whole research work needs to be divided into different phases. Each phase should specify the job to be executed during the phase. Example of division of work into different phases is given below:

16.9.1 Phase I

In the first phase, the investigator has to specify research work to be undertaken, for example,

- Selection of sample and size of sample and sub-sample
- Preparation of preliminary draft of the tools for collection of data
- Reviewing of related literature.

16.9.2 Phase II

This phase involves:

- Drafting, finalization and fine tuning of tools to be utilized for the present study.
- Finalization of schedule for the collection of data

16.9.3 Phase III

This phase is concerned with:

- Collection of data-Primary as well as secondary data.
- Transportation of data of spread-sheet (Independent and dependent variables)
- Scoring, tabulation and classification of data.

16.9.4 Phase IV

This phase involves:

- Identification and application of appropriate statistical techniques for the analysis of data.
- Using descriptive and inferential statistics for obtaining results

16.9.5 Phase V

This phase is concerned with:

- Findings and conclusions of the study in light of given objectives and hypotheses/research questions
- Discussing findings of the study in light of findings of other studies conducted earlier
- Suggestions/recommendations for policy implications

16.10 MAIN POINTS ABOUT RESEARCH DESIGN

1. Measurement of multiple outcomes is preferable to single outcomes. In other words, use more than one dependent variable: for example, achievement, attitudes, and transfer to a new process. Result: if no differences are obtained on one, differences on another may prove equally valuable and relevant.
2. Begin with dependent variables each having sufficient criterion reliability to minimize the probability that measurement error, *per se*, will make a significant difference actually present in the outcomes.
3. Select appropriate independent variables such that they are relevant and are arranged in realistic combination with each other to take advantage of interaction relationships. For example, it makes little sense to study class size as a variable unless one also brings in its relationship to teaching method, pupil characteristics, and other factors.

4. Allow for the relationship between personality characteristics and validation criteria in a flexible, rather than a fixed, fashion. For instance, rather than using the Strong Inventory to select medical school candidates across the broad, look for the additional sub-patterns which fall outside the "typical" medical interest profile but would predict success in some of the less prominent specialty fields as medical research, and medical school instruction. Otherwise, there is a risk of selecting out potentially successful candidates and creating professional stereotypes that are absolute rather than relative.
5. Emphasize the interaction between individual difference and particular learning principles or methods. Too much reliance has been placed on randomization, equate groups and formal statistical controls; too little reliance on controls by individual differences. In other words, instead of seeking general principles of education applying to everyone, seek empirically established principles about how to deal with people of particular types. (Isaac and Michael, 1972)

References

Bailey, K.D. (1987). *Methods of Social Research.* 3rd. edn. New York: Free Press.

Best, J. and Kahn, J. (2009). *Research in Education.* 10th edition, Needham Heights: Allyn and Bacon.

Cozby, P. (2009). *Methods in Behavioural Research.* 10th edition, Bemont: Wadsworth.

Festinger, L. and Katz, D. (1976) (eds.). *Research Methods in the Behavioral Sciences.* New Delhi: Amerind Publishing Co.

Good, Carter V. (1966). *Essentials of Educational Research: Methodology and Design.* New York: Applleton-Century Crofts.

Goode, W.J., and Hatt, P.K. (1990). *Methods in Social Research.* New Delhi: McGraw-Hill.

Guthrie, G. (2010). *Basic Research Methods.* New Delhi: Sage.

CHAPTER

17

Sampling Procedures

17.0 DEFINING THE POPULATION

Residents in a region, account holders of a bank, educational institutions in a state, employees in public sectors, students in colleges of education, etc., are considered to be different populations. The population may be all the individuals of a particular type, or a more restricted part of that group. Population, on the other hand, refers to the total items about which information is required. A population is any group of individuals that have one or more characteristics in common that are of interest to the researcher. The attributes that are the object of study is called characteristics and the units that are used are called the elementary units. The aggregate of all such units is the population.

The universe or population is of two types, finite and infinite, if the population contains fixed number of elements so that it is possible to list them in totality, it is called the finite population. For example, what is total population of teachers in higher education in Jammu city? The population where we cannot make out the total number of items, it is called infinite population. For example, it is impossible to list the number of stars in the sky.

The population of concrete individuals is called existent population, while the collection of all possible ways in which an event can materialize, as a hypothetical population. All the 200 students of M.Ed. of Jammu City is an example of existent population And the population of heads and tails obtained by tossing an infinite number of times is an example of hypothetical population.

17.1 SAMPLING

It is not possible to gather information from everyone or everything of a population. The primary purpose of research is to discover principles that have universal application. But study of whole population would be impracticable if not impossible. Some populations are so large that their characteristics cannot be measured, before the measurement could be completed, the population would have changed. For example, it is very difficult to conduct a reading experiment of fifth grade students in English subject of private and government schools in India. In this study, a large number of manpower would be required. A lot of cost would be involved. Researchers and students working hours would also be required in the conduct of such a huge experiment. Time, money manpower involved in complete enumeration is very, very high. The goal of finding a representative sample (or subset) of population, therefore, becomes necessity. Hence, a small proportion of a population called sample is selected for observation and analysis. In other words, a finite part of a statistical population is selected whose properties are studied to gain information about the whole. (Webster, 1085).

Sampling, therefore, is a process concerned with the selection of a relatively small portion of population to draw valid inferences or generalization on the basis of careful observation and analysis. A measured value based upon sample is a *statistic*. A population value inferred from a statistic is a *parameter*. The sampling process comprises several stages namely:

- *Defining the population of concern*: Any group of individuals that have one or more characteristics in common that are of interest to the researcher. It involves, (a) elements, (b) sampling units, (c) extent, and (d) time.
- *Specifying a sampling frame*: A set of items or events possible to measure. In order to select a sample from given population it is necessary to have a complete, accurate, and up-to date list of all the units of population. A sample should be selected in such a way that it has all the characteristics of the population. Such a list is known as sampling frame. If sampling frame is not available at the time of investigation, it would be difficult to conduct investigation or survey. It is therefore, essential to prepare sampling frame beforehand.
- *Specifying the sampling unit*: The sampling unit is the basic unit that contains elements of the target population.

- *Determining the sample size*: Researcher can actually calculate the required size using the following formula: $N = ((K \times S)/E)^2$ where K is desired confidence level, S is sample standard deviation, and E is the required level of precision.
- *Selecting Sampling Methods*: Probability or Non-Probability Sampling Method.
- Implementing the sampling plan: collection of data, analysis of data and replication of results.

17.2 SAMPLING METHODS

Sampling methods can be classified into *probability sampling* and *non-probability sampling* methods.

17.2.1 Probability Sampling

A probability sampling is one in which every unit in the population has a chance (greater than zero) of being selected in the sample, and this probability can be accurately determined. The combination of these traits makes it possible to produce unbiased estimates of population total, by weighting sampled units according to their probability of selection. In other words, in probability sampling the units of population are not selected at the discretion of the researcher but by means of certain procedures which ensure that every unit of a population has one fixed probability of being included in the sample.

When every element in the population *does* have the same probability of selection, this is known as an 'equal probability of selection' (EPS) design. Such designs are also referred to as 'self-weighting' because all sampled units are given the same weight. These various ways of probability sampling have two things in common:

1. Every element has a known non-zero probability of being sampled, and
2. It involves random selection at some point.

Probability sampling is based on the principles of randomization which has two important applications in research:

1. Selecting a group of individuals for observation who are representative of the population about which the researcher wishes to generalize; or
2. Equating experimental and control groups in an experiment. Assigning individuals by random assignment is the best method of providing for their equivalence.

A random sampling is not necessarily an identical representation of population. Characteristics of successive samples drawn from the population may differ to some degree, but it is possible to estimate their variation from the population characteristics and from each other. The variation is known as sampling error which refers to the chance variations that occur in sampling with randomization. These variations are predictable and taken into account in data analysis techniques.

Probability sampling methods are: (1) Simple Random Sampling, (2) Stratified Sampling, (3) Systematic Sampling, (4) Cluster Sampling, and (5) Multistage Sampling.

17.2.2 Simple Random Sampling

A random sample involves what is called probability sampling, which means that every member of the population has a nonzero probability of being selected for the sample. In other words, all members of the population have some chance of being included in the sample.

In a Simple Random Sample (SRS) of a given size, all such subsets of the frame are given an equal probability. Each element of the frame thus has an equal probability of selection: the frame is not sub-divided or partitioned. Furthermore, any given *pair* of elements has the same chance of selection as any other such pair (and similarly for triples, and so on). This minimizes bias and simplifies analysis of results. In particular, the variance between individual results within the sample is a good indicator of variance in the overall population, which makes it relatively easy to estimate the accuracy of results. Simple random sampling has three plus points:

(i) A simple random sample is an unbiased sample, which means that those individuals selected vary only as they would be due to random fluctuation;
(ii) There is nothing in the sample that would make this sample different from other samples; and
(iii) It is the representative of the population from which it is selected.

However, Simple Random Sampling can be vulnerable to sampling error because the randomness of the selection may result in a sample that doesn't reflect the make-up of the population. For instance, a simple random sample of ten people from a given country will *on average* produce five men and five women, but any given trial is likely to over represent one sex and under represent the other. Systematic and stratified techniques, discussed below, attempt to overcome this problem by using information about the population to choose a more representative sample.

Simple random sampling is always an 'equal probability of selection' (EPS) design, but not all EPS designs are simple random sampling. A more convenient way of selecting a random sample in experiment is by the use of a Table of random numbers. Many such Tables have been generated by computers.

17.2.3 Random Selection and Random Assignment

Random selection and random assignment are not the same, but they are both used to obtain representativeness and eliminate possible bias. In random selection, the individuals are randomly selected representing a population and in random assignment the individuals are randomly assigned to groups or treatments.

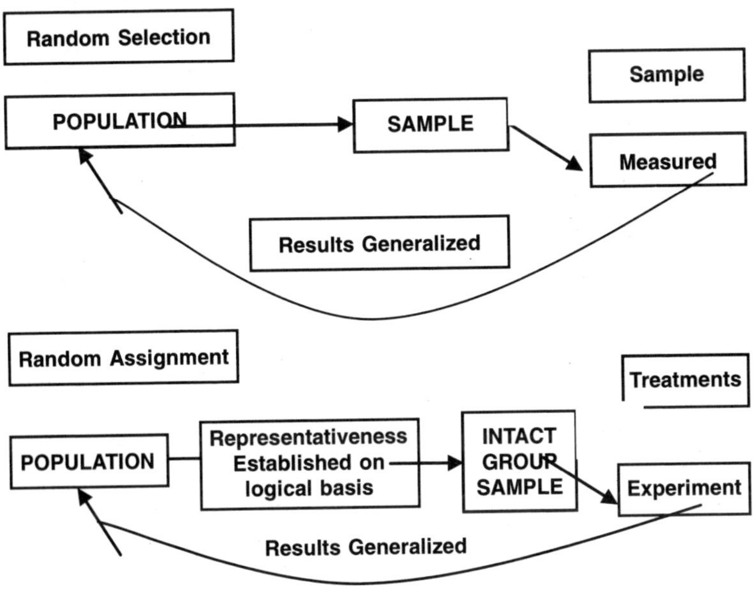

17.2.4 Simple Random Sampling Method: Lottery Method

If we wish to draw a sample of 50 individuals from a population of 600 students enrolled in a school, we could place the 600 names in a container and, blindfolded, draw one name at a time until the sample of 50 was selected. This procedure is cumbersome and is rarely used.

17.2.5 Simple Random Sampling with Replacement

In this method of sampling each unit of the population has the equal probability of being selected as a 'n' units of the sample given by the following formula:

The probability of selection of each unit = 1/N

The selection of the unit from the sample can be done using either (1) Random Number Table or (2) manually or (3) computer generated number or (4) using Monte-Carlo simulation.

The Random Number Table contains four digit numbers in rectangular format with rows and columns. The steps of the simple random sampling with replacement are:

1. If N is a three-digit number, i.e. 835
2. Suppose a sample of 20 is to be selected
3. Fix the initial position in the random number table (for example, 101)
4. Read the first three digits of the number and select the unit from the population
5. Decide the direction of movement for selecting the next number
6. Accordingly, select the first three digits of the next number in the random number table
7. Then select the unit from the population with corresponding serial number as the second unit of the sample. Later replace that unit in the population
8. Repeat steps 5-7 until the required number of units of the sample are selected from the population.

When using table of random numbers:

(a) One must number the population numbers serially.
(b) Numbers above 835 and below 101 are to be deleted.
(c) Repeated numbers are also not to be included in the sample.

The procedure of selection can be illustrated by an example.

Random Number Table (Tippett)

2952	6641	3992	9792	7979	5911
3170	5624	4167	9525	1545	1396
7203	5356	1300	2693	2370	7483
3408	2769	3563	6107	6913	7691
0560	5246	1112	9025	6008	8126

If we randomly decide to read the table numbers from left to right, starting from the first row itself, we obtain the following numbers: 295, 266, 413, 992, 997, 279, 795, 911, 317, 056, 244, 167, 952, 515, 451, 396, 720, 353, 561, 300, 269, 323, 707, 483, 340.

Selected numbers are : 295, 266, 413, 279, 795, 317, 244, 167, 515, 451, 396, 720, 353, 561, 300, 269, 323, 707, 483 and 340 (n = 20).

17.2.6 Random Assignment

These 20 numbered members of the population as mentioned are selected randomly. This sample can be further divided into two equated groups of 10 each for experimentation. Then selection of each group of 10 members can be done on the basis of assigning odd numbers to one group and even numbers to other group.

17.2.7 Simple Random Sampling without Replacement

In this method of sampling, each unit of the population has a varying probability of being selected as a unit of the sample. Formula for the selection of sample in this context is:

The probabilty of selection of the first unit = 1/N
The probability of selection of the second unit = 1/N–1
The probabilty of selection of the nth unit = 1/N–(n–1)

The units of the sample are selected from the population based on the respective probability given above using Monte-Carlo simulation.

Steps of Monte-Carlo simulation are:

1. Find the probability , 1/N. If N=10, then 1/N is 0.1.
2. Find the cumulative probabilities of the N intervals.
3. Find a two digit random number from the Random Number Table and check the range in which it lies in Table.

TABLE 17.1
Cumulative Probabilities

Unit of Population	*Probability*	*Cumulative Probability*	*Cumulative Probability Range*
1	0.1	0.1	0.0-0.09
2	0.1	0.2	0.10-0.19
3	0.1	0.3	0.20-0.29
4	0.1	0.4	0.30-0.39
5	0.1	0.5	0.40-0.49
6	0.1	0.6	0.50-0.59
7	0.1	0.7	0.60-0.69
8	0.1	0.8	0.70-0.79
9	0.1	0.9	0.80-0.89
10	0.1	1.0	0.90-0.99

4. Select the corresponding unit of the population and include it as the first unit of the sample.
5. Find the probability 1/(N–1) and repeat steps 2-4 to select the secound unit of the sample from the population.
6. like this, repeat steps 2-4 until all the remaining units are selected from the third unit till the nth unit of the sample are selected from the population using probabilities, 1/(N–2)......1/(N - (n–1), respectively.

17.2.8 Stratified Sampling

Simple Random Sampling may also be cumbersome and tedious when sampling is from an unusually large target population. In some cases, investigators are interested in research questions specific to sub-groups of the population. For example, researchers might be interested in examining whether cognitive ability as a predictor of job performance is equally applicable across racial groups. Simple Random Sampling cannot accommodate the needs of researchers in this situation because it does not provide sub-samples of the population

Where the population embraces a number of distinct categories, the frame can be organized by these categories into separate "strata". Each stratum is then sampled as an independent sub-population, out of which individual elements can be randomly selected. There are several potential benefits to stratified sampling.

First, dividing the population into distinct, independent strata can enable researchers to draw inferences about specific sub-groups that may be lost in a more generalized random sample.

Second, utilizing a stratified sampling method can lead to more efficient statistical estimates (provided that strata are selected based upon relevance to the criterion in question, instead of availability of the samples).

Third, sometimes data are more readily available for individual, pre-existing strata within a population than for the overall population; in such cases, using a stratified sampling approach may be more convenient than aggregating data across groups.

Finally, since each stratum is treated as an independent population, different sampling approaches can be applied to different strata, potentially enabling researchers to use the approach best suited (or most cost-effective) for each identified sub-group within the population.

A stratified sampling approach is most effective when three conditions are met :

1. Variability within strata is minimized
2. Variability between strata is maximized
3. The variables upon which the population is stratified are strongly correlated with the desired dependent variable.

The stratified sampling focuses on:

(i) important subpopulations and ignores irrelevant ones;
(ii) use of different sampling techniques for different sub-populations;
(iii) the accuracy/efficiency of estimation, and
(iv) greater balancing of statistical power of tests of differences between strata by sampling equal numbers from strata varying widely in size.

17.2.9 Post-stratification

Stratification is sometimes introduced after the sampling phase. This process is called "post-stratification". This approach is typically implemented due to a lack of prior knowledge of an appropriate stratifying variable or when the experimenter lacks the necessary information to create a stratifying variable during the sampling phase. Although the method is susceptible to the pitfalls of post hoc approach, it can provide several benefits in the right situation. Implementation usually follows a simple random sample. In addition to allowing for stratification on an ancillary variable, post-stratification uses weightage which can improve the precision of a sample's estimates

17.2.10 Choice-based Sampling

Choice-based sampling is one of the stratified sampling strategies. In choice-based sampling, the data are stratified on the target and a sample is taken from each strata so that the rare target class will be more represented in the sample. The model is then built on this biased sample. The effects of the input variables on the target are often estimated with more precision with the choice-based sample even when a smaller overall sample size is taken, compared to a random sample. The results usually must be adjusted to correct the oversampling.

17.2.11 Probability Proportional to Size Sampling

In some cases the sample designer has access to an "auxiliary variable" or "size measure", believed to be correlated to the variable of interest, for each element in the population. This data can be used to improve accuracy in sample design. One option is to use the auxiliary variable as a basis for stratification.

Another option is probability-proportional-to-size ('PPS') sampling, in which the selection probability for each element is set to be proportional to its size measure, up to a maximum of 1. In a simple PPS design, these selection probabilities can then be used as the basis for proportional sampling. However, this has the drawbacks of variable sample size, and different portions of the population may still be over or under-represented due to chance variation in selections. To address this problem, PPS may be combined with a systematic approach.

Example: Suppose we have seven colleges of different streams populations of 5461, 1850, 2092, 3508, 2112, 318 and 482 students respectively (total 15823 students–N), and we want to use student population as the basis for a PPS sample of size. To do this, we could allocate .05% to each strata. Total sample (n) would be 792 (Round figure). Each strata would get proportional representation through random sampling.

TABLE 17.2
Showing Sample Size by Strata

Strata (college)	*Strata (size)*	*Sample size by strata*	
Arts & Science	5461	5461×.05= 274	
MBA	1850	92	
Medical	2092	105	
Education	3508	175	
Engineering	2112	106	
Law	318	16	
Pharmacy	482	24	
Total	15,823= N	792= n*	.05% of the population

The PPS approach can improve accuracy for a given sample sizes by concentrating sample on large elements that have the greatest impact on population estimates. PPS sampling is commonly used for surveys of characteristics of school populations of different strata, where element size varies greatly and auxiliary information is often available for instance, a survey attempting to measure the learning outcomes of different educational institutions.

There are, however, some potential drawbacks of using stratified sampling. First, identifying strata and implementing such an approach can increase the cost and complexity of sample selection.

Second, when examining multiple criteria, stratifying variables may be related to some, but not to others, further complicating the *design*, and potentially reducing the utility of the strata.

Finally, in some cases (such as design with a large number of strata, or those with a specified minimum sample size per group), stratified sampling can potentially require a larger sample (although in most cases, the required sample size is not larger than would be required for simple random sampling.

17.2.12 Disproportional Stratified Sampling

If the variances are not equal, then disproportional stratified sampling should be used. For example, there are three different strata: 1. Schools in rural areas =500, 2. Schools in semi-urban areas = 400, and 3. Schools in urban areas = 300. Variance of these locations on 0-10 scale are 49, 16, and 4 respectively. Sample size is 90. Sample unis for each stratum is determined as given below in Table 17.3.

TABLE 17.3
Disproportional Stratified Sampling

Stratum Number	*Size of Stratum*	$p=N\cdot/N$	σ_1	$p\sigma_1 n$	$p_1\sigma_1$	$p\sigma_1 n/\Sigma p\sigma_1$
1	500	0.416	7	262.5	2.92	55
2	400	0.333	4	120.00	1.33	25
3	300	0.25	2	45.00	0.50	10
Total					$\Sigma p\sigma_{1-}$ 4.75	90

1. p_1= 500/1200= 0.42, p_{2-} 400/1200= 0.33 and so on
2. Sample : n=90
3. σ_1= under root of variance and given on 0-10 scale.

Thus, sample selected under disproportionate stratified sampling for each stratum is: Schools in rural areas=55, Schools in semi-urban areas=25, Schools in urban areas = 10.

17.2.13 Cluster Sampling

Cluster sampling is a sampling technique in which population is divided into different clusters. Numbers within each cluster are dissimilar (heterogeneous) in terms of their attributes, but different clusters are similar to each other. This leads to the inference that each cluster can be treated as a small population which possesses all the attributes of the population. First clusters are selected. All the units of that cluster are selected randomly to arrive at inference about the population. Some of the points to be considered for cluster sampling are:

1. Use when the studied population is spread across a wide area such that simple random sampling would be difficult to implement in accessing the selected sample.
2. Divide the population into a set of different coherent areas.
3. Select areas randomly to assess various attributes.
4. Access all subjects in the selected areas. If it is not possible, select a significant random sample and use the same selection rules in each cluster.

For example, in a study of the opinions of homeless across a country, rather than study a few homeless people in all towns, a number of towns are selected and a significant number of homeless people are interviewed in each one.

17.2.14 Multistage Sampling

In a large scale survey covering the entire nation/sub-continent, the size of the sampling frame will be too large which leads to more time and cost of the study. In such study, multi-stage sampling technique is used in designing a smaller sampling frame. This will make the study feasible, practical in terms of cost and time.

Multi-stage sampling is a complex form of cluster sampling in which two or more levels of units are embedded one in the other. For example, consider the study of quality of teacher education in India. It is not feasible to conduct study on a very large sample frame. Hence, multi-stage sampling technique is used for selection of sample. Following steps are used in the multi-stage sampling.

- In the first stage, different states of the country are sampled from each region using stratified sampling consists of constructing the clusters that will be used to sample from.
- In the second stage, a sample of districts from the selected states is selected using cluster sampling technique.
- In each selected district, primary units, i.e. a sample of colleges of education is randomly selected from each district.

This study involves three stages of sampling. The highest levels of sampling units are states, and the lowest levels of sampling units are colleges of education. This technique, thus, is essentially the process of taking random samples of preceding random samples. It probably solves more of the problems inherent to random sampling. Moreover, it is an effective strategy because it banks on multiple randomizations. As such, it is extremely useful.

17.2.15 Systematic Sampling

Systematic sampling relies on arranging the target population according to some ordering scheme and then selecting elements at regular intervals through that ordered list. Systematic sampling involves a random start and then proceeds with the selection of every *k*th element from then onwards. It is important that the starting point is not automatically the first in the list, but is instead randomly chosen from within the first to the *k*th element in the list. A simple example would be to select every 10th name from the telephone directory (an 'every 10th' sample, also referred to as 'sampling with a skip of 10').

As long as the starting point is randomized, systematic sampling is a type of probability sampling. It is easy to implement and the stratification induced can make it efficient, if the variable by which the list is ordered is correlated with the variable of interest. When population can be accurately listed and finite, a method of systematic selection will provide a sample which approximates a random sample.

For example, let the size of the population (N) be 1000 and the sample size be 50. The units of the sampling frame are divided into a number of intervals based on the ratio N/n as shown below:

> Sampling intervals width, I= N/n =1000/50= 20. The sampling frame consists of units with serial numbers from 1 to 1000. This range is divided into 40 intervals viz., 1-20, 21-40, 41-60, 61-80, 81-100 and so on———— 981-1000. Then a number from the first interval 1-20 is selected randomly. Let the randomly selected unit form the first interval of population is 15. Then, the second unit of the sample is the unit in population with serial number 35 which is obtained by adding 20 to 15. As per these guidelines, the units of the population with serial numbers 55, 75, 95, 105 and so on ——— 995 are treated as the third, fourth, fifth, sixth——49th units of the sample respectively.

However, systematic sampling is especially vulnerable to periodicities in the list. If periodicity is present and the period is a multiple or factor of the interval used, the sample is especially likely to be unrepresentative of the overall population, making the scheme less accurate than simple random sampling.

Example: Consider a street where the odd-numbered houses are all on the north (expensive) side of the road, and the even-numbered houses are all on the south (cheap) side. Under the sampling scheme given above, it is impossible' to get a representative sample; either the houses sampled will all be from the odd-numbered, expensive side, or they will all be from the even-numbered, cheap side.

Another drawback of systematic sampling is that even in scenarios where it is more accurate than simple random sampling, its theoretical properties make it difficult to *quantify* that accuracy. (In the two examples of systematic sampling that are given above, much of the potential sampling error is due to variation between neighbouring houses—but because this method never selects two neighbouring houses, the sample will not give us any information on that variation.)

17.3 NON-PROBABILITY SAMPLING

Non-probability sampling is any sampling method where some elements of the population have *no* chance of selection (these are sometimes referred to as 'out of coverage'/'under covered'), or where the probability of selection can't be accurately determined. It involves the selection of elements based on assumptions regarding the population of interest, which forms the criteria for selection. Hence, because the selection of elements is non-random, non-probability sampling does not allow the estimation of sampling errors. These conditions place limits on how much information a sample can provide about the population. Information about the relationship between sample and population is limited, making it difficult to extrapolate from the sample to the population. In non-probability sampling the units of population are selected at the discretion of the researcher.

Non-probability Sampling includes: Convenience Sampling, Quota Sampling, Purposive Sampling, Judgment Sampling, and Snowball Sampling.

17.3.1 Convenience Sampling

Convenience sampling (sometimes known as *grab* or *opportunity sampling*) is a type of non-probability sampling which involves the sample being drawn from that part of the population which is close to hand. That is, a sample population selected because it is readily available and convenient. The researcher using such a sample cannot scientifically make generalizations about the total population from this sample because it would not be representative enough. For example, if the interviewer was to conduct such a survey at a shopping center early in the morning on a given day, the people that he/she could interview would be limited to those given there at that given time, which would not represent the views of other members of society in such an area, if the survey was to be conducted at different times of day and several times per week. This type of sampling is most useful for pilot testing.

In most of the conditions, the following may be true in case of convenient sampling :

- The sampling units may be distributed sparsely
- Many respondents will refuse to fill the questionnaire
- Some respondents will not cooperate in filling the questionnaires
- Some of the interviewers may not be serious in selecting the sampling units as per the assumed sampling plan.

Several important considerations for researchers using convenience samples include:

1. Are there controls within the research design or experiment which can serve to lessen the impact of a non-random, convenience sample whereby ensuring the results will be more representative of the population?
2. Is there good reason to believe that a particular convenience sample would or should respond or behave differently than a random sample from the same population?
3. Is the question being asked by the researcher that can adequately be answered using a convenience sample?

17.3.2 Quota Sampling

In quota sampling, the population is first segmented into mutually exclusive sub-groups, just as in stratified sampling. Then judgment is used to select the subjects or units from each segment based on a specified proportion. For example, an interviewer may be told to sample 200 females and 300 males between the age of 45 and 60. Let percetage of males and females between the age of 45 and 60 is 25% and 20% respectively. The sample size of males will be 50 and 60 for females. (i.e. 0.25n for males and 0.20n for females).

It is this second step which makes the technique one of non-probability sampling. In quota sampling the selection of the sample is non-random. For example interviewers might be tempted to interview those who look most helpful. The problem is that these samples may be biased because not everyone gets a chance of selection. This random element is its greatest weakness and quota *versus* probability has been a matter of controversy for many years.

17.3.3 Purposive Sampling

Purposive sampling targets a particular group of people. When the desired population for the study is rare or very difficult to locate, purposive sampling may be the only option. For example, you are interested in studying cognitive processing speed of young adults who have suffered closed head brain injuries in automobile accidents. This would be a difficult population to find. Your city has a well-established rehabilitation hospital and you contact the director to ask permission to recruit from this population. The major problem with purposive sampling is that the type of people who are available for study may be different from those in the population who can't be located and this might introduce a source of bias. For example, those available for study through the rehabilitation hospital may have more serious injuries requiring longer rehabilitation, and their families may have greater education and financial resources (which resulted in their choosing. Similarly, purposive sampling technique is used in the study of mentally retarded children.

17.3.4 Judgment Sampling

The judgment sampling is non-probability sampling in which the sampling units are selected on the advice of some experts or by the institution or opinion of the researcher himself. Steps involved in the selection of sampling units are:

In the first case, an expert who is familiar with the sampling frame guides the researcher in selecting the sampling units from the sampling frame.

In the second case, researcher applies his or her intuitive judgment and previous experience in selecting the sampling units.

In this sampling method, there is more chance of biases. If the exercise is done more seriously, it would lead to better results. This sampling is also called purposive sampling when sampling units are identified from the population selectively. This sampling technique is applied for sampling the population related to rare events in which the members of the population are not equally qualified to become the member of the sampling frame and hence the members of the sample. For instance, people living below poverty line and their educational problems.

17.3.5 Snowball Sampling

The snowball sampling is a restrictive multi-stage sampling in which initially certain numbers of sampling units (respondents) are randomly selected. Later, additional sampling units are selected through referral process. This means that the initially selected respondents provide addresses of additional respondents for the interviewers.

Initial respondents may be randomly selected, for example, from the information contained in telephone directories. Similarly, students are identified randomly from the classroom attendance register, and additional students are included on the basis of information from the already selected sample. This is an inexpensive and convenient non-probability sampling method which suits the situations where the development of sampling frame is difficult and time-consuming task.

17.4 CHARACTERISTICS OF A GOOD SAMPLE

(1) A good sample adheres to sampling procedures and well defined processes. These are:

- Defining the population of concern
- Specifying a sampling frame, a set of items or events possible to measure
- Specifying a sampling method for selecting items or events from the frame
- Determining the sample size
- Implementing the sampling plan
- Sampling and data collection
- Reviewing the sampling process and

(2) A good sample is based upon a good sampling design and takes into account the following points:

- Relate to the objectives of the investigation;
- Design should be practical and achievable;
- Design should be cost-effective in terms of equipment and labour;
- Provide estimates of population parameters that are truly representative and unbiased; and
- Adequately provide answers to research questions.

(3) A good sample is ideally a representative sample of the population from which it has been drawn. It ensures randomization of selection, i.e. it should be:

- Taken at *random* so that every member of the population of data has an equal chance of selection;
- Large enough to give sufficient *precision*; and
- Unbiased by the sampling procedure.

These also need to be noted in the design as otherwise a wrong interpretation may arise from the results.

(4) A good Sample allows sufficiently reliable information about the particular population under investigation.

- The type of sampling or rather where the sampling occurs determines how much control; the investigator has over the individuals studied. If the sampling is to take place in the laboratory then the investigator has much greater control in the design of the experiment. Design is critical in determining the sampling strategy and analysis of results.
- When estimating population parameters from sample statistics, the sample size is important; larger sample size usually result in greater statistical reliability. However, optimum sample size is a balance between statistical and practical considerations.
- Selection of sample is based upon population. Therefore, reliable source of population should be used, for example census records, telephone directories, school records etc.

(5) A good sample is *based upon a large sample*. Where the frame and population are identical, statistical theory yields exact recommendations on sample size. Where it is not straightforward to define a frame representative of the population, is more important to ensure that all sources of variation are embraced in the frame. Large number of observations is of no value if major sources of variation are neglected in the study.

- Researcher can actually calculate the required size using the following formula:

$$N = ((K \times S)/E)^2$$

where K is desired confidence level, S is sample standard deviation, and E is the required level of precision. In case the researcher is not interested in using the above formula, he can, however, use a 'sample size calculator' where the only things you need to know are: the population size; the confidence interval what range you will accept above and below the mean, i.e. 0.05 or 0.01 confidence level.

(6) Good sample should take note of dispersion factor. Universe may be homogeneous or heterogeneous in nature. If the universe is homogeneous, a small sample can serve the pupose. But if the nature is hetrogeneous, a large sample will serve the pupose.

Required Sample Size

Levels Population	*Confidence*		
	95% C.L. *±5% C.L.*	*99% C.L.* *±5% C.L.*	*99% C.L.* *±1% C.L.*
30	28	29	insufficient
100	80	87	99
500	217	286	485
1,000	278	400	943
5,000	357	588	3845
10,000	370	624	6247
50,000	381	657	12486
100,000	383	661	14267
1,000,000	384	665	16369

(7) For technical surveys where items are to be intensively and continuously studied, a good sample should contain small numbers.

(8) A good sample falls within precision limits. Precision is the range within which the population average lies in accordance with the reliability specified in the confidence level as a percentage of the estimate of as a numerical quantity. Moreover, the sample mean should be closer to true mean (population mean).

(9) A good sample is manageable. It is time bond, cost effective, and accessible.

(10) A good sample ensures minimum level of sampling and non-sampling errors. Sampling errors are caused by sampling design. It includes:

(a) *Selection error*: Incorrect selection probabilities are used.
(b) *Estimation error*: Biased parameter estimate because of the elements in these samples.

Non-sampling errors are caused by the mistakes in data processing. It includes:

(a) *Over coverage*: Inclusion of data from outside of the population.
(b) *Under coverage*: Sampling frame does not include elements in the population.
(c) *Measurement error*: The respondents misunderstanding the question.
(d) *Processing error*: Mistakes in data coding.
(e) *Non-response.*

(11) Standard Error

(a) The standard error helps in testing the difference between the observed and the expected frequencies that may arise due to chance. The criterion usually adopted is that if the difference is less than three times the standard error and it has a chance of failing, it is called a significant difference.

(b) The standard error gives an idea about the realiability and requirement of a sample. The smaller the standard error, the greater is the uniformity of sampling distribution. Therefore, greater is the reliability of the sample. Likewise, the greater the standard error, the greater is the difference between the observed and the expected frequencies. In such a situation, non-reliability of the sample and it varies inversely with the size of the sample.

(c) The standard error enables the researcher to specify the limits within which the parameters of the population are expected to lie with a specified degree of confidence level.

References

Aggarwal, Y.P. (1988). Better Sampling—Concepts, Techniques and Evaluation. New Delhi: Sterling Publications.

Best, J. and Kahn, J. (2009). *Research in Education.* 10th edition, Needham Heights: Allyn and Bacon.

Chaudary, A. and Stenger, H. (1992). Survey Sampling: Theory and Methods. New York: Marcel Dekker.

Cochran, W.G. (1984). Sampling Techniques. New Delhi: Wiley Eastern.

Deming, W.E. (1960). Sample Design in Business Research. New York: John Wiley and Sons.

Hennerson, M.E., Morris, E.E. and Fitz-Gubbon, C.T. (1988). How to Measure Attitudes, New Delhi: Sage.

Kothari, C.R. (2004). Research Methodology: Methods and Techniques. New Delhi: New Age International Publishers.

Koul, L. (2009). *Methodology of Educational Research.* Vikas Publishing House, New Delhi.

Panneersevam, R. (2004). Research Methodology. New Delhi: Prentice-Hall of India.

Plutchik, R. (1968). Foundations of Experimental Research. New York: Harper and Row.

CHAPTER

18

Psychological Tests : Development and Standardization

18.0 PSYCHOLOGICAL TESTS

Psychological tests are instruments designed to describe and measure a sample of certain aspects of human behaviour or traits. These tests are used for the purpose of selection, classification, prediction, and guidance and evaluation of educational programmes. They are used:

1. to describe status or a prevailing condition at a particular time,
2. to measure changes in status produced by modifying factors, and
3 to predict future behaviour on the basis of present performance.

Psychological tests are mostly employed as tools in school surveys, school appraisal programmes, experimental investigations, complex causal relationship studies and prognostic research. These tests can be employed in different situations or conditions after necessary modifications. Psychological tests are standardized instruments; therefore, results derived from the large sample can be generalized or replicated.

Psychological tests yield objective and standardized descriptions of behaviour, quantified by numerical scores. Data gathered from these tests are easy to score, tabulate and can be statistically analyzed. Statistical Package for Social Science Research (SPSS) is time saver and cost effective for the analysis of data gathered from psychological tests.

18.1 TEST CATEGORIES

Psychological tests may be classified into four categories:

1. *Performance tests and Paper-pencil tests*: in performance tests the individual is required to manipulate objects or mechanical apparatus while their actions are observed and recorded by the examiner. Paper-pencil tests require the subjects to mark their response on a prepared sheet.
2. *Individual tests and Group tests*: individual testes are administered to the subjects individually whereas group tests are administered to the subject in a group
3. *Power tests and Speed tests*: power tests observe no time limit and the subjects attempt progressively more difficult tasks as long as they can, while speed tests involve the element of power where time limit is also observed.
4. *Standardized tests and Non-standardized tests or Teacher-made tests*: standardized tests are expertly designed and standardized through establishing their reliability and validity by careful statistical controls, whereas non-standardized tests are teacher-made tests and are based on the best logic and skill that the teacher can command. These are used to test the students' academic performance.

18.2 TYPES OF TESTS

Tests may be classified into six types namely, (1) Tests of Intelligence, (2) Achievement tests, (3) Aptitude tests, (4) Interest inventories, (5) Personality inventories, and (6) Projective devices.

18.2.1 Tests of Intelligence

Conceived of an inborn general ability which enters into performance of all activities and which differs in quantity from person to person, intelligence is a factor which determines a good deal of education outcomes. In experimental designs, intelligence is a significant variable which stands in need of being controlled. In studies of the causal relationship kind, intelligence of the subjects is a factor which has often to be reckoned. Intelligence test may be classified into:

(1) Performance test and verbal tests;

(2) Oral tests and paper-pencil tests;
(3) Group test and individual tests;
(4) Omnibus tests and battery of tests; and
(5) Point-scales and age-scales.

Whatever the types, an intelligence test is marked by the following characteristics:

(1) It measures the quality termed intelligence only indirectly through testing the person's present performance in situation where intelligence operates.
(2) The items in any intelligence test are numerous and varied. They test many different abilities which are supposed to constitute intelligence.
(3) The items are, as far as possible, knowledge-fee.
(4) The items are, as far as possible, culture-fee.
(5) Objective and unambiguous directions for administrating answering, scoring and interpreting the test invariably accompany it.
(6) The same test of intelligence supplies different norms for different age-level and group. Norms calculated for different ages and group are essential factor in the use and interpretation of test scores.

18.2.2 Achievement Tests

Achievement tests attempt to measure an individual learning outcome, or to measure degree of learning that has taken place as a result of exposure to a relatively defined learning experience. A test of achievement may be standardized nationally (IIT/IIM/NET), or regionally (State Level Eligibility Test) or locally, or it may be not be standardized at all.

Most tests used in school or colleges are achievement tests. Individual or group status in academic learning is determined through these tests. They are generally used in the promotion of student to next grade and the grouping of students for instructional purposes. Achievement scores are helpful in the grading of students. Data gathered can also be used for selection, placement of an individual, for appraisal of educational institution or assessing comparative status of different educational institutions, or between urban and rural schools, or between districts of the state, or between states of the country.

In research, achievement scores are used in ascertaining the effectiveness of the teaching methods or innovative practices as well as in evaluating the influences of courses of study. They are used for identifying and classifying children with learning difficulties and used for getting admission into special school services.

Measures of general achievement are used to survey learning in one or more academic areas. Tests that cover a number of academic areas are typically divided into several sub-tests and are referred to as "achievement batteries" Such batteries may be individually administered or group-administered. Sub-tests may comprise of reading, writing, vocabulary, mathematics, science and social studies. Achievement batteries are considered as standardized instruments.

Content validity is critical for all measures of achievement tests. Concurrent validity might be used to help establish a new achievement test's validity. For reliability coefficient, test-retest stability over test items, and standard error of measurement are used in multiple choice items. For test that also have items requiring some degree of subjectivity (e.g., easy-type answers) inter-scorer reliability is needed.

18.2.3 Aptitude Tests

Aptitude tests are prognostic tests, which are typically used to make predictions. Aptitude tests attempt to predict an individual's capacity to acquire improved performance with additional training. Aptitude tests tend to focus more on informal learning or life experiences as their subject matter, whereas achievement tests tend to focus on the learning that has occurred as a result of relatively structured input. For example,

(A) if s =9,what is its variance-v?
(a) 18, (b) 81, (c) 27(d) 72. (b) is a correct choice and is dependent on learning experience, hence achievement item)

(B) o is to O as x is to
(a)/(b) %, (c) X, (d) Y (c) is a correct choice and is based on informal learning, hence aptitude item).

Aptitude tests draw on a broader fund of informal abilities and are typically used to predict broader variables. The aptitude test in contrast to the achievement test is the utilization of the task that is not formally taught in the schools such as figural analogies and number series.

Aptitude tests are used to predict individual's capacity for specific profession or occupation. For example, selection for medical, law, management, engineering, art, music courses. Aptitude tests may be used to classify students into relatively homogenous groups for instructional purposes, screen individuals for particular educational programmes or guide individuals into the area where they can develop their potentials to the optimum level. For example, the Graduate Record Examination (GRE), the Scholastic Aptitude Test (SAT), the General Management Aptitude Test (GMAT), the Common Aptitude Test (CAT), National Eligibility Test (NET), the Medical College Admission Test, the Law School Admission Test (LSAT) are some of the standardized aptitude tests.

For the standardization of the test, predictive and construct validity is important. Test-retest reliability, stability over test items, and the standard error of measurement are critical in case of group-administered paper-pencil test with multiple choice items. Test items with some degree of subjectivity-inter-scorer and inter-tester reliability are needed.

18.2.4 Diagnostic Tests

Diagnostic tests are used to get "diagnostic information" or used for "diagnostic purposes". Student's difficulty or deficiency in specific area is identified and remedial measures are suggested for overcoming the difficulty. For example, a diagnostic reading test may contain a number of sub-tests each designed to diagnose specific deficiency or lack of skill in reading. Diagnostic tests in mathematics are designed to diagnose difficulties with mathematics concepts. The Key Math Revised Test, for example, contains 13 sub-tests designed to assess areas such as basic concepts (including knowledge of symbols, numbers, and fractions), operations (including skill in addition, subtraction, division, multiplication, and mental computation), applications (numerical problems employing variables such as money and time). Diagnostic information is obtained from an evaluation of the individual's performance in the various areas, subtests, and items. Total test scores are translated into grade equivalents, area performance may be translated into a general pattern of functioning, and sub-tests performance may be translated into a profile illustrating strengths and weaknesses. Information gathered from items may be useful in determining the skills or new practice to be included in a remedial programme.

Diagnostic Adaptive Behavior Scale (Tammy Reynolds, Zupanick & Mark Dombeck, 2010) is used to measure adaptive behavioural skills (conceptual skills, social skills, and practical life skills) and may help to determine the intensity and types of supports needed to maximize independent functioning and quality of life. However, a more useful and appropriate test for that purpose is the Supports Intensity Scale (AAIDD, 2004). Tests of IQ and adaptive functioning provide a sufficient basis for making a diagnosis of intellectual disability. Other tests (e.g., neuropsychological tests) may provide further detail, but are not necessary for diagnosis. All the relevant information (test scores, medical history, familial history, social history, educational history, interviews, and psychological testing information) is gathered together and taken into account before a diagnosis is made. Diagnosticians have some discretion. The test scores are weighted heavily but are not the sole basis for a diagnosis of intellectual disability. For instance, if a child appears to be smarter or more adaptive than the testing indicates this would be taken into account along with all the other data. The diagnostician then compares all this data to the diagnostic criteria for intellectual disabilities (intellectual developmental disorder, formerly mental retardation) before determining that an intellectual disability is present.

18.2.5 Interest Inventories

These attempt to measure the types of activities that an individual has a tendency to like and to choose. These related activities have been identified by careful analysis with Interest Inventories. One kind of instrument is to identify the interest patterns of successful practitioners in a number of vocational fields. A distinctive pattern has been discovered to be characteristic of each field. The assumption is that an individual is most satisfied, well-adjusted and successful in the profession of his or her liking.

Another inventory is based on the correlation between a number of activities from the areas of school, recreation, and work and his or her mechanical, computational, scientific, persuasive, artistic, literary, musical, social service, and clerical areas of interest. By sorting the subjects stated likes and dislikes into various interest areas, one can choose areas of highest interest.

Interest blanks or inventories are examples of self-report instruments in which individuals note their own likes and dislikes. These self-report instruments are really standardized interviews in which the subjects, through introspection, indicate feelings that may be interpreted in terms of what is known about interest patterns. Two commonly used interest inventories used to help individuals decide on the type of jobs they might want to pursue are the Kuder Preference Record and the Strong Campbell Interest Inventory.

Content validity is usually important in this context as are predictive and construct validity. Test-retest, stability over items, and standard error of measurement are the relevant forms of reliability.

18.2.6 Projective Devices

A projective instrument enables subjects to project their internal feelings, attitudes, needs, values, or wishes to an external object. Thus, the subjects may unconsciously reveal themselves as they react to the external object. The use of projective devices is particularly helpful in counteracting the tendency of subjects to try to appear in their best light, to respond as they believe they should. Projection tests include the Rorschach, the Thematic Apperception Test, and the Children's Apperception Test.

Projection may be accomplished through a number of techniques:

1. *Association Technique*: The respondent is asked to indicate what he or she sees, feels, or thinks when presented with a picture, cartoon, ink blot, word, or phrase. The Thematic Apperception Test, the Rorschach Ink Blot Test, and various word-association tests are familiar examples.
2. *Completion Technique*: The respondent is asked to complete an incomplete sentence or task. A sentence—completion instrument may include such items as:
   My greatest ambition is———————————
   My greatest fear is————————————
   I most enjoy———————————————
3. *Role-playing Technique*: Subjects are asked to improvise or act out a situation in which they have been assigned various roles. The researcher may observe such traits as hostility, frustration, dominance, sympathy, insecurity, prejudice or the absence of such traits.
4. *Creative or constructive Technique*: Permitting subjects to model clay, finger paint, play.

With dolls, play with toys, or draw or write imaginative stories about assigned situations may be revealing. The choice of color, form, words, and other reactions may provide opportunities to infer deep-seated feelings.

Construct validity is critical. Inter-scorer and inter-tester forms of reliability need to be established. Predictive validity also is probably important, whereas content validity is most likely not relevant. Test-retest reliability may also be pertinent.

18.2.7 Personality Measures

For the measurement of certain personality traits, various instruments have been devised in recent years. Personality testing, however, is yet in its formative years and more research is being carried out towards constructing and improving such tools. Personality measures are mainly of two kinds:

(1) *Personality measures are like interest inventories requiring the subject*: to self-report on their personality patterns. The individuals check response to certain questions or statements designed to measure certain personality traits or tendencies. Possessing many of the characteristics of inquiry forms like questionnaire and rating-scale they can be considered tests only to the extent that they are carefully standardized and yield quantitative measures. An inventory which has often been used as research device to identify and describe certain personality trait among students is the Mooney Problem Check list. It is an inventory (in two forms) to be used by students in reporting their own problems of adjustment. This inventory list a number of possible problems, classified in different categories from which the students have to check those which, from their own viewpoint, trouble them. These responses yield not only a verbal picture of individual's adjustment problems but also quantitative of difficulty he feels he is experiencing in his adjustment. The Mooney Problem Check list seems to have set the pattern for constructing more personality inventories by researchers in psychology and education.

The validity of these direct personality measures called inventories, however, is limited because individuals are sometimes unable to report their own reaction accurately or objectively. Lack of insight into their own selves, the emotional involvement of an individual with his own selves, the emotional involvement of an individual with his own problems and the tendency to withhold embarrassing responses-all these limit the effectiveness of such personal-adjustment scales.

(2) *Somewhat free from the limitation of personality inventories are the projective tests of personality* : The individual unconsciously projects his personality through his responses to given situations. Rorschach's ink-blot test, T.A.T., C.A.T. Rosenzeweig's picture-frustration study, are all projective techniques where, in reaction to vague visual pictures or symbols, individuals project their own personalities. Tautophone and Word-Association Tests present various sounds and words respectively as stimuli for the purpose of recording reactions which are later interpreted, according to set scheme of interpretation, to get a picture of the individual's personality. Tests and techniques of this category, however, present problems of more or less developmental and promotional try-out. Sentence-completion, story-completion, argument-completion, etc.

are other similar devices which depend on a good deal of subjective judgment and skill of interpretation.

(3) *Holtzman Inkblot Test (HIT)*: This test is a modification of of the Rorschach Test mentioned above. This test consists of 45 inkblot cards (and not 10 inkblot cards as we find in the case of Rorschach test) which are based on color, movement, shading and other factors involved in inkblot perception. Only one response per card is obtained from the respondent and responses are interpreted at three levels of form appropriateness. Form responses are interpreted for knowing the accuracy (F) or inaccuracy (F-) respondent's percepts, shading and colour for ascertaining his affectional and emotional needs; and movement responses for assessing the dynamic aspects of his life.

(4) *Tomkins-Horn Picture Arrangement Test*: This test is designed for group administration. It consists of 25 plates, each containing three sketches that may be arranged in different ways to portray sequence of events. The respondent is asked to arrange them in a sequence which he considers as reasonable. The responses are interpreted as providing evidence confirming certain norms, respondent's attitudes, etc.

The rationale of the projective method is to make the individual organize a series of unstructured situations, or objects in some way. Obviously there is no one 'right' set of responses. The investigator is interested in the pattern that develops from the respondent's responses. He then interprets this pattern according to valid and reliable categories that have been developed for the test.

18.2.8 Measures of Specific Intellectual Abilities

There are certain intellectual abilities and talents, one such ability is creativity, the components of creativity include numerous variables related to general intellectual ability (such as originality in problem-solving, originality in perception, originality in abstraction, ideational fluency, and inductive reasoning abilities), measures of creativity may also be thought of as tools for assessing aspects of intellectual functioning.

Guilford (1967) drew a distinction between the intellectual processes of convergent and divergent types of thinking. Divergent thinking involves a reasoning process in which thought is permitted the freedom to move in many different directions, making several solutions possible. Divergent thinking requires flexibility of thought, originality, and imagination. There is much less emphasis on recall of facts than in convergent thinking. Guilford's model has served as a stimulus to focus research attention on not only the products of creative thought but the process as well.

A number of tests and test batteries designed to measure creativity in children and adults are available. Test battery, the structure-of-intellect abilities, are consequences and unusal uses subtests, four Christensen-Guilford Fluency Tests (word fluency, ideational fluency, expressional fluency, and associational fluency), and other verbally-oriented subtests (such as simile interpretation) as well as relatively non-verbal subtests (such as sketches, making objects, and decorations).

Based on the work of Medwick (1962) , the Remote Associates Test (RAT) presents the test taker with three words , and the task is to find a fourth word that is associated with the other three. The Torrance (1966, 1987a, 1987c) Tests of creative thinking consists of word-based, as well as picture-based and sound-based, test materials.

Creativity tests are typically divided into four main components: Divergent thinking, Convergent thinking, Artistic assessments and Self-assessments.

(a) Divergent thinking is the ability to consciously generate new ideas that branch out to many possible solutions for a given problem. These solutions or responses are then scored on four components:

(1) *Originality*—statistical infrequency of response
(2) *Fluency*—number of responses
(3) *Flexibility*—the degree of difference of the responses, in other words do they come from a single domain or multiple domains
(4) *Elaboration*—the amount of detail of the response
Guilford's Alternative Uses Task (1967)
Wallas and Kogan (1965)
Torrance Test of Creative Thinking (TTCT) (1974)

(b) Convergent thinking is the ability to correctly hone in the single correct solution to a problem. In creativity convergent thinking often requires taking a novel approach to the problem, seeing the problem from a different perspective or making a unique association between parts of the problem. These solutions are scored either correct or incorrect.

Insight Problems : An insight problem is a problem that requires the examinee to shift his or her perceptive and view the problem in a novel way in order to achieve the solution. There are several types of insight problems. The three predominant types are verbal, mathematical, and spatial (Dow & Mayer, 2003).

(c) Artistic assessments are the evaluations of an artistic product (e.g., painting, story, poem, musical composition, collage, drawing etc.). Evaluations are typically done by two or more judges that must be in near agreement on the creativity of the product. The Barron-Welsh Art Scale is a Freudian-based assessment in which the examiner is asked to draw images. The images are then scored on scales that contain primary processes such as ego functioning and libidinal drives such as symbolization and substitution. The scales also contains personal style and social attitudes.

Self-assessments are person's responses to the amount of creativity a personal feels they exhibit persons responses to the amount of creativity a person feels they exhibit. Khatena-Torrance Creative Perception Inventory, Creativity Assessment Packet (Williams, 1980) and Profile of Creative Ability (Gail, 2007) are tests of creativity.

18.3 TEST DEVELOPMENT

The process of developing a test includes six stages :

1. Test conceptualization, 2. Test construction, 3. Test try out, 4. Test analysis, 5. Final Draft, and 6. Test revision.

18.3.1 Test Conceptualization

Review of literature on existing tests designed to measure a particular construct sometimes provides substantial evidence of gaps and inconsistency in the tests. Secondly, test earlier designed might require certain modifications to suit the new situation. Thirdly, an emerging social phenomenon or pattern of behaviour might serve as the stimulus to the development of a new test.

18.3.2 Emergence of Some Questions

Regardless of stimulus for developing the new test, the test developer must have clear view of the following querries before going for the construction of new test. (Cohan and Swerdlick, 2002)

1. What is the test designed to measure?
2. What is the objective of the test?
3. What is a need for this test?
4. Who will use this test?
5. Who will take the test?
6. What content the test cover?
7. How the test be administered?
8. What is the ideal format of the test?
9. What special training will be required of test users for administering or interpreting the test?

10. What types of responses will be rquired by test-takers?
11. Who will be bebefited from administeration of this test?
12. What are ethical considerations for the administration of the test?
13. How will meaning be attributed to scores on this test?

18.4 TEST CONSTRUCTION

18.4.1 Writing Items

In the process of test construction, writiing of the test items go hand in hand with scaling. Three important questions which should be considered by the prospective test developer are:

(a) For psychological tests designed for use by school psychologists, interviews with teachers, administrative staff, experts and others may be invaluable. Review of literature may be fruitful sources of inquiry. Items should comprehensively sample the domain of the test.

(b) Item format refers to the form, plan, structure, arrangement, or layout of individual test item.

(c) Number of items at the priliminary stage should be double because half of these items will be eliminated in the test's final version.

18.4.2 Test Tryout

Having selected the pool of items, the test developer will go for tryout of the test.

- The test should be tried out on the subjects for whom the test was designed.
- Subjects for tryout should be selected randomly.
- All other things being equal, ten subjects per test items are recommended.
- The test tryout should be executed under conditions that are as identical as possible to the conditions under which the standardised test will be administered.
- The test booklets along with their answers should be collected and scored with the help of a scoring key

18.4.3 Item Analysis

The criteria for the best item may differ as a function of the test developer's objectives. Various indices are, therefore used to analyze and select items. These are—Item-Difficulty Index, Item-Validity Index, Item-Reliability Index, and Item-Discrimination Index.

Item-Difficulty Index

An index of an item's difficulty is obtained by calculating the proportion of the number of test-takers who got the item right. For example, if 50 test-takers out of total 100 mark item one correct, then the level of difficulty will be 0.5 (p_1 = 50/100). The level of difficulty ranges between 0 and 1. In true-false item, the probability of guessing correctly on the basis of chance alone is ½, or 0.5. therefore, the optimal item difficulty is half way between 0.50 and 1.00 or 0.75 (0.50+1.00/2=0.75).

For a five-option multiple-choice item, the probability of guessing correctly on item on the basis of chance alone is equal to 1/5 or 0.20 and the optimal item difficulty is therefore 0.60 (i.e., .02+1.00/2 = 0.60)

Item-Validity Index

The item-validity index can be calculated once the following two statistics are known:

- The item-score standard deviation.
- The correlation between the item score and the criterion score.

The item-score standard deviation of item 1 (S_1) can be calculated:

S_1 = under root of p_1 (1–p_1)

An item-validity index is product of item-score standard deviation and the correlation between the item score and the criterion score. ($S_1 r_{ic}$)

Item-Reliability Index

The item-reliability index reveals the internal consistency of a test, the higher this index, the greater the test's internal consistency. This index is equal to the product of the item score standard deviation and the correlation between the item score and the total test score.

Item-Discrimination Index

From the arranged answer sheets, 27% within "upper" and "lower" scores are considerered for item discrimination index (Kelley, 1939). Suppose a test was administered to 100 people. The upper (U) and lower (L) 27% of the test in each group was calculated. Data and item-discrimination indices for item 1 through 5 are presented in Table 18.1.

TABLE 18.1

Item-Discrimination Indices for Five Hypothetical Items

Item	*U*	*L*	*U-L*	*n*	*d (U-L)/n*
1	18	15	3	27	.11
2	22	8	14	27	.52
3	27	0	27	27	1.00
4	18	18	0	27	0.00
5	0	27	-27	27	-1.00

Item 1 discrimination index is equal to .11, is probability a reasonable item because more members of U than of the L group answered it. Item 2 is better than item 1 because it has higher discrimination index i.e., .52. Item 4 and item 5 having zero and negative discrination cannot be considered good items to be included in the test.

Item analysis is a procedure to increase the reliability and validity of a test by separately evaluating each test item to determine whether or not that item discriminates in the same way the overall test is intended to discriminate. For example, given a test of academic aptitude or achievement, will students in the top half of the test score distribution also tend to get a particular item correct and students in the bottom half of this distribution tend to miss this same item? If so, such an item has favorable discriminating power and contributes to the overall reliability and validity of the test.

Example A : Steps in the Item Analysis of a True-False or Multiple Choice Aptitude or Achievement Test:

1. Rank orders the distribution of test scores from high to low.
2. Divide these ranked scores into two contrasting groups. The division point is arbitrary but common practice is to split the data in half, forming the Top and Bottom Halves; or, to increase the contrast, compare Upper and Lower Quarters. For ease of computation, use two groups of equal size.
3. Contrast a four-fold table based on two pairs of categories. The first pair is simply the category Wrong-Right (for a specific test item); the second pair is the category High Scorers-Low Scorers (depending on how the ranks were divided):

	Wrong	*Right*
High		
Low		

4. Calculate the chi square (χ^2) value of the resulting proportions .
5. If χ^2 is significant, it can be concluded that a dependable difference exists in the proportion of high and low scoring subjects who gave correct answers. Items that meet this criterion should be retained; items that fail to meet it should be discarded.

Example B—Steps in the Item Analysis of a Three-Choice Interest Inventory:

Interest or personality inventories often attempt to discriminate between the preferences of two sub-groups on a given series of items. For instance, if the following item is given to a groups of Art and Science students of degree college to check.

* A, Agree; ?, Undecided; D, Disagree.

1. Divide the data into two groups; art and science groups.
2. Contrast a 2 × 2 contingency table:

	Disagree	*Agree*
Art		
Science		

3. Calculate χ^2
4. If χ^2 is significant it can be concluded that a dependable difference exists in the proportion of Art and Science students on item.

The selected items are put in the final draft of the test. Then test is administered to as large a sample as is practical for ascertaining the parameters of reliability, validity and norms.

18.4.4 Test Revision

Whenever there is need for the revision of the test, an exercise for the development of new test can be undertaken. Test developer considers aspects of test revision in the context of modifying an existing test to create a new edition.

18.5 INTERPRETING TEST SCORES

To interpret a test score, two things must be known:

1. The nature of the score itself—what kind of scoring or scaling system was used in its calculation?
2. The basis for comparison underlying the score—what reference population or norm group does it represent, if any?

18.5.1 Types of Test Scores

1. *Raw Scores*—Simply the total number of points an individual earns on a test before it is converted to any formal or standardized scoring system. A raw score, by itself, is uninterpretable, since there is no way of knowing how it compares with anything else.
2. *Percentile (Centile) Ranks and Percentiles (Centiles)*—Raw scores begin to have meaning when they are rank ordered from high to low. Because this procedure ignores the sample size, a convenient solution is to convert the scores into percentage values. There are two statistics used for this purpose: (1) the percentile (centile) rank of any given score, which is a number between 0 and 100 indicating the percent of cases in a norm group falling at or below that score; and, conversely, (2) the percentile (centile), which is a point on a scale of scores at or below which a given percent of the cases fall. For example, an individual obtaining a score on a test with a percentile rank of 68, or whose score lies at the 68th percentile, can be said to be doing as well as, or better than, 68 percent of the persons to whom he is being compared. Percentiles of 25, 50 and 75 divide a distribution of scores into four quarters and are called the first, second, and third quartiles, respectively. The 50th percentile, or second quartile, is also the median percentile ranks and percentiles have three important advantages: (1) they are easily understood by the lay audiences; (2) they allow exact interpretation; and (3) they are more appropriate for markedly skewed data than scores based on the normal probability curve. There are also some disadvantages. Because a percentile scale consists of 100 points, it is misleading to report results in percentage terms when the sample size is under 100, a distortion which increases as the sample size approaches zero. Furthermore, percentile ranks and percentiles only permit statements about rank (greater than, equal to, or less than) and the intervals between units are not equal (the interval between the 60th and 70th percentiles is not equal to interval

between the 80th and 90th percentiles). Because the intervals are unequal, their values are misleading near the center of a distribution where they exaggerate small difference (the raw score difference between the percentiles of 50 and 55 may be infinitesimal) and especially misleading at the extremes of a distribution (the raw score difference between the percentiles of 98 and 99 may be quite large). The distortion is apt to be greatest when dealing with several percentiles reported as 99 where raw score differences can vary tremendously (a "brilliant" student may answer twice as many questions as a "bright" student, but both might be reported as having percentiles of 99, if the two performances fall in the top one percent of the reference group). The same is true at the opposite end of the scale. As a general rule of thumb, percentiles between 10 and 90 reflect minimal distortion; beyond these limits in either direction they should be interpreted with the distortion factor in mind.

3. *Stamine Score*—Stanine ('standard nine') scores combine the understandability of percentages with the properties of the normal curve of probability. A scale is created with nine intervals, each interval representing half of a standard deviation. The middle interval (5th stanine) straddles the midpoint of the distribution, encompassing the middle 20 percent of cases. The 4th, 3rd, 2nd, and 1st stanines, moving from the centre to the extreme lower end of the distribution in increments of one-half of a standard deviation, encompass respectively, 17, 12, 7, and 4 percent of the cases. Correspondingly, the 6th, 7th, 8th and 9th stanines, moving from the centre to the extreme upper end of the distribution in like increments, also encompass respectively, 17, 12, 7, and 4 percent of the cases. Examination of the chart graphically illustrates these characteristics and allows direct comparisons to other scales. A stanine is not a point on a scale like a percentile but a relatively broad interval. It is, therefore, insensitive to sizeable differences within a stanine interval and misleadingly sensitive to small difference on either side of the point separating adjacent stanine intervals. Neverthless, stanine scores are coming into increasing use because of their simplicity and utility.

4. *Standard Scores*—The most powerful scores, statistically, are standard scores derived from the properties of the normal probability curve and preserving the absolute differences between scores, a feature percentile or stanine scores do not posses. Furthermore, they can be used in calculating averages and correlation yielding the same results as the original raw scores. Standard scores from a variety of tests also have the advantage of being directly comparable if the reference groups are equivalent. Their major disadvantages are two: if data are markedly skewed, they are inappropriate, and, because of their dependence on the standard deviation, they are difficult to explain to lay audiences.
   (a) *Z-Scores*—If a mean and standard deviation are computed for a given set of raw scores, each raw score can be expressed in terms of its distance from the mean in standard deviation units or Z-Scores:

$$\text{Z-Score} = \frac{\text{Raw Score} - \text{Mean}}{\text{Standard Deviation}} = \frac{X - M}{\sigma}$$

   z-scores at the mean have a value of zero. Since 99.97 percent of all scores in a normal distribution fall between a range of three standard deviations above the mean and three standard deviations below the mean. The z-score above the mean carries a plus sign; below the mean, a minus sign. The utility of z-scores comes from their relationship to properties of the normal curve of probability. Using a table for the area underneath a normal curve, statements can be made about the proportion of cases above or below any z-score value or between any two z-socres values.
   (b) *T-Scores*—Because z-scores have a mean of zero and involve decimals as well as plus and signs. T-scores get around this problem by arbitrarily setting a new mean equal to 50 and the standard deviation equal to 10.
   (c) *Other Standard Scores*—Many other scoring systems are based on properties of the normal probability curve. The College Entrance Examination Board (CEEB) simply multiplies the T-scores system by 10, creating a mean of 500 and a standard deviation of 100. Tests of intelligence set the mean IQ at 100 and

their standard deviations at 15, 16, or 20, depending on the test. These difference in standard deviations further complicate comparisons of IQs between tests which differ in this respect.

Chart comparing various test scores their correspondence to each other is shown in Figure 18.1.

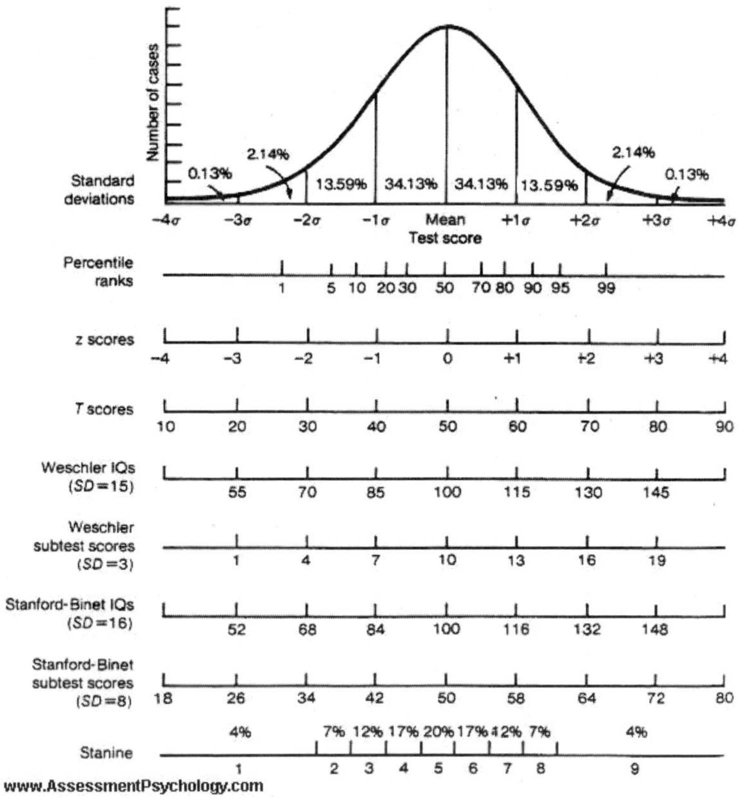

Figure 18.1 : Various Test Scores Correspondence to each other on Normal Curve

18.6. IMPROVING TEST RELIABILITY

Reliability means the consistency between measurements in a series. The reliability coefficient tells what proportion of the test variance is non-error variance. The coefficient of reliability of a set of test scores is related to a number of other characteristics of the test and of the group tested. Typically, the reliability coefficient will be greater for scores as mentioned below:

1. The reliability coefficient increases with the length of the test, a relationship which is much less pronounced for validity. The Spearman-Brown formula indicates the theoretical relation between test reliability and test length. This is shown in Table 18.1.

TABLE 18.1
Relation of Test Reliability to Test Length

Item	*Reliability*
5	.20
10	.33
20	.50
40	.67
80	.80
160	.89
320	.94

2. Homogeneity of test content tends to enhance test reliability. For example, a one hundred-item test in arithmetic is likely to be more reliable than a one hundred-item test covering all aspects of achievement in high school.
3. The items in homogeneous tests tend to have higher indices of discrimination than items in tests covering more diverse content and abilities. But item discrimination is also heavily dependent on the technical quality of the item—on the soundness of the idea identifying them, the clarity of the expression and in the case of multiple choice items, the adequacy of the correct response.
4. The difficulty of a test item affects its contribution to test reliability. An item which all examinees answer correctly or all miss contributes nothing to test reliability. Items of middle difficulty, that is, from 25 to 75 per cent correct response, are all capable of contributing much to test reliability. Items which more than 90 per cent or fewer than 10 per cent of the examinees answer correctly cannot possibly contribute as much.
5. The reliability coefficient for a set of test scores depends also on the range of talent in the group tested. If an

achievement test suitable for use in the middle grades of an elementary school is given to pupils in the fourth, fifth, and sixth grades, the reliability of the complete set of scores will almost be higher than the reliability of the scores for pupils of any one grade. Thus, increasing the range of talent, hence the true score variance, tends to increase the reliability coefficient.

6. Scores from a test given to a group under highly speeded conditions will ordinarily show a higher reliability coefficient than would be obtained for scores from the same test given to the same group with time limit. But most of the increased reliability of speeded test scores is spurious. Therefore, dependable estimates of test score reliability can be obtained from a test only if the speed at which an examinee works is not important factor in determining his score.

Validity

Validity refers to a judgment concerning how well a test does in fact measure what it purports to measure. More specifically, it is a judgment based on evidence about the appropriateness of inferences drawn from test scores. An inference is a logical or deduction in reasoning process. In other words, does the test serve specific purpose for which it is designed. For istance, the test prepared for the measurement of intelligence really measures the intelligence or a test for measurement of anxiety infact measures the same for the purpose it is designed. Validation is a process of gathering and evaluating validity evidence. In other words, it must validate the test specific purpose. There are three main categories through which tests can validated. Table 18.2 shows three types of validity.

The term "face validity" often is used to indicate whether the instrument, on the face of it, appears to measure what it claims to measure. Will persons making use of this instrument, accept it as a valid measure in the everyday sense of the word? While face validity is not a rigorous concept, its importance never can be ignored on that basis. Its presence, in conjunction with the above categories of validity, reinforces overall acceptance. It also is true that face validity, in the absence of these other standards, can be dangerously misleading, just as its absence, when these other validities are, in fact, present, can lead to disbelieving and frustrating resistance among potential users.

TABLE 18.2

Three Types of Validity (Isaac and Michael, 1972)

	Question	*Method*	*Common Use*	*Example*
(1)	*(2)*	*(3)*	*(4)*	*(5)*
Content validity	How well does the content of the test sample the kinds of things about which conclusions are to be drawn?	Logically conclude whether or not the test content comprises an adequate definition of what it claims to measure.	Achievement tests.	A test of school readiness is examined to see whether the content relates to knowledge and skills expected of first grade children following the kindergarten program.
Criterion-related Validity[2]	Does the test compare well with external variables considered to be direct measures of the characteristic or behaviour in question	Give the test and compare it with the criterion variable. The later may be obtained concurrently or predicted, and then obtained in the future, depending on the recommended use of the original test.	Test used in place of a more complicated procedure; or to select and classify persons.	Diagnosis of mental instability based on a card-sorting test compared with a more elaborate psychiatric examination; intelligence test scores used to predict future performance.
Construct Validity	To what extent do certain explanatory concepts or qualities account for performance on the test?	Based on the theory underlying the test, set-up hypotheses regarding the behavior of persons with high or low scores. Test the hypothesis.	Tests used for description, or in scientific research.	A test of personality types is studied to see how well theoretical implications of the typologies account for actual results obtained.

18.7 FACTORS AFFECTING THE VALIDITY OF A TEST

The validity of a test is tied to :

(a) the test bias;
(b) the rating error; and
(c) the test fairness.

18.7.1 Test Bias

It refers to prejudice and preferential treatment. For psychometricians, bias is a factor inherent within a test that systematically prevents accurate, impartial measurement for instance, "flip-coin test" (FCT). Coin will have one side "head" and the other side "tail" FCT will be considered bias if its one side appears frequently than it would by chance alone. A valid test must be free from bias.

18.7.2 Rating Error

Simply stated, a rating error is a judgment resulting from the intentional or unintentional misuse of a rating scale. For example, a leniency error arises from the tendency on the part of the rater to be lenient in marking. At the other extreme is a severity error. In this case rater is on the either of extreme side. (strickest on rating). Other type of error is a central tendency error. In this case, the rater is confined to centre. Another type of error is on account of halo effect. These rating errors needs to be checked to increase the validity of this test.

18.7.3 Test Fairness

Test fairness means a test is used in an impartial, just and equitable manner. Unfairness in the use of a test is due to:

(a) test usage guidelines are not clear,
(b) test is not used properly in practice, and
(c) administrative regulations are not followed properly.

References

Anastasi, A. Susana,W. (2008). *Psychological Testing.* New Delhi: Dorling Kindersley.

Best, J. and Kahn, J. (2009). *Research in Education.* 10th edition, Needham Heights: Allyn and Bacon.

Cohan, R.J. and Swerdlick, M.E. (2002). *Psychological Testing & Assessment: An Introduction to Test and Measurement.* New York: McGraw Hill.

Freeman, F.S. (1965). *Theory and Practice of Psychological Testing.* New Delhi: Oxford and IBH Publishing.

Jackson,C. (2001). *Understanding Psychological Testing.* New Delhi: JAICO Publishing House.

Kanji, K. (2006). *100 Statistical Tests.* 3rd edition, New Delhi: Vistaar.

Kline, P. (1976). *Psychological Testing: The Measurement of Intelligence Ability and Personality.* London: Malaby Press.

Kline, P. (2005). *Psychological Testing: A Practical Approach to Design and Evaluation.* New Delhi: Vistaar.

Koul, L. (2009). *Methodology of Educational Research.* Vikas Publishing House, New Delhi.

Isaac, S., Michael, W.B. (1972). *Handbook in Research and Evaluation.* San Diego, California : Robert R. Knapp Publisher.

Thorndike, R.L. and Hagen, E.P. (1977). *Measurement and Evaluation in Psychology and Education.* 4th ed. New York: John Wiley and Sons.

CHAPTER

19

Questionnaire

A questionnaire is an essential instrument for getting factual, reliable and valid information for research purpose. A questionnaire consists of a set of well formulated questions to probe and obtain responses from respondents. When opinions rather than facts are desired, an opinionnaire or attitude scale is used. The purpose is to gather requisite information in written form from the target group or groups. Gathered information is further analysed to find answers to research questions. A precise and feasible procedure of getting requisite information is followed for finding solution of problem under investigation.

19.1 QUESTIONNAIRE

Questionnaire can be defined as :

- A device for securing answers to questions by using a form which a respondent fills himself. (Goode & Hatt, 1952)
- A systematic compilation of questions to a sample of population from which information is desired. (Barr & Johnson, 1953).
- A questionnaire is a series of questions asked to individuals to obtain statistically useful information about a given topic. (Best and Kahn, 2007)
- A questionnaire is series of questions which are seriously framed and administered on a sampled population to get requisite data for further analysis and conclusions. (Oppenheim, 1992)

- A questionnaire is to gather factual data or to get information about opinions, attitudes, and interest.

19.2 FORMS OF QUESTIONNAIRE

Questionnaire may be of closed form or opened form. For example:

19.2.1 The Closed Form

Closed-Ended Form Contains Questions with Option

Respondent has to pick an answer from a given number of options:

There are four types of response scales for closed ended questions:

- **Dichotomous,** where respondent has two options,
  Example: Do you like your teacher? Yes/No
- **Nominal-polytomous,** where the respondent has more than two unordered options.
  Example: I like my teacher because—1. He helps me, 2. His method of teaching is good, 3. He has command over the subject .Give the order of preference.
- **Ordinal-polytomous,** where the respondent has more than two ordered options.
  Example: In your view, what are the three characteristics of an effective teacher in order of preference?
- **Continuous,** where the respondent is presented with a continuous scale.
  Example: Rank your language teacher as Best=1, Good = 2, Average = 3, Poor= 4

19.2.2 The Open Form

The open-form or unrestricted questionnaire calls for a free response in the respondent's own words. An example of open-form item which is to be responded by the respondent in his or her own writing is given below:

Why did you choose teaching as a profession?

In this open-form item no clue is given. Thus, it provides for greater depth of response. Respondent is also free to make use of his or her experience or imagination. Therefore, it requires greater effort on the part of the respondent. Information thus gathered is unstructured; the researcher sometimes encounters difficulty in interpreting, tabulating and summarizing the research report.

19.3 QUESTIONNAIRE DESIGN

Research issue and objectives hypotheses are kept in view while designing questionnaire. Hence, they should be clearly identified and defined properly. If researcher is not clear about the kind of measurement to be made, then the questionnaire will suffer from ambiguous questions. The following points are to be kept in mind while designing questionnaire:

- Researcher must be clear what information he requires so that appropriate questions are asked to get appropriate responses in the light of objectives and hypotheses of the study. He must ensure that information relates to the purpose of research questions.
- Nature of the expected responses should be defined and retained for interpretation of the responses, be it attitudinal, behavioural, attributes, beliefs, feelings, or standards of action.
- The type of scale, index, or typology to be used should be determined.
- The types of questions (closed, multiple-choice, open) should fit the statistical data analysis techniques available and goals of present investigation.
- Questions and prepared answers to choose from should be based on the principle of neutrality.

I. Decisions about Question Content

- Is this question necessary? Just how will it be useful?
- Do respondents possess the knowledge or have access to information necessary for giving a correct answer?
- Are several questions needed on the subject matter of the question?
- Does the question need to be more concrete, specific and closely related to the respondent's personal experience?
- Is the question content sufficiently general and free from spurious concreteness and specificity?
- Do the replies express general attitudes and only to be as specific as they sound?
- Is the question content biased or loaded in one direction without accompanying questions to balance the emphasis?
- Will the respondents give the information that is asked for?

The meaning should be clear. Ambiguous words, equivocal sentence structures and negatives may cause misunderstanding, possibly invalidating questionnaire results.

II. Decisions About Question Wording

- Can the question be misunderstood? Does it contain different or unclear phraseology?
- Does the question adequately express the alternatives with respect to the point?
- Is the wording biased? Is it emotionally loaded or slanted toward a particular kind of answer?
- Is the question wording likely to be objectionable to the respondent in any way?
- Would a more personalized or less personalized wording of the question produce better results?

The wording should be kept simple; no technical or specialized words be used which may confuse the respondent

III. Avoid following types of questions

- **Complex terms and language**—big words can offend and confuse. If they're not necessary, why use them? Compare the two following agree/disagree statements: 'Polysyllabic linguistic terminology can act to obscure connotations.
- **Ambiguous questions**—It's very easy to write ambiguous questions because frames of reference can be highly divergent. For example, consider the question: How big is your family? Or 'Do you use drugs? Families can be nuclear or extended, or for children of separated parents, may include two households, similarly, 'drugs' can be an ambiguous term. Some respondents will only consider illegal drugs, while be impossible to know whether alcohol or cigarettes were also considered'.
- **Double negatives**—a significant proportion of respondents get confused when faced with double negatives. Consider the following agree/disagree statement: 'You are not satisfied with your job'. To state that you are satisfied in your job means that you need to choose disagree, which can be quite confusing.
- **Double-barrelled questions**—this is when you ask for only one response to a question with more than one issue. For example, take the question: 'Do you consider the president to be an honest and effective leader?' Respondents may think yes, effective—but definitely not honest.
- **'Ring true' statements**—these are statements that are easy to agree with simply because of their 'ring true tone'. A

couple of examples might be 'You really can't rely on people these days' or 'Times may be tough, but there are generally people around you can count on'. Both of these are likely to get a high percentage of agree responses.

- **Hard to disagree with statements**–these are statements where your respondent is likely to think 'yes that's true, but..' They are not, however, given a chance to elaborate and are forced to either agree or disagree. For example, 'The elderly are often a burden to society'.
- **Leading questions**–consider how the wording of the following questions on abortion might affect responses: 'Do mothers have the right to murder an unborn child'? *vs.* 'Do women have the right to make choices about their own bodies'?
- **Recall dependent questions**–these are questions that rely on memory. For example, 'How many jobs have you held? Without boundaries such as an occupational field or timeframe, this question can be easy to answer 'incorrectly'.
- **Offensive questions**–if respondents take offence to a question or a series of questions, not only are they likely to skip those items, they may just throw out the entire survey. Offensive questions can range from 'what did you do to make your husband leave you?' to 'How old are you'?
- **Questions with unwarranted assumptions**–respondents are likely to be at a loss when it comes to answering a question that contains an assumption they do not agree with. For example, Muslims are liberal. Respondend may be uncomfortable in agreeing with the statement.
- Avoid questions which evoke predictable response biases and obscure objective information.

IV. Decisions About Form of Response to the Question

- If a check list is used, does it cover adequately all the significant alternatives without overlapping and in a defensible order? Is it of reasonable length? Is the wording of items impartial and balanced?
- Is the form of response easy, definite, uniform, and adequate for the purpose?
- Is the answer to the question likely to be influenced by the content of preceding questions?

- Is the question led up to in a natural way? Is it in correct psychological order?
- Does the question come too early or too late from the point of view of arousing interest and receiving sufficient attention, avoiding resistance, etc.?
- Are possible responses mutually exclusive or not overlapping?

V. Appropriate Sequence of Questions

A preferred sequence of questions is given below:

- First few questions relating to personal details of the respondents.
- Introductory questions to establish a rapport with the respondents:
    - o Simple and direct questions to build an opinion that questionnaire is simple to answer,
    - o Focused questions relating to objectives and issues of the research, and
    - o Main body of the questionnaire should contain questions to obtain needed information.

VI. Follow

- Study other questionnaires, and keep in mind the characteristics of a good questionnaire.
- Get all the help you can and make all preparation for planning and constructing your questionnaire.
- Submit your questionnaire items for criticism to your friends and colleagues.
- Try your questionnaire on a few representatives of population to be studied for the purpose of selection and deletion of items.
- Use closed or the open end form. But objectivity is important. Lengthy, subjective, open-ended answers are difficult for the respondents to answer and for the investigator to evaluate.
- Questions should be asked in such a way that they minimize the evaluation task, eliminating unnecessary processing steps and interpretation problems.
- Be careful of inadequate alternatives, for example: Married or unmarried.
- Phrase questions so that they suit all respondents, for example: How many days per week do you send your student-teachers for practice teaching? may not suit all respondents as each college follows its own pattern.
- Design questions that will give a complete response, for

example: Do you read the India Today? Would not reveal much information about the reading habit of the respondent.

- Provide for systematic quantification of responses, for example, first choice (3 points), second choice (2 points), third choice (1 point).

19.4 PRE-TESTING OF QUESTIONNAIRE

Once the questionnaire is ready, it should be pre-tested through a pilot survey involving the respondents in the proposed sampling frame. This exercise is mainly intended to test the degree of understanding the meaning of the questions, difficulty in understanding the questions and check the relevance of the questions. Sometimes peer review of the questions or expert opinions are considered.

19.4.1 Review of Questionnaire for Improvements

The purpose of pre-testing of questionnaire is to obtain information to improve its contents, format, and sequence for final use in the survey.

19.5 ADMINISTERING THE QUESTIONNAIRE

19.5.1 Getting Permission

It is essential that approval of the head of the institution should be got in advance specifying the day, date and the purpose of the study. In certain sensitive cases (drug abuse) parental and student consent is essential.

If the desired information is delicate or intimate in nature, the student needs not to mention his or her name. The anonymous instrument is most likely to produce objective and honest responses.

Respondents must be convinced that their responses will be held in strict confidence.

19.5.2 The Cover Letter

A courteous, carefully constructed cover letter should be included to explain the purpose of the study. Confirmation of the visit for the administration of the questionnaire should be obtained verbally or in written form. The cover letter should assure the respondent that all information will be kept in strict confidence or that the questionnaire is anonymous.

19.6 STANDARDIZATION OF QUESTIONNAIRE

For standardization, statistical validity and reliability of the questionnaire need to be established. Following points may be considered:

19.6.1 Validity

The validity of a questionnaire and of its parts may be judged by following types of evidence:

1. Is the question on the specified subject or construct?
2. Is the question perfectly clear and unambiguous?
3. Does the question get at something stable, which is typical of the individual or of the situation?
4. Does the question pull or have extractive power? Will it be answered by a large enough proportion of respondents to have validity?
5. Do the responses show a reasonable range of variation?
6. Is the information consistent, in agreement with what is known, and is agreement with expectancy?
7. Is the item sufficiently inclusive?
8. Is there a possibility of obtaining an external criterion to evaluate questionnaire?
9. Is questionnaire internally validity established?

19.6.2 Reliability

Reliability is the degree of consistency that the instrument demonstrates. It merely connotes something that is consistent—not necessarily consistently good or bad, but simply consistent.

19.7 SOURCES OF ERROR VARIANCE

(a) *Test Construction:* one source of variance during test construction is item sampling or content sampling, a term refers to variation among items within a test, as well as to variation among items between tests.

(b) *Test administration:* sources of errors variance that occur during test administration may influence the test-taker's attention or motivation. For example, physical environment—seating arrangement, ventilation, light and noise, examiner interference—favourable or unfavourable, test-taker's mind-set, etc.

(c) *Test scoring and interpretation:* manual scoring sometimes causes error. In open ended questions errors are expected in the interpretation.

Other sources of error: certain type of assessment situations lend themselves to particular varieties of systematic and non-systematic error. For example, assessing the degree of agreement between partners regarding abusive behaviour. Sources of non-systematic error in assessment situation include forgetting, failture to notice abusive behaviour and misunderstating instructions regarding reporting. Systematic error include underreporting or overreporting of perpetration of abuse

References

Birdie, D.R. and Aderson, J.F. (1974). Questionnaires—Design and Use. New Jersy: Scarecrow Press.

Likert, R. (1967). *The Method of Constructing an Attitude Scale: Readings in Attitude Theory and Measurements.* New York: John Wiley &Sons.

Oppenheim, A.N. (1982). Questionnaire—Design and Measurements. London: Heinemann.

Oppenheim, A.N. (1992) Questionnaire Design, Interviewing and Attitude Measurement. London: Pinter.

Thorndike, R.L. and Hagen, E.P. (1977). *Measurement and Evaluation in Psychology and Education.* 4th ed. New York: John Wiley and Sons.

Thurstone, L.L. (1959). *Measurement of Values.* Chicago: University of Chicago Press.

Torgerson, W. (1958). *Theory and Methods of Scaling.* New York: John Wiley and Sons.

CHAPTER

20

Scales and its Construction

20.0 SCALES FOR MEASUREMENT OF VARIABLES

There are different methods of quantification of data. Measurement scales are used to categorise and/or quantify variables. Scientists have suggested four scales of measurement as given below.

20.1 NOMINAL SCALE

A nominal scale is the least precise method of quantification. It consists of assignment of facts/choices to various alternative categories which are usually exhaustive as well mutually exclusive. A nominal scale describes differences between things by assigning them to categories—such as males or females; boys or girls; married or unmarried: professors, associate professors, assistant professors, etc. The statistics which can be used with nominal scales are in the non-parametric group. The most likely ones would be: mode, cross-tabulation—with chi-square

20.2 ORDINAL SCALE

Ordinal scale is the simplest attitude measuring scale. The numbers possess the property of rank order. The rating of certain attributes/characteristics as deemed important by the respondent is obtained through the scale. The criterion for highest to lowest ordering is expressed as relative position or rank in a group. For example, positions in the final examination can expressed as 1st rank, 2nd rank, 3rd rank, 4th rank and 5th rank. Ordinal data would use non-parametric statistics. These would include: Median, mode and rank order correlation

20.3 INTERVAL SCALE

Interval scale assumes equal distance between various categories. The interval scale is also known as rating scale. An interval scale has an arbitrary zero point with further numbers placed at equal distance. A very good example of interval scale is thermometer. Such scale permits the researcher to say that position 5 on the scale is above the position 4. The distance between position 4 and position 5 is same. This scale does not permit that position 4 is twice as strong as position 2. Data can be used to derive mean and standard deviation.

Interval scale data would use parametric statistical techniques: Mean and standard deviation Correlation—r, Regression, Analysis of variance and Factor analysis.

20.4 RATIO SCALE

A ratio scale has also equal interval properties of interval scale. In addition, ratio scale has a true zero. The numerals of the ratio scale have the qualities of real numbers and can be added, subtracted, multiplied, divided and expressed in ratio relationships. For example, 5 grams is half of 10 grams.

Interval scale data would use parametric statistical techniques: Mean and standard deviation Correlation–r, Regression, Analysis of variance and Factor analysis.

20.5 RATING SCALE

Rating is a term applied to expression of opinion or judgment regarding some situation, object or character. Opinions are usually expressed on a scale of values. Rating techniques are devices by which such judgments may be quantified. (Barr, Davis & Johnson, 1953).

Rating scale is a very useful device in research in assessing quality or values when these variables are difficult to measure objectively. For example, how good was your performance in the classroom? Or how do you enjoy this lecture? These are the questions which hardly can be answered objectively. There are number of options or degree of difference in answering questions, for instance, performance may be low, moderate, high excellent or cannot say. Therefore, rating scales indicate the degree or amount of preference/opinion. Descriptions of different degrees of quality are arranged along a line from high to low or described on a scale.

For example: How good was your performance in the

classroom? This can be shown in form given below for getting information from the respondent.

Excellent V. Good Good Average Below Average

20.5.1 Construction of Rating Scale

1. The researcher should be more careful in the construction of rating scale. Rating Scale may include three factors:
   (i) The subjects or phenomena to be rated,
   (ii) The continuum along which it will be rated, and
   (iii) The judges who will do the rating.
2. The subjects or phenomena to be rated are usually a limited number of aspects of a thing, or of traits of a person. Only the most significant aspects for the purpose of the study should be chosen.
   (i) The usual way to get qualitative-cum-quantitative judgments on the selected aspects of a thing.
   (ii) Another procedure, however estabblishes position in term of specific behavioural situational description. For instance, instead of deciding whether the individual's leadership qualities are superior or above average, it may be easier to place on the scale-most stimulating to lest stimulating or authoritative to democratic.
3. In writing and arranging these descriptions it is better to have the judgment and agreement of several people.
4. Items may be arranged in ascending or descending order from left to right. Ordinarily an odd number of steps should be used and the average or usual quality should be kept in the middle of the scale.
5. Qualified and experienced persons should be selected for rating where technical competency is required.
6. Pooled judgments increase the reliability of any rating scale. Employ several judges, depending on the rating situation, to obtain desirable reliability.

20.6 ATTITUDE SCALE

Attitude scales are generally used in education, psychology and other social sciences. Focus is on the study of perception, preference, and motivation of individuals. Scaling methods are classified into subject-centered approach, stimuli-centered approach, and response approach. In the subject-centered approach, the variation across the respondents is studied. The stimuli-centered approach examines the systematic variation across stimuli. In the response approach, the variation across subjects as well as the variation across stimuli is studied.

Different scales used in attitude measurement are summarized in Table 20.1.

TABLE 20.1
Attitude Measurement Scales

Category	*Purpose*	*Name of Scale*
1.	Scaling Stimuli	(a) Thurstone's case V scale
		(b) Osgood's semantic differential scale
2.	Scaling Respondents	(a) Summated scale
		(b) Q-sort technique
3.	Scaling Stimuli and Respondents	(a) Cumulative scale/Scalogram analysis

20.7 THURSTONE OR EQUAL-APPEARING INTERVAL SCALES

These scales not only place the individual somewhere along an agreement continuum for a given attitude but also scale the attitude items themselves. Each item is assigned a *scale value* indicating the strength of attitude for an agreement response to them. For example:

Sl.No.	*Statement*	*Scale value*
1.	This institution treats its teachers better than any other institution	10.2
2.	Doing it all over again, I would still teach for this institution	8.5
3.	The teacher and the institution take equal advantage of each other	5.0

The person taking this test simply checks the items with which he agrees, the points corresponding to those items are totaled and then divided by the number of answered items to yield an average scaled value.

20.7.1 Steps in the Construction of an Equal-appearing Interval Scale

1. Collect a series of short, concise statements reflecting the attitude of an individual towards a group, institution, idea or practice.

2. These statements are submitted to a panel of twenty or more judges who are asked to arrange them in eleven groups-ranging from one extremely favourable to another extremely unfavourable position.
3. For each item, plot the distribution of scaled value (1-11) assigned by the various judges, locating the median of this distribution (its scaled value).
4. Those items which bring out marked disagreement between the judges in assigning a position are discarded.
5. Check for irrelevance by presenting the remaining items to a group of respondents, asking them to mark those statements with which they agree. Items with poor internal consistency, statistically, are then eliminated.
6. Select from those items remaining the statements whose scale values are equally spaced along the attitude continuum.

20.8 OSGOOD'S SEMANTIC DIFFERENTIAL SCALE

Osgood's semantic differential scale is used to convert raw data obtained using quantitative-judgement procedure into interval scaled data. This interval scaled data can be further analyzed through factor analysis. The semantic differential scale reflects the direction and intensity of respondents' attitude concerning institution, service, usage of ICT or learning resources, etc.

For example, as per this scale, the respondents are expected to rate an educational institution on a set of bipolar objectives. This is shown in Table 20.2 as given below.

TABLE 20.2
Semantic Differential Scale

		-2	*-1*	*0*	*1*	*2*	
Student care	: Inferior	——	——	——	——	——	Superior
Infrastructure	: Inferior	——	——	——	——	——	Superior
Student Progression	: Poor	——	——	——	——	——	Good
Syllabus	: Old	——	——	——	——	——	Latest
Faculty base	: Poor	——	——	——	——	——	Good

20.8.1 Steps of Semantic Differential Scale

1. Identify the attributes on which the organizations are judged by the respondents.
2. Decide on the number of descriptive phrases and define

them. Also decide on the numerical weights of the descriptive phrases.

3. Design a questionnaire containing semantic differential scale for each organization.
4. Administer the questionnaire to the respondents and seek their judgement for all the organizations.
5. For each organization, sum the judgement scores of each attribute across respondent and find its average.
6. For each organization, plot the average score of each attribute on the semantic differential scale as shown in Table 20.3 as given below.

TABLE 20.3
Semantic Differential Scale

		-2	*-1*	*0*	*1*	*2*	
Student care	: Inferior		A			B	Superior
Infrastructure	: Inferior			B	A		Superior
Student Progression	: Poor		A		B		Good
Syllabus	: Old			B		A	Latest
Faculty base	: Poor				A, B		Good

In Table 20.3 the institution A is perceived as inferior students care, poor student progression, but with good infrastructure, good faculty base and very latest syllabus; the institution B is perceived as superior students care, good student progression and good faculty base but with neither inferior nor superior infrastructure and neither old nor latest syllabus.

20.8.2 Analysis of data collected through the Semantic Scale

1. Compute a t-test or a Median test of the significance of a difference between group means or medians for individual scales or for all scales summed.
2. Profile analysis using the sign test. By plotting the profiles of mean response patterns between comparison groups down a set of scales, similarities and dissimilarities in the profiles can be observed.

3. Distance-cluster analysis of semantic space: Given Osgood's three axes of semantic—evaluative, potency and activity, it is possible to drive a measure of distance along each axis for each concept.

20.9 LIKERT METHOD OF SUMMATED RATINGS

This device of attitude measurement is carried out without the panel of judges necessary for the Thurstone Scale. Likert- Scale yields scores very similar to those obtained by the Thurstone-scale. The coefficient of correlation between the two scales is reported as high as .92 in one study. (Edward and Kenny, 1946).

20.9.1 Steps of Construction of Summated Scale

1. Formulate possible number of statements about the attitudinal object which is to be studied.
2. Ensure that the number of favourable statements is almost equal to the number of unfavourable statements.
3. Assume the following directional intensity descriptors of the items of the attitudinal object:

1	2	3	4	5
Strongly Agree	Agree	Undecided	Disagree	Strongly disagree

4. Assign scale values to the degree of agreement/ disagreement as stated below:
   (a) For favourable statements (items), the scale values from left to right are assumed as 5, 4, 3, 2, 1
   For unfavouable statements (items), the scale values from left to right are assumed as 1, 2, 3, 4, 5
   OR
   (b) For favourable statements (items), the scale values from left to right are assumed as +2, +1, 0, - 2, -1
   For unfavouable statements (items), the scale values from left to right are assumed as -2, - 1, 0, +1, +2
5. Test should be administered to a small group to test the internal consistency of the assembled statements (items) and the items found ambiguous or irrelevant should be deleted.
6. Calculate the total attitude scores of each respondent by summing the scores assigned to each of the items by that respondent.
7. If an attitude scale or opinonnaire consisted of 30 Statements, the following score value would be revealing:

30×5 = 150 Most favourable responses possible
30×3 = 90 A neutral attitude
30×1 = 30 Most unfavoueable attitude
The scores for any individual would fall between 30 to 150
Above 90 scores would be favouable
Below 90 scores would be unfavourable OR

8. (i) In case of assumed scale values +2, +1, 0, -1, -2 for favouable and -2, -1, 0, +2, +1 for unfavourable items as mentioned above, find the highest quartile group (first quartile) and the lowest quartile(fourth quartile) of the respondents on the basis of total scores. High scores can be assumed to be with the favourable attitiudes and the low scores can be assumed to be with unfavorable attitudes.
   (ii) Find the mean difference between the highest quartile and the lowest quartile group for each item. If an iem is a good one, then the mean score of the favouable group will be more than that of the unfavourable group. For an item, if the mean score across the two groups are equal or near equal, then that item is to be excluded from the scale.
9. Mix favouable and unfavourable items in random order.
10. Administer the scale to the respondents to study or assess their attitudes towards specific idea, or institution or phenomenon which ever is the subject of your investigation.

20.10 GUTTMAN-TYPE OR CUMULATIVE SCALES

This scale consist of a relatively small set of homogeneous items that are supposedly unidimensional, measuring only one attribute. Such scales get their name from the cumulative relation between items and the total scores of individuals. Items can be ordered in difficulty, complexity, or value-loading (from low to high) so that to answer correctly. Approval of the last implies success or approval on all the preceding ones; or, to miss or disapprove a middle item implies failure or disapproval of all the subsequent items. When the scale is cumulative and we know a subject's total scores, we can predict his answering pattern.

Cumulative scales have limited application. They are appropriate where a single clear-cut attribute or stimulus dimension is involved. A well constructed scale may yield reliable measures of a number of psychological variables: cognitive complexity, tolerance, conformity, group identification, acceptance of authority, or permissiveness. Furthermore, these scales are particularly useful with children because of their simplicity and brevity. They may also be adapted as a rating device for an observer.

(A) Some statements are given below as an example 1:

1. Would you object to such a person living in your community?
2. Would you object to him working where you are employed?
3. Would you object to inviting him into your house?
4. Would you object to his marrying a member of your family?

Answer "Yes" to item 1 predicts "Yes" answers to 2, 3, and 4; a "No" answer to item 4 predicts "No" answer to 3, 2, 1; a "No" answer to item 1 but "Yes" to item 2 predicts "Yes" for items 3 and 4.

(B) Some multiplication problems are given below as an example 2.

What is 3 × 4?	Seven multiplication problems at the left illustrate
What is 7 × 9?	Achievement items ordered according to difficulty
What is 7 × 34?	Or complexity level with similar implications if an item is
What is .7 × .6?	passed or failed
What is .09 × .008?	
What is 15% of 160?	
What is .25 of 175?	

Table 20.4 shows scalogram analysis with ideal P.

TABLE 20.4
Scalogram Analysis with Ideal P

Respondent category	*Questions in terms of difficulty index*						*Scale score*
	6	*5*	*4*	*3*	*2*	*1*	
I	X	X	X	X	X	X	6
II		X	X	X	X	X	5
III			X	X	X	X	4
IV				X	X	X	3
V					X	X	2
VI						X	1
VII							0

20.11 TEST OF SOUND MEASUREMENT

Sound rating scale of measurement must meet the tests of validity, reliability and practicability. Validity refers to the extent to which a test measures what we actually wish to measure. Reliability has to do with the accuracy and precision of measurement procedure. Practicability is concerned with a wide range of factors of economy, convenience, and interpretability. (Thorndike and Hagen, 1977).

20.11.1 Validity

Validity refers to a judgment concerning how well a test does in fact measure what it purports to measure. More specifically, it is a judgment based on evidence about the appropriateness of inferences drawn from test scores. An inference is a logical or deduction in reasoning process. In other words, does the test serve specific purpose for which it is designed. For instance, the test prepared for the measurement of intelligence really measures the intelligence or a test for measurement of anxiety in fact measures the same for the purpose it is designed. Validation is a process of gathering and evaluating validity evidence. In other words, it must validate the test specific purpose. There are three main categories through which tests can be validated:

- *Content validity:* content is scrutinized to establish validity
- *Criterion-related validity:* test scores obtained is correlated to criterion to establish validity of the test.
- Two types of validity evidence are subsumed under 'criterion-related validity' namely—*Concurrent validity and Predictive validity.*
- *Construct validity:* comprehensive analysis is done in the light of theoretical framework of the construct to establish the validity.

20.11.2 Reliability

The test of reliability refers when a scale is used it must give consistent results. Two aspects of reliability namely stability and equivalence need to be ensured. The stability aspect is concerned with securing consistent results with repeated measurements of the same person and with the same instrument. The equivalence aspect considers how much error may get introduced by different investigators or different samples of the items being studied. Reliability can be improved in the following ways:

- Ensure that external sources of variation such as boredom, fatigue, stress, etc. to be minimized to the extent possible.

- Directions for measurement should be carefully designed with no variation from group to group.
- Scholar should be trained in using instructional manual.

20.11.3 Test of Practicability

Test of practicability refers to economy, convenience and interpretability.

- *Economy implies*—if instrument of measurement should be within the allocated budget as well as of appropriate length.
- *Convenience test suggests*—measuring instrument should be easy to administer
- *Interpretability demands*—detailed instructions for administering the test, scoring, evidence about the reliability, and interpreting the results

References

Andrich, D. (1997). 'Rating Scale Analysis', in J.P. Keeves (ed.), Educational Research, Methodology, and Measurement: An International Handbook, 2nd edn. Oxford ; Elsevier. pp. 874-80.

Edwards, A.L. (1957). *Techniques of Attitude Scale Construction.* New York: Appleton-Century-Crofts.

Green, B.F. (1956). A Method of Scalogram Analysis using summary statistics. *Psychometrika,* 21, 79-89.

Jahoda, M. and Warrer, N. (eds.) (1966). Attitudes: Selected Readings. Middlesex: Penguin Books.

Likert, R. (1967). *The Method of Constructing an Attitude Scale: Readings in Attitude Theory and Measurements.* New York: John Wiley & Sons.

Shaw, M.E. and Wright, J.M. (1967). Scales for the Measurement of Attitudes. New York: McGraw-Hill

Thorndike, R.L. and Hagen, E.P. (1977). *Measurement and Evaluation in Psychology and Education.* 4th ed. New York: John Wiley and Sons.

Thurstone, L.L. (1959). *Measurement of Values.* Chicago: University of Chicago Press.

Torgerson, W. (1958). *Theory and Methods of Scaling.* New York: John Wiley and Sons.

CHAPTER

21

Observation as a Research Tool

21.0 OBSERVATION

From the earliest history of scientific activity, observation has generally been used a method of inquiry. The accumulated knowledge of biologists, physicists, astronomers and other natural scientists is built upon centuries of systematic observation, much of it of phenomena in their natural surrounding rather than in the laboratory. Observation as a research tool in the psychology and the social areas came into prominence during the last century, with marked progress in educational studies during the second quarter of the century. However, observation continues to characterize all research: experimental, descriptive, and qualitative. Among the factors favourable to the wider use of observation as an investigational procedure were the demand of the newer or progressive education. Reasons were : (1) to probe aspects of behaviour not accessible to the conventional paper-pencil-test, interview or laboratory technique, (2) to obviate certain of the judgment errors likely to enter into the customary rating procedures, (3) establishment of centers for research in child development laying emphasis on the need for studying children in natural or social situations, (4) for observing the child (including his social and emotional behaviour), rather than relying exclusively on cross-sectional measurements of mental and physical growth, and (5) understanding the behaviour of children with special needs.

In experimental or laboratory research, systematic observations are made. In order to get precise results of the observation, the investigation is done under carefully arranged and controlled conditions. But many important aspects of human behviours cannot be observed under controlled conditions. Researches in education and social sciences are conducted under less rigid control and more natural conditions to understand the behaviour of the subject.

In descriptive research, direct observation is used as a data gathering device. Certain information can best be obtained through direct examination by the researcher. For instance, observation of infrastructure—classroom, seating capacity, ventilation, furniture and equipments and this process is relatively easy and may consist of classifying, measuring. or counting. But when the process involves the study of a human subject in action, it is much more complex.

In qualitative research, social scientists are literally surrounded by their subject matter that they have to open their eyes and observe their fellow men and women, and the institutions and societies they have created, in action (Kalton, 1977). Besides subject matter, method must be suitable for investigating the problem in which the social scientist is interested; it must be appropriate to the populations and samples he wishes to study; and it should be reasonably reliable and objective. *The Concise Oxford Dictionary* defines it as 'accurate watching and noting of phenomena as they occur in nature with regard to cause and effect or mutual relations'.

Observation as a research technique, in order to be most reliable and valid tool for data gathering, must be systematic, directed by a specific purpose, carefully focused, and thoroughly recorded. Because human behaviour is complex and many important traits and characteristics are difficult or impossible to observe directly, they must be carefully defined in precise operational form. Operational definition helps in measuring those traits and characteristics objectively. Instruments such as stopwatches, mechanical counters, audio and videotape recorders, note-book computers and other devices make observations more precise and meaningful. In brief:

1. Information required is obtained directly, rather than through the reports of others; in the case of behaviour one finds out what the individual does, rather than what he says he does.
2. Observation as a research tool is used in understanding, measuring, prediction and modification of human behaviour. If future conditions can be simulated on a sample basis, the behaviour of the sample may provide a good indicator of future behaviour.

3. It is to observe the behaviour of persons in appropriate situations-controlled or uncontrolled.
4. It is conducted purposively, systematically, carefully focused and thoroughly recorded to get reliable and valid results.
5. For accuracy in measuring and recording, variables are operationally defined and tools such as check-list, score-card or some other inquiry forms are utilized along with cameras and tape-recorder.

21.1 ISSUES REGARDING OBSERVATIONS

1. *Deciding who is to be studied and in what situations*: The researcher first has to decide on the type of individual to study, for instant, special children, adolescents, or children at different levels of education, or children with different socio-economic status, etc. If school children are selected, then the observations might occur inside a classroom, or on playing field. They are needed to be observed in their natural settings.
2. *Formal Groups, Informal Groups or Occasional Groups*: There are different kinds of group one can study. A formal group is stable, with the same people serving as nucleus, such as a class, a family, a team, etc. Formal Groups are aware about the rules, procedures, boundaries and limitations. Informal group do not meet regularly. An occasional group consists of who might come together on certain specific function. All types of groups have their specific objectives, problems, and mode of operation. The researcher might look for different things in each.
3. *Gaining Access*: If studies are conducted in schools, gaining access is often difficult. In the current scenario, many schools officials are reluctant to let outsiders enter the schools. The researcher has to submit detail plans outlining what he wants to do and how much time he will take doing it. He has to seek prior permission for the classroom observations.
4. *What to study*: There are numerous aspects, traits, characteristics which can be observed, but it is not desirable to study each and every aspects. Identify the most significant and meaningful variables specific to your study in the process of observation.
5. *Frequency and length of time*: Frequency and length of

observation depends upon the nature of the study. Time involved in observation should be reasonable and may not tantamount to undue interference in the regular class-work. If the research study is of intensive nature and requires more than one sitting, it is suggested that each session should not be more than 30 minutes duration.

Researcher has to decide as per prevailing situation whether to go for participant or non-participant observation in order to get more reliable and valid results.

21.2 PARTICIPANT OBSERVATION

In participant observation, the observer becomes a member of the group which is to be observed. In this process, he has to be an attentative listener, and an eager learner. He has to spin and reel at the same time i.e., simultaneously interacting, registering, observing, recording and interpreting behaviour of the group. The observer gets the feel of what the various activities of a group mean to the members and tries to understand the frame of reference of the group he is investigating, primarily, by joining the members in their daily activities in order to experience things as they do. The observer does not rely on intuition. This process of observation has built-in validity.

The social scientist observes the life of community as a whole, the relationship between its members and its activities and institutions. The community may be as small as family or as large as a city. It may be a 'closed' community, like a family or a tribe, or an 'open' one, such as a factory, a town or a village. An important difference between the two is that in the 'open' community an observation can sometimes remain unnoticed, while in 'closed' this is not possible.

The observer's task is to place himself in the best position for getting complete and unbiased picture of the life of the community, and this at once raises the question; what is the best role for the observer to adopt in the community. The successful utilization of observation method calls for:

- The observer should be skilled and experienced and be fully aware of the risks of getting a biased and unrepresentative picture.
- The observer should ensure that the behaviour of the community not become self-conscious and untypical.
- The observer should have prolonged stay in the community to have authentic and trustworthy inquiry.

- Lastly, the materials obtained by observation should be supported where necessary by other methods.

Participation observation is commonly used in an exploratory studies, at least in the initial stage. Becker (1958) distinguished three stages in the field work:

- The first being the selection and definition of problems, concepts, and indices. The participant observer's early observations help to develop his ideas on these subjects.
- The second stage involves checking of the numerous preliminary ideas which are worth pursuing. This is done by collecting further data to check on the frequency and distribution of phenomena in the community.
- The third stage of fieldwork consists of attempting to incorporate the individual findings into a model of the social system under study.
- After the fieldwork, the final systematic analysis, checking the models and rebuilding them if necessary, is conducted.
- An important feature of the procedure is its sequential nature, the observer beginning with speculations suggested by observation and developing his ideas until he can try to build a general model.

Participant observation is a somewhat individual method. One canot expect it to yield a completely faithful and objective picture, nor suppose that several observers studying the same situation would bring back identical pictures. (Paddock, 1961).

21.3 NON-PARTICIPANT OBSERVATION

In process of observation, researcher or observer is not a part of the group under study. Observer tales position outside where his or her presence is least observed. He is surreptitious or unobtrusive observer. If one observes in cyberspace, the observer is completely unknown or unnoticed. This method is mostly used in observing infants, children and abnormal persons. Validity increases by keeping the setting as natural as possible and not letting the subjects be unduly influenced by the presence of the observer or by his measuring or recording devices.

21.4 STEPS OF OBSERVATION

1. Planning

Mechanisms involved in observation

- Identify and define specifically the activities or aspects of behaviour to be observed.

- Realistically consider access/acceptance to the group/ situation/activities you wish to observe.
- Familiarize yourself and plan for any potential language and/or cultural issues likely to affect the process.
- Consider the presentation of self, including what role you will take and how involved you will be.
- Decide about the process of observation whether it is participant or non-participant

2. **Temporal course of observation**
   - Decide approximately how long you think you will be observing and whether the process will be covert or candid.
   - Fix time, date and number of observations to be undertaken.
   - Identify the conditions of observation, variations in subjects, and variations in apparatus.

3. **Consider strategies for ensuring credibility**
   - Replication of observations to achieve repetitiveness.
   - Designing the study in order to increase the number of observations.
   - Identify statistical techniques to be used.

4. **Tools for recording**
   - Prepare an observation schedule/checklist based on relevant themes which are to be explored.
   - Identify apparatus to be used for recording and its limitations.

5. **Seek ethics approval**
   - Freedom, and dignity of the subjects should be kept in mind.

6. **Conducting the Observations**
   - Ease into the observation situation. If structured and candid, this will be similar to the opening stages of an interview where you need to be on time, set-up and check any equipment, introduce the study, and establish rapport. If your study involves greater immersion into a culture, early stages will require you to sit back, listen, attempt to gain trust, and then establish rapport.
   - Use all your senses, and possibly your intuition, to gather data.

- Because you will not be directing the process, you need to be prepared to invest significant time in your observations.
- The observer has to decide what to focus on. In some settings, there may be several different things happening at the same time, and you will need to set some priorities Ther is no right thing to look at. One has to decide what is challenging or interesting to study.
- Look for saturation (your observations no longer yield new knowledge) before ending the process.

7. **Recordings**
   - Observations need to be recorded in a timely manner. If using schedules, they should be filled in while observations occur. If you are more immersed in your research context, you may want to your observations when removed from the situation either on data sheets or in a journal. Your record may also include photographs and video/audio recordings. Checklists, rating scales, scorecards, and scaled specimens provide systematic means of summarizing or quantifying data collected by observation.
   - Attempt to record your data in a systematic fashion that will ease future analysis.

8. **Reviewing**
   - Review the process and note any difficulties encountered, i.e. access, time taken, engagement, cultural 'ignorance', comfort zones, recording/note-taking, roles, objectivity, etc.
   - Review your observation records and note any difficulties you might encounter in making sense of your record.
   - See if you can confirm your record by checking with an insider, asking another observer to compare notes, or triangulating your observational data with other data types.

9. **Refining**
   - Make modifications based on your own review of the process and the quality of the data generated.
   - Observation takes practice, keep reviewing and refining until you are comfortable with the process and data collected.

10. **Other Issues**
    - Observer should know, what is his role? Does he want to

participate in the interaction? Does he want to remain aloof? Can he behave one way one time and another way another time? It is up to the observer to choose what he wants to do.

- There are two options before the observer, either one should have narrow focus or look at every things. Better way is to strike balance. Basic purpose is to uncover deep meaning rather than surface structure.
- Exercises that involve observing the same phenomenon—for example, looking at films, videos, discussing what you have observed with others, and then looking again at the same videos will heighten your power of observation. In this process one is trained to focus on details or look at the whole.

11. **Analyzing Data**
    - Work through data management and analysis. Treatment of data is according to the nature of research problem-qualitative, quantitative or experimental. Use appropriate techniques for the analysis of data.

21.5 CHARACTERISTICS OF GOOD OBSERVATION

Observation as a research data gathering process, demands rigorous adherence to the spirit of scientific inquiry. The following standards should be observed in the process of observation :

- Observation is carefully planned specifying who is to be studied, what is to be studied and in what situation, where, and frequency and length.
- Observation is based upon the nature of study- whether it is qualitative of quantitative, participative or non-participative.
- Temporal course of observation is planned in advance specifying time, date and venue.
- Strategies for ensuring creditability, reliability and validity are chalked out.
- Tools of observation such as camera, videos, tape-recorder, audio-meter (recording instruments) as well as Checklists, rating scales, scorecards, and scaled specimens are selected carefully and used appropriately.
- Observation is conducted as per objectives, hypotheses and design of the study.
- Observation is checked and verified whenever possible by

repetition or by comparison with those of other competent observers. The process of observation is, therefore, continuously revised and refined.

- Observation should be objective, free from biases and based upon the principle of neutrality.
- Observations are carefully and expertly recorded. Information gathered is systematized, quantified and analyzed to arrive at logical conclusions.
- Good observation presents the holistic view of the phenomenon.
- Good observation is based upon the foundations of freedom, liberty, and dignity of the subject (individual who is to be observed).

21.6 RELIABILITY OF OBSERVATION

In qualitative research Trustworthiness is the fundamental criteria because it is deliberated parallel to the positivist criteria that are internal validity, external validity, reliability and objectivity (Guba & Lincoln, 1989). The trustworthiness criteria comprise four quality standards: the credibility (via member checking), transferability (via thick description), dependability (via outside reviewer), and conformability (conformability data audit).

Authenticity is about conversation between researcher and participants, and the situations and emotional compassion that arise during the investigation (Ellis & Bochner, 2000). The authenticity criteria contain: ontological authenticity (understanding social milieu), educative authenticity (appreciating others' perspectives), catalytic authenticity (acting for change), and tactical authenticity (empowering members for action) (Bryman, 2008).

There are some points to be kept in mind:

- Sample should be adequate and well defined
- Variables of observation should be objective, specific and properly defined
- Methods of recording appropriate to the situation should be predetermined
- There should be a simple and understandable interaction
- The observer should follow the principle of neutrality (unbiasedness)
- Anxiety is a source of distortion and its adequate handling is a major problem in refining the human instrument for gathering reliable data
- Manageable time-schedule should be designed

- Impact of the observer should be minimized
- Observer should be trained as how to observe as well as how to handle apparatus

21.7 VALIDITY OF OBSERVATION

- The truly significant incidents of behaviour must be identified and sampled
- Seek the help of experts in identifying significant incidents of behaviour which are based on sound, established theories
- Criterion-related and construct validity may also be necessary, depending on the purpose of study and inferences made regarding behaviour.
- Contextual content of the observation is validated through internal validity criterion.

21.8 MERITS

- Observation is an appropriate research instrument in qualitative, experimental and descriptive research
- Significant aspects of personality which express themselves in behaviour can be best studied directly through observation rather than indirectly through questionnaire and interview.
- Physical aspects can be measured and compared with standard norms
- Processes and procedures can be assessed and compared with quality norms
- Impacts of various programmes can be assessed through research tool of observation
- Observation in the classroom is made to analyze learning behaviour which is a more complex phenomenon, to improve classroom performance. Most of the classroom interactions are observed through observations.
- Longitudinal studies are conducted on the basis of continuous observation of specific phenomenon.
- It is more reliable, very flexible and extremely searching.
- It discloses the minute, delicate and hidden facts , usually at lesser expense
- For accuracy in measuring and recording, tools such as check-list, and score-card or some other inquiry form are utilized along with camera and tape-recorder and measuring instruments like thermometer, audio-meter, stop-watch, binocular, etc.

- Observation is repeated by the same individual or by simultaneous observation done by many individuals.

References

Angrosumo, M.V. and May-de-Perez, K.A. (2000). 'Rethinking observation' in N.K. Denzin and Y.S. Lincoln (eds.), *Handbook of Qualitative Research*, 2nd edn., Thousand Oaks, CA & London : Sage, pp. 673-702.

Crol, P. (1986). *Systematic Classroom Observation.* London & Philadelphia: Falmer Press.

Jackson, P.W. (1968). *Life in Classrooms,* New York : Holt, Rinechart & Winston.

Rolfe, S.A. (2001). 'Direct Observation' in G. Macnavigaton, S.A. Rolfe & I. Siraj—Blatechford (eds.) , *Doing Early Childhood Research: International Perspective on Theory and Practice,* Buckingham: OVP. pp. 224-39.

Sanger, J.l. (1996). *The Complete Observer : A Field Guide to Observation*, London: Falmer Press.

CHAPTER

22

Interview as a Research Tool

Interview as a research tool is an oral type of questionnaire or schedule to gather information in a face to face relationship. It is a face to face interaction or an intimate contact between interviewee and interviewer to get information for the solution of the problem. It is a causal interaction between expert and interviewee where interviewee is willing to get interviewed. It is also an in-depth contextual understanding of the problem through interaction with the interviewee.

The dynamics of interviewing, however, involve much more than an oral questionnaire. Interview is relatively more flexible tool than any written inquiry form. It provides ample scope for explanation, adjustment and variation according to the situation. In order to make it more reliable, authentic and trustworthy, it is essential that physical, cultural and communication barriers are to be narrowed down. The interviewee and the interviewer should come on the same waive-length so that more authentic and more trustworthy information may come forth spontaneously.

Interview as a research tool is used both in quantitative and qualitative research. In case of quantitative approach, interview is used when sample size is large, interview schedule is structured, and statistical techniques are used to draw inferences. It is also used as a research tool where it is not possible to get requisite information through questionnaire, for example, from illiterate or who cannot write or understand written words, small children who have not gone through formal education. Most data-collection methods in behavioral research are moderately indirect. The indirect approach is more useful where anxiety or conformity pressures are apt to conceal true response tendencies.

Three cardinal principles of qualitative research are: (1) Each research question is uniquely defined by a specific set of circumstances. (2) There can be no attempt to answer a question without deep knowledge of the specific contextual parameters defining those circumstances, (3) Such deep knowledge comes only to those who have paid their dues. Therefore, interview occupies a very significant place in the conduct of qualitative research. This tool is invariably used in ethnographic, phenomenological, case studies and grounded theory. It gives large margin to 'in-depth analyses of the problem. Interview technique as a research tool produces spectacular results in terms of depth. It allows the reader to gain deeper understanding of, and empathy for, lives lived and values held in a very different fashion from one's own eyes (Lareau and Shultz, 1996). Being an exploratory device and contextual, it helps in understanding numerous variables and their relationships having impact on the phenomenon.

Interview is, therefore, a two person conversation initiated by the researcher on content specified by research objectives of systematic description, prediction or explanation. The data from in-depth or open-ended interviews consist of direct question from people, their experiences, opinions, feelings and knowledge.

22.1 INTERVIEW SCHEDULE

22.1.1 Unstructured Interview Schedule

The client-centered counseling technique of Carl Rogers illustrates the unstructured approach, giving the respondent broad freedom to express himself in his own way and at his own time. The interviewer may have a general or specific objective which he feels can best be met without imposing a structure on the respondent. Usually the information involved is of a highly personal and potentially threatening nature. Of the three interview structures, this one is the most vulnerable to subjective bias or errors of inexperience.

22.1.2 Semi-structured Interview

These are built around a core of structured questions from which the interviewer branches off to explore in depth. Again, accurate and complete information is desired with additional opportunity to probe for underlying factors or relationships which are too complex or elusive to encompass in more straight-forward questions. Semi-structured interviews require more training and skill both to probe significant points and to avoid biasing tendencies.

22.1.3 Structured Interviews

The interviewers follows a well-defined structure resembling the format of an objective questionnaire, allowing clarification and elaboration within narrow limits. These tend to be factually oriented, aimed at specific information, and relatively brief. Structured interviews are suitable when accurate and complete information from all respondents is important and when the type of information sought fits readily into a structured inquiry.

22.2 TYPES OF INTERVIEW

Types of interview are given in Figure 22.1.

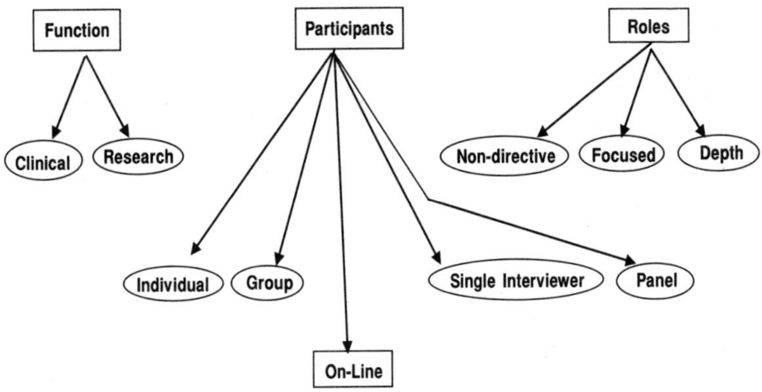

Figure 22.1 : Types of Interview

22.2.1 The Clinical Interview

In clinical work some form of the interview or personal contact has been used in many kinds of situations to secure information about the client and to understand his problems. The two major purposes of the interview in clinical work are diagnosis and treatment. Social workers employ the interview to secure information about the client's problem, his past history, family relations, and job adjustment. Classical interview is conducted when the client is a child, a mental defective, or a psychotic, or when there are unusual discrepancies in the client's presentation of data about himself.

During the clinical interview, certain non-verbal behaviour on the part of the patient has useful diagnostic value, including gait, expression posture, speech, topics avoided, digressions, and word choice. In addition to the general techniques that apply to any interview situation, special procedures may be needed to deal effectively with the problems that arise in the several types of clinical interviews: for example, the intake or admission interview, diagnostic interview, to arrive at a judgment concerning the patient's condition; interviews before and after psychological test administration, and as a means of introducing the patient to therapy; the interview to assist friends and relatives in their dealings with the patient; and the exit or termination interview to facilitate the patient's discharge or transition from hospital to home.

22.2.2 Research Interview

Research interview is used both in quantitative and qualitative research. In quantitative research, structured interview schedule is used to gather certain facts about large number of persons. Data thus collected is put to statistical analysis so as to derive inferences. In qualitative research, in-depth open interview schedule is used in case studies, ethnographic and phenomenological studies. Data thus collected are interpreted by the investigator to identify pattern and draw conclusions.

22.2.3 Non-Directive Interview

In non-directive interview, the interviewer has full freedom to make suitable alterations in questions to suit a particular situation. He may also revise the order or paraphrase the questions to suit the needs of the respondents. According to the roles assumed by the interviewer and interviewee in relation to the socio-psychological process of interaction non-directive implies uncontrolled, unguided, or unstructured interview. The non-directive interview includes questions of open-end form and permits much freedom to the interviewee to talk freely about the problem under study.

22.2.4 Focused Interview

In this type of interview, the investigator focuses on a specific problem or event or experience rather than on general lines of inquiry about it. The interviewer presents a set of well defined questions, pictures, or video to get response from the interviewee on specific experience and records the answers of the respondents in logical way. In general the focused interview employs non-directive procedures in encouraging the respondent to structure the stimulus situation. Non-direction in the focused interview means reliance on unstructured questions, but varying degrees of structure may be present. Interviewee is placed in concrete situation, field of inquiry and hypotheses are clearly stated, and the inner feelings and emotional attitudes of the interviewee *vis-a-vis* given problem or situation are given particular attention.

For instance, Rolf Oerter (1995) developed the "adulthood interview" for studying concepts of human nature and adulthood in different cultures (United States, West Germany, Indonesia, Japan and Korea) The interview was divided into four main parts. In the first part, general questions about adulthood were asked. The second part dealt with the three main roles of adulthood: family, occupational and political. The third part drew attention to the past of the interviewee, asking for developmental changes during previous two or three years. The last part dealt with the near future of the interviewee, asking for his or her goals in life and his or her development.

The successful carrying out of focus interview depends on: The interviewer's situational competence which can be increased by practical experience of making decisions necessary in interview situation, in rehearsal interviews, and interview training. Specific, reliable, authentic and trustworthy information may be obtained by more depth (deep probing) and spreading the range (by introducing new topics or the next question of the interview guide) and with the different solutions at each point.

22.2.5 In-depth Interview

The depth interview is an intensive and searching type of interview with emphasis on such psychological and social factors as attitudes, emotions or convictions. It determines the respondent's degree of attachment or detachment towards an experience or an activity. It usually involves flexibility of interview situation, focus on feelings and restatement of implied or expressed feelings. It helps in understanding the behaviour of an individual which is otherwise not possible through questionnaire. The procedures of such depth interviewing are as follows:

(a) Interview Situation

Flexible interviews encourage orientation to stimulus situation, rather then to interviewer, thus facilitating depth and curbing stereotyped reports.

(b) Retrospective Focus

Focus on past experience, through reinstatement of stimulus situation, promotes elaboration of reported responses.

(c) Focus on Feelings

Asking questions explicitly referring to affective aspects (e.g., "How did you feel when . . . ?" These may encourage reports of depth responses.

(d) Restatement of Implied or Expressed Feelings

Occasional restatements of implied or expressed feelings prove effective (1) inviting progressive elaboration of response, and (2) establishing common ground for understanding.

22.2.6 Group and Individual Interviews

The size of the group should not be so large that it is unwieldy or inhibits participation by most members, and should not be so small that it lacks substantially greater coverage than in the individual interview. The optimum size is approximately 10 to 12 persons. Social, intellectual, and educational homogeneity are important for effective participation of all group members. A circular seating arrangement, with the interviewer as one of the group, is conducive to full and spontaneous reporting and participation.

22.2.7 Single Interviewer or Panel

Both individual and group interviews may be conducted by a single interviewer or panel of interviewers, according to the design and purpose of the interview. For instance, interviews for selection and treatment purposes are held by the panel of experts in different and related fields. Interview for research purposes are usually held by a single investigator.

22.2.8 On-Line Interview

The purpose of on-line interview is to gather information from a participant on a particular topic. On-line interview is considered to be cost effective and dominant data collection method. On-line interview is without face to face experience; therefore, an on-line interviewer might need to develop a new set of techniques or skills. On-line sampling provides some interesting challenges. If e-mail is used as a means of interviewing, there is no issues regarding travelling, recording or transcribing. On-line sampling also makes possible interviewing people who are geographically dispersed. Telephones, mobiles, teleconferencing, and web-based on-line can be used for conducting interviews.

Usually, on-line interview is preplanned. A participant is selected who agrees to be interviewed at a particular time and with the use of a particular technology. Both interviewer and participant agree to be online at the same time, and the interview questions are posed by the interviewer and responded by the participant.

E-mail, Instant Messenger, Online chat, Face Book or Social Networking can be used. Because it is not planned, you will need to think about how you can capture ideas that are available.

High speed internet connections link many people to the Web and potentially to each other, conducting focus group interview online offers a new alternative to the traditional type of focus group setting. In this process, huge information can be gathered and analyzed to find solution of the specific problem.

22.3 STEPS FOR CONDUCTING AN INTERVIEW

Interviewing is an art which requires appropriate training and experience. Careful preparation of questions for the interview is as important as has been emphasized in preparing the questionnaire. A well-conducted interview is not just a haphazard series of questions and answers of a pleasant conversation. The interviewer should have a set of carefully prepared questions to serve as a thread conversation. Although he may vary the order of the questions to adapt to special circumstances.

22.3.1 Planning an Interview

(a) Define the purpose of the study—its background, theoretical basis, general goals, possible applications of results, and reasons for using the interview method.
(b) Translate the general goals into detailed and specific objectives which can be fitted to the particular interview pattern you plan to follow, constructing questions yielding useful information.
(c) Develop a tentative guide to be used during the interview, exploiting the advantages of the interview technique.
(d) Develop a satisfactory method of coding and/or recording responses. Generally, responses can be pre-categorized in a pilot study to anticipate the most frequent response patterns. Only responses falling outside these general categories would need to be written out. Tape recording of the interview may offer advantages, unless the nature of the interview is highly personal and produces guarded responses. A written summary of information recorded during or following the interview is not advised. Because of the pace of an interview, the act of writing either slows the interview unnecessarily or causes the interviewer to be

selective in the kind and amount of information he records, at the risk of introducing bias. Therefore, interviewer should:

- Realistically consider issues of representation and access.
- Develop a contingency plan in case key interviews fall through.
- Familiarize yourself with, and plan for, any potential language and/or cultural issues likely to affect the process. Find and trial a good translator if necessary.
- Consider the presentation of self, including what role you will take and how involved you will be in conversations.
- Decide approximately how long you think the interviews should take.
- Make appointments early. Plan travel time, interview time, and wait around time.

22.3.2 Framing Questions for the Interview

(a) Questions must be framed in language that ensures effective communication between the interviewer and the respondent. Omit all ambiguous vocabulary.

(b) Make certain respondent appreciates the purpose of each questions he is asked. Avoid arousing any suspicion or resistance.

(c) Ascertain whether the population from which the respondents have been selected actually has the information sought by the interview and that the questions permit the reasonable recovery of this information.

(d) Avoid leading questions (questions which suggest a desirable or preferred answer).

(e) Ensure that the frame of reference surrounding each question is clear so that each respondent hears the question in the same way, avoiding misinterpretations.

(f) Pretest the interview in a pilot study to eliminate weaknesses and experiment with alternative items or techniques.

(g) Carefully read questions and consider whether they might be considered confusing, leading, or problematic in any way for the interviewee.

(h) Rewrite the questions in relation to considerations above and run them past a few peers/supervisor for their assessment. Repeat this step as many times as necessary to get each question as right as possible.

(i) Attempt to put your questions into an order that is logical and will ease respondents into the interview.

22.3.3 Pilot Study

(a) Attempt a pilot interview with a couple of respondents whose background is similar to those in your 'sample'.

(b) Note any difficulties encountered, i.e. access, time taken, pacing, comfort zones, recording/note-taking, roles, objectivity, conversational flow, ambiguities, etc.

(c) Get feedback from the interviewees on the above and anything else they wish to discuss.

(d) Attempt to make sense of your notes and/or transcribe your data.

22.3.4 Modification and Revision

(a) Make modifications based on your own reflections, the feedback from the interviewees, and the quality of the data generated.

(b) If modifications are substantial, start again from step one.

(c) Get ethical clearance for the final interview schedule/ question/themes.

22.3.5 Executing the Interview

(a) The initial task of the interview is securing the confidence of the interviewee through establishing rapport with him. This process involves expertise of interviewer and art of communication.

(b) Interviewer should secure desired information through asking the planned sequence of questions. It should not be conducted in a rigid manner. Interviewer should inform, inspire and involve respondents and provide necessary explanation wherever required.

(c) The recording devices selected should be used without distracting the interviewee.

A check list for conducting the interview

(a) An interviewer generally should open an interview by asking factual non-threatening questions.

(b) The interviewer should locate the major data by unstructured head questions.

(c) The interviewer should make use of occasional guide questions.

(d) The interviewer should make an effort to pick up leads.
(e) The interviewer should cut through generalities with well-formulated probes.
(f) The interviewer should stick with the fruitful areas once they open up.
(g) The interviewer should reflect on the meaning of emerging data and ask questions that clarify or amplify their meaning for the research problem.
(h) The interviewer should be especially alert to follow-up only areas where the respondent shows emotional involvement.
(i) The interviewer should try to redirect the interview to more faithful topics when useful data are not emerging.
(j) The interviewer should be alert to "touchy" subject matters and just blunder in.
(k) The interviewer should try to turn back respondent's direct questions.
(l) The interviewer should wind up the interview before the respondent becomes tired.
(m) Whether an interviewer should take notes depends on the situation.

Inadequate responses which call for probing or secondary questions may be partial response, non-response, irrelevant response, inaccurate response, or verbalized response. In addition to problems of motivation and conflict of motives, the following things are to be sorted out and be given due consideration by the interviewer:

(a) The respondent may fail to understand the purpose of the question or the kind of answer needed.
(b) The language or concepts may go beyond the respondent's comprehension.
(c) The respondent may lack the information or background necessary to answer the question.
(d) The respondent may not remember the information requested.
(e) The respondent may not be able to verbalize his feelings, as in the case of intimate "depth" questions or materials.
(f) The respondent may feel that the question does not fit the purpose of the interview.
(g) The respondent may regard a question as going beyond the limits of what he is willing to confide in the interviewer.
(h) The respondent may feel that the interviewer is unable to understand his true feelings.

22.3.6 Recording and Interpretation of the Responses

(a) It is best to employ, if possible, a device of recording which would retain the actual wording of the responses. Tape-recording is convenient but ensures that it may not be nuisance. More sophisticated and high frequency gadgets are now available for recording which could be used for recording the interview.

(b) The responses to the questions in the interview have to be noted down on a diary. In case it is not recorded on spot, then should be noted down immediately after the interview. The former is often found to be of a distracting nature while the latter often fails in being complete in detail. For using either of these devices successfully a skilful and practiced hand is necessary.

(c) Sometimes, instead of recording responses, the interviewer tend to record his evaluation of them as the interview goes on it is, however, advisable to interpret and evaluate the responses later on the basis of the recording of responses rather than simultaneously

(d) In order to ensure the validity of the interview, it is essential that apparent and hidden biases should be identified and eliminated.

(e) Authenticity of interview is about conversation between researcher and participants, and the situations and emotional compassion that arise during the investigation (Ellis & Bochner, 2000). The authenticity criteria contain: ontological authenticity (understanding social milieu), educative authenticity (appreciating others' perspectives), catalytic authenticity (acting for change), and tactical authenticity (empowering members for action) (Bryman, 2008).

(f) The recordings of the interview should be interpreted in such a way that the whole phenomenon under study is understood as a complex system that is more than sum of its parts; focus on complex interdependencies and system dynamics that can not meaningfully be reduced to a few discrete and linear, cause-effect relationships.

References

Atkinsons, J.A. (1968). A Handbook for Interviewers. HMSO, London.

Gillham, B. (2005). Research Interviewing: The Range of Techniques. Maidenhead: Open University Press.

Gubrium, J.F. and Hostein, J.A. (2003). Postmodern Interviewing, London: Thousand Oaks, CA: Sage.

Hyman, H.H. (1954). *Interviewing in Social Research.* Chicago; University of Chicago Press.

Kahn, R.L., and Cannel, C.F. (1957). *The Dynamics of Interviewing : Theory, Techniques and Cases.* New York: John Wiley and Sons.

Kreuger, R., and Casey, M. (2009). Focus Group: A practical Guide for Appplied Research. 4th edition, Thousand Oaks: Sage.

Kvale, S. (2008). Doing Interviews. London: Sage.

Merton, R.K., Fiske, M., and Kendall, P.L. (1956). The focused interview: A manual problems and procedures. Glencoe: Free Press.

Mishler, E. (1986). Research Interviewing. Cambridge, MA: Harvard University Press.

Oppenheim, A.N. (1992). Questionnaire Design, Interviewing and Attitude Measurement. London: Pinter.

Schostak, J.F. (2010), Interviewing and Representation in Qualitative Research Projects, Buckingham and Philadelphia: University Open Press.

CHAPTER

23

Sociometric Techniques

23.0 SOCIOMETRY

The word *sociometry* comes from the Latin "socius", meaning social and the Latin "metrum," meaning measure. This implies sociometry is a way of measuring the degree of relatedness among people. Measurement of relatedness can be useful not only in the assessment of behaviour within groups, but also for interventions to bring about positive change and for determining the extent of change. For a work group, sociometry can be a powerful tool for reducing conflict and improving communication because it allows the group to see itself objectively and to analyze its own dynamics. It is also a powerful tool for assessing dynamics and development in groups devoted to therapy or training.

A useful working definition of sociometry is that it is a methodology for tracking the energy vectors of interpersonal relationships in a group. It shows the patterns of how individuals associate with each other when acting as a group toward a specified end or goal (Criswell in Moreno, 1960, p. 140). Moreno himself defined sociometry as "the mathematical study of psychological properties of populations, the experimental technique of and the results obtained by application of quantitative methods" (Moreno, 1953, pp. 15-16).

In order to study group conflict and interpersonal relations, Bogardus (1928) and Moreno (1934), developed quantifying measuring techniques, which were later to be called 'sociometrics'.

Sociometry is a technique used for measuring the social relationships that exist among the members of a group. It is a study to measure social choices that people make. Subjects can also be asked to rank others members of the group using sociometric technique. Members of a group or organization can be asked to rate each other using one or more criteria. It is also used to identify communication and interaction patterns of individuals in groups. It has also been called a means of studying the attracting and repulsions of members of groups. In brief, sociometry is quantitative study of social relationships and interactions, social attitudes, and social preferences.

According to Helen Jennings (1952), sociometry may be described as a means of presenting simply and graphically the entire structure of relations existing at a given time among members of a given group. The major lines of communication, or the patterns of attraction and rejection in its full scope, are made readily comprehensive at a glance.

For example, a person is asked to choose one or more other persons according to one or more criteria supplied by researcher. With whom would you like to work? With whom would you like to play? He then makes one, two, three or more choices among members of his own group or of other groups. This method works well for kindergartners as well as for atomic scientists. Such techniques are used in various educational situation to study social adjustment, group dynamics, learning, motivation, discipline, leadership behaviour, social interaction and development, and index of popularity.

Sociometric techniques have been used in the studies of mainstreaming of differently abled children and their integration in regular classroom; social, economic, and cultural discriminations among students; peer relations—issues in assessment and interventions; classroom climate and its effects on academic achievement; children as being 'socially at risk'; interaction pattern of sub-group, cliques and specific friendship and group conflicts; study of academic culture in higher education; identification of level of friendship, and anxiety; and evaluation of teachers on sociometric scale.

23.1 SOME PRINCIPLES OF CRITERION SELECTION

- The criterion should be as simple and straightforward as possible.
- The respondents should have some actual experience in reference to the criterion, whether *ex post facto* or present

otherwise the questions will not arouse any significant response.

- The criterion should be specific rather than general or vague. Vaguely defined criteria evoke vague responses. (Note for example that "friendship" is actually a cluster of criteria.)
- When possible, the criterion should be actual rather than hypothetical.
- A criterion is more powerful if it is one that has a potential for being acted upon. For example, question for freshers— "Whom would you choose as a roommate for the year?" has more potential of being acted upon than the question "Whom do you trust?"
- Moreno points out that the ideal criterion is one that helps further the life-goal of the subject.

"It is easy to gain the cooperation of the people tested as soon as they come to think of the test as an instrument to bring their wills to a wider realization, that it is not only an instrument for exploring the status of a population, but primarily an instrument to bring the population to a *collective self-expression* in respect to the fundamental activities in which it is or is about to be involved." (Moreno, 1953, pp. 680-81).

As a general rule questions should be future oriented, imply how the results are to be used, and specify the boundaries of the group (Hale, 1985). And last but not least, the criteria should be designed to keep the level of risk for the group appropriate to the group's cohesion and stage of development.

23.2 APPLICATION OF SOCIOMETRY IN THE WORK SETTING

The typical process for a sociometric intervention in an organization follows these basic steps: (1) Identify the group to be studied, (2) Develop the criterion, (3) Establish rapport/warm-up, (4) Gather sociometric data, (5) Analyze and interpret data, (6) Feed-back data, either: (a) to individuals, prior to group meeting, or (b) in a group setting, (7) Develop and implement action plans, and (8) Post-test (optional).

Numerous sociometric techniques are used to measure social interaction within groups, but sociogram, sociometric matrix, guess— who technique and social distance scale are most frequently used in educational research. Methods of socimetric analysis include:

(1) Sociometric matrices,
(2) Sociograms, and
(3) Sociometric indices.

23.2.1 Sociometric Matrix

Sociometric Matrix is a rectangular array of numbers or other symbols indicating the choices made by the members of a group. Choices or preferences are ploted in columns of the matrix. It is convenient to write sociometric matrices. For example, suppose a group of five members has responded to the sociometric question. With whom would you like to work? The responses to the sociometric question are of course, choice. If a group member chooses another group member, the choice is represented by 1 & 0 i.e. '1' indicates a member choose other member in a group and '0' in case member does not choose another. Sociometric Choice Matrix is shown in Table 23.1.

TABLE 23.1
Sociometric Choice Matrix

	A	*B*	*C*	*D*	*E*
A	0	1	0	0	1
B	1	0	0	0	1
C	0	0	0	1	1
D	0	1	0	0	1
E	1	1	0	0	0
Σ	2	3	0	1	4

Criteria : Each member has to make two choices out of 5 members of the group on a specific question.

Three kinds of choices will emerge as given below:

A simple—One way choice: 'D' chooses 'E' and 'E' does not choose 'A'.

Mutual—Two-way choice: A chooses 'B' and 'B' chooses 'A'.

No choice—Zero choice to member of a group: for instance 'C' chooses 'D' and 'E', but 'C' fails to get choice from other members of the group.

'E' gets maximum choices (4). Two mutual and two independent.

'B' gets 3 choices two mutual and one independent.

'A' gets two mutual choices.

'D' gets one choice.

'C' could not figure on the choices.

Evidently C is not at all popular because no one chooses him. D is not popular because he receives single choice.

In this matrix we find 'most popular' on one hand and 'isolate' on the other, isolates having least social interaction. This gives rise to the in-depth study of isolates so that effective strategies can be evolved to bring about desirable behavioural modification. Variables of 'most popular' individuals can further be studied in relation to leadership development theories.

23.2.2 Sociogram

Sociogram is a map of interpersonal relationships and interpersonal lines of communication. Sociometric choices may be represented graphically on a chart known as a sociogram. There are many versions of the sociogramm pattern. For instance, it can be presented in different symbols indicating boys and girls or teachers and boys. A choice may be represented by a single-pointed an arrow and mutual choices by an pointing in opposite directions. Those chosen most often are referred to as stars, those not chosen as isolates. Small groups made up of individuals who choose one another are cliques or cohesive group.

Sociogram is a diagram or chart of the choices made in groups. This is shown in Figure 23.1.

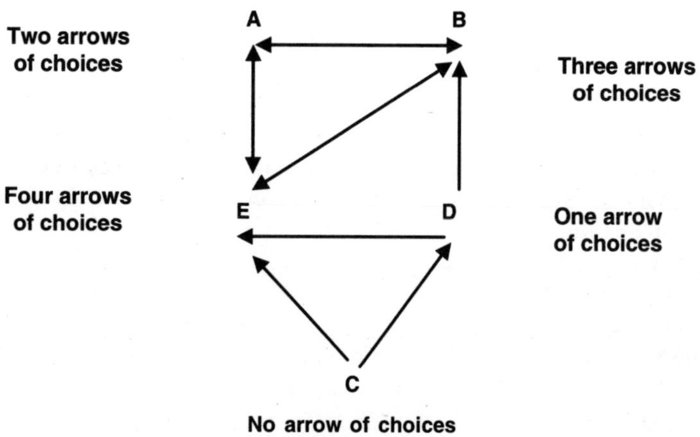

Figure 23.1

- 'E' got maximum choices (4). Therefore, E is the center of choice. We might call him leader.
- A, B and C choose each other. This is a clique. We define a clique as three that A, B, E choose each other.

— 'C' is not chosen, it reflects that he is either isolate or neglected.

Number of sociograms can be constructed at different period of time to identify changes in interactions or relationships from time to time in order to bring isolates or individuals at social risk into the mainstream or to transform cliques into more general group membership. Peer group interactions and relationships help in understanding the nature of the members of the group.

Sociogram is feasible only for small group for descriptive purposes or graph and is E excellent means of summarizing group relations. For larger group (larger than 20 members) and move analytic purpose, it is not suitable. It becomes difficult to construct and difficult to interpret.

23.2.3 Sociometric Indices

Sociometric indices reveal the choice status of Person, and Group cohesiveness.

A simple but useful index is:

$CS_E = C_E/M\text{-}1 = CS_E = 4/4 = 1.00$

CS_E = Choice status of 'E' persons

C_E = choice given to E

M-1 = Total number – 1

Similarly $CS_a = Ca/M\text{-}1 = 2/4 = .50$ and

$CS_b = Cb/M\text{-}1 = 3/4 = .75$

$CS_c = Cc/M\text{-}1 = 0/4 = 0$ (zero)

$CS_d = Cd/M\text{-}1 = 1/4 = .25$

Group sociometric measures are perhaps more interesting. It is a measure of the cohesiveness of a group. Group cohesiveness is represented by sum of mutual choices or mutual pairs. This useful index is the proportion of mutual choices to the total number of possible pairs. It is a five member group, the total number of possible pairs 5 things taken 2 at a time.

Total number of possible pairs = 10/2 =5

There were three mutual choices in case of A↔B, B↔E, E↔A, therefore, group cohesiveness is:

= 3/5 = .60 a substantial degree of cohesiveness.

23.3 APPLICATIONS OF SOCIOMETRY

1. Sociometric techniques are useful in classifying individual and groups,
2. In identifying the leader or popular student in the class,

3. In identifying group cohesiveness,
4. In identifying isolates or rejected,
5. In devising strategies to bring isolates or rejected into mainstream,
6. In mainstreaming of differently abled children and their integration in regular classroom,
7. In identifying social, economic, and cultural discriminations among students,
8. Peer relations—issues in assessment and interventions,
9. ST are used in identifying,
10. Identifying children as being 'socially at risk',
11. Interaction pattern of sub-group, cliques and specific friendship and group conflicts,
12. In study of academic culture in higher education,
13. In identification of level of friendship, anxiety, cildren at risk, and
14. In evaluating of teachers on sociometric scale.

References

Hale, Ann E. (1985). *Conducting Clinical Sociometric Explorations: A Manual.* Roanoke, Virginia: Royal Publishing Company.

Kerlinger, F. (1986). *Foundations of Behavioral Research.* 5rd edition, Orlando: Harcourt Brace.

Kothari,C.R. (2004). *Research Methodology: Methods & Techniques.* New Delhi: New Age International Publishers.

Koul, L. (2009). *Methodology of Educational Research.* Vikas Publishing House, New Delhi.

Leedy, P., Ormrod, J. (2010). *Practical Research: Planning and Design.* 9th edition, Needham Heights: Allyn Bacon.

Paneerselvam, R. (2004). *Research Methodology.* New Delhi: Prentice-Hall of India

Punch, K.F. (2009). *Introduction to Research Methods in Education.* New Delhi: Sage.

Rolfe, S.A. (2001). 'Direct observation' in G. Macnavigaton, S.A. Rolfe & I. Siraj–Sanger, Jl (1996). *The Complete Observer?* A Field Guide to Observation, London: Falmer Press.

CHAPTER

24

Reliability and Validity of Instruments of Measurement

24.0 INTRODUCTION

True Score *vs.* Observed Scores

Observed score on an ability test differs from true score. In other words observed score contains true score plus error (not related to test-taker's ability). This can be explained in an simple equation:

$$X = T + E$$

X represents observed score; T represents true score, and E represents error.

In statistics , it can be expressed as Variance from true differences is true variance, and variance from irrelevant, random sources is error variance, and total variance is true variance plus error variance.

Total Variance = True Variance + Error Variance

The true variance and error variance is shown in Figure 24.1.

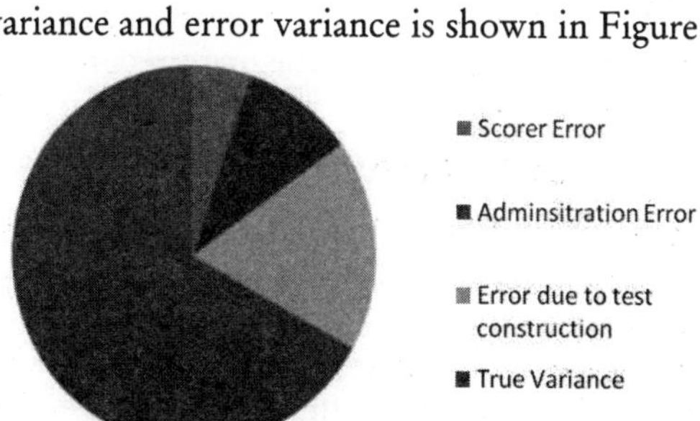

Figure 24.1

Reliability

The term reliability refers to the proportion of the total variance attributed to true variance. The greater the proportion of the total variance attributed to the true variance, the more reliable the test is. Because the true differences are assumed to be stable, they are presumed to yield consistent scores on repeated administration of test as well as on equivalent forms of tests. Broadly speaking, Reliability is the degree of consistency that the instrument demonstrates. It merely connotes something that is consistent—not necessarily consistently good or bad, but simply consistent.

24.1 SOURCES OF ERROR VARIANCE

1. Test Construction

One source of variance during test construction is item sampling or content sampling, a term refers to variation among items within a test, as well as to variation among items between tests.

2. Test Administration

Sources of errors variance that occur during test administration may influence the test taker's attention or motivation. For example, physical environment-seating arrangement, ventilation, light and noise, examiner interference—favourable or unfavourable, test-takers' mind-set, etc.

3. Test scoring and interpretation

Manual scoring sometimes causes error. In open ended questions errors are expected in the interpretation.

4. Other Sources of Error

Certain type of assessment situations lend themselves to particular varieties of systematic and non-systematic error. Sources of non-systematic error in assessment situation include forgetting, failure to notice behaviour and misunderstating instructions regarding reporting. Systematic errors include underreporting or overreporting of perpetration of abuse

24.2 RELIABILITY ESTIMATES

24.2.1 Test-Retest Reliability (stability over time)

For example, an accurate ruler (12 inches scale) when put to test and retest would give the same results. The reliability of this instrument of measurement may also be said to be stable over time. This approach to reliabilty estimation is called test-retest reliabilty. Test-retest reliability is obtained by correlating pairs of scores from the same people on two different administrations of the same test.

Variables affecting the Coefficient of stability are: (a) the time interval between administration of the same test, (b) training or counseling, (c) emotional instability, physical environment or disturbance, (d) various factors such as experience, practice, memory, fatigue, and motivation may intervene and confound an obtained measure of reliabilty.

24.2.2 Pararel-Forms and Alternate-Forms Reliability Estimates

- Parallel forms of the test exist when for each form of the test, the mean and the variance of observered test scores are equal. In theory, the mean of scores obtained on parallel forms correlate equally with the true score.
- Alternate forms are simply different version of a test that has been constructed so as to be parallel. i.e. typically designed to be equivalent with respect to variables such as content and level of difficulty.

Additional source of error vaiance has been observed in alternate or parallel forms is item sampling, i.e. test-takers may do better or worse on a specific form of the test, not as a function of their true ability, but simply because of the particular items that were selected for inclusion in the test (Atkinson, 1981).

24.2.3 Split-Half Reliability Estimates (stability of items, i.e. internal-consistency)

An estimate of split-half reliability is obtained by correlating two pairs of scores obtained from equivalent halves of a single test. The computation of a coefficient of split-half reliability generally involves four steps:

- Dividing the test into two equivalent halves: one acceptable way is to split a test randomly into two equal halves. A second acceptable way is to assign odd numbered items to one-half of the test and even numbered items to other half, i.e. odd-even reliability.
- Mini-parallel-forms can be created for the calculation of split-half reliability.
- Computing a Pearson's between scores on the two halves of the test.
- Adjusting the half-test reliability using Spearman-Brown formula.

24.3 THE SPEARMAN-BROWN FORMULA

The Spearman-Brown Formula is used to calculate Split-half Reliability Coefficient. Formula for estimation of split-half reliability of the whole test is given below:

$$r_{SB} = \frac{2rhh}{1+rhh}$$

r_{SB} is Spearman-Brown Farmula for Split-Half Reliability.

rhh stands for the Pearson r scores in the two half tests.

The reliabilty of the instrument could be raised by increasing test length, by determining the number of items needed to attain a desired level of reliabilty, creating new items, clarifying the tests administration, or simplifying the scoring rules.

This Spearman-Brown farmula is considered inappropriate for measuring reliability of heterogeneous tests and speed tests.

24.4 KUDER-RICHARDSON-20 FARMULA

Kuder-Richardson 20 farmula is used for determining the inter-item consistency of dichotomous items, for example, right or wrong. If test items are more heterogeneous KR-20 will yield lower reliability estimates than the split-half method. The KR-20 used for calculation of reliabilty is given below:

$$r_{KR} = \left(\frac{k}{k-1}\right)\left(\frac{1-\sum pq}{\sigma^2}\right)$$

r_{KR20} stands for Kuder-Richardson-20 farmula

k is the number of test items

σ^2 is the variance of total test scores

p is the proportion test-takers who pass the item, q is the proportion people who fail the item, and Σpq is of the pq products over all items.

24.5 COEFFICIENT ALPHA (CRONBACH, 1951)

Coefficient alpha (Cronbach, 1951) is the mean of all possible—the good along with the bad-split-half correlations, corrected by the Spearman-Brown farmula. (Kaiser and Michael, 1975) The KR-20 is appropriate for use on tests with dichotomous items. Besides, coefficient alpha is appropriate for use on tests containing non-dichotomous items.The farmula for coeffieicent alpha is:

$$r_{\alpha} = \left(\frac{k}{k-1}\right)\left(\frac{1-\sum \sigma_i^2}{\sigma^2}\right)$$

r_α stands for Cronbach farmula for reliability, k is number of test items.

σ_i^2 is the variance of one item,

$\Sigma\sigma_i^2$ is the sum of variance of each item, and σ^2 is the variance of the total test scores.

Today, computer is generally used for analysis of data, therefore, coefficient alpha is the preferred statistic for obtaining an estimate of internal consistency reliability.

24.6 THE NATURE OF THE TEST

Which test is to be used, basiclly depends on the nature of the test such as whether:

(1) test items are homogeneous or heterogeneous (The Spearman-Brown or The KR-20);
(2) trait being measured is presumed to be dynamic or static (internal consistency meaures for dynamic trait and the test-retest fot static trait;
(3) the range of test scores is or not restricted (Bayley Scales,1993);
(4) the test is a speed or a power (test-retest or alternate-forms reliability); and
(5) the test is or is not criterion-referenced (Hambleton & Jurgensen, 1990).

24.7 FACTORS AFFECTING RELIABILITY ESTIMATES

(1) Range of scores
(2) The time interval between testing
(3) The effects of practice and learning
(4) Reliability of sub-tests
(5) Consistency of scores and

I. *Lasting and General Characteristics of the Individual*
   1. General skills (e.g. reading).
   2. General ability to comprehend instructions, testwiseness and techniques of taking tests.
   3. Ability to solve problems of the general type presented in this test.
   4. Attitudes, emotional reactions or habits generally operating in situations like the test situation (e.g., self-confidence).

II. *Lasting and specific characteristics of the individual*
   1. Knowledge and skills required by particular problems in the test.

2. Attitudes, emotional reactions, or habits related to particular test stimuli (e.g. fear of high places brought to mind by an inquiry about such fears on a personality test).

III. *Temporary and general characteristics of the individual (systematically affecting performance on various tests at a particular time)*
1. Health, fatigue, and emotional strain.
2. Motivation, rapport with examiner.
3. Effects of heat, light, and ventilation.
4. Level of practice on skills required by tests of this type.
5. Present attitudes, emotional reactions, or strength of habits (insofar as these are departures from the person's average or lasting characteristics, e.g. political attitudes during an election campaign.

IV. *Temporary and specific characteristics of the individual*
1. Changes in fatigue or motivation developed by this particular test (e.g. discouragement resulting from failure on a particular item).
2. Fluctuations in attention, coordination, or standards of judgment.
3. Fluctuations in memory for particular facts.
4. Level of practice on skills or knowledge required by this particular test (e.g. effects of special coaching).
5. Temporary emotional states and strength of habits, related to particular test stimuli (e.g. a question calls to mind a recent bad dream)

24.8 CONCEPT OF VALIDITY

Validity refers to a judgment concerning how well a test does in fact measure what it purports to measure. More specifically, it is a judgment based on evidence about the appropriateness of inferences drawn from test scores. An inference is a logical or deduction in reasoning process. In other words, does the test serve specific purpose for which it is designed. For instance, the test prepared for the measurement of intelligence really measures the intelligence or a test for measurement of anxiety infact measures the same for the pupose it is designed. Validation is a process of gathering and evaluating validity evidence. In other words, it must validate the test specific purpose. There are three main categories through which tests can validated:

- *Content validity*: content is scritinized to establish validity.
- *Criterion related validity*: test scores obtained is correlated to criterion to establish validity of the test. Two types of validity evidence are subsumed under 'criterion-related validity' namely—*Concrrent validty and Predictive validity.*
- *Construct validity*: comprehensive analysis is done in the light of theoretical framework of the construct to establish the validity.

24.8.1 Content Validity

Content validity describes a judgment concerning how adequately a test samples behaviour representative of the universe of behaviour the test was designed to sample. This form of validity is estimated by evaluating the relevance of the test items, individually and as a whole. At the same time, it is essential that the content not be compounded by introducing irrelevant materials.

For example, a test of spelling ability should not place any weight on rates of writing. A test of arithmetical problems may not be 'contaminated' with reading ability. With respect to educational achievement tests, it is customary to consider a test a content-valid measure when the proportion of material covered by the test approximates the proportion of material covered in the course. One widely used method of measuring 'content validity' was developed by C.H. Lawshe (1975) developed a formula termed the Content Validity Ratio (CVR). He proposed that each rater on the judging panel respond to the following questions for each item: Is the skill or knowledge measured by this item-Essential/Useful but not essential/ Not essential. On the basis of panelists judgement, CVR is calculated to establish the content validity of the test. For example:

$$CVR = \frac{n_e - N/2}{N/2}$$

where CVR= content validity ratio; n_e =number of panelists indicating 'essential,' and N= total number of panelists=10.

1. Negative CVR, when fever than half the panelists indicate "essential" i.e.

$$CVR = \frac{3-(10/2)}{10/2} = \frac{-2}{5} = -0.4$$

2. Zero CVR, when exactly half of the panelists indicate "essential"

$$CVR = \frac{5-(10/2)}{10/2} = 0$$

3. Positive CVR, assume eight of ten indicated "essential"

$$CVR = \frac{8 - (10/2)}{10/2} = .60$$

The CVR .60 is significant. This item can be retained.

24.8.2 Criterion Related Validity

Criterion validation establishes validity through a comparison with some criterion external to the test. The criterion is, in essence, the standard against which the validity of the test will be judged. If the scores of the measure being validated relate highly to the criterion, the designed measure is valid. Validating scores of post-graduate admission test to graduate average grade scores is an example of criterion validity.

1. One should be careful in selection of criterion measure. Like test scores, the criterion scores should be reliable. The reliability of the criterion and the reliability of the test each limit the magnitude of the validity coefficient. This relationship can be explained by the farmula given below:

   $$r_{xy} = \sqrt{(r_{xx})(r_{yy})}$$

   r_{xy} is the vailidity coefficient (correlation between the test and the criterion measure), r_{xx} is the test reliability, and r_{yy} is the criterion reliability.
2. If one test (Y) is being used as the criterion to validate the test (X), then evidence should exist that test (y) is valid.
3. If the criterion used is a rating made by a panel of judges, then evidence should exist that the rating is valid.
4. A psychological test that had been validated using some sort of criterion involving data is obtained from psychologists.

Two types of validity evidence are subsumed under the "criterion-related validity" namely :

24.8.3 Concurrent Validity

Concurrent Validity is used if data on the two measures, test and criterion, are collected at or about the same time. Statements of concurrent validity indicate the extent to whch test scores may be used to estimate an individual's present standing on a criterion. If for example, scores (classifications) made on the basis of a psychodiagnostic test to be validated against a criterion of already diagnosed psychiatric patients, the process would be one of concurrent validity.

Sometimes a researcher explores whether a test that had been validated with adults could be used with adolecents. Or a test that had been validated on data from schools of U.K. could be used on Indian students.

24.8.4 Predictive Validity

Predictive Validity is measures of the relationship between the test scores and a criterion measure. In other words, the predictive validity is how accurately scores on the test predict some criterion measure. Measures of the relationship between college admission tests and freshman grade point averages, for example, provide evidence of predictive validity of the admission tests. Or relationship between marks obtained by the students of professional college in the terminal examination and their placement in future provide evidence of predictive validity of the terminal examination. Judgement of criterion-related validity, whether concurrent or predictive, are based on two types of statistical evidence: validity coefficient and expectancy data.

24.8.5 The Validity Coefficient

The validity coefficient can be derived by using:

1. Pearson (r) correlation coefficient to determine the validity of the two measures.
2. In case of preferences or self-ranking, Spearman rho rank-order correlation would be employed. Use of the method of correlation depends upon the type of data, the sample size, and the shape of the distribution.

Cronbach and Gleser (1965) argued that validity coefficients need to be large enough to enable the test user to make accurate decisions.

24.9 CONSTRUCT VALIDITY

Construct Validity is a judgment about the appropriateness of inferences drawn from test scores regarding individual standings on a variable called a "construct". A construct is an informed, scientific idea developed or hypothesized to describe behaviour. "Intelligence" is a construct that may be invoked to describe why a student performs well in school. "Anxiety" is a construct that may be invoked to why a psychiatric patient paces the floor. Other examples of constructs are "personality", "self-concept", "motivation", "creativity" etc.

The researcher investigating a test's construct validity must formulate hypotheses about the expected behaviour of high scores and low scores on the test. From these hypotheses arises a tentative theory about the nature of the construct the test was designed to measure. If the test is a valid measure of the construct, the high and the low scores will behave as predicted by the theory. If high and low scores do not behave as predicted, the investigator will need to re-examine hypotheses made about the construct.

One possible reason for obtaining results contrary to those that would have been predicted by the theory is that the test simply is not a valid measure of the construct. Alternative explanation if supported by substantial evidence would provide ample scope that theory (construct) needs to be re-examined. Thus, although, confirming evidence contributes to a judgement that the test is indeed a valid measure of some construct, contrary evidence—on the bright side—provides a stimulus for the discovery of new facts of the constuct or alternative way to measure it.

Construct validity has been viewed as the unifying concept for all validity evidence, all types of validity evidence, including the content and criterion-related validities, are forms of construct validity.

24.9.1 Evidence of Construct Validity

Construct validity is established on the basis of different kinds of evidence. For example:

1. *Evidence of homogeneity*: The test is homogeneous, measuring a single construct.
2. *Evidence of changes with age*: If the test score is to be considered a valid measure of a construct, it should show the progressive changes with age. Other things being same, the scores of children in grade 9th and 8th would be higher over 6th and 7th grade children for a test of eighth grade vocabulary.
3. *Evidence of pre-test/post-test changes*: Evidence showing that test scores change as a result of some experience between a pre-test and post-test can be evidence of construct validity.
4. *Evidence from distinct groups*: Test scores obtained by people from distict groups vary as predicted by theory is an example of construct validity.
5. *Convergent evidence*: If scores on the test undergoing validation tend to correlate highly in the predicted direction with scores on old or already validated tests to measure the same construct is an example of construct validity.

6. *Discriminated evidence*: Test should provide discriminant evidence of construct validity.
7. *Factor analysis*: Both convergent and discrinant evidence of construct validity can be obtained by the use of factor analysis.

24.10 FACTORS AFFECTING THE VALIDITY OF A TEST

The validity of a test is tied to

(a) the test bias :
(b) the rating error
(c) the test fairness

24.10.1 Test Bias

It refers to prejudice and preferential treatment. Intelligence test too difficult for one group as compared to another is an example of bias. For psychometricians, bias is a factor inherent within a test that systematically prevents accurate, impartial measurement

For instance, "flip-coin test" (FCT). Coin will have one side "head" and the other side "tail". FCT will be considered bias if its one side appears frequently than it would by chance alone. A valid test must be free from bias.

24.10.2 Rating Error

Simply stated, a rating error is a judgment resulting from the intentional or unintentional misuse of a rating scale. For example, a leniency error arises from the tendency on the part of the rater to be lenient in marking. At the other extreme is a severity error. In this case rater is on the either of extreme side. (strickest on rating). Other type of error is a central tendency error. In this case, the rater is confined to centre. Another type of error is on account of halo effect.

24.10.3 Test Fairness

Test fairness means a test is used in an impartial, just and equitable manner. Unfairness in the use of a test is due to:

(a) test usage guidelines are not clear;
(b) test is not used properly in practice; and
(c) administrative regulations are not followed properly.

1. Relationship between reliability and validity:

(a) For a test to predict a particular criterion, predictive (criterion-related) validity is more important than reliability. When predictive validity is satisfactory, low reliability is not a serious problem.

(b) Given two test measuring the same thing, the test with the higher reliability will also have the higher validity coefficient.

(c) Rule for the limit reliability places on validity. The correlation between the test and independent criterion can never be higher than the square root of the product of the reliability of the test and the reliability of the criterion variable.

REFERENCES

Anastasi, A. and Susana, W. (2008). *Psychological Testing.* New Delhi: Dorling Kindersley.

Cohan, R.J. and Swerdlick (2002). *Psychological Testing and Assessment: An Introduction to Test and Measurement.* New York: McGraw Hill.

Jackson, C. (2001). *Understanding Psychological Testing.* New Delhi: JAICO Publishing House

Kline, P. (2005). *Psychological Testing: A Practical Approach to Design and Evaluation.* New Delhi: Vistaar.

UNIT IV

METHODS

CHAPTER

25

Qualitative Research Method

Three cardinal principles of qualitative research are:

(1) Each research question is uniquely defined by a specific set of circumstances.
(2) There can be no attempt to answer a question without deep knowledge of the specific contextual parameters defining those circumstances.
(3) Such deep knowledge comes only to those who have paid their dues

The main characteristics of qualitative research are:

(1) It is intuitive–it involves deep knowledge to explore the real world;
(2) It is holistic–research needs to explore systems because the whole is often seen as more than the sum total of the parts;
(3) It is subjective–researchers acknowledge being value-bound;
(4) Methods are often inductive–the process moves from specific observations;
(5) It is dependable–uses systematic and rigorous approaches to research instead of method of reliability;
(6) It is auditable–verifiable through full and transparent explication of method; and
(7) Its findings are idiographic–may not be able to generalize, yet have their own intrinsic worth.

Unpredictability and uncertainty are recognized as crucial aspects of the research situation. It reflects the real world situations as they unfold naturally without any manipulation and pre-determined constraints or outcomes.

Thinking, seeing and messing about ideas in order to change the world. Truth is to be understood in systemic circular relations. Aim is to question the assumed educational, theoretical or moral superiority of particular world-views or dominant paradigms in educational research and practice. It involves deconstruction and reconstruction of ideas. Deconstruction is one which seeks to interrogate these constructed 'texts'. The process might involve the deconstruction of language, drawing on linguistics and literary theory, of actions, drawing on anthropology and cultural studies, drawing on sociology and social psychology. It recognizes multiple views and multiple voices and turns its attention to the 'margins' rather than 'centre' in order to the 'vicious binaries' by which society is constructed and defined. It is more like a prism which refracts multiple images of 'realities'.

Researcher challenges the existing paradigms, i.e., the areas of certainty, objectivity, validity and truth. Involve him in the in-depth understanding and active participation of the subjects. Scholar who 'produce data' are complex creatures whose perceptions and communications are shaped at every turn by the context in which they find themselves.

25.1 QUALITATIVE RESEARCH APPROACH

25.1.1 Biographical Studies

In biographical studies the investigator begins with an objective set of experiences in the subject's life, noting life course, stages and experiences.

25.1.2 Ethnographical

This is concerned with studying an entire culture of the group of people or known as cultural anthropology or more recently a naturalistic inquiry. It is a method of field study that became popular in the later part of the nineteenth century. It is a method for carrying out qualitative observational research. It has continued to show significant development, suggesting promising techniques for the study of behaviour in educational situation.

25.1.3 Phenomenological

It is concerned with the study of the structures and essence of experience of particular phenomenon for people. It is personal experience of a phenomenon and the essential experience of others who have also experienced this phenomenon intensely. How X ideological perspective is manifested in this phenomenon? This focuses on the subjective experiences of people over a long period of time.

25.1.4 Case-based Research

This is concerned with case study. A case may be an individual or institution. The case study is an intensive examination of "single case of a particular phenomenon". Andrew Bennett expanded the term to "include both within case analysis of single cases and comparisons between or among a small number of cases. In the case-based research a wide array of different data sources and a number of different analytic strategies are utilized. The case study examines units of analysis that are not drawn from a well-demarcated population.

25.1.5 Grounded Theory

Grounded theory is a research strategy whose purpose is to generate theory from data. The focus of grounded theory approach is on the development of inductive, "bottom-up" theory that is "grounded" directly in the empirical data. Analytical and interpretive procedures are used for analyzing and conceptualizing data through coding (open coding, axial coding and selection coding), non-statistical sampling, writing of memos, diagramming of conceptual relationships, written and verbal reports. The findings of grounded theory are not arrive at by means of statistical procedures or other means of quantification, but are derived from the data gathered by a variety of means including 'observation' interview, documents, and videotapes.

25.2 RESEARCH DESIGN

"In a qualitative study, the activities of collecting and analyzing data, developing and modifying theory, elaborating or refocusing research questions, identifying and dealing with validity threats are usually going on more or less simultaneously, each influencing all of others. In addition, the researcher may need to reconsider or modify any design decision during the study in response to new developments" (Maxwell, 1998). Research designs may be formulated to achieve the goals of the research.

At the centre of the design of a study is its logic or rationale—the reasoning, or the set of ideas by which the study intends to proceed in order to answer its research questions. (Punch, 2009).

The research design should respond to the following queries:

1. What will be the conceptual framework? (i.e. the conceptual framework that determines how much pre-specified structure of a study will have). It includes: (a) Identification of problem; (b) Research questions; (c) Research tools to be used; (d) collection and analysis of qualitative data-subjects, contents and context; (e) connecting research questions to data; and (f) interpretations of results.
2. What will be the methodology? This comprises: (a) sampling for the research; (b) approach-qualitative or mixed; (c) content and context, and (d) tools and procedures for data collection.
3. How data will be analyzed? The main components are: (a) data reduction—without loss of significant information; (b) data display—the process to organize, compress and assemble information (graphs, charts, and Venn diagrams, causal models, etc.); and (c) drawing and verifying conclusions.

They link theoretical frameworks, research questions, presentation goals, methods, and generalization. Their realization is the result of evidence obtained in the research process.

25.3 METHODOLOGY

Method

25.3.1 Inductive

Research questions are formulated and modified in the process of observations in the field. Hypotheses are more likely to emerge from the data than to be formulated prior to the research.

25.3.2 Sampling

In qualitative research:

- Features of the basic population are not known
- Extension of the basic population is not known in advance
- Repeated drawing of sampling elements with criteria to be defined again in each step
- Sample size is not defined in advance
- Sampling is finished when theoretical saturation has been reached

Therefore, the purposive sampling method is generally used in qualitative research.

25.3.3 Purposeful Sampling

Purpose is to get insight about phenomenon, not empirical generalization from a sample to a population. Qualitative research cannot be conducted through *a-priori* samples only. Sampling goes on throughout research, through various sampling techniques, such as, typical case sampling, intensity sampling, critical case sampling, sensitive case sampling, convenience sampling, primary selection and secondary selection.

25.3.4 Tools and Techniques of Qualitative Research

Tools and techniques of qualitative research are innumerous, such as, observation, interview, triangulation, Focus Group Discussion, Reflective Dialogue.

- *Observation* is a technique of data collection in which one or more persons observe the happenings in a relevant situation on the basis of pre-determined scheme. It could be participant observation in which the observer participates himself in said situation. In non-participant observation the observer observes the behaviour in real life situation. Data from observations consist of detail description of people's activities, actions, and the full range of interpersonal interaction and organizational processes that are part of observable human experience.
- *Interview* is a two person conversation initiated by the researcher on content specified by research objectives of systematic description, prediction or explanation. The data from in-depth or open-ended interviews consist of direct question from people, their experiences, opinions, feelings and knowledge.
- *Triangulation* uses two or more methods to investigate to get a more complete, accurate picture of human behaviour. This can be done through convergence of gathering data from different sources through different methods.
- *Focus Group Discussions* are organized group discussions which are focused around a single theme. The group is a purposive sample-based on certain pre-determined criteria. Statement(s) of one person initiates a chain reaction of comments/responses from other respondents. When a group deliberates over a theme/problem, many a time, there is an excitement among participants to put forward their views.

- *Email-Facilitated Reflective Dialogue* may be used to engage human service practitioners as partners in research about sensitive areas of front line work which otherwise can be difficult for a range of reasons, such as, time constraints, geographic limitations, trust in the research relationship, issue of privacy, and fear of professional judgment.
- *Written documents*: document analysis in qualitative inquiry yields excerpts, quotations, or entire passages from organizational or programme records, memoranda and correspondence, official publications and reports, personal diaries, or open-ended written responses to questionnaires and surveys.

Qualitative Research cannot be conducted through static tools and techniques, because very often the researcher employing qualitative research methodology does not have a sound theoretical base related to the reality. Theory in fact is the product of enquiry. Data are created by human efforts; put more prosaically, the way in which information is collected affects the content of the data themselves; scholar who 'produce data' are complex creatures whose perceptions and communications are shaped at every turn by the context in which they find themselves; and both the content and the quality of data are prime concerns.

It is in-depth analysis of contextually-bound data. It involves the subjectivity of the researcher.

25.4 INTERPRETATION OF RESULTS

The whole phenomenon under study is understood as a complex system that is more than sum of its parts; focus on complex interdependencies and system dynamics that can not meaningfully be reduced to a few discrete and linear, cause-effect relationships.

25.5 CRITERIA FOR EVALUATION

Criteria are : (1) Trustworthiness, (2) Authenticity.

25.5.1 Trustworthiness

Trustworthiness is the fundamental criteria because it is deliberated parallel to the positivist criteria that are internal validity, external validity, reliability and objectivity (Guba & Lincoln, 1989). The trustworthiness criteria comprise four quality standards: the credibility (via member checking), transferability (via thick description), dependability (via outside reviewer), and conformability (conformability data audit).

25.5.2 Authenticity

Authenticity is about conversation between researcher and participants, and the situations and emotional compassion that arise during the investigation (Ellis & Bochner, 2000). The authenticity criteria contain: ontological authenticity (understanding social milieu), educative authenticity (appreciating others' perspectives), catalytic authenticity (acting for change), and tactical authenticity (empowering members for action) (Bryman, 2008). Findings are qualitative, valuable and idiographic or transferable.

References

Anfara and Mertz (2006). *Theoretical Frameworks in Qualitative Research.* Thousand Oaks, C A: Sage.

Bailey, K.D. (1987). *Methods of Social Research.* 3rd. edn. New York: Free Press.

Bassey, M. (2001). A solution to the problem of generalisation in educational research: Fuzzy prediction. *Oxford Review of Education*, 27(10), pp. 5-22.

Best, J. and Kahn, J. (2995). *Research in Education.* 10th edition, Needham Heights: Allyn and Bacon.

Cozby, P. (2009). *Methods in Behavioural Research.* 10th edition, Bemont: Wadsworth.

Denzin, N.K. and Lincoln, Y.S. (2000). *Handbook of Qualitative Research*, London: Sage.

Feldman, N. (ed.) (2001). Strategies for Interpreting Qualitative Data. Thousand Oaks, CA: Sage.

Flick, U. (2007c). *Designing Qualitative Research* .Thousand Oaks, CA: Sage.

Goode,W.J., and Hatt, P.K. (1990). *Methods in Social Research.* McGraw-Hill, New Delhi.

Guthrie, G. (2010). *Basic Research Methods.* New Delhi: Sage.

Marshall, C., and Rossman, G.B. (2006). *Designing Qualitative Research.* 4th edn., New Delhi: Sage.

Maxwell, J.A. (1996). *Qualitative Research Design: An Interaction Approach.* Thousand Oaks, CA: Sage.

Neuman, W.L. (1994). *Social Research Methods: Qualitative and Quantitative Aproaches.* 2nd Edn. Boston: Allyn and Bacon.

Punch, K.F. (2009*). Introduction to Research Methods in Education.* New Delhi: Sage.

Singh, J. (2008). *Methodology and Techniques of Social Research.* New Delhi: Kanishka Publishers.

Somekh, B., and Lewin, C. (2005). *Research Methods in the Social Sciences.* New Delhi. Vstaar Publications.

Wallen, N.E. and Fraenkel, J.R. (1991). *Educational Research: A Guide to the Process.* New York: McGraw-Hill.

Zeller, R.A. (1996) 'Validity', in J.P. Keeves (ed.), *Educational Research, Methodology, and Measurement: An International Handbook.* 2nd edn. Oxford: Elsevier. pp. 822-9.

CHAPTER

26

Field Studies and Field Experiments

26.0 FIELD STUDIES

Field studies involve the efforts to gain understanding by observing naturally—occurring events. Field studies are based on *three cardinal principles* of social research:

(1) Each research question is uniquely defined by a specific set of circumstances.

(2) There can be no attempt to answer a question without deep knowledge of the specific contextual parameters defining those circumstances.

(3) Such deep knowledge comes only to those who have paid their dues

26.1 FOCUS IS ON

- Detached observation or principle of neutrality;
- Getting on 'insider's view of reality'; and
- Striving to maintain unobtrusiveness.

26.2 COMPOSITION

- Ethnographical or phenomenological studies, grounded theory and case studies of communities. (data collection for hypotheses testing)

26.3 NEED AND IMPORTANCE

- Quite useful when necessary to preserve the 'whole' events to immerse oneself in a situation
- When subjects are unable/unwilling to participate in the surveys

26.4 PROCESSES OF FIELD STUDIES

26.4.1 Selecting Topic/Setting

- Topic should be close at hand where researcher can readily fit in
- Topic should be doable

26.4.2 Access

- Researcher should know the importance of 'Gate-keepers' in group setting
- Sometimes need to become accepted member of group or developing 'key informants'.

26.4.3 Presentation and eEstablishment of Roles

- Covert 'research vs. group membership' (peripherial, action or complete)
- Methodological empathy

26.4.4 Note-taking

- 'Field jottings' and daily field notes, daily diary

26.4.5 Analysis

- Grounded theory development
- Coding in quantitative situations

26.4.6 Reporting

- Identifying larger meaning of findings

26.5 LIMITATIONS OF FIELD STUDIES

While field research can be an extremely useful method for gaining first-hand cultural knowledge, but it entails some difficulties:

- It is costly (time and money)
- Situation of interest may be fleeting
- It requires excellent observational/interpretive skills
- Risk of 'going native' in participative observation
- Lack of external validity (especially when subjects are selected on the basis of availability or convenience)

26.6 FIELD EXPERIMENTS

Field experiment is the most systematic and fruitful form of research in social science. Field experiments, as surveys, differ widely in their objectives, designs, and limitations. A field experiment is an experiment performed outside the laboratory, in the 'real' world. Unlike case studies and observational studies, a field experiment still follows all of the steps addressing research problems and generating hypotheses. The focus is on the typical experiment, and designs calls for measurement of people's physical, behavioural, or cognitive (informational or attitudinal) characteristics before, perhaps during, and after the experimental intervention of an innovative social service, such as programmes for literacy, health, family planning, nutrition and the like. The community study explores the intricate relationships and unique interactions of critical variables in a particular setting. However, there is the difficulty of generalizing the findings. Processes of field experiment:

- Allows for maximum control over extraneous variables through the employment of control and stimulus groups.
- An experiment manipulates the hypothesized cause and observes the consequences on the hypothesized effect, in a context in which other potential causes of that effect can be equally operable in a control group.
- All of the remaining forms of data collection seek to emulate the experimental method.
- Data are analyzed scientifically to obtain substantial evidence.
- Principles of scientific inquiry are followed:
  The field experiment attempts to incorporate the advantages of the laboratory experiment (random assignment to achieve controls, use of a control group for comparison of effects, experimenter manipulation of supposed causes and measurement of supposed effects) with the advantages of field surveys and case studies (representative sample in naturalistic setting with unobtrusive, non-reactive, non-sensitizing measurement).

26.7 BASIC FIELD EXPERIMENTAL REQUIREMENTS

A description of situational and generalizable variables is a legitimate scientific objective. Validating cause and effect relationship of such variables is even more central to the goals of science: prediction and control. The real-world validity of cause and effect relationship is the controlled field experiment. It attempts to eliminate the influence of unknown variables. Some of the essential devices to improve the internal validity (precision of results) and external validity (generalization of results) of field experiments are:

1. Random selection of population units (schools) to ensure comparability of experimental and control groups. The sample of units is randomized in order to offset the effects of the experimenter's own biases, the biases of other unknown or unwanted variables.
2. Random selection of subjects (students) within the experimental and control groups randomization is necessary to equate the groups in case of non-randomization; the treatments will be 'contaminated' through the interaction of the groups.
3. Avoidance of self-selection samples, such as samples of subjects who volunteer for participation and who thereby may be typical of the study population. For example selection of students of high I.Q. levels.
4. Avoidance of inappropriate samples and treatments (i.e. inappropriate for the objectives of the study). For example, literacy programme in which already literates are included in the experimental groups.
5. Avoidance of insensitive or irrelevant measures that is too gross to detect real changes. Or conversely, avoidance of subjects for whom change due to experimentation either will be nil or difficult to detect.
6. Use of unobtrusive, non-sensitizing measurement: meaning that the impact of measurement of subjects should not be such that measurement itself produces a change.
7. Control of other sources of measurement biases influencing treatment results. such extraneous biases are: (1) reactive measures which through pre-treatment administration may increase or decrease subjects responsiveness to the treatment; (2) 'instrumentation' weaknesses; and (3) 'experimental set', i.e. awareness of their participation in the experiment may influence the results.

26.8 PROBLEMS OF FIELDS EXPERIMENTS

- The inaccessibility of significant groups;
- The inability to define relevant populations, to compile sampling frame, or to define important characteristics of the study units;

- The lack of previous application and testing of social science principles and theories in the present culture.
- The extreme heterogeneity of sub-cultures;
- The ability to know, assess and control sources of variability; and
- The limitations of budget and resources.

26.9 STEPS OF FIELD EXPERIMENTS

26.9.1 Identification of Problem

- Problem can be identified from existing theories epistemological and philosophical approaches and problems experienced in the field.

26.9.2 Objectives/Research Questions

A hypothesis/research question may not be appropriate if:

- You do not have a hunch or educated guess about a particular situation;
- You do not have defined variables;
- Your question centers on phenomenological descriptions; and
- Your question centers on ethnographic study of a cultural group.

Researcher should check

- Is the question right for the researcher?
- Is the question right for the field?

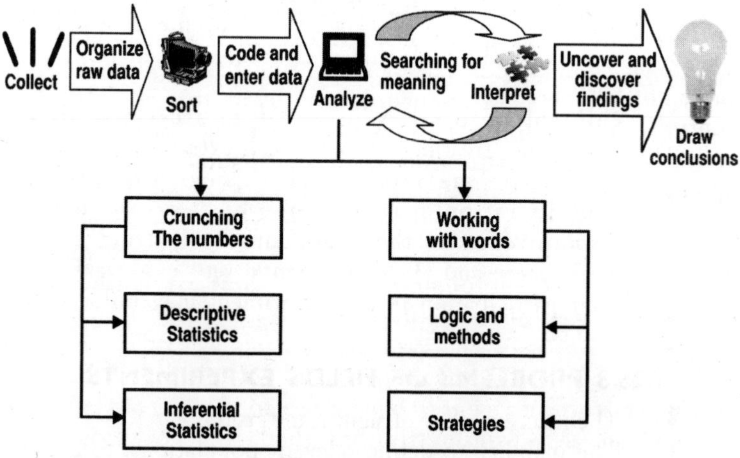

Figure 26.1 : Illustration of Objectives/Research Questions/Hypotheses

- Is the question well articulated?
- Is the question doable?
- Does researcher get the tick of approval from those in the know?

26.9.3 Methodology

(A) Research Design

- Defining of experimental and control groups
- Defining of independent and dependent variables (causes and consequent effects)
- Specifying of treatments
- Analysis of data to identify impact of field experiment

(B) Sampling design

- Random selection of population units (schools)
- Random selection of subjects (students)

(C) Instruments of Measurement

- Selection of unobtrusive, non-sensitizing and non-reactive measurement
- Selection of appropriate instruments of measurement, and
- Verification of secondary data.

Underlying all experiments is evaluation of the significance of the cause-effect relationships being studied with respect to the advancement of social science theory and to the usefulness for problem-solving.

26.10 EXTERNAL AND INTERNAL VALIDITY

26.10.1 Internal Validity

Where extraneous variables can be completely ruled out as the cause of a particular experimental outcome (importance of internal controls).

Threats to internal validity in field experiments are:

- *History*—Environmental changes during experiment that affect outcome
- *Maturation*—Subject changes during experiment that affect outcome
- *Testing effects*—reactions to measurement process
- *Instrumentation*—unwanted changes in characteristics of instrument/procedure
- *Regression to mean*—normalization of extreme scores ('learning')
- *Selection*—systematic differences in composition of control and experiment groups

- *Differential attritions*—loss of subjects in experiment, resulting homogeneity of remaining subjects (obscuring differences between control and stimulus groups.

External validity—When outcomes are generalizable to contexts outside of the particular experiment (importance of sound sampling and capacity to replicate).

References

Campbell, Donald T., Julian C. Stanley (1963). *Experimental and Quasi-experimental Design for Research.* Chicago: Rand-McNally Co.

Denzin, N.K. and Lincoln, Y.S. (2000). *Handbook of Qualitative Research,* London:Sage.

Feldman, N. (ed.) (2001). Strategies for Interpreting Qualitative Data. Thousand Oaks, CA: Sage.

Flick, U. (2007c). *Designing Qualitative Research* .Thousand Oaks, CA: Sage.

Goode,W.J., and Hatt, P.K. (1990). *Methods in Social Research.* McGraw-Hill, New Delhi.

Guthrie, G. (2010). *Basic Research Methods.* New Delhi: Sage.

Marshall, C., and Rossman, G.B. (2006). *Designing Qualitative Research.* 4th edn., New Delhi: Sage.

Maxwell, J.A. (1996). *Qualitative Research Design: An Interaction Approach.* Thousand Oaks, CA: Sage.

Neuman, W.L. (1994). *Social Research Methods: Qualitative and Quantitative Aproaches.* 2nd. Edn. Boston: Allyn and Bacon.

Punch, K.F. (2009). *Introduction to Research Methods in Education.* New Delhi: Sage.

Singh, J. (2008). *Methodology and Techniques of Social Research.* New Delhi: Kanishka Publishers.

Somekh, B., and Lewin, C. (2005). *Research Methods in the Social Sciences.* New Delhi. Vstaar Publications.

Whitting, G.C., and Cesar, G.H. (1976). Types of Field Experiments. In Gerald Hursh, Cesar, and Prodipto Roy (eds.) *Third World Surveys: Survey Research in Developing Nations.* New Delhi: Macmillan Company of India.

CHAPTER

27

Case Study Method

27.0 CASE STUDY

Case Study is usually used by social scientists (social interaction and the social construction of meaning). In education, it may be a 'case' of curriculum development, or a 'case' of innovative teaching, or a 'case' of effective teacher or 'a case' of an effective institution. In others, such as, medical science, criminology, psychology, emphasis is on studying the 'the case'. What is common to all approaches is the stress on study-in depth. A case study derives much of its rationale and methods from ethnography and its constituent theoretical discourses-symbolic interactionism, phenomenology and ethno-methodology, (Atkinson *et. al.*, 2001). Case study is contextual analysis of a limited number of events or conditions and their relationships. Focus is on understanding the case rather than generalizing to a population at large. A case study, thus, is particular, descriptive, inductive, and ultimately heuristic—it seeks to 'illuminate' the reader understanding of an issue. (Parlett and Hamilton, 1972).

Case study is a research design rather than an approach to the collection or analysis of data, and case studies must involve utilization of a wide array of different data sources and a number of different analytic strategies. Second, the case study examines units of analysis that are not drawn from well-demarcated population. Finally authors must, therefore, be prepared to defend their methods against the slings and arrows of their critics.

27.1 CARDINAL PRINCIPLES OF CASE STUDIES

Three cardinal principles of a case study are:

- Each case study is uniquely defined by a specific set of circumstances.
- Each case study has the specific contextual parameters defining those circumstances.
- Each case requires in-depth understanding of the case.

27.1.1 When a case study is appropriate method of research?

In this context number of situations exist:

- When it promises to yield fundamental insight into a rare but important process or event that offers no obvious point of comparison (March, Sproul & Tamuz,1991; Adams, Clemens, & Orloff, 2005).
- When it addresses an ambiguous, obscure, or otherwise inhospitable population that is difficult to reach through traditional methods (Geis, 1991).
- When it explores a crucial, deviant, or negative case that will shed light on an established theory (Emigh, 1997).
- When a case study approach is used in conjunction with a large-n statistical study to flesh out underlying causal mechanism (Kurtz & Barnes, 2002).
- When it is combined with a small-n comparative approach to asses necessary causal conditions or conditional theoretical statements (Paige, 1999).
- When it can be evaluated against an established body of theory that offers multiple observable implications (Campbell, 1975).
- When on adequate body of theory exists, and the relevant hypothesis or control group is therefore unclear (Walton, 1992).

27.2 IDENTIFICATION OF 'A CASE' FOR STUDY

Some times we experience that a particular institution is not performing to the expected level, or an individual performance is very low in the organization, or there is high level of attrition among teachers, or in other words, a particular institute has edge over other institutes in the similar area or a particular teacher gives good learning results as compared to others. These cases require in-depth study to find tangible solution of problems. In order to identify case studies, it is essential to find out what has been written before and read important articles about case studies. This will enable the researcher aware about the existing problem that needs solving or you may come across new interesting idea. For example, a case of an institution in which we may have well qualified staff and adequate infrastructure but could not set good results.

27.2.1 A case study method in education and allied sciences is an empirical enquiry that is conducted

- within a localized boundary of space and time (i.e. a singularity);
- into interesting aspects of an educational activity, or programme, or institution, or system;
- mainly in its natural context and within an ethic of respect for persons;
- in order to inform the judgements and decisions of practitioners or policy-makers, or of theoreticians who are working to these ends;
- in such a way that sufficient data are collected which may enable researches to :
  - (a) explore *significant* features of the case;
  - (b) create *plausible* interpretations of what is found;
  - (c) test for the *trustworthiness* of these interpretations;
  - (d) construct a *worthwhile* argument or story;
  - (e) relate the argument or story to any relevant research in the literature;
  - (f) convey *convincingly* to an audience this argument or story; and
  - (g) provide an audit trail by which other researchers may validate or challenge the findings, or construct alternative arguments.

27.3 AT LEAST THREE TYPES OF CASE STUDIES CAN BE CONCEIVED

- *Theory-seeking and theory-testing case studies*: are particular studies of general issues—aiming to lead to fuzzy propositions (more tentative) or fuzzy generalizations (less tentative) and conveying these, their context and the evidence leading them to interested audiences.
- *Storytelling and picture-drawing case studies:* are narrative stories and descriptive accounts of social and educational events, projects, programmes, institutions or systems, which deserve to be told to interested audiences, after careful analysis.

- *Evaluative case studies:* are enquiries into educational and social systems, projects or events to determine their worthwhileness, as judged by analysis by researchers, and to convey this to interested audiences.

27.4 RESEARCH DESIGN

Following queries need to be satisfied while designing research study:

- Statement of the case in clear specific term.
- What are the boundaries of the case under study?
- Time framework—how much time can be spent in each field work.
- What methods of investigation to be employed?
- The logic of case study approach—depth *verses* coverage.
- Whether exploratory or explanatory or descriptive.
- Holistic i.e., single unit of analysis or embedded, i.e. multiple units of analysis.

27.4.1 There are some generic demands that must respond to, namely

- *Transparency*: The logic by which theory, evidence, and methods are connected must be explicit.
- *Causal logic*: It explains variations in the attributes of different units of analysis by developing a multivariate analysis. This approach is frequently grounded in, and draws strength from positivism.
- *Phenomenological logic*: It assumes that social reality is constructed by and through symbolic and cultural interpretations. It is customarily associated with field observations of real-life situations, participant observations, and ethnographic and the interpretation of key texts. Lubeck and Alford note that the open-ended, negotiated, self-conscious character of social interaction means that causation is not linear, relations are contingent and subject to continual change.
- *Historical-Dialectical logic*: It assumes that all relationships and processes are interdependent and change over time in relation to one another. The essential concepts are totality, conjunctures, and chronology.
- *Clarity*: It refers to internal logic or architecture of the study. The clarity question can be tested by asking two or three people to read proposal and explain to you, in a few sentences, or the central problem and central claim.

- *Methodology precision*: It asserts the importance of focusing on the 'how' question. How large must the sample be? How will the sample be selected? How can one assume the reliability and validity of the data? How exactly can evidence be collected?, etc.
- Theory driven expectations are perhaps counterintuitive and somewhat controversial. But theoretical tradition provides something more than a context for the research during review of literature.
- *Doability*: It highlights practical considerations and provide substantial evidence for the policy implications.

Research Design should consider:

- Overview of the study project (objectives, issues, readings, literature and research)
- Field procedures (access to field sites, sources of information)
  Case study questions posed to Investigators; key classifications; suggestions for likely sources of evidence (not the literal questions to be asked)
- A guide for the case study report.

27.5 METHODS

The most commonly employed methods are: (a) interviews—structured or semi-structured, (b) documentary analysis—video or audio, and (c) observation—participant or non-participant

27.6 CONDUCTING A CASE STUDY

27.6.1 Desired skills of the investigator

- Good knowledge of the phenomenon (collection procedures are not routinized)
- Sensitivity for novel and unexpected issues in data collection
- Asking good questions
- Being a good "listener"
- Adaptiveness and flexibility

27.6.2 Important to identify different levels of questions

(A) Single case-level

1. Questions asked of specific interviewees
2. Questions asked of the individual case

(B) More general levels

1. Findings across multiple cases
2. Findings across an entire study (including reviewed literature)
3. Normative questions about policy recommendations and conclusions.

27.6.3 Collecting the evidence

Six sources of evidence:

(1) Documents (letters, agendas, progress reports)
(2) Archival records (Service records, organizational charts, budgets, etc.)
(3) Interviews (typically open-ended, but also focused, structured and surveys are possible)
(4) Direct observations (formal or casual; useful to have multiple observers)
(5) Participant observation (assuming a role in the situation and getting an inside view of the events)
(6) Physical artifacts

27.6.4 Three principles of data collection

(1) Use multiple sources of evidence

Triangulation = searching converging findings from different sources - increases construct validity

(2) Create a case study database

A database separate from the final report to be written, containing.

- Case study notes (clear and available for later use)
- Case study documents
- Tabular materials (collected and created)
- Narratives (initial open-ended answers to the study questions suggested by investigators).

(3) Maintain a chain of evidence

- The link between the initial study questions and the case study procedure should be pointed out in the case study protocol, as also the circumstances of the evidence to be collected
- Putting the data collection to practice on the basis of the protocol
- Actual evidence storage in the database for later checks (specific collection circumstances indicated)
- Sufficient citing of the case study data base and evidence in the final report and conclusions to be drawn.

27.7 ANALYZING THE EVIDENCE

Analysis of evidence is one of the most difficult aspects of doing case studies. Most important is to have a general analytic strategy, which helps to choose among different techniques.

27.7.1 Two general analytic strategies

(1) Relying on *theoretical propositions*: theoretical orientation guiding the analysis; following theoretical propositions that have formed the design of the case study—helps to focus attention on certain data and to ignore other data.

(2) Developing a case *description*: a descriptive framework for organizing the case study; analysis organized on the basis of description of the general characteristics and relations of the phenomenon in question.

27.7.2 : (1) *Pattern matching* (explanatory/descriptive) Comparing empirically-based patterns with predicted one(s).

Expected outcomes as a pattern: comparing if the initially predicted results have been found and alternative patterns are absent.

Rival explanations as patterns: searching if some of the theoretically salient explaining conditions might be articulated in empirical findings; then the presence of certain explanation should exclude the presence of others.

Simpler patterns: pattern matching is possible also with only few variables, if the derived patterns are predicted to have enough clear differences.

(2) *Explanation-building* (mainly explanatory).

Analyzing case study data by building an explanation about the case and identifying a set of causal links.

Explanation is the result of series of iterations:

Initial theoretical statement—Comparing findings of an initial case to other additional cases.

(3) *Time-series analysis.*

"How"—and "why"—questions about relationships and changes of events over time.

Identifying theoretically proposed sequences of an event that are expected to lead to a certain outcome; identification of events must be done before the onset of the investigation.

Comparing this trend with the trend of empirical data points.

(4) *Analysis should show that:*

It relied on all the relevant evidence;

All major rival interpretations are dealt;

Most significant issue of the study is addressed; and
Prior expert knowledge is brought to the study.

Analytic memoes were used to draw interpretations. Relationships among variables are analyzed. Sometimes theoretical orientation guides the analysis. In descriptive case studies, a descriptive framework for organizing the case study is developed. Analysis is done on the basis of the general characteristics and relations of the phenomenon in question. In explanation building a set of causal links is identified on the basis of result of series of iterations.

27.8 CHARACTERISTICS OF GOOD CASE STUDY

First, the outcomes must be trustworthy. Case study should also be reasonably reliable and valid.

- Has there been prolonged engagement with data sources?
- Has there been persistent observation of emerging issues?
- Have raw data been adequately checked with their sources?
- Has there been sufficient triangulation of raw data leading to analytical statements?
- Has the working hypothesis, or evaluation, or emerging story been systematically tested against the analytical statements?
- Has a critical friend thoroughly tried to challenge the findings?
- Is the account of the research sufficiently detailed to give the reader confidence in the findings?
- Does the case record provide an adequate audit trail?

Second, the conduct of the enquiry and its report must be ethical, particularly in terms of respect for persons.

- Has permission been given to conduct the research in terms of the identification of an issue, problem, or hypothesis, in this particular setting?
- Have arrangements been agreed for transferring the ownership of the record of utterances and activities to the researcher, thus enabling the researcher to use these in compiling the case record?
- Have arrangements been agreed for either identifying or concealing the contributing individuals and the particular setting of the research in the case report?
- Have arrangements been agreed for negotiating permission to publish the case report?

Third, an outcome of the research must be that it says something significant to someone (teacher, manager, policy-maker, parent, learner, etc.), thereby informing her or his work and potentially helping to improve it.

Fourth, the research must be reported in forms which are meaningful and readable to the various audiences.

Fifth, *Case record* should contain the agreed interview transcripts or reports and observation reports, the final versions of analytical statements, the interpretative writings, the final draft of conceptual background statements, the day-by-day journal of the research, etc. This compilation of working records, edited to be suitable for public access, shows in detail how the researcher has collected data, analysed it, interpreted it, tested findings and so on. There may be only one copy of this document, kept by the researcher.

Sixth, this is the academic report which in principle should be subject to peer scrutiny by academic referees to vouch for its trustworthiness and probity. It should be published in an academic journal.

27.9 LIMITATIONS

- The weakness of case study is that it is not possible to generalize statistically from one or small number of cases to the population as a whole, even though good case studies appeal to the capacity of the reader for 'naturalistic generalization'. (Stake, 1994).
- A case may not be statistically representative of the population as a whole.
- Drawing boundaries of a case is not straightforward and involves crucial decisions, i.e. what to include and what to exclude and, thus, what is the claim to knowledge that is being made.
- Case studies lack scientific vigour and reliability.
- Case study is sometime coloured or influenced by subjectivity

References

Bassey, M. (1981). *Case Study in Educational Settings*. Buckinghum: Open University Press.

Bennett, Andrew (2001). "Case Study: Methods and Analysis." pp. 1513-19 in *International Encyclopedia of the Social and Behavioural Sciences,* edited by Neil J. Smelser and Paul Baltes. Amsterdam, The Nneitherlands: Elsevier.

Murphy, R. and H. Torrance, (eds.) [1987]. *Evaluating Education: Issues and Methods.* London: Paul Chapman Publishing.

Ragin, C. and Becker, H. (eds.) [1992]. *What is a Case?* Cambridge: Cambridge University Press.

Reynolds, J. (1981). *Case Method in Education : A Qualitative Guide for Effective use.* International Labour Office, Geneva.

Stake, R. (1995). *The Art of Case Study Research.* Thousand Oaks, CA: Sage.

Stenhouse, L. (1984). The conduct, analysis and refooting or case study in educational research and evaluation; In R. Murphy and H. Torrance (eds.) *Evaluating Education: issues & methods.* London: Paul Chapman Publishing, pp. 74-80.

Walker, R. (1974). The Conduct of Educational case studies : Ethics, Theory and Procedures, Buckingham: Open University Press.

Yin, R.K. (!994). *Case Study Method : Design and Research.* New Delhi: Sage.

CHAPTER 28

Discourse Analysis

Discourse Analysis, or Discourse Studies, is a general term for a number of approaches to analyzing written, spoken, signed language use, or any significant semiotic event.

28.1 OBJECTIVES OF DISCOURSE ANALYSIS

Discourse, writing, talk, conversation, communicative event, etc.—are variously defined in terms of coherent sequences of sentences, propositions, speech acts or turns-at-talk. Contrary to much of traditional linguistics, discourse analysts not only study language use 'beyond the sentence boundary', but also prefer to analyze 'naturally occurring' language use, and not invented examples. This is known as corpus linguistics; text linguistics is related. The essential difference between discourse analysis and text linguistics is that it aims at revealing socio-psychological characteristics of a person/persons rather than text structure.

Discourse analysis has been taken up in a variety of social science disciplines, including linguistics, sociology, anthropology, social work, cognitive psychology, social psychology, international relations, human geography, communication studies and translation studies, each of which is subject to its own assumptions, dimensions of analysis, and methodologies.

28.2 TYPES OF DISCOURSE ANALYSIS

Types or theories of Discourse Analysis are:

1. Jacques Derrida's "Deconstruction" is one;

2. Michel Foucault's Genealogy and social criticism and analysis of the uses of discourse to exercise power (such as his analysis of how "Knowledge" is created in our societies and with what purpose or effect);
3. Fredric Jameson's Marxist analysis of Postmodernism itself would provide another interesting reading on the dominant discourse of our time; and
4. Julia Kristeva's 'Feminist interpretations of current social practices'.

Example: Take the question of gender. What toys are considered suitable for girls? And what toys are purchased for girls? Ask your friends: would you gift a Barbie doll to a 4 year old boy? Or a set of carpenter's tools to a girl? Notice that dolls are invariably considered suitable for girl children and tools/guns for boys.

The point is dolls become signs of the feminine, and therefore are given to girls. Girls and dolls become interchangeable as signs of the feminine. Just as tools/guns become signs of masculinity.

It is not that girls cannot use tools. Or that dolls are essentially feminine. It is just that the values associated with these objects govern their use. The language of tools and dolls must therefore be read and interpreted within the context of culture of community's notions of femininity and masculinity. 'Dolls=feminine' and 'tools= masculine' is a language in that culture. These meanings are naturalized.

The interpretation looks at the language of toys and the discourse within which we interpret them. What are the discourses we can detect in the above example?

- That girls are delicate and weaker; and
- That grooming and care are feminine qualities/duties.

These discourses are patriarchal and treat women as weaker, gentler and requiring protection and to be given particular tasks. These discourses govern suitable play material because games and play are also elements within the same society. As a result, the discourses decide what is suitable or not suitable for girls and boys. It then becomes natural to give dolls to girls and tools to boys.

28.3 ISSUES OF RELIABILITY AND VALIDITY

Discourse or Critical Analysis always remains a matter of interpretation. As there is no hard data provided through discourse analysis, the reliability and the validity of one's research/findings depends on the force and logic of one's arguments. Even the best constructed arguments are subject to their own deconstructive reading and counter-interpretations. The validity of critical analysis is, therefore, dependent on the quality of the rhetoric. Despite this fact, well-founded arguments remain authoritative over time and have concrete applications.

28.4 USES OF DISCOURSE ANALYSIS

The contribution of the post-modern Discourse Analysis is the application of critical thought to social situations and the unveiling of the hidden (or not so hidden) politics within the socially dominant as well as all other discourses (interpretations of the world, belief systems, etc.).

Discourse Analysis can be applied to any text, that is, to any problem or the situation. Since Discourse Analysis is basically an interpretative and deconstructing reading, there are no specific guidelines to follow. One could, however, make use of the theories of Jacques Derrida, Michel Foucault, Julia Kristeva, or Fredric Jameson, as well as of other critical and post-modern thinkers.

Again, the purpose of Discourse Analysis is not to provide definite answers, but to expand our personal horizons and make us realize our own shortcomings and unacknowledged agenda/ motivations—as well as that of others. In short, critical analysis reveals what is going on behind our backs and those of others and which determines our actions.

For example, Discourse Analysis applied to the theory of Library Science, would not argue for or against the validity and "truth" of a certain research method (qualitative or quantitative), statement, or value (i.e. the Library Bill of Rights, or policies concerning free speech). Rather, discourse analysis would focus on the existence and message of these texts and locate them within a historical and social context.

Discourse Analysis aims at revealing the motivation and politics involved in the arguing for or against a specific research method, statement, or value. The concrete result will be the awareness to the qualities and shortcomings of each and the inception of an informed debate. Though this debate will never be settled, it allows for the correction of bias and the inclusion of minorities within the debate and analyzed discourse.

REFERENCES

Blommaert, J. (2005). *Discourse*. Cambridge: Cambridge University Press.

Carter, R. (1997). *Investigating English Discourse*. London: Routledge.

Gee, J.P. (2005). *An Introduction to Discourse Analysis: Theory and Method.* London: Routledge.

Gee, J.P., Michaels, S. and O' Connor, M.C. (1992). 'Discourse analysis', in M.D. LeCompte, W.L. Millroy and J. Preissle (eds.), The Handbook of Qualitative Research in Education. San Diego, CA: Academic Press. pp. 227-91.

Halliday, M.A.K., and Greaves, W.S. (2008). *Intonation in the Grammar of English*, London, Equinox.

Halliday, M.A.K., and C.M.I.M. Matthiessen (2004). *An introduction to functional grammar*, 3d ed. London, Arnold.

Harris, Zellig S. (1991.) *A Theory of Language and Information: A mathematical approach.* Oxford & New York: Clarendon Press, xii, 428 pp.; illustr.

Johnstone, B. (2002). *Discourse analysis*. Oxford: Blackwell.

Miscoiu, S., Craciun, O., Colopelnic, N. (2008). *Radicalism, Populism, Interventionism. Three Approaches Based on Discourse Theory*. Cluj-Napoca: Efes.

Renkema, J. (2004). *Introduction to discourse studies*. Amsterdam: Benjamins.

Schiffrin, D., Deborah Tannen, & Hamilton, H.E. (eds.) (2001). *Handbook of Discourse Analysis*. Oxford: Blackwell.

CHAPTER

29

Grounded Theory Method

29.0 GROUNDED THEORY

Grounded theory is a research method whose purpose is to generate theory from data. The phrase "grounded theory" refers to theory that is developed inductively from a corpus of data. If done well, this means that the resulting theory at least fits one data set perfectly. Grounded theory tries to study a phenomenon and a set of data in context through which the theory emerges. Most significant contributions of social sciences have been concepts rather than causal inferences. Most fecund concepts have originated in case-based rather proceeding with a preconceived theory and set of hypotheses. Grounded theory conceptualizes the latent social patterns and structures of area of interest through the process of constant comparison.

Grounded theory methods consist of systematic, yet flexible guidelines for collecting and analyzing qualitative data to construct theories. Analytical and interpretive procedures are used for analyzing and conceptualizing data through coding (open coding, axial coding and selection coding), non-statistical sampling, writing of memos, diagramming of conceptual relationships, written and verbal reports. The findings of grounded theory are not arrive at by means of statistical procedures or other means of quantification, but are derived from data gathered by a variety of means including 'observation' interview, documents, and videotapes. Axial coding is the process of relating codes (categories and properties) to each other, via a combination of inductive and deductive thinking. Grounded theorists emphasize causal relationships, and fit things into a basic frame of generic relationships. The frame consists of elements, such as, phenomenon, causal conditions, context, intervening conditions, action strategies and consequences. In contrast, selective coding is the process of choosing one category to be the core category. Grounded theory calls for:

- Simultaneous involvement in data collection and analysis
- Constructing analytic codes and categories from data, not from preconceived logically deduced hypotheses
- Using the constant comparative method, which involves making comparisons during each stage of the analysis
- Advancing theory development during each step of data collection and analysis
- Memo-writing to elaborate categories, specify their properties, define relationships between categories, and identify gaps
- Sampling aimed toward theory construction, not for population representativeness
- Conducting the literature review *after* developing an independent analysis.

29.1 CONDUCTING GROUNDED THEORY

The methodological stages are:

29.1.1 Identify Area of Research

Examples of substantive areas included dying (Glaser, 1967), online learning (Scott, 2007), a cafe (Rosenbaum, 2006), nursing practice (Nathanial, 2007), management studies (Holton, 2007), work processes (Gynnild, 2207), interdisciplinary teams (McCallin, 2007). Your study will be about the perspective of one (or more) of the groups of people of the substantive area who will comprise your substantive population, e.g. patients, doctors, nurses and social workers (Glaser, 1967), online learners (Scott, 2007), nurses who have practiced in direct contact with patients (Nathanial, 2007), knowledge workers (Holton, 2007) journalists (Gynnild, 2006), health professionals (McCallin, 2007).

29.1.2 Collection of Data

A Grounded Theory may use qualitative data, quantitative data (e.g. Glase, 1964 and Glaser, 2008) or a mixture of the two. How researchers use methods matter. Methods are merely tools. Some tools are more useful than others. Decisions about methods do have consequences. How you collect data affects which phenomena researcher will see, how, where, and when he will view them, and what sense he will make of them.

29.2 TOOLS

29.2.1 Interviews

Open-ended, intermediate, and ending questions should be used for a good interview. The current interview protocol should span the entire range of the sample questions.

29.2.2 On Online Data

Now Internet research offers endless opportunities for textual analysis and poses methodological issues. On the Internet, participants may alter what we define as basic information—age, gender, race, ethnicity, and social class origin—as well as the specific content of their responses. These include :

- collecting observations of the substantive area itself and activities occurring within the substantive area;
- accessing public or private record irrespective of form (e.g. photograph, diary, painting, sculpture, biography, television broadcast, news report, survey, government or organisational document, etc.); and
- conversing with individuals or a group of individuals, face-to-face or remotely [synchronously (e.g telephone, text chat) or asynchronously (e.g. email or wiki)].

29.3 INITIAL CODING

Initial coding should stick closely to the data. Try to see actions in each segment of data rather than applying preexisting categories to the data. Initial coding can prompt researchers to see areas in which they lack needed data. Realizing certain gaps—or holes in data—is part of the analytic process. Open coding simply means code everything and more on that in the getting started. Eventually the core category and the main concern become apparent; where the core category explains the behaviour in the substantive area, i.e. it explains how the main concern is resolved or processed.

29.3.1 A Code for Coding Implies

- Remain open
- Stay close to the data
- Keep your codes simple and precise
- Construct short codes

- Preserve actions
- Compare data with data
- Move quickly through the data

Charmaz (2006) stresses that initial coding "moves researcher toward fulfilling two criteria for completing a grounded theory analysis: fit and relevance." The study fits the empirical world when researcher has constructed codes and developed them into categories that crystallize participants' experience. It has relevance when he offers an incisive analytic framework that interprets what is happening and makes relationships between implicit processes and structures visible.

29.3.2 Incident-by-incident coding works well, for example, with observational notes. Following methods may be used.

29.3.3 In-vivo codes

Typically, these are "codes of participants' special terms." They: "help us to preserve participants' meanings of their views and actions in the coding itself" and "serve as symbolic markers of participants' speech and meanings". They are "characteristic of social words and organization settings."

29.3.4 Focused Coding

Involve "more directed, selective, and conceptual" codes than in-vivo or initial coding. "Focused coding means using the most significant and/or frequent earlier codes to sift through large amounts of data ... [which] requires decisions about which initial codes make the most analytic sense to categorize your data incisively and completely."

29.3.5 Axial Coding

The purpose of which is to "relate categories to sub-categories," is not clearly denoted in the phase flow of this section; however, is placed between focused and theoretical coding.

29.3.6 Theoretical Coding

Theoretical Coding was introduced by Glaser to conceptualize "how the substantive codes may relate to each other as hypotheses to be integrated into a theory." These not only "specify existing relationships between categories" from focused coding, but, according to Glaser, preclude the need for axial coding.

29.4 COMPARATIVE METHODS

'Constant Comparative Methods' (Glaser & Strauss, 1967) are used to establish analytic distinctions—and to make comparisons at each level of analytic work. At first, data are compared with data to find similarities and differences.

29.5 MEMOS

Write memos throughout the entire process. The development of theory is captured in memos; few memos—thin theory. Method memos chronicle tussles with the method and help write the chapter on method. But most importantly theoretical memos are written about codes and their (potential) relationships with other codes. It's a low risk activity, so don't be concerned about writing 'bad' memos; memos will mature in the process as skill and theory develop.

In general, memos should contain some raw data, make comparisons, define, detail, or ask questions about codes or categories, offer conjectures to check in the field, and use supporting raw data of definitions or analytic claims. Memo-writing frees you to explore your ideas about your categories. Treat memos as *partial, preliminary, and provisional.* They are immediately correctable. Just note where you are on firm ground and where you are making conjectures. Then *go back to the field and check your conjectures.*

29.6 CONDUCT SELECTIVE CODING AND THEORETICAL SAMPLING

In this process, the core category and main concern are recognised; open coding stops and selective coding—coding only for the core category and related categories are considered. Further sampling is directed by the developing theory (who do I need to ask to learn more about these issues?) and used to saturate the core category and related categories. *Memos are sorted out to find the Theoretical Code(s)* which best organises substantive code. This leads to formation of theory.

29.7 REVIEW OF LITERATURE

Review the literature and integrate with your theory through selective coding.

(i) Synthesize the literature for making connections between the parts identified, and showing new patterns and arrangements among them. (Hart, 1998, 110).

(ii) Consider the convergence and divergence of the findings, theories, methods, and implications that are found in the literature.

(ii) The dialectical process of thesis-antithesis-synthesis as a framework for developing synthesis in the literature review may be followed (Burton and Steane, 2004).

(iv) The whole approach is organised around the principle that theory that is developed will be grounded in data

29.8 WRITE UP YOUR THEORY

The quality of that theory will depend upon your skills and the skills you develop as you research. A theory should consist of a set of basic statements called the axioms of theory, which tell us what the theory is all about. Such axiomatic statements or postulates as they are called include primitive terms. These are terms that are intuitively understood and cannot be otherwise completely defined. The criterion by which a theory is judged is not its truth or falsity, but rather its usefulness.

29.9 IMPORTANCE OF GROUNDED THEORY RESEARCH

(1) Theory is generated on the basis of data; the theory will, therefore, be grounded in data. Grounded theory explicitly address the question of how to generate theory in research.
(2) It represents a coordinated, systematic and flexible overall research strategy to generate theory from the corpus of data.
(3) It brings a disiplined and organised approach to the analysis of qualitative data.
(4) Its contributions in the area of medical sociology and education have been well recognised.
(5) Grounded theory is found very useful in the identification of research problems from professonal practice, and from organisational and institutional contexts. In these situations, a traditional hypothesis-testing approach is not appropriate.

REFERENCES

Bryant, A. and Charmaz, K. (eds.) (2007). *The Sage Handbook of Grounded Theory.* Thousand Oaks, CA: Sage.
Charmaz, K. (2006). *Constructing Grounded Theory.* Thousand Oaks, CA: Sage.
Feldman, N. (ed.) (2001). Strategies for Interpreting Qualitative Data. Thousand Oaks, CA: Sage.
Glaser, B. (1992). *Basics of Grounded Theory Analysis: Emergence* vs. *Forcing.* Mill Valley, CA: Sociology Press.
Glaser, B. and Strauss, A. (1967). *The Discovery of Grounded Theory: Strategies for Qualitative Research.* Chicago: Aldine.
Strauss, A. and Corbib, J. (1994). Grounded Theory Methodology: An overview. In N.K. Denzin and Y.S. Lincoln (eds.). *Handbook of Qualitative Research.* Thosand Oaks, CA: Sage. pp. 273-85.

CHAPTER

30

Method of Ethnographic Research

30.0 NATURE OF ETHNOGRAPHY RESEARCH

Ethnography has its roots planted in the fields of anthropology and sociology. The Random House Dictionary of the English Language defines ethnography "A branch of anthropology dealing with the scientific description of individual culture". An ethnography is a written description of a particular culture–the customs, beliefs, and behaviour-based on information collected through fieldwork. (Harris and Johnson, 2000). Ethnography in educational research implies a process of providing scientific descriptions of educational systems, processes, and phenomena within their specific contexts. Psychological and social elements are also embedded in ethnographical studies. The emphasis in ethnographic research is on describing the context in qualitative terms without superimposing the researcher's (observer's) own value system on the situation. Thus, ethnographic research takes a qualitative-phenomenological approach. Some of the features of ethnographic studies are:

- Ethnographic research may use either qualitative or quantitative or mixed approach.
- Ethnographic research involves field research and hypotheses are more likely to emerge from the data than to be formulated prior to the research.
- Ethnographic research is the contextualization, which requires that all data be interpreted only in the context of the situation or environment in which they were collected;

- Ethnographic research is often not concerned about generalization. Of course, generalization of results depends on the correspondence between the context under study and other situations.

Experimentation and survey research traditionally have involved *a priori* hypothesis formation, followed by specific procedures designed to test hypotheses. In contrast, ethnographic research proceeds from the position that hypotheses may emerge as the data collection occurs or ethnographic research does not begin from specified, preconceived hypotheses; it relies heavily upon description as the research proceeds. The observer attempts to suspend any preconceived ideas or notions that might undesirably influence the interpretation of what is being observed. The observer wishes to concentrate on the entire context and thus maintains a holistic view, rather than focusing on bits and pieces. The ethnographic researcher attempts to maintain a perspective on the totality of the situation. Ethnographic research takes a general and holistic perspective. Theory is considered only as it appears relevant.

- Ethnographic research is conducted in the field setting, based on the premise that the situation influences people's interpretations, thoughts, and actions. The researcher attempts to interpret the situation from the perspective of the individuals being studied, and the researcher is involved in the situation as a participant-observer. (Geertz, 1973).
- The methodology of ethnographic research is different from that of experimental research. For example, statistical procedures for analysis are usually not so complex, nor are they so clearly specified beforehand as they are in experimental and survey research. Some of the key elements in ethnographical research are:

Key Elements of Ethnographical studies

- The shared cultural meanings of the group are crucial to understanding its behaviour;
- Insider's perspective on those events, actions and contexts are essential;
- The group will be studied in its natural setting;
- It is an unfolding and evolving sort of study rather than pre-structured;
- Ethnography is eclectic not restricted;
- It relies on the field of anthropology for its theoretical base;

- It addresses issues of gaining access, role of observer, power crisis; and
- If often uses words of participants in written presentations.

Ethnographic studies also focus on organizations, which consist of defined groups of people who interact in regular and structured ways. An organization can be viewed as consisting of cultures. For example, a school has a student culture (possibly more than one student culture), a faculty culture, an administrative culture (assuming that the school is large enough), and possibly a teacher aid culture and a maintenance personnel culture. A culture consists of the collective understandings among the members of a group that are related to their particular role. Whatever makes up the parts of a culture, there is coherence and consistency among these parts. We will call the makeup culture perspectives. In nutshell, Organizations are considered to be composed of cultures, and cultures are made up of perspectives.

30.1 THE PROCESS OF ETHNOGRAPHIC RESEARCH

The process of ethnographic research is an integrated process in which procedures are evolved and conducted concurrently.

30.2 IDENTIFICATION OF THE PHENOMENON TO BE STUDIED

Some of the statements identifying the phenomenon to be studied as social interaction of high school students are:

(A)
1. Interaction among the students across races.
2. Interaction among the students across the sexes.
3. Faculty social systems.
4. Role of the faculty in the social interaction of students.

Typical ethnographic studies in education might have the following research statements.

(B)
1. A study of life in an urban classroom.
2. A study of decision-making in an inner-city high school.
3. A study of peer interactions in racially mixed classrooms of a suburban high school.
4. A study of interaction patterns among faculty in a private pre-primary schools.
5. A study of socialization within a rural high school.

30.3 IDENTIFICATION OF SUBJECTS

Subjects to be studied must be identified; this often includes specifying conditions so that the study may become feasible. For example, a study of interaction patterns among faculty (subjects) in private colleges.

30.4 HYPOTHESIS GENERATION

As the data collection proceeds in an ethnographic study, hypotheses may be formulated and modified. A study may begin with few if any specific hypotheses, but the data may imply hypotheses as the study goes along. The ethnographic researcher is very amenable to introducing new hypotheses and discarding hypotheses that are not supported. There are no a priori limits on the number or nature of hypotheses. Hypothesis generation is continuing activity throughout an ethnographic study. Unlike survey research or experimentation, for which hypotheses are initially specified and then tested, ethnographic research may begin with no hypotheses, and hypotheses may be formulated and modified along the way.

30.5 DATA COLLECTION

Typical ethnographic research employs three kinds of data collection: interviews, observation, and documents. This in turn produces three kinds of data: quotations, descriptions, and excerpts of documents, are resulting in one product: narrative description. This narrative often includes charts, diagrams and additional artifacts that help to tell "the story" (Hammersley, 1990).

30.6 OBSERVATION

Observation in ethnographic research is comprehensive – that is, continued and total. The observer attempts to record all relevant information in an unobtrusive way. Consequently, observation is quite unstructured. The emphasis is on capturing the perspective of the individuals being observed, which requires careful listening to pick up subtle cues and nuances. Observation is a continuing process; it is not limited to one or two sessions. The recordings made by the observer while actually conducting the observations are recorded in the field notes/diary. An observer may be identified openly as a researcher or may be in a disguised role. Whatever the case, observers try to be as unobtrusive as possible so that they do not interfere with normal activities. An important part of observation relates to the idea of contextualization; that is, to understand behaviour, the observer must understand the context in which individuals are thinking and reacting. The observer must have the option of interpreting events. Thus, observation extends beyond objective recording of what happens. The participant-observer attempts to assume the role of the individuals under study and experience their thoughts, feelings, and actions.

30.7 INTERVIEWING

Interviewing might be quite casual and informal, or it might be quite structured. Questions might be asked of those being observed in an attempt to clarify what is happening or in an attempt to capture the feelings of those observed. Formal structured interviews may be conducted with a predefined set of questions. In the social interaction example, a number of students might be interviewed. Faculty and administrators might also be interviewed. Other people, such as cooks lunchroom and attendants might be interviewed to obtain their perceptions of the student's social interaction. Such interviews would be helpful in determining the tone of the social interaction, which might not be entirely apparent from observing behaviour. Interviewing may be used, and supportive quantitative data may be brought to bear from internal or external sources. Whatever the source, however, the data should reflect the perspectives of the subjects under study.

30.8 OTHER SOURCES

In addition to participant observation and interviews, ethnographers may also make use of various documents in answering guiding questions. When available, these documents can add additional insight or information to projects. Because ethnographic attention has been and continues to be focused on both literate and non-literate peoples, not all research projects will have site documents available. It is also possible that even research among a literate group will not have relevant site documents to consider; this could vary depending on the focus of the research. Thinking carefully about your participants and how they function and asking questions of your informants helps to decide what kinds of documents might be available.

Possible documents include: budgets, advertisements, work descriptions, annual reports, memos, school records, correspondence, informational brochures, teaching materials, newsletters, websites, recruitment or orientation packets, contracts, records of court proceedings, posters, minutes of meetings, menus, and many other kinds of written items.

30.9 ANALYSIS

Analysis in ethnographic research consists of synthesizing the information from the observations, interviews, and other data sources. The analysis of the data involves interpretation of the meanings and functions of human actions and mainly takes the form of verbal descriptions and explanations, with quantification and statistical analysis playing a subordinate role at most. However, there are proportions and percentages that can be computed, based on classifications of items from interviews or types of activities and events observed.

30.10 INTERPRETING AND REPORTING FINDINGS

Remember that the researcher is the detective looking for trends and patterns that occur across the various groups or within individuals (Krueger, 1994). The process of analysis and interpretation involve disciplined examination, creative insight, and careful attention to the purposes of the research study. Analysis and interpretation are conceptually separate processes. The analysis process begins with assembling the raw materials and getting an overview or total picture of the entire process. The researcher's role in analysis covers a continuum with assembly of raw data on one extreme and interpretative comment on the other. Analysis is the process of bringing order to the data, organizing what is there into patterns, categories, and basic descriptive units. The analysis process involves consideration of words, tone, context, non-verbal, internal consistency, frequency, extensiveness, intensity, specificity of responses and big ideas. Data reduction strategies are essential in the analysis (Krueger, 1994).

Interpretation involves attaching meaning and significance to the analysis, explaining descriptive patterns, and looking for relationships and linkages among descriptive dimensions. Once these processes have been completed the researcher must report his or her interpretations and conclusions

30.11 RELIABILITY

- In a specific study, internal reliability would depend on the extent to which two or more observers agree on what they saw and how they interpret what they saw.
- The use of multiple data collection procedures, along with triangulation, tends to enhance reliability.
- External reliability is a matter of degree, and some would argue that nothing can be replicated exactly.

30.12 VALIDITY

A research study may be both internally and externally reliable yet lack validity

30.12.1 Internal Validity

- Because ethnographic research is conducted in the natural setting, it does not have this option of control.
- Establishing internal validity is a process that involves both deduction and induction; the researcher systematically reasons through the possible causes responsible for the data.

30.12.2 External Validity

- External validity can be strengthened by multisite studies. If a phenomenon seems to be consistent across a number of studies, its generalizability is increased.
- Even if there is inconsistency in the phenomenon, a study of the differences between the sites may reveal the limitations or special conditions of generalization.

30.13 TRIANGULATION

Triangulation is qualitative cross-validation. It can be conducted among different data sources or different data collection methods. Basically, triangulation is comparison—Comparison of information to determine whether or not there is corroboration. It is a search for convergence of the information on a common finding or concept. To a large extent, the triangulation process assesses the sufficiency of the data. If the data are inconsistent or do not converge, they are insufficient. The researcher is then faced with a dilemma regarding what to believe. Denzin (1978, p. 308). Triangulation is qualitative cross-validation. It assesses the sufficiency of the data according to the convergence of multiple data sources or multiple data collection procedures. Figure 30.1 shows the process of cross-validation.

Figure 30.1 reveals convergence of multiple data sources or multiple data collection procedures for cross-validation. For example, students are examined by the counselor and faculty to know their level of participation in extracurricular activities. Other multiple data sources and procedures such as school records, faculty interview and field observation, are used to cross-validate or authenticate the results. In reviewing school records, one type of information checked was the composition of the students' caste-wise and gender-wise in extracurricular activities, such as athletics and clubs. For activities in which ninth-grade students participated, the records showed that the

Triangulation Involving Multiple Data Sources

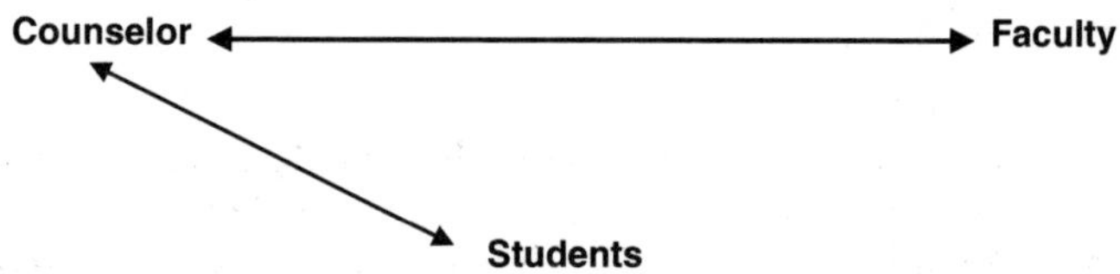

Triangulation Involving Multiple Data Sources

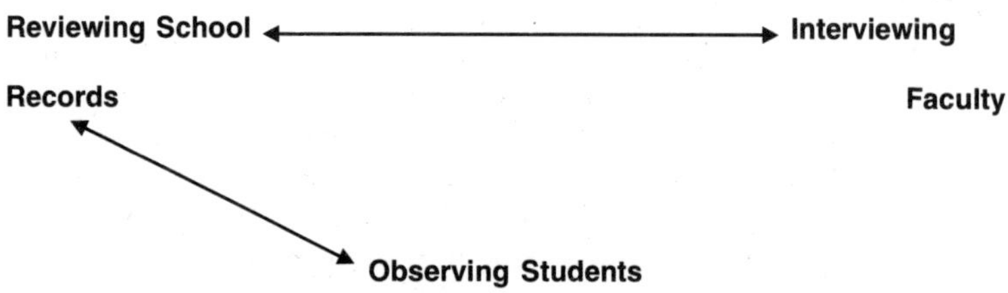

Figure 30.1 : Triangulation (the process of Qualitative Cross-Validation) for the Social Interaction

proportional incidence of both high and low caste ninth-grade boys being involved in predominantly male-oriented activities was greater than the corresponding proportional incidence for high and low caste ninth-grade girls in predominantly female-oriented activities. Supportive evidence for the hypothesis also confirmed the hypothesis. The results of the triangulation so appeared were consistent.

In this study, triangulation of the interview with questionnaires, observations and document analysis as well as triangulation of interviews with one another rendered a holistic understanding of the situation and generally converging conclusions. As Fielding and Fielding (1986) stated, "Triangulation puts the researcher in a frame of mind to regard his or her own material critically, to test it, to identify its weaknesses, to identify where to test further doing something different".

Creswell (2002) added, triangulation is the process of corroborating evidence from different individuals, of methods of data collection. This ensures that the study will be accurate because the information is not drawn from single source, individual, of process of data collection. In this way, it encourages the researcher to develop a report that is both accurate and credible.

Triangulation is also used as a strategy for improving the quality of qualitative research by extending the approach to the issue under study. This can be done in four ways:

(1) The first way is to use additional methods (e.g. two qualitative methods of by adding a quantitative approach) or using two methodological approaches in one method;
(2) The second way is to include different sorts of data in your project;
(3) The third way is to take a different theoretical perspective—studying the issue under study with more than one research perspective in qualitative research; and
(4) The fourth way is to involve two or more researchers in the project with different theoretical-methodological background. (Denzin, 1986b)

References

Agar, M. (1996). *Professional Stranger: An Informal Introduction to Ethnography*, (2nd ed.). New Delhi: Academic Press.

Atkinson, P., Coffey, A., Delamont, S. Lofland, J. and Lofland, L. (eds.) (2001). *Handbook of Ethnography*. London: Sage.

Fetterman, D.M. (1989). *Ethnography step by step*. Newbury Park, CA: Sage.

Hammersley, M. and Atkinson, P. (1995). *Ethnography: Principles in Practice*. 2nd edn. London: Routledge.

Harris, M. and Johnson, O. (2000). *Cultural Anthropology*, (5th ed.), Needham Heights, MA: Allyn and Bacon.

Krueger, A.R. (1994). *Focus Groups: A Practical Guide for Applied Research*, Thousand Oaks, CA: Sage Publications.

Woods, P. (1986). *Inside Schools: Ethnography in Educational Research*. London: Routledge & Kegan Paul.

CHAPTER

31

Phenomenological Method

The phenomenological movement was initiated by Husserl (1936/1970) based upon philosophical discipline. Later theorists, such as Heidegger (1927) and Merleau-Ponty M. (1962), have recast the phenomenological project, moving away from a philosophical discipline. They focused on consciousness and hermeneutic (interpretive) dimensions. Social scientists have observed that methods and assumptions of the natural sciences are inappropriate to the study of man. The natural sciences deal with matter whereas phenomenology deals with phenomena. For example, atoms and molecules do not have consciousness. Matter simply reacts 'unconsciously' to external stimuli. Unlike matter, man has consciousness—thoughts, feelings, meanings, intentions, and an awareness of being. Man reacts 'consciously' to internal stimuli. Phenomenological approach, therefore, offers a better alternative to the study of man.

Applied to research, phenomenology is the study of phenomena: their nature and meanings. The focus is on lived experience. The phenomenological researcher aims to provide a rich textured description of lived experience. The lived experience comprises the world of objects around us as we perceive them. It is an experience of our self, body and relationships. It is the "locus of interaction between ourselves and our perceptual environments and the world of experienced horizons within which we meaningfully dwell together" (Von Eckartsberg, 1998, cited in Garza, 2007, p. 314).

It can be defined as the world that is lived and experienced—a world "that appears meaningfully to consciousness in its qualitative, flowing givenness; not an objective world 'out there', but a humanly relational world" (Todres *et. al.,* 2006, p. 55). Merleau-Ponty famously explains, "man is in the world, and only in the world does he know himself." (1962, xi).

There are certain essential features of the life world, such as a person's sense of selfhood, embodiment, sociality, spatiality, temporality, project, discourse and mood-as-atmosphere (Ashworth, 2003, 2006). These interlinked 'fractions' (Ashworth, 2003) act as a lens through which to view the data. The task of the researcher is to bring out these dimensions and show the structural whole that is socially shared while also experienced in individual and particular ways. "The overall aim of life world research", says Dahlberg *et al* (2008, p. 37) is "to describe and elucidate the lived world in a way that expands our understanding of human being and human experience."

The important phenomenological concept is intentionality, i.e. relationship between the person and the meanings of the things they're focusing on and experiencing. For example, one woman's lived experience of divorce and its impact on her relationship with her children were studied. The intentional, embodied relationship between a mother and her children was highlighted. The challenge for phenomenological researchers is two-fold: how to help participants express their world as directly as possible; and how to explicate these dimensions such that the lived world is revealed.

31.1 APPROACHES

31.1.1 Different schools have emerged which focus more explicitly on the life world (Ashworth, 2003; Dahlberg *et al,* 2008) and lived experience (van Manen, 1991). *Hermeneutic* variants highlight the researcher's role and horizons of interpretation such as in the Reflective Lifeworld Approach (Dalhlberg *et. al.,* (2008), Interpretative Phenomenological Analysis (IPA) (Smith and Osborne, 2003), Embodied Enquiry (Todres, 2007), Critical Narrative Analysis (CNA) (Langdridge, 2007) and in the Dallas' approach to phenomenological research (Garza, 2007). For example, a *lifeworld researcher* would ask 'What is the lifeworld of one who feels lost?' Collecting and analysing interview data, they would focus on existential themes such as the person's sense of self-identity and embodied relations with others when experiencing a feeling of being lost.

31.1.2 With the *heuristic approach* adopted by Moustakas (1990), the researcher's role in self-reflection towards producing a creative synthesis to explicate lived experience is brought to the fore. For example, the *heuristic researcher* could well focus more intensely on the question: 'What is my experience of feeling lost?' While they might draw on a range of data from stories, poems, artwork, literature, journals, they would also look inward, attending to their own feelings/experiences by using a reflective diary. They would aim to produce a composite description and creative synthesis of the experience.

31.1.3 In relational research approaches (Finlay and Evans, 2009), attention is paid to the researcher's journey and the research process focusing on how data emerges out of embodied dialogical encounters between researchers and co-researchers. One variant of such relational research is the dialogue research approach (described by Halling and Leifer, 1991 and Rowe *et al.*, 1989) where groups of phenomenologists investigate a phenomenon, dwelling in and negotiating layered meanings together. For example, the *researcher* might similarly interview just one person ask 'What is it like to feel lost?'. They might focus on the co-researchers' self-identity and 'creative adjustment' (their sense of self, their being-in-the-world and the defensive way they've learned to cope). The research data would be seen to be co-created in the dialogical research encounter and the relational dynamics between researcher and co-researchers would be reflexively explored.

31.1.4 A *descriptive empirical phenomenologist* might well ask: 'What is the lived experience of feeling lost?' They might compare the protocols (written descriptions) offered by participants about one instance of feeling lost and attempt to identify the essential or general structures underlying the phenomenon of feeling lost.

A *lifeworld researcher* would ask 'What is the lifeworld of one who feels lost?' Collecting and analysing interview data, they would focus on existential themes such as the person's sense of self-identity and embodied relations with others when experiencing a feeling of being lost.

The *IPA researcher* would focus on 'What is the individual experience of feeling lost?' They would aim to capture individual variations between co-researchers. Thematic analysis would involve some explicit interpretation on the part of both co-researcher and researcher.

The *Critical Narrative Approach researcher* would ask 'What story or stories does a person tell of their experience of feeling lost?' having interviewed perhaps just one person. The analysis would be focused on the narrative produced and how it was co-created in the research context.

All the variants of phenomenology above share a similar focus on describing lived experience and recognising the significance of our embodied, inter-subjective lifeworld. Giorgi (1989) indicates certain core characteristics hold across the variations, namely that the research is *descriptive*, explores the *intentional relationship* between persons and situations, uses *phenomenological reductions* and provides knowledge of psychological *essences* or structures of meanings immanent in human experience through imaginative variation (Wertz, 2005). Other phenomenologists argue that the project to identify essences and to use phenomenological reductions may be less central. Some methodologies, for example, the explicitly hermeneutic and idiographic approach of IPA, downplays (or even rejects) these features.

31.2 GATHERING AND ANALYSING PHENOMENOLOGICAL DATA

Method

31.2.1 Inductive

Research questions are formulated and modified in the process of observations in the field. Hypotheses are more likely to emerge from the data than to be formulated prior to the research.

31.2.2 Sampling

Purposeful Sampling: Purpose is to get insight about phenomenon, not empirical generalization from a sample to a population. Qualitative research cannot be conducted through *a-priori* samples only. Sampling goes on throughout research, through various sampling techniques, such as, typical case sampling, intensity sampling, critical case sampling, sensitive case sampling, convenience sampling, primary selection and secondary selection.

31.2.3 Tools and Data Collection

The most common tools used include the use of: narratives in interviews, diaries and protocols; participant observation; questionnaires; and reflective diaries or researcher's own introspective accounts. Supplementary techniques such as repertory grids, artwork or use of external literary or documentary sources may also be used to explore meanings further.

Phenomenologist doing interviews, for example, will tend to ask participants to describe their experience concretely by posing such questions as: 'Could you describe a typical day?' or 'Can you describe that particular incident in more detail?'. This way of opening a dialogue is valued over and above asking more general abstract questions such as 'what is your role?' or 'What is depression?'

Participant observations need to be conducted in a natural setting and with openness. "Openness is the mark of a true willingness to listen, see, and understand. It involves respect, and certain humility toward the phenomenon, as well as sensitivity and flexibility." Dahlberg *et. al.* (2001, p. 97). The aim is to allow the phenomenon to present itself to us instead of us imposing preconceived ideas on it. This openness needs to be maintained throughout the entire research process, not just at the start.

A questionnaire consists of a list of preset questions to which respondents asked to supply answers. Questions should be open-ended. Open-ended questions allow the respondent to compose his own answer rather than choosing between a number of given answers. This may provide more valid data since he can say what he means in his own words. However, this kind of response may be difficult to classify and quantify.

31.3 ANALYSIS

The analytical method suggested by Wertz (1983) and Giorgi (1985) is used i.e. (1) systematic readings of the transcript are undertaken by first dwelling on the phenomenon (through empathetic immersion and reflection), (2) then describing emergent psychological structures (i.e., constituents and recurrent themes).

In contrast, with dialogic analysis (Rowe *et. al.*, 1989), researchers prefer to use open, spontaneous, fluid dialogue in a group context rather than adhering to any explicit procedures. Whichever the approach, researchers are involved in "an extreme form of care that saves the situations described in a slow, meditative way and attends to, even magnifies, all the details", Wertz (2005, p. 172).

Significant themes or narratives emerging from the data are identified. Each type of analysis and way of presenting the data simultaneously reveals and conceals. Different analyses highlight particular nuances and indicate various immanent possibilities of meaning as *figural* against a *ground* of other possible meanings. The analytical process invariably involves a process of reflective writing and rewriting. This process aims to create depth: multiple layers of meaning are crafted to lay bare certain truths while retaining the ambiguity of experience.

31.4 RELIABILITY AND VALIDITY OF PHENOMENOLOGICAL STUDIES

The phenomenological study can be judged in its relative power to draw the reader into the researcher's discoveries allowing the reader to see the worlds of others in new and deeper ways. Polkinghorne (1983) offers four qualities to help the reader evaluate the power and trustworthiness of phenomenological accounts: *vividness, accuracy, richness and elegance.*

Many qualitative researchers embrace the use of *participant validation* as a way to 'prove' the validity of their research. When the participant agrees with the researcher's assessment, it is seen as strengthening the researcher's argument. As Dahlberg *et. al.* (2008, p. 94) warn, researchers need to be "careful not to make definite what is indefinite". Lifeworld research is characterised by its capacity to present the paradoxes and integrate opposites demonstrating holism (Dahlberg *et al,* 2008). Sources of error, bias, and invalidity need to be identified in order to make the study most trustworthy and authentic.

References

Ashworth, P.D. (1993). Participant agreement in the justification of qualitative findings. *Journal of Phenomenological Psychology,* 24: 3-16.

Ashworth, P.D. (2003). An approach to phenomenological psychology: the contingencies of the lifeworld. *Journal of Phenomenological Psychology,* 34 (6):145-56.

Dahlberg, K., Dahlberg, H. and Nystrom, M. (2008) (eds.). *Reflective Lifeworld Research.* 2nd edition. Lund, Sweden: Student Literature.

Feldman, N. (ed.) (2001), *Strategies for Interpreting Qualitative Data.* Thousand Oaks, CA: Sage.

Finlay, L. (2003a). The intertwining of body, self and world: a phenomenological study of living with recently-diagnosed multiple sclerosis, *Journal of Phenomenological Psychology,* 34(2), 157-78.

Finlay, L. (2003b). Through the looking glass: inter-subjectivity and hermeneutic reflection. In L. Finlay and B. Gough (eds.) *Reflexivity: A Practical Guide for Researchers in Health and Social Sciences.* Oxford: Blackwell Publishing.

Finlay, L. (2005). Reflexive embodied empathy: a phenomenology of participant-researcher inters subjectivity, *Methods Issue: The Humanistic Psychologist,* 33(4), 271-92.

Garza, G. (2007). Varieties of Phenomenological Research at the University of Dallas, *Qualitative Research in Psychology,* 4(4), 313-42.

Giorgi, A. (1985). Sketch of a psychological phenomenological method. In A Giorgi (ed.) *Phenomenology and Psychological Research.* Pittsburgh, PA: Duquesne University Press.

Giorgi, A. (1994). A phenomenological perspective on certain qualitative research methods. *Journal of Phenomenological Psychology,* 25:190-220.

Giorgi, A. and Giorgi, B. (2003). Phenomenology. In J.A. Smith (ed.) *Qualitative psychology: a practical guide to research methods.* London: Sage.

Halling, S., and Leifer, M. (1991). The theory and practice of dialogic research. *Journal of Phenomenological Psychology*, 22(1), 1-15.

Heidegger M. (1962). *Being and Time*. New York: Harper and Row.

Hertz, R. (1997) Introduction: reflexivity and voice. In R. Hertz (ed.) *Reflexivity and voice*. Thousand Oaks, CA: Sage.

Husserl, E. (1931), *Ideas: general introduction to pure phenomenology*. (Boyce Gibson, W.R. Trans.). London: George Allen and Unwin. (Originally published, 1913).

Langdridge, D. (2007). *Phenomenological psychology: theory, research and method*. Harlow, England: Pearson Prentice Hall.

Linda Finlay (2007). Introducing phenomenological research (DOC) retrieved from Google.com under heading phenmenological research method.

Moran, D. (2000). *Introduction to phenomenology*. London: Routledge.

Smith, J.A. and Osborn, M. (2003) Interpretative phenomenological analysis. In J.A. Smith (ed.) *Qualitative psychology: a practical guide to research methods*. London: Sage Publications.

Todres, L. (2007). *Embodied enquiry: phenomenological touchstones for research, psychotherapy and spirituality*. Palgrave: Macmillan.

van Manen, M. (1990). *Researching Lived Experience: Human Science for an Action Sensitive Pedagogy*. New York: State University of New York Press.

Vedder, B. (2002). On the Meaning of Metaphor in Gadamer's Hermeneutics, *Research in Phenomenology*, 32(1): 196-209.

Wertz, F.J. (2005). Phenomenological research methods for counseling psychology, *Journal of Counseling Psychology*, 52(2), 167-77.

CHAPTER

32

Mixed Methods Research

32.1 INTRODUCTION

Mixed methods research is empirical research that involves the collection and analysis of both quantitative and qualitative data. It has been noted that such terms as 'multimethod', 'integrated', 'blended' and 'combined' have been used, along with 'multitrait-multimethod research', 'methodological triangulation', and 'mixed method research' (Creswell & Clark, 2007, 5-6). It is consistent and systematic use of the term 'mixed method' to describe research. A mixed method of research involves:

- Multiparadigms-qualitative and quantitative
- Pragmatic approach-methods to be used in research to determine the questions asked
- Potentially complementary forms of empirical inquiry
- The investigation of natural *versus* artificial settings
- An inductive *versus* a deductive approach
- The identification of cultural patterns as against seeking scientific laws.

32.2 MAIN DIMENSIONS (GRESWELL & CLARK, 2007)

1. *The timing dimension :* What will the timing of qualitative and quantitative methods be? In which order will the researcher collect and use the data? Will it be concurrent (both sets of data are collected at the same time or sequential (one set is collected before the other)?

2. *The weighing dimension*: what will be the relative importance and, weight, or priority given to? The general possibilities are equal weighting to both approaches, or unequal weighting, with one approach carrying more weight.
3. *The mixing dimension*: how will qualitative and quantitative methods be mixed, and especially how will the two data sets be mixed? The possibilities are that the two data can be merged, one can be embedded within the other, or they can be connected in some other way.

32.3 MIXED METHODS DESIGNS

There are four mixed methods designs:

1. *Triangulation Design*: A triangulation design involves the current but separate collection and analysis the two types of data, which are then merged, perhaps through data transformation, or perhaps at the interpretation of result stage. For example, on the general topic of teaching effectiveness, both methods would focus on the different aspects of teaching effectiveness.
2. *Embedded Design*: This design takes cognigence that a single data set is not sufficient. Different types of questions require different types of data to answer them. For example, qualitative data is collected as a part of correlational study to trace the relationships between independent variables and teaching effectiveness as the dependent variable.
3. *Explanatory Design*: This is a two-phase mixed method design, where qualitative data are used to help explain, or to built upon, initial quantitative results. Quantitative results guide the selection of sub-samples for follow-up in-depth investigation in the second phase. For example, quantitative survey is followed by qualitative in-depth study in order to gain a fuller understanding of both the nature as well as the factors influencing teaching effective.
4. *Exploratory Design*: In this two-phase mixed method design, qualitative data are collected in the first and quantitative data in the second. For example, a researcher explores some phenomenon of teaching effectiveness in-depth before going for the constructing of tool for the measurement of teaching effectiveness.

32.4 STEPS OF MIXED METHODS RESEARCH

Identification of Topic: The researcher may select topic through inductive and deductive seasoning. It should be based on the logic of the research proposed, and ensure that methods chosen are appropriate to the questions asked.

Research Questions: Researcher should check–Is the question right for the researcher?, Is the question right for the mixed methods research?, Is the question doable?

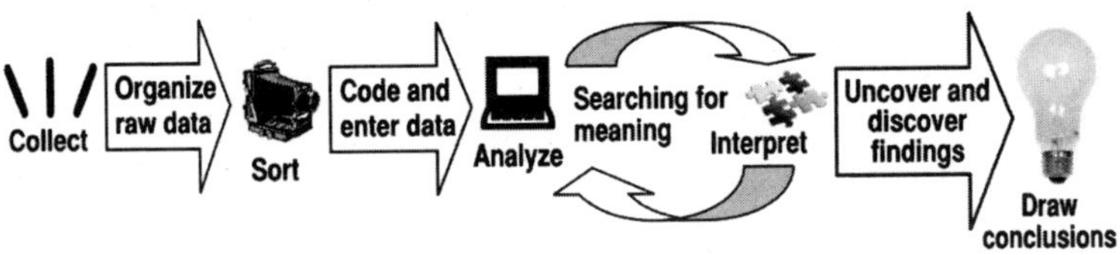

Figure 32.1 : Objectives/Research Questions/Theory

32.5 METHODOLOGY

32.5.1 Research Design

The researcher has to decide what type of research would be-triangulation, embedded, explanatory or exploratory.

32.5.2 Sampling and Measurement Procedures

Procedures for sampling and collection of data for both quantitative data and qualitative data should be clearly specified, and defined

32.6 DATA ANALYSIS

Approaches (soft-wares or manual) to the analysis of both quantitative and qualitative data need to be explained, i.e. how data are to be analyzed to find meaningful answers to the research questions.

32.7 RESULTS AND CONCLUSIONS

Johnson (2009) proposed a set of guidelines that is more inclusive and might better represent research in education. These guidelines are:

- Identify important problems and pose questions that can be investigated empirically or through other potentially useful approaches. Continuously generate, discover, describe, and construct new knowledge, and test knowledge claims.
- Separately and interconnectively explore, reflect upon,

describe, predict, and explain the natural world and meaningful social and personal 'worlds' and experiences.

- Explicate researcher and research values, purposes, commitments, and key background assumptions.
- Use method and strategies that, separately or in combination, can produce warranted investigation of particular research questions.
- Rely on sources of evidences.
- Link exploratory research to relevant theory through theory generation, theory testing, and ongoing theory modification.
- Describe nomological (i.e., general law like) knowledge domain, but also describe ideographic, local and contextual knowledge domains, and interconnect these to continually produce meaningful "practical theory".
- Replicate, document mediating and moderating processes, delineate conditions of generalization, and identify broad generalizations when possible, but also identify complex contextual interactions to aid in particular understanding and practical application of education/social theory.
- Articulate, explicate, develop, and test "manualized models, "practice-based models, middle-level theoretical models, met-models (i.e., models of models) and trastheoretical and transdisciplinary models of educational phenomena, and interconnect these continually for scientific learning.
- Explicate creative and formal reasoning processes (i.e., deductive, inductive, abductive, critical-theory) to help situate and warrant findings and value choices.
- Fully disclose research processes and findings to encourage professional and societal scrutiny.
- Continually encourage self-examination and critique and ongoing improvement of the education scientific enterprise.

32.8 RELIABILITY AND VALIDITY

Eisenhart and Howe (1992) proposed five criteria namely, (a) ensuring a fit between research questions, data collection, procedures, and analytic techniques, (b) ensuring the effective application of specific data collection and analytic techniques; (c) being alert to and cognizant of prior knowledge; (d) being cognizant of both internal and external value constraints; and

TABLE 32.1
Criteria for Mixed Method of Research*

Quantitative Term	*Qualitative Term*	*Strategy Employed*
Internal validity	Credibility	• Prolonged engagement in field • Use of peer debriefing • Triangulation • Member checks • Time sampling
External validity	Transferability	• Provide thick description
Reliability	Dependability	• Purposive sampling
Objectivity	Confirmability	• Create an audit trail • Code-recode strategy • Triangulation • Peer examination • Triangulation • Practice reflexivity

*Educational Researcher, Vol. 35, No. 9, p. 30.

(e) assessing a study's comprehensiveness.

REFERENCES

Best, J. and Kahn, J. (1995). *Research in Education.* 10th edition, Needham Heights: Allyn and Bacon.

Bryant, A., and Charmaz, K. (eds.) (2007a). *The Sage Handbook of Grounded Theory.* London: Sage.

Cozby, P. (2009). *Methods in Behavioural Research.* 10th edition, Bemont: Wadsworth.

Denzin, N.K. and Lincoln,Y.S. (2000). *Handbook of Qualitative Research,* London: Sage

Feldman, N. (ed.) (2001). Strategies for Interpreting Qualitative Data. Thousand Oaks, CA: Sage.

Flick, U. (2010). *An Introduction to Qualitative Research.* 4th edn., New Delhi: Sage.

Marshall, C., and Rossman, G.B. (2006). *Designing Qualitative Research.* 4th edn. New Delhi: Sage.

Maxwell, J.A. (2002). Literature Review of, and for, Educational Research: A Commentary on Boote and Beile's "Scholars Before Researchers". *Educational Researcher*, Vol. 35, No. 9, pp. 28-31.

Merkens, H. (2004). Selection, Procedures, Sampling, Case Construction. In U. Flick, E.V. Kandroff and I. Steinke (eds.), *A Comparison to Qualitative Research.* London: Sage.

Tashakhori, A. and Teddlie, C. (eds.) (2003). *Handbook of Mixed Methods in Social and Behavioral Research.* Thousand Oaks. CA: Sage.

CHAPTER

33

Descriptive Research Method

33.0 NATURE OF DESCRIPTIVE RESEARCH

A descriptive study describes and interprets what is. It is primarily concerned with present, although it often considers past events and influences as they relate to current conditions. It is concerned with conditions or relationships that exist, opinions that are held, processes that are going on, effects that are evident, trends that are developing. Descriptive Research studies are also used both in quantitative and qualitative research.

The literature and terminology of descriptive investigations include such expressions as descriptive survey, normative, survey status, and trend. Descriptive studies may include present facts or current conditions concerning the nature of a group of persons, a number of objects or a class of events. It may involve the procedures of induction, analysis, classification, enumeration, or measurement. The term survey and status suggest gathering of evidence relating to current events or conditions. The expression 'normative, sometimes is applied to descriptive investigations because the purpose is to determine normal or typical condition or practice, as in comparing local test results with a city, state, or national norms (central tendency). For instance, there are norms for assessing the status or quality of an institution/organization.

Many descriptive studies are highly analytical in character. For the purposes of an analytical study the interest may be in matters of form, pattern, or organization or it may be concerned with the dynamics of the school, as illustrated by pupil-teacher relationships or teacher-principal relationships.

Assessment describes status of a phenomenon at a particular time without value judgment. It attempts no explanation of underlying reasons and makes no recommendations for action. It may deal with prevailing opinion, knowledge, practices, or conditions. Assessment studies may include: the survey, public opinion surveys, national and international surveys, activities analysis, and trend studies.

Descriptive research studies are designed to obtain pertinent and precise information concerning the current status of phenomena and, whenever possible, to draw valid general conclusions from the fact discovered. They are restricted not only to fact finding but may often result in the formulation of important principles of knowledge and solution of significant problems concerning local, state , national and international issues. They collect data which provide three types of information i.e. (1) where are we at present with regard to specific variables under study? (present status) (2) what is our standing *vis-à-vis* established norms, or what experts consider to be desirable, and what is our position in relation to others? (mis-match between anticipated and actual), and (3) how can we achieve goals by exploring possible ways and means? (strategies to correct mis-match). Descriptive studies provide us insights to evolve strategies for the solution of the problem.

33.1 DESCRIPTIVE RESEARCH

33.1.1 Quantitative Descriptive Research

Depending upon the nature of data and use of techniques, descriptive research can broadly be either 'quantitative descriptive research' or 'qualitative descriptive research'. Quantitative research mostly uses statistical method in drawing comparison between concepts, ideas, products or packages, etc. Quantitative research involves quantifications based on numbers. Thus, it is easier to identify, classify the variables to predict the results. The internal and external validity can be easily established. Sometimes, it is known as non-experimental or co-relational research. In descriptive research studies, the researcher does not manipulate the variable, decide who receives the treatment or arrange for events to happen. Such descriptive research also involves events that have already taken place and may be related to a present condition and deals with the relationships between variables, the testing of hypotheses, and the development of generalizations, principles, or theories that have universal validity as well prediction of future phenomenon.

33.1.2 Qualitative Descriptive Research

Descriptive studies investigate phenomena in their natural setting. Their purpose is to provide information useful to the solution of local problems and at times provide data to form the basis or research of a more fundamental nature. Qualitative Descriptive Research includes : (1) Ethnographic: the culture of the group of people or more recently a naturalistic inquiry; (2) Phenomenological: the structures and essence of experience of particular phenomenon for people; and (3) Case-based Research: set of symbols and give meaning to people's interactions, understanding the system as a whole, (4) Grounded Theory: the findings of grounded theory are not arrive at by means of statistical procedures or other means of quantification, but are derived from data gathered by a variety of means including 'observation' interview, documents, and video tapes.

The method of descriptive research, in contrast to an experiment, is relatively less scientifically sophisticated. Here the researcher does not manipulate the variables or arrange for events to happen. In fact, the events that are observed and described by him would have happened even though there had been no observation. (*ex-post-facto*)

33.2 TYPES OF DESCRIPTIVE RESEARCH

The descriptive research studies may be classified in the following three categories:

33.2.1 Survey Studies

In survey studies detail information is gathered to understand the present status or detail description of phenomena to know where we are and to make intelligent plan for what we intend to achieve. Survey studies describe and specify the properties of educational phenomena. They include: School surveys which may be categorized into three types: (1) the investigative, evaluative or status survey which serves primarily to evaluate existing condition, (2) deliberative, developmental, or planning survey, which is intended primarily to make proposals for development and improvement, with a minimum criticism of present circumstances, and (3) the implementive survey, which not only makes suggestions for development but also attempts to create conditions in the conduct of the survey which will enhance the prospects of actually achieving survey recommendations. (Cooper, 1946; Reller, 1942)

The scope of school surveys is large and varied. A single comprehensive school survey may be composed of various constituent surveys. These include: (1) survey testing, (2) school appraisal, (3) status studies, (4) financial studies, (5) curriculum studies, and (6) school infrastructure survey.

School Surveys—Used to gather data concerned with internal or external characteristics of a school system.

Job Analysis—Used to gather information to be used in structuring a training program for a particular job.

Documentary Analysis—Closely akin to historical research; deals with documenting present situations.

Public Opinion Surveys—Used to enhance the decision-making process by government officials.

Community Surveys—Used to gather data concerned with internal or external characteristics of a community.

33.2.2 Interrelationship Studies

These studies are to discover relationship between various facts of existing phenomena. These include case study, *ex-post facto* or causal-comparative studies, correlation and prediction studies, and cross-cultural and comparative studies.

33.2.3 Case Study and Field Studies

Purpose of the case or field studies is to study intensively the background, current status, and environmental interactions of a given social unit: an individual, group, institution, or community. For example, Piaget's studies of cognitive growth in children; an in-depth study of a pupil with a learning disability by a school psychologist; an intensive study of the 'inner city' culture and living conditions in a large metropolitan environment; and an anthropologist's exhaustive field study of cultural life on a remote Indian reservation in the Southwest.

33.2.4 Ex-post facto or causal-comparative studies

Purpose of ex-post facto or causal comparative studies is to investigate possible cause-and-effect relationships by observing some existing consequence and searching back through the data for plausible causal factors. This is in contrast to the experimental method which collects its data under controlled conditions in the present. In the *ex-post facto* studies there is no scope for the manipulation of the independent variables to identify the effect on dependent variable.

33.2.5 Correlation and Prediction Studies

Correlation studies are concerned with determining the extent of relationship existing between variables. These are used to obtain description of existing phenomenon and enable a researcher to ascertain the extent to which variations in one variable are associated with variations in another. The magnitude of the relationship is dtermined through the use of the coefficient of correlation.

Correaltion studies are particularly useful in making prediction. Guilford (1965, pp. 356-57) has conceptualised four types of predictions in psychology and education. These are predictions of (i) attributes from other attributes, such as predicting incidence of criminality from a knowledge of sex, caste, or race; (ii) attributes from measurements, such as predicting criminality from known scores on tests of ability or other behaviour traits; (iii) measurements from attributes, such as predicting probable tests scores from a knowledge of sex or socio-economic status; and (iv) measurements from other measurements, such as predicting achievment test scores from known aptitude test scores. Generally 'regression equations' are used in making predictions.

33.2.6 Cross-cultural and Comparative Studies

With the growth of social sciences in the late nineteenth century, the dynamic relationship between education and society was recognised. Behaviourists emphasized the importance of many cross-cultural studies relating to education. Anthropologists studied the relationship between child rearing practices in various countries and cultures, the inculcation of moral values, drug abuse and crime rate. The recent examples of cross-cultural studies are the relationship between the content of the folk tales and agression relationship between acievement motivation in folk tales and need achievement, relationship between various techniques of education and development of super ego and other manifestations of personality.

33.2.7 Comparative Studies

Comparative studies have been undertaken to compare school-state relationships, educational reforms, the problems and causes of wastage and stagnation, the accessibility to higher education, education of children with special needs, education of deprived and margainalised section of the society, educational system prevailing in different countries and their implications, innovative practices across the various countries and their application in the local conditions, curriculum framework of developed and developing countries, pattern of investment in education and it impact on economy across the world, globalisation, privatisation and liberalisation impact on educational deveelopment, etc., a number of reports on the comprehensive comparative studies relatiing to education of marginalised population, illitracy, right to education, juvenile delinquency have been published by UNESCO. These reports have proved helpful in the development of planning models. Sharing of experiences and learning resources among countries have futher strengthened the education system of various countries of the world.

33.2.8 Developmental Studies

Such studies are concerned not only with present status and interrelationships of variables but also with changes that take place as a function of time. Developmental studies may include: 1. growth studies, 2. follow-up studies, and 3. trend studies.

Growth Studies—May be either longitudinal or cross-sectional. The longitudinal technique is the most satisfactory for studying human development. The cross-sectional technique is more commonly used because it is less expensive.

Trend Studies are used to make predictions from social trends, economic conditions, technological advances, etc. to project future trends.

Follow-up studies are undertaken for system development. These are based on a thorough determination of the present situation or system and the goals.

33.3 EVALUATION

The purpose of evaluation is to see if a given programme is working; if an institution is successful according to the goals set for; if practices, processes, procedures and activities are effectively.

33.4 STEPS IN CONDUCTING DESCRIPTIVE RESEARCH

Identification of Problem : Familarity with the area and the sub-areas of the field is prerequisite. Researcher's inquisitiveness would help him to identify the right topic. He can make use of his personal experience, opinion of experts in the area of his interest, interacting with resource persons in the identification of research problem of his or her choice. When topic of research is identified, need arises to explain and justify why do you like to undertake this research study? What are the expected outcomes of the proposed research study? What are its practical implications?

Review of Literature is the fundamental task of dissertation and research preparation. Literature reviewing should be a central focus of pre-dissertation course work, integrated throughout the programme.

'Comprehensiveness' and 'Broadness' are two of the criteria assessing the 'Coverage'. First, is a standard for evaluating the literature review, and Second is the discussion part of the dissertation.

Statement of Problem is one or two sentences claim that outlines the problem that the study addresses. Statement of the problem should be specific, clear and researchable. A research worthy problem statement is the description of an active challenge faced by researchers and/or practitioners that does not have adequate solution. The research worthy problem statement should address all six questions; what, how, where, when, why and who.

Objectives of the Study : After selecting the topic and defining the research problem, the researcher should mention the objectives of the research. Objectives of the study provide clear direction to research. They should reflect the basic purpose of the study, i.e. what we want to achieve. Objectives of the study should provide necessary safeguards in collection of requisite information. Quantitative or qualitative data thus collected are analyzed and interpreted *vis-a-vis* earmarked objectives or outcomes of the research project.

Methodology should include research design, sampling procedures, instruments for the collection of data. Research design gives the outlines of the research work. Research design is the plan, structure and strategy of investigation conceived to obtain answers to research questions. The researcher should explain the method he is going to use. Sampling procedures should explain the details of sample for the conduct of study. The research should ensure that standardized tools should be used for the collection of data.

Data Analysis : Specify the procedures you will use, and label them accurately (e.g., General Linear Model (quantitative) or Qualitative or Mixed Methods of analysis of data).

Limitations and Delimitations : Limitations identify potential weaknesses of the study. Explain in clear terms about your analysis, the nature of self-report, your instruments, the sample and threats to internal validity that may have been impossible to avoid or minimize. Delimination address how a study will be narrowed in scope, that is, how it is bounded. This is the place to explain the things that you are not doing and why you have chosen not to do them—the literature you will not review (and why not), the population you are not studying (and why not), the methodological procedures you will not use (and why you will not use them). Limit your delimitations to the things that a reader might reasonably expect you to do but that you, for clearly explained reasons, have decided not to do.

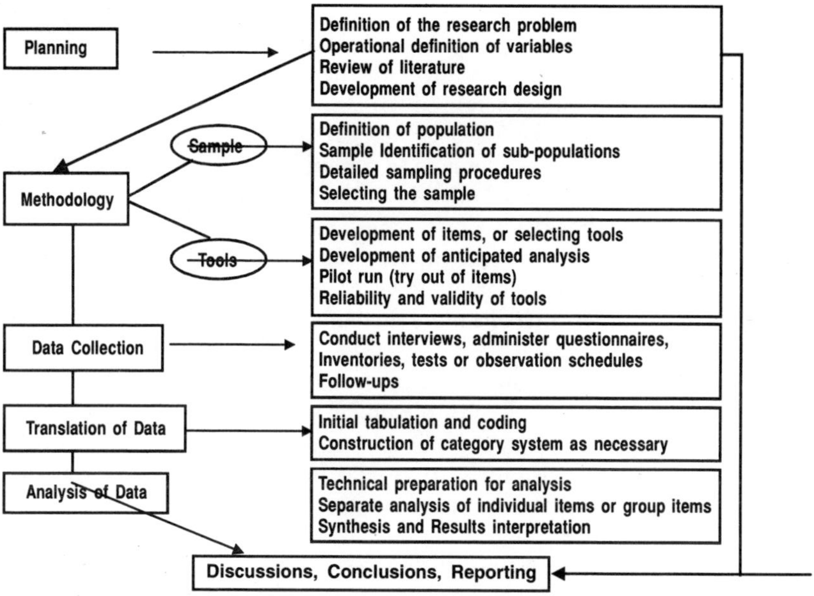

Implications : This can be a difficult section to write. Think about *implications*—how results of the study may affect scholarly research, theory, practice, educational interventions, and policy.

33.5 MERITS OF THE DESCRIPTIVE STUDIES

- To secure evidence concerning the existing situation or current condition.
- To identify standards or norms with which to compare present condition in order to plan the next step.
- To determine how to take the next step (having determined where we are and where we wish to go. Worthwhile descriptive studies collect three types of information: (a) of what exists by studying and analyzing important aspects of present situations; (b) of what we want by clarifying goals and objectives possible through a study of the conditions existing elsewhere or what experts consider to be desirable, and (c) of how to get there through discovering the possible means of achieving the goals on the basis of experiences of other or the opinions of the experts.
- Descriptive research is very important for professionals, administrators, policy planners and teachers. As it brings

into focus our attention to existing educational problems and also suggests ways of solving them.

- It is concerned not with the characteristics of individuals but with generalized statistics of the whole population or a sample thereof.
- It involves planning, a careful analysis and interpretation of the data and a logical and skilful reporting of the findings.
- It provides information useful to the solution of local problems. It may, however, provide data to form the basis of research of a more fundamental nature. It also determine the present trends.
- It secures historical perspective through a series of cross-sectional pictures of similar conditions at different times. When survey studies are repeated annually or at other intervals, such cross-section pictures of conditions at different time periods provide the data for historical studies.
- Descriptive investigations are undertaken for comparison, to know the level or standing of one's country against others in terms of the objectives of education.
- It helps reconstruct or redesign the tools with which we do research in measuring relationship between variables.
- It contributes to advancement of knowledge because it affords insight into the nature of what one is dealing with, for instance, teaching and learning for making it more effective.

33.6 LIMITATIONS OF THE DESCRIPTIVE STUDIES

Descriptive research is widely used, particularly in the behavioural sciences. In education this method is used, because it is impracticable to manipulate such variables as aptitude, intelligence, personality traits, cultural variables. However, its limitations should be recognized :

- Information that is not known to the respondents cannot be obtained;
- Information that is not salient to the respondents cannot be obtained, for instance, seeking information from the young about the life experiences of old persons;
- A request for information that is considered secret cannot be entertained;

- The independent variables cannot be manipulated;
- Subjects cannot be randomly, or otherwise assigned to treatment groups; and
- Causes are often multiple than single. Moreover, information obtained from a single survey is less reliable than trend data derived from two or more consecutive surveys made by the same methods.

References

Bailey, K.D. (1987). *Methods of Social Research.* 3rd. edn. New York: Free Press.

Best, J. and Kahn, J. (2009). *Research in Education.* 10th edition, Needham Heights: Allyn and Bacon

Cozby, P. (2009). *Methods in Behavioural Research.* 10th edition, Bemont: Wadsworth.

Festinger, L. and Katz, D. (1976). (eds.). *Research Methods in the Behavioral Sciences.* New Delhi: Amerind Publishing Co.

Goode,W.J., and Hatt, P.K. (1990). *Methods in Social Research.* New Delhi: McGraw-Hill,

Guthrie, G. (2010). *Basic Research Methods.* New Delhi: Sage.

Kerlinger, F. (1986). *Foundations of Behavioural Research.* 5th edition, Orlando: Harcourt Brace.

Koul, L. (2009). *Methodology of Educational Research.* Vikas Publishing House, New Delhi.

Punch, K.F. (2009). *Introduction to Research Methods in Education.* New Delhi: Sage.

Singh, J. (2008). *Methodology and Techniques of Social Research.* New Delhi: Kanishka Publishers.

Somekh, B., and Lewin, C. (2005). *Research Methods in the Social Sciences.* New Delhi. Vstaar Publications.

William Wiersma (1986). *Research Methods in Education: An Introduction.* Allyn and Bacon, Inc. London.

CHAPTER

34

Experimental Research Method

34.0 EXPERIMENTAL RESEARCH

Experimental research is the description and analysis of what will be or what will occur, under carefully controlled conditions (Best, 1993). Its basic assumption rests on J.S. Mill's law of the single variable which states that if two situations are similar in very respect, and one element is added or subtracted from one but not the other, any difference that develops is the result of the operation of that element added or subtracted. This procedure is distinctly different from the historical and the normative survey methods.

Purpose of experimental research is to investigate cause-and-effect relationships by exposing one or more experimental groups to one or more treatment conditions and comparing the results to one or more control groups not receiving the treatment.

Examples:

1. To investigate the effects of two methods of teaching a twelfth grade history program as a function of class size (large and small) and levels of student intelligence (high, average, low), using random assignment of teachers and students-by-intelligence level to method and class size.
2. To investigate the effects of a new drug abuse prevention program on the attitudes of junior high school students using experimental and control groups who are either exposed or not exposed to the program, respectively, and using a pretest-posttest design in which only half of the

students randomly receive the pretest to determine how much of an attitude change can be attributed to pretesting or to the educational program.

3. To investigate the effects of two methods of pupil evaluation on the performance of children in the twenty-three elementary schools of a given sub-urban district.

34.1 PROCESSES OF EXPERIMENTAL RESEARCH

1. Experimental research requires rigorous management of experimental variables and conditions either by direct control manipulation or through randomization.
2. Experimental research typically uses a control group as a baseline against which to compare the group(s) receiving the experimental treatment.
3. Experimental research concentrates on the control of variance:
   (a) to maximize the variance of the variables associated with research hypotheses;
   (b) to minimize the variance of extraneous variables that might affect the experimental outcomes, but are not themselves the object of study; and
   (c) to minimize the error or random variance, including so-called errors of measurement.

The best solution is random selection of subjects, random assignment of subjects to groups, and random assignment of experimental treatment to groups.

34.1.1 Internal Validity

Internal validity is the *sine qua non* of research design and the first objective of experimental methodology. It explains the significant difference (dependent variable) on account of experimental manipulation (independent variable). Extraneous variables that might affect the experimental outcomes are : (a) experimental setting, (b) age, fatigue, or interest, (c) pretesting procedures, (d) measuring instruments, (e) groups selected on the basis of extreme scores, (f) differential selection of subjects, and (g) differential experimental mortality, etc.

34.1.2 External Validity

External validity is the second objective of experimental methodology. It explains the representativeness of the findings and results can be generalized to similar circumstances and subjects. When examining the external validity of a design, the experimenter should check the threats to representativeness, for instance, (a) interaction effects of selection biases, (b) reactive effect of pretesting, (c) reactive effect of experimental procedures, and (d) multiple treatment interference.

In classic experimental design, all variables of concern are held constant except a single treatment variable which is deliberately manipulated or allowed to vary. Advances in methodology such as factorial design and the analysis of variance now allow the experimenter to permit more than one variable to be manipulated or varied concurrently across more than one experimental group. This permits the simultaneous determination of :

(1) the effect of the principal independent variables (treatments),
(2) the variation associated with classificatory variables, and
(3) the interaction of selected combinations of independent and or classificatory variables.

34.2 STEPS IN EXPERIMENTAL RESEARCH

1. Survey the literature relating to the problem.
2. Identify and define the problem.
3. Formulate a problem hypothesis, deducing the consequences, and defining basic terms and variables.
4. Construct an experiment plan:
   (a) Identify all non-experimental variables that might contaminate the experiment, and determine how to control them.
   (b) Select a research design.
   (c) Select a sample of subjects to represent a given population, assign subjects to groups, and assign experimental treatments to groups.
   (d) Select or construct and validate instruments to measure the outcome of the experiment.
   (e) Outline procedures for collecting the data, and possibly conduct a pilot or "trial run" test to perfect the instruments or design.
   (f) State the statistical or null hypothesis.
5. Conduct the experiments.
6. Reduce the raw data in a manner that will produce the best appraisal of the effect which is presumed to exist.
7. Apply an appropriate test of significance to determine the confidence one can place on the results of the study.

34.3 INTERACTION BETWEEN VARIABLES

34.3.1 Patterns of Interaction

The current emphasis in behavioural research is upon interactions between variables. What method works best? Or What factor is the most important? has given way to questions specifying, what variables? in what combinations and amounts? under what conditions? with what subjects? and to meet what objectives?

34.3.2 Interaction-proneness

Some factors are more interaction-prone than others. It is important to look for the interaction between variables, combining them to optimize outcomes.

34.3.3 Main Effects Versus Interactions

In cases of 'effectiveness', however, a main effect of one variable is to be judged more likely than the interaction of two other variables. More generally, main effects are more likely than interactions. If every highest order interaction is significant, if every effect is specific to certain values on all other potential treatment dimensions, then a science is not possible. If generalizations are ever possible, it is because the great bulk of potential determining factors can be discarded.

34.3.4 Use of Appropriate Independent Variables

It is useful to select independent variables such that they are relevant and arranged in realistic combinations with each other to take into account the interaction relationships. If one questions whether he has defined his variables properly, he is likely to discover new things. Often the researcher selects what appears to be obvious and important variables as if they were independent of the others. If an interaction relationship exists between two or more of these independent variables, however, he is apt to overlook highly important and useful information.

Examples: Class size is an important independent variable only in relationship with different teaching methods; to consider it separately is to miss its relevance to teaching. Another example of interaction between independent variable comes from Gage's research on the Minnesota Teacher Attitude Inventory (MTAI). This is a well-developed test based on the conception that teachers who are warm, gentle, democratic, and child-centered, have a superior relationship with the class and it has validity ratings near. However, when Gage developed another test of cognitive *versus* emotional orientation and compared "interpersonal relations-valuing" classes with "cognitive learning-oriented" classes—classes where the teacher and pupil are collaborating in a learning enterprise—MTAI predictive validities remained around 40 for the former but fell to zero in the latter case. Thus, an over simple conception of the independent variable led apparently to a false interpretation of previous results.

34.3.5 The Fixed Treatment Assumption

The fixed treatment assumption has certain limitations in the validation of test. Instead of predicting whether type A does better than type B in a given treatment, look for ways to change the treatment to fit individuals of different kinds. It is important to ask: What teaching methods work best for what kinds of students under what conditions?

34.4 CRITERIA FOR A WELL-DESIGNED EXPERIMENT

1. Adequate experimental control;
2. No artificial or atypical characteristic of a experiment to cause the experimental effects;
3. Basis for comparison;
4. Adequate information from the data;
5. Uncontaminated data;
6. No confounding of relevant variables;
7. Representativeness; and
8. Parsimony

34.5 MERITS

1. Experimental method is widely used in educational research with considerable success in the classroom where within certain limits, significant factors or conditions can be controlled;
2. Experimental research is used to determine and evaluate the adequacy and effectiveness of educational aims and objectives through measurement of outcomes;
3. It serves as a basis for the formulation, execution and modification of educational practices and programmes;
4. Experimental research ascertains the effect of any change in the normal educational programme or practices;
5. In many educational areas like teaching and learning, pedagogy, superiority of particular method of instruction, impact of ICT and innovative practices on learning outcomes can be examined; and
6. Experimental research has contributed significantly in the field of special education.

34.6 LIMITATIONS

1. Since in the field of education, complex human beings are the subjects and it is unlikely that all variables can be successfully controlled.
2. Some moral and psychological principles do stand in the way of strict experimentation.
3. The control group and the experimental group are never as identical as they aught to be for an exact experiment.
4. Another difficulty, in principle at least, arises from the fact that educational experiments are carried through with human beings and affect mental processes and attitudes. Gestalt psychology and related research have shown that the introduction of any specific influence, however, well and exactly defined, intended to change one specific type of mental process or attitude- will change the "whole field" of mentality, often in aspects and ways that escape the control of experimenter.

34.7 DIFFERENT EXPERIMENTAL RESEARCH DESIGNS

34.7.1 True Experimental Design

Randomized Control Group: Pretest-Posttest Design

Group	*Pretest*	*Treatment*	*Posttest*
Experimental Group (R)*	T_1	X	T_2
Control Group (R)	T_1	–	T_2

* Random assignment.

Design Procedure

1. Selecting subjects from a population by random method.
2. Assigning subjects to groups and the treatment (X), or non-treatment to groups by random method.
3. Pretest the groups on the dependent variable (T_1), finding the mean pretest score for both the experimental and control groups.
4. Keeping all conditions the same for both groups, except for exposing only the experimental group to X, the experimental treatment (independent variable) for a specified period of time.
5. Test the groups on T_2 the dependent variable, and find the mean post test score for both groups.

6. Finding the difference between the T_1 and T_2 means for each group separately (T_2—T_1)
7. Compare these differences to determine whether the application of X is associated with a change favouring the experimental group over the control group (which was not expose to X)
8. Apply an appropriate statistical test to determine whether the difference in the scores is significant—that is, if a difference is large enough to reject the null hypothesis that the difference is simply a chance occurrence. Design can be extended to two or more than two independent variables. For example:

First Experimental Group	T_1 Xa	(Method a)	T_2
Second Experimental Group	T_1 Xb	(Method b)	T_2
Control Group	T_1	—	T_2

34.7.2 Randomized Solomon Four-Group Design

Group	*Pretest*	*Treatment*	*Posttest*	*Difference**
1. Pretest (R)**	T_1	X	T_2	1D = T_1, X, M, H
2. Pretest (R)	T_1		T_2	2D = T_1, M, H
3. Unpretest (R)		X	T_2	3D = X, M, H
4. Unpretest (R)			T_2	4D = M, H

**(R) Random assignment.

*D—The difference between T_1 and T_2 mean scores represent the effects of various combination of variables, such as pretesting T_1, independent variable X, history H, Maturation M,. To find the effect of X alone,substract 4D from 3D. To find the effect of pretesting, subtract 4D from 2D. To find the effect of the interaction of pretesting and X, add 2D and 3D and subtract the sum for 1D.

34.7.3 Counterbalanced Experimental Design

When random assignment of subjects is not possible and intact groups must be used, a limited number of subjects is available , no pretest is given and, more than one varation of X is tested, then counterbalanced design is used.

Replication	*Treatment Variations*			
	Xa	*Xb*	*Xc*	*Xd*
1.	A	B	C	D
2.	B	D	A	C
3.	C	A	D	B
4.	D	A	B	C

Column Mean Scores:

Design Procedures

1. Each group of subjects (A, B, C, D) is exposed to each variation of X (or absence of X, if control group is used) at different times during the experiment. In the above example, there are four variations of X applied to four different groups in such a way that: (a) a different X is presented to each group each time, and (b) each *x* precedes and follows each other X an equal number of times.
2. After all the experimental sessions are completed, the column mean for each variation of X is computed. A column mean represents the average score for all groups when exposed to the particular X in the column heading. A comparison of these column mean scores reveals what effect the different Xs have upon group performance.

34.7.4 Control-Group Time Series Design

	Pretest	*Treatment*	*post-test*
Experimental Group:	$T_1\,T_2\,T_3\,T_4$	X	$T_5\,T_6\,T_7\,T_8$
Control Group:	$T_1\,T_2\,T_3\,T_4$		$T_5\,T_6\,T_7\,T_8$

Procedure

1. Selecting subjects from a population by random method.
2. Assigning subjects to groups and the treatment (X), or non-treatment to groups by random method.
3. Pretest the groups on the dependent variable (T_1, T_2, T_3, T_4), finding the mean pretest score for both the experimental and control groups.
4. Keeping all conditions the same for both groups, except for exposing only the experimental group to X, the experimental treatment (independent variable) for a specified period of time.
5. Test the groups on T_5, T_6, T_7, T_8, the dependent variable, and find the mean post test score for both groups.
6. Finding the difference between the means for each group separately.
7. Compare these differences to determine whether the application of X is associated with a change favouring the experimental group over the control group (which was not expose to X).
8. Apply an appropriate statistical test to determine whether the difference in the scores is significant—that is, if a

difference is large enough to reject the null hypothesis that the difference is simply a chance occurrence.

34.7.5 The 2X2 Factorial Design

Teaching method (X_1)	*Lenth of Period (X_2)*		*Mean*	*Difference*
Lecture	A	B		
Discussion	59.0	58.0	58.5	+1.0
	C	D		
	82.0	84.0	83.0	+2.0
Mean	70.5	71.0		
Difference	23	26		

This is the simplest factorial design, permitting the study of the effects of two Xs (treatments), each of which is varied in two ways (level or values).

Example:

1. Let X_1 represent two teaching methods and X_2 represents two length of time for a class period.
2. Assign subjects at random to each of the four possible combinations of experimental treatment. Group A is exposed to 50-minute lecture periods, Group B to 30-minute discussion periods.
3. After a redetermined period of time, the achievement of each subject is measured and the mean score of each of the groups are recorded in their appropriate cells (e.g., Group A = 59.0, Group B = 58.0, etc.) and C = 820, D = 847.
4. Mean scores are also computed for the pairs of groups exposed to the lecture method (A to B = 58.5) and the discussion method (C and D = 83.0); the 50 minute period (A and C = 70.5) or the 30-minute period (B to D = 71.0). These combined means are placed in their respective row or column margins.

Design Information

1. What is the main effect of teaching method (X_1) on achievement scores? Answer: A comparison of the mean score of two lecture groups (58.5) with that of the two discussion groups (83.0) appears to favour the latter as more effective.
2. What is the main effect of length of class (X_2) on achievement scores? Answer: A comparison of the mean

score of two groups with 50-minute periods (70.5) and the two groups with 30-minutes (71.0) suggests no particular difference.

3. What is the interaction effect, if any, of teaching method and length of class period on the achievement scores? Answer: If there is an interaction, the effect that a teaching method has on the achievement scores will differ for 30 and 50 minute classes. If the discussion method, for example, is more effective with one length of class then it is with the other, there is an interaction. If there is no interaction, the effect of teaching method on achievement scores will be the same for both lengths of class periods. The data in the above example, therefore, reveal no appreciable interaction effect.

34.7.6 Extended Factorial Designs

Factorial designs are more complex than the 2 x 2 model. For example: *2 x 3 design*—two independent variables: one varied in two ways; the other varied in three ways. Example:

First variable: Sex *(male or female)*

Second variable: Methods of teaching reading (*reading experience approach, phonics approach, and world recognition approach).*

3 X 3 Design—three independent variables: each varied three ways. Example:

First variable: Intelligence *(Above 110 IQ, Between 90-110 IQ, and Below 90 IQ)*

Second variable: Problem-solving Approach *(individual, small group, and large group)*

Third variable: Time allotment (2 *hours without interruption*, 2 1 *hour session with a 1 hour break*, 2 1 *hour sessions with a* 24-*hour break*).

2 x 2 x 2 Design: three independent variables: each varied two ways. Example:

First variable: Age (12 *year old and* 15 *year old*)

Second variable: Sex (*boys and girls*)

Third variable: Counseling atmosphere (*directive or non-directive*)

Note: This design requires eight treatment groups ($2 \times 2 \times 2 = 8$) and can answer the following seven questions: What is the main effect on (for example) achievement scores of (1) X_1, (2) X_2 and (3) X_3? What is the interaction effect on the achievement scores of (4) X_1 and X_2 (5) X_1, and X_3, (6) X_2 and X_3 and (7) X_1, X_2 and X_3?

Designs of greater complexity than the above illustrations are possible, through they tend to be unwidely and highly sophisticated.

An important characteristics of a factorial designs is that several hypothesis can be tested simultaneously, releasing researchers from the rigidity of classical designs. Whereas classical designs allowed only the study of a single variable at a time, factorial designs permit several variables to be investigated in one experiment. An example of this multi-factor approach would be an experiment investigating simultaneously the following question: What effect does teacher personality (X_1) have on student when using a particular teaching method (X_2) in a particular classroom situation (X_3) with students of particular ability level (X_4)?

References

Ackoff, R.L. (1962). *Scientific Method.* New York: John Wiley & Sons.

Best, J.W. and Kahn, J.V. (2008). *Research in Edcation.* Pearson, Prentice Hall, Inc. and Dorling Kindersley Publishing, Inc. (India).

Brodbeck, M. (1963). Logic and scientific method in research on teaching. In N.L. Gage (ed.), *Handbook of Research on Teaching* (pp. 44-93), Chicago: Rand McNally.

Englehart, Max D. (1972). *Methods of Educational Research.* Chicago: Rand McNally.

Festinger, L. and Katz, D. (1976). (eds.) *Research Methods in the Behavioral Sciences.* New Delhi: Amerind Publishing Co.

Freedman, P. (1960). *The Principles of Scientific Research.* 2nd ed., New York: Pergamon Press.

Plutchik, R. (1968). *Foundations of Experimental Research.* New York: Harper and Row.

CHAPTER

35

Ex-post Facto Research Method

35.0 EX-POST FACTO RESEARCH

In behavioural sciences many problems cannot be solved by the experimental methods, because of the complexity and nature of social phenomena. One cannot always select and control the factors necessary to study cause and effect relations in artificial laboratory situations. If an experimenter controls variations in all but a single independent experimental—variable, he may prevent the simultaneous functioning of the variables that naturally found operating together. This may free the independent variable from the influence. Hence, an analysis what actually does happen in a natural situation may be more satisfactory way to study causes. Therefore, *ex-post facto* is an alternative method of empirical inquiry for establishing causal relationships between events and circumstances.

Kerlinger (1986) defines ex-post facto research as systematic, empirical inquiry in which the scientist does not have direct control of independent variables because the manifestations have already occurred. The researcher starts with observation of a dependent variable or variables. He then studies the independent variables in retrospect for their possible relations to, and effect on, dependent variable or variables. Inferences about relations among variables are made, without direct intervention, from concomitant variation of independent and dependent variables.

Ary, Jacobs, and Razavleh (1972) stated that *ex-post-facto* research is to discover or establish causal or functional relationships among variables, and that 'careful investigators prefer to speak of functional rather than causal relations.

Tuckman (1972) defined it as an experiment in which the researcher examines the effect of a naturalistically occurring treatment after that treatment has occurred rather than creating the treatment itself. The experimenter attempts to relate this after-the-fact treatment to an outcome of dependent measure. The treatment is included by selection rather than manipulation.

In the context of social and educational research the phrase means 'after-the-fact' or 'retrospectively' and refers to those studies which investigate possible cause-and-effect relationships by observing an existing condition or state of affairs and searching back in time for plausible causal factors. In effect, researchers ask themselves what factors seem to be associated with certain occurrences, or conditions, or aspects of behaviour. *Ex-post facto* research, then, is a method of teasing out possible antecedents of events that have happened and cannot, therefore, be engineered or manipulated by the investigator. It implies some type of subsequent action. The variables are studied in retrospect, in search of possible relationships of effects. The independent variables of an *ex-post facto* study usually are identified before the data are collected and are of such nature that they have occurred in the situation. Socio-economic level is an example of a possible independent variable in an *ex-post facto* study. A researcher can not randomly assign socio-economic level to individuals. A researcher can randomly select individuals from categories, i.e. upper, middle and lower socio-economic levels.

35.1 RESEARCH APPROACHES

Listed below is the whole range of research approaches that can be used in *ex-post* research studies.

35.1.1 Historical Research Design

Sukhia, Mehrotra and Mehrotra (1974) placed this method in historical perspective within logic. This method is based on Mill's canon of Agreement and Disagreement which states that causes of given observed effect may be ascertained by noting elements which are invariable present when the result is present in which is invariably absent when the result is absent. The purpose is to collect, verify, synthesize evidence to establish facts that defend or refute your hypothesis. It uses primary sources, secondary sources, and lots of qualitative data sources such as logs, diaries, official records, reports, etc. The limitation is that the sources must be both authentic and valid.

35.1.2 Causal Comparative Research Design

Causal comparative approach differs from historical. Historical approach finds out the causes of past events whereas, causal comparative deals with the present events only. This research design attempts to explore cause and affect relationships where causes already exist and cannot be manipulated. It uses what already exists and looks backward to explain why.

35.1.3 Case and Field Research Approach

Case and Field Research Approach makes observations under normal field conditions and discovers the causes of observed phenomena. It is also called ethnographic research. It uses direct observation to give a complete snapshot of a case that is being studied. It is useful when not much is known about a phenomenon. It uses few subjects.

35.1.4 Descriptive or Survey Research Design

It attempts to describe and explain conditions of the present by using many subjects and questionnaires to fully describe a phenomenon. It is mainly concerned with status and trends. Survey research design/survey methodology is one of the most popular for *ex-post facto* research studies.

35.1.5 Correlational or Prospective Research Design

It attempts to explore relationships to make predictions. It uses one set of subjects with two or more variables for each.

35.1.6 Developmental or Time Series Research Design

Data are collected at regular time intervals. There is an emphasis on time patterns and longitudinal growth or change.

35.1.7 Quasi Experimental Research Design

Quasi-experiment design is *ex-post facto* experiment in which a particular characteristic of a given group is investigated with a view to identifying its antecedents. The *ex-post facto* experiment begins with a given effect and seeks the experimental factor that brought it about. And there is no control over situations that have already occurred

35.2 STEPS IN CONDUCTING EX-POST FACTO RESEARCH

35.2.1 Define the Research Problem

Identify important problems and pose questions that can be investigated empirically or through potentially useful approaches. Problem selected should be significant and contribute to the solution of practical problem or to bridge mismatch between expectations and experiences. Variables are to be operationally defined.

35.2.2 Survey of Literature

'Comprehensiveness' and 'Broadness' are two of the criteria assessing the 'Coverage'.

The centrality of relevance also needs to focused in surveying literature. The primary purpose is not only to synthesize and summarize but also to inform and support some decisions.

35.2.3 Formulation of Hypotheses/Research Questions

Hypotheses or research questions should state relationships between different variables. It must state the expected relationships between variables. Research questions or hypotheses should be clear, accurate to draw logical conclusions.

35.2.4 Assumptions

Listing the assumptions upon which the hypotheses and procedures will be based. Assumptions may be concerning the nature of social reality, or concerning human nature and agency, and knowledge which a researcher can observe, measure, and quantify it.

35.2.5 Designing the Approach

Ex-post facto studies are of two kinds, neither of them involving actual manipulation of the experimental variable. In the first comparison is made of two groups, which are equated as closely as possible by matching and adjustment, but where only one group has some past time been exposed to the predictor variable. The hypothesis of interest is tested by comparing the incident of the predictant variable in the two groups. This research looks from the past to the present, and is generally termed as a *cause-to-effect design.*

In the second kind, two groups differing in the predictant variable, but as nearly as possible equated in other respects by matching and adjustment, are compared; the researcher then look back for possible explanations of the difference. This is the *effect to cause design.*

The researcher has to keep these points while designing research:

- Selection of appropriate subjects and source materials,
- Selection or construction of techniques for data collection,
- Establishing categories for classifying data that are unambiguous, appropriate for the purpose of the study, and capable of bringing out significant relationships, and
- Selection of correlational/quasi-experimental approach.

35.2.6 Reliability and Validity of Instruments of Measurement

Instruments of measurement must meet the tests of validity, reliability and practicability. Validity refers to the extent to which a test measures what we actually wish to measure. Reliability has to do with the accuracy and precision of measurement procedure. Practicability is concerned with a wide range of factors of economy, convenience, and interpretability.

35.2.7 Treatment of Data

Gathering of data on factors invariably present in cases where the given result occurs and discarding of those elements which are not universally present.

Gathering of data on factors invariably present in cases where the given effect does not occur.

Comparing two sets of data, in effect, subtracting one from the other to get at the causes responsible for the occurrence or otherwise of the effect. (Sukhia, *et al.*, 1974)

35.2.8 Analysis of Data

The following statistical techniques are used for analysis of data:

- t-test, ANOVA, ANCOVA when two or more groups are compared.
- Regression analysis when there are multiple independent variables.
- MANOVA and multivariate regression, when there are multiple dependent variables.
- Path analysis and structural equation modeling when the theoretical causal paths are being investigated.

35.2.9 Findings, Interpretation and Discussion

This is concerned with description, discussion and interpretation of the findings in clear, precise terms.

35.3 MERITS OF EX-POST FACTO RESEARCH METHOD

(1) The *ex-post facto* Research is appropriate in many circumstances where the more powerful experimental method is not possible:

(a) When it is not possible to select, control, and manipulate the factors to study cause and effect relations directly;

(b) When the control of all variations except independent variable may be highly unrealistic and artificial, preventing the normal interaction with other influential variables; and

(c) When laboratory controls for many research purposes would be impractical, costly or ethically questionable.

(2) It yields useful information concerning the nature of phenomena: what goes with what, under what conditions, in what sequences and patterns, and the like;

(3) Improvement in techniques, statistical methods, and designs with partial control features, in recent years, have made these studies more feasible; and

(4) It is a research approach which analyses the relationship between data, between variables and some results in such a way that the underlying patterns of relationships becomes clear.

If a tally of sound and important studies in psychology, sociology, and education were made, it is likely that *ex-post facto* studies would outnumber and outrank experimental studies. (Kerlinger, 1986).

35.4 LIMITATIONS OF EX-FACTO RESEARCH METHOD

(1) The main weakness of any ex-post facto design is the lack of control over independent variables. Failure to introduce the common elements of control, randomization makes them extremely vulnerable from the scientific point of view;

(2) The difficulty in being certain that the relevant causative factor is actually included among the many factors under study;

(3) No single factor is cause of an outcome. Combination and interaction of factors go together under certain conditions and yield a given outcome;

(4) A phenomena may not result only from multiple causes but also from one cause in one instance and from another cause in another instance;

(5) When a relationship between two variables is discovered, determining which is the cause and which is the effect may be difficult;

(6) Locating existing groups of subjects who are similar in all respects except for their exposure to one variable is extremely difficult;

(7) Classifying subjects into dichotomous groups for the

purpose of comparison, is fraught with problems, since categories like these are vague, variable and transitory. Such investigations often do not yield useful findings; and

(8) Comparative studies in natural situations do not allow controlled selection of subjects. Locating existing subjects who are similar in all respects except for their response to observable is extremely difficult.

References

Ary, D., Jacob, L.C., and Razavleh, A. (1972). *Introduction to Research in Education.* New York: Halt, Rinehart and Winston.

Bailey, K.D. (1987). *Methods of Social Research.* 3rd. edn., New York: Free Press.

Festinger, L. and Katz, D. (1976) (eds.). *Research Methods in the Behavioural Sciences.* New Delhi: Amerind Publishing Co.

Kerlinger, F. (1986). *Foundations of Behavioural Research.* 5rd edition, Orlando: Harcourt Brace.

Laws, S. (2003). *Research for Development.* New Delhi: Vistaar Publications.

Leedy, P., Ormrod, J. (2010). *Practical Research: Planning and Design.* 9th edition, Needham Heights: Allyn Bacon

Lord, H.G. (1973). Exp-Post Facto Studies as a Research Method. Special Report No. 7320. Bureau of Education for Handicapped. Washington: D.C. Media Services.

Ozga, J. (2000). *Policy Research in Educational Settings.* Buckingham,UK: Open University Press.

Sukhia, S.P., Mehrotra, P.V. and Mehrotra, R.N. (1974). *Elements of Educational Research.* New Delhi: Allied Publishers.

Tuckman, B.W. (1972). *Conducting Educational Research.* New York: Harcourt.

CHAPTER

36

Historical Research Method

36.0 WHAT IS HISTORICAL RESEARCH?

History is not merely a list of chronological events but a truthful integrated account of the relationships between persons, events, times and places. History is used to understand the past and tries to understand present in light of past events and developments. It is a flowing, dynamic account of past events that involves an interpretation of the events in an attempt to recapture the nuances, personalities, and ideas that influenced these events. In Collingwood's language, "Scissors-and-paste historians study periods; they collect all the extant testimony about a certain limited group of events, and hope in vain that something will come of it. Scientific historians study problems; they ask questions, and if they are good historian they ask questions which they see their way to answering."

History is not a discipline of direct observation or experimentation. It utilizes the reports of observation that cannot be repeated. The historian cannot recall the actors of the past to reproduce the famous scenes of history on the stage of today. (Good, 2008). The historian depends on the observations of others.

The process of historical research is one of critical inquiry, and the product of this research is the narration or description of past events and facts. The historian seeks to test the truthfulness of the reports of observations made by others. Historian like scientist examines data, formulate hypotheses, and test the hypotheses against the evidence until acceptable conclusions are reached. Since historical research involves a description of past events, there is no possibility of control or manipulation of variables in the experimental sense. As control and manipulation of variables are essential to the experimental approach, so is critical inquiry essential to historical research. Historical research is the process of critical inquiry into past events to produce an accurate description and interpretation of those events.

It involves the systematic search for documents and other sources that contain facts relating to the historians' questions about the past. (Borg and Gall, 1983). In other words, historical research is to reconstruct the past systematically by collecting, evaluating, verifying, and synthesizing evidence to establish facts. Purpose is to reach conclusions, often in relation to particular hypotheses. It is rigorous, systematic, exhaustive, disciplined collection of appropriate, reliable, or unbiased information.

36.1 NEED FOR HISTORICAL RESEARCH

The following are the important reasons for conducting historical research (based on Berg, 1998, as cited in Johnson & Christenson, 2005):

- To uncover the unknown (i.e., some historical events are not recorded),
- To answer questions (i.e., there are many questions about our past that we not only want to know but can be useful from knowing),
- To identify the relationship that the past has to the present (i.e., knowing about the past can frequently give a better perspective of current events), and
- To record and evaluate the accomplishments of individuals, agencies, or institutions.

36.2 NATURE OF HISTORICAL RESEARCH

- The historian cannot generalize on the basis of past events.
- Historical analysis depends on the reported observations of others.

Although the nature of historical data—that is, events that cannot be observed first-hand often makes it more difficult to meet these standards, historical research still requires standards of objectivity that are as demanding as those for other methods of educational research.

- History does not operate in a closed system such as may be created in the physical science laboratory.

- It is rigorous, systematic, exhaustive, disciplined collection of appropriate, reliable, or unbiased information.

36.3 PURPOSE OF HISTORICAL RESEARCH

- Historical research provides us evidence in the light of which school theories and plans can be evaluated.
- It helps us in understanding trends, patterns, practices and development in education at different levels
- In understanding the contemporary problems in education
- In understanding educational problems of marginalized section of the society in historical perspectives.
- Understanding school as molder of regional and national character, academic freedom, pupil dropout, relationship between political and educational pattern, shifts in educational leadership, and value pattern in education
- Longitudinal analysis of the socialization process in educational institutions, changes in student and faculty value system, emergence of educational institutions, and impact of social-class background upon educational motivation and achievement.
- Application of historical research in comparative education to identify the impact of various systems of education across the world
- A research study consisting entirely of historical research provides a perspective for interpreting a part of the contemporary educational context. Historical research provides information that aids in making educational decisions.
- In the field of psychology many genetic, biographical, autobiographical, case, and clinic studies are essentially historical in approach
- Development of various schools of thoughts and their impacts on the contemporary society is one of the purposes
- The life, character, achievements of important educators and their impact on learning community can be examined
- Historical research also seeks to study the legal basis of educational institutions by different agencies, relation between state and center governments with regard to education, legal status of students and teachers, administration of private aided schools, etc.
- Historical research takes up the studies of institutions and

organizations, for example, one may study the history of growth and development of Vishwa Bharti University, Banaras Hindu University, Aligarh Muslim University, etc.

36.4 TYPES OF HISTORICAL RESEARCH

36.4.1 Bibliographic Research

Bibliographic Research reflects truthfully the important facts about the life, character, and contributions of important educators. In Indian context, one may study the contribution of Gandhi, Tagore and other leading educationists and their influence on current educational practice and thought.

36.4.2 Legal Research

It aims at to study the legal basis of educational institutions run by different religions and castes, relation between center and state governments with regard to education, legal status of teachers and students, administration of private-aided schools, school finance and participation of students in the administration of universities, etc.

36.4.3 History of Ideas

It includes the study of the origin and the development of major philosophical or scientific thoughts. Their impact on theories and practices, aims and objectives of education, relevant curriculum contents, teaching methods and evaluation techniques may be studied in historical perspectives. The evolution of current concepts like team teaching, the problem-solving approach, mastery-learning approach, value education, inclusive schooling, etc. provide important topics of historical studies.

36.4.4 History of Institution or Organizations

Case studies of schools, universities, and other educational institutions may be undertaken to see their contributions in the field of education.

36.5 STEPS IN THE CONDUCT OF HISTORICAL RESEARCH

36.5.1 Identification of Problem

Ideas for historical research topics can come from many different sources such as current issues in education, the accomplishments of an individual, an educational policy, or the relationship between events. In this context, library is obviously a central location for finding the topic for the study. Libraries typically have three main research domains—the main library catalogue, the journal catalogue and the electronic resources index. A review of related literature is necessary for any research study, and in a sense this itself is historical research for the identification of problem as well as to deduce research hypothesis.

- Researcher may select a problem pertaining to individuals, institutions, organizations, law, curriculum, administration, teacher education, important concepts and thoughts that have influenced education during a specific period of time in a given culture or sub-culture.
- He may delimit his study to an era of events in a local, regional or national setting.
- He may study the trend of events in different areas, different societies or different cultures.
- He may identify topic going through the gaps and inconsistencies in the existing historical data to get more satisfactory explanation of past events.
- The problem may not be too broad or too narrow. Moreover, it should be worthwhile, researchable and adequate data are available to arrive at logical conclusions.

36.5.2 Review of Literature

Essentially, review of literature provides a context for conducting the research and interpreting the results. On a larger scale, to meet this function adequately, the information must be accurate and must be viewed in the context of when the events occurred the researcher may proceed from the best general treatises to specialized volumes and printed collection of sources, then to calendars of documents, expert bibliographies, and reviews in historical and other appropriate journals. (Good, 1960). This step involves identifying, locating, and collecting information pertaining to the research topic. The information sources are often contained in documents such as diaries or newspapers, records, photographs, relics, and interviews with individuals who have had experience with or have knowledge of the research topic. Interviews with individuals who have knowledge of the research topic are called oral histories.

36.5.3 Formulation of Hypotheses

The hypotheses for historical research may not be formal hypotheses to be tested. Rather, they are written as explicit statements that tentatively explain the occurrence of events and conditions. In historical research, the researcher may formulate research questions that are more appropriate to the past events he is investigating and then direct his research towards seeking answers to those questions with the help of evidences. Hypotheses should be based on accurate assumptions, but failure to do so can occur, and a false assumption is almost certain to lead to an erroneous conclusion.

Best and Kahn (2002) have also remarked that although hypotheses are not always *explicitly* stated in historical investigations, they are usually implied. The historian gathers evidence and carefully relates its trustworthiness. If evidence is compatible with consequences of the hypothesis, it is confirmed. If the evidence is not compatible, or negative, the hypothesis is not confirmed. It is through such synthesis that historical generalizations are established.

For example, for the 'Study of DAV and Missionary Convent Schools of Education in British Period', questions may be:

1. What were the similarities between the two schools?
2. What were the differences between the two schools?
3. What impact did the schools have on Indian society?

36.5.4 Methodology

Methodology of historical research is essential for designing and the conduct of historical study. Deep understanding of the philosophy of history is also needed as a defense against errors of procedure and of content. Moreover, some appreciation of the influence of social and cultural factors is important if the findings are to seen in broad context.

36.5.5 Method

Historical research may be qualitative or quantitative or mixed. The type of approach depends on theme of the study and the data available. For example, research on the relative school performance during the British period as compared to post-independent period would probably include a quantitative analysis of the school performance data from the two time frames. On the other hand, the life and work of Mahatma Gandhi is appropriately qualitative.

36.5.6 Sample

The researcher, in the historical research, has little control over sampling. As historical data are the closed class of data located along a fixed temporal locus, and historian has no choice of sampling his data. He is supposed to include every type of data that comes his way.

36.5.7 Collection of Data

Data is gathered from rich mine of historical resources—primary and secondary sources, remains or relics and documents.

1. A primary source is an original or firsthand account of the event or experience. These are documents or remains, the first witness to the event, with only the mind of the observer or eye witness coming between the original event and the user of the source. They are available in written, pictorial and mechanical forms as under:

Personal records: Diaries, autobiographies, certificates, affidavits, declarations, letters, wills, deeds, contracts, and original drafts of speeches, articles, books and pamphlets.

Official records or documents: Legislative, judicial or executive documents such as constitutions, laws, charters, court proceedings and decisions; data preserved by missionaries, and other religious organizations; the information compiled by central or state education or planning departments; records of various commissions and committees, school surveys, annual reports, and other records maintained by centers of learning.

Oral testimony of traditions and events: Such as folklore, legends, ballads, tales, anecdotes, sagas, traditions, customs, manners, burials, ceremonials, social institutions, and language.

Pictorial records: Photographs, movies, micro-films, drawings, paintings, coins and sculpture.

Mechanical records: Tape recordings of interviews, meetings and speeches.

Remains or relics: Fossils, skeletons, tools, clothing, historical sites, furniture, utensils, art objects, and museum pieces.

2. *Secondary Sources* are indirect sources or second hand information, i.e. the accounts of an event provided by a person who did not directly observe the event, object, or condition. It may record of the statements of contemporaries. Information thus gathered are subject to an inherent danger of inaccuracy and distortion. Most history textbooks and encyclopedias are examples of secondary sources.

A newspaper editorial concerning the problem would be a secondary source. In a study including, among other things, the relationships between teachers and community members in nineteenth-century America, Clifford (1978) used teachers' written accounts of living with community families. These accounts were primary sources. A report on the same topic by another author would be a secondary source. The writings of John Dewey are primary sources of his views, whereas an interpretation by his students would be considered a secondary source.

36.6 THE STEPS IN DOCUMENT ANALYSIS

Plan

1. Create a list of documents you wish to explore.
2. If any documents are considered 'sensitive', seek ethics approval.

3. Do preliminary groundwork to determine whether they will be accessible.
4. Consider and plan for any translation needs.
5. If there are too many documents for analysis, develop an appropriate sampling strategy.
6. Consider what types of data you wish to gather from the documents.

Gather

7. Gather relevant documents—be prepared for hiccups.
8. Develop and employ a scheme for organizing and managing the documents.
9. Make copies of original documents that can be annotated.

Review

10. Assess the authenticity and credibility of the 'text'.
11. Explore the 'agenda' of the document and look for any biases.

Interrogate

12. Extract background information on author, audience, purpose, style.
13. Explore content—this can be done by occurrence, or by themes and issues.
14. Look for 'writing evidence' (what the document was meant to impart) and 'unwitting evidence' (everything else you can glean from the documents).

Reflect/Refine

15. View document analysis as an iterative and ongoing process.
16. Reflect on any difficulties associated with gathering the data, reviewing the sources, and exploring the content.
17. Modify the plan based on your reflections.
18. Gather, review, and interrogate additional documents as needed.

The methodology of historical research can be summarized in four steps namely, identification of research problem which may include the formulation of hypotheses or questions, collection and evaluation of source materials which include internal and external criticism, synthesis of information from source materials and finally analysis, interpretation, and drawing conclusion. The four steps are diagrammed in Figure 36.1.

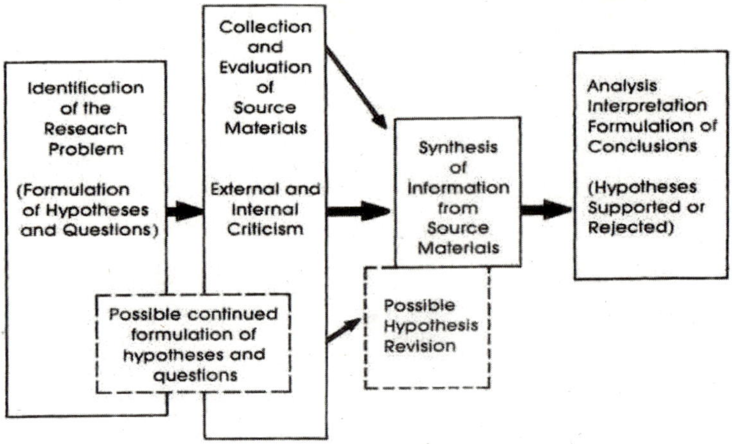

Figure 36.1 : Steps of Investigation in Historical Research Method (Wievsma, 1986)

36.7 COLLECTION OF SOURCE MATERIALS

The collection of source materials does not consist of simply assembling all available documents that appear to have some relevance to the research problem. A basic rule of historical research is to use primary sources whenever it is possible to locate them. The researcher must decide which are primary and which secondary sources are. This requires an analysis of the sources.

36.8 EVALUATION OF SOURCE MATERIALS

36.8.1 External Criticism

Source materials must be subjected to external criticism. It is the tool for establishing the validity of the document. The question to be answered is, "Is the document genuine, authentic, and what it seems to be?" External criticism in historical research evaluates the validity of the document—that is, where, when, and by whom it was produced.

Establishing the validity of materials involves several possible factors, any of which could make the document invalid. With written material, the status of the author in the context of the event is important. Was the author in a position to make a valid record of the event? Was the author an on-the-spot observer, if the document appears to be a primary source? Are factors such as time and place consistent with what is known about the event?

Since the practice of using ghost writers is common, a document that appears to be the product of a direct observer may in fact be a secondary source. The ghost writer's unique contributions may inadvertently or deliberately threaten the validity of the document, and there are also possibilities of inadvertent mechanical errors.

A word may be mistranslated or an error made in typing or transcribing documents. For source materials produced before the advent of printing, copy errors in reproduced documents are not unusual. Printing has not eliminated the possibility of such errors, but it has reduced their likelihood.

According to a common practice when code is used, words are often composed or slightly different words are used in order to protect the security of the code. The scholar should be careful and must avoid pitfalls occurring during decoding of the words.

Forged or copied documents are easily available in the market. Critics observed that the text of the document contained a number of 'aberrations'. The scholars should not be tempted to use them without verifying their originality or authenticity.

While evaluating originality or authenticity of the source materials, the scholar must have scientific bent of mind and should not endorse its originality without reliable and valid evidence. For instance, when Alexander the great was listening to an account of how he slew his opponent's elephant with a single blow of his spear, the young conqueror's sense of historical accuracy could not condone such exaggerated hero worship, and he snatched the book and threw it into the water with the comment that the author of such untruth also should be ducked.

36.8.2 Internal Criticism

The second part of critical evaluation is internal criticism, which establishes the meaning of the material along with its trustworthiness. In other words, it weighs the testimony of the document in relation to the truth. There may be some overlap between external and internal criticism, but the shift in emphasis is from the actual material as a source to the content of the material. To some extent, external criticism precedes internal criticism in the sequence, since there is little point in dealing with the content of the material if its authenticity is doubtful. However, consider the external criticism directed toward the author of what appears to be a historical document. In establishing the author's status, it may very well be necessary to evaluate some of the content. This essentially becomes internal criticism. Internal criticism in historical research evaluates the meaning, accuracy, and trustworthiness of the content of the document.

The basic principles of internal criticism (Woody, 1953, p. 19) are:

1. Do not read into earlier documents the conceptions of later times,
2. Do not judge an author ignorant of certain events,
3. Underestimating a source is no less an error than overestimating it in the same degree,
4. Direct, competent, independent witnesses should be accepted for the point of their agreement, and
5. Official testimony, oral or written, must be compared with unofficial testimony whenever possible.

Internal criticism is concerned with questions of the real meaning as distinguished from the literal meaning, the competence of the observer for careful and accurate reporting, and good faith of the observer in making statements without bias or prejudice. (Good, 1959).

The competency and accuracy or the truthfulness and honesty of the observer is a negative aspect of internal criticism, in that every possible reason for disbelieving is sought and every statement is questioned as long as any doubt remains.

The test of truthfulness and honest include evaluation of the observer's characteristics and statements in relation to personal or vested interest race, nation, party, region, sect, social level, economic group, profession, conventional formulas rather than true sentiments, vanity or boosting, attempt to please some individual or group, exaggerations, and embellishments.

The author is an important factor in evaluating the content of a document as well as in establishing the authenticity of the document. A pertinent question of internal criticism is whether the author was predisposed, because of position or otherwise, to present a biased rather than an objective account. Biographies and autobiographies may tend to shift the emphasis from the event to the person. Fictitious details may be included by the author because of some personal factor. An author who was opposed to an existing educational policy might have emphasized different factors than one who was favourable toward the same policy at the same time. For these kinds of situations, the position or status of the author is very important in ascribing meaning to the content.

An analysis of the author's style and use of rhetoric is important for internal criticism. Does the author have a tendency to color the writings by eloquent but misleading phrases? Is part of the writing figurative rather than a record of the real event? If the question of figurative and real meaning arises, the researcher must be able to distinguish between the two. Does the author borrow heavily from documents already in existence at the time of his/her writing? If so, is the document an objective restatement of the facts, or do the author's own interpretations come into the writings? The latter is more likely the case. The researcher should check the reporting of the author for consistency with the earlier sources. This process should also give indications of the separation of fact and interpretation.

The concern for accuracy is basic to all internal criticism (as well as external criticism). There are two parts of the question of the accuracy of a specific author: Was the author competent to give an accurate report and, if competent, predisposed to do so? A competent reporter may, for some reason, give a distorted account of an event. In checking several authors, there may be inconsistencies even about such facts as the date of a specific event. In such a case, the researcher must weigh the evidence and decide which account is more accurate.

A single document, even a primary source, can seldom stand on its own. Internal criticism involves considerable cross-referencing of several documents. If certain facts are omitted from an account, this should not be interpreted to mean that the author was unaware of them or that they did not occur. Each document should be evaluated in its chronological position—that is, in the light of the documents that preceded it, not in the light of documents that appeared later. If several sources contain the same errors, they are likely to have originated from a common erroneous source. If two sources are contradictory, it is certain that at least one is in error, but it is also possible that both are in error. The discounting of one account does not establish the trustworthiness of another. A specific document

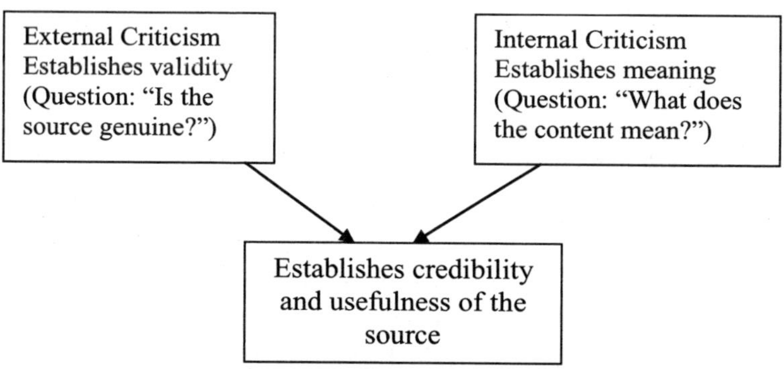

Figure 36.2 : External and Internal; Criticism in the Evaluation of Source Materials for Historical Research

may prove valuable for certain parts of the overall research problem and essentially useless for other parts.

Both external and internal criticisms are necessary for establishing the credibility and usefulness of the source. If the source is not authentic, it cannot be used. Even if it is authentic, if its content is not relevant to the research problem, it would be useless. The functions of external and internal criticism are summarized in Figure 36.2.

36.9 SYNTHESIS OF INFORMATION

Synthesis refers to selecting, organizing, and analyzing the materials collected into topical themes and central ideas or concepts. These themes are then pulled together to form a contiguous and meaningful whole. The materials have now been reviewed and their authenticity established, at least to the satisfaction of the researcher. The relative value of the various sources must be considered. For example, a primary source may be considered more important than a secondary one. If contradictory accounts appear, the inconsistencies must be resolved, which may require developing a case for discounting one version of the event.

Central ideas or concepts must be pulled together and continuity between them developed. If a substantial period of time—say, several years—is covered by the research study, the ideas can often be organized chronologically. In fact, chronological ordering is often required to avoid confusion between possible cause and effect among events. Several accounts of the same event may be included in the source materials. If the accounts are consistent, they provide historical support, and the researcher can summarize the information from these accounts with respect to the point being made.

As the researcher reviews the source materials and synthesizes the information from them, it may be necessary to formulate additional hypotheses or revise initial ones. Evidence may appear that refutes initial hypotheses; unanticipated information may support new hypotheses; and the materials may also generate new questions relevant to the research problem. If hypotheses and questions are not included but the research proceeds from a statement of purpose, it may be advantageous to introduce hypotheses when synthesizing the information. In any event, hypotheses should be introduced when they prove useful, especially as they provide direction for the research and assist in synthesizing information. Once the hypothesis has been established satisfactorily against the evidence, it may become a central thesis, unifying theme, or principle of interpretation.

It is essential to give appropriate emphasis to all causal factors or forces in a synthetic or eclectic treatment of data, rather than to follow narrowly a single school of interpretation that might exclude some part of the evidence.

Sound historical perspective in using evidence enables us to evaluate events and personages, distant in time or space, in term of the contemporaneous standards and conditions then prevailing rather than comparison with our present day time and culture.

Effective historical writing demands evidence of scholarship, mastery of materials and style of writing (literary excellence). This is a matter of expositional strategy which calls for creativity in addition to the qualities of imagination and ingenuity. The scholar must be elegant and objective in his style of writing the research report.

The final step of historical research methodology is characterized by decision-making about the research problem. Historical research relies heavily on a logical analysis of the information from the documents. This may include statistical information from the period under study. Such information occasionally is generated by random samples of documents from the period. As an example, in a study reported by Ringer (1978), a random sample of entries was selected from major biographical encyclopedias for Germany, France, England, and the United States. The entries were those for males born between 1810 and 1899 who might have reached advanced educational institutions between 1830 and 1930. All possible entries could not have been checked because of time limitations, so a random sample was used.

At the final step, the conclusions are formulated, and any hypotheses introduced earlier are either supported or rejected. Of course, it is necessary to make interpretations of the information, and the researcher should recognize the possibility of alternative explanations of the results if such explanations are reasonable. A case should be made for the most likely interpretation, but if other possible interpretations exist, they should at least be recognized. For all interpretations, the author should remain as objective as possible.

Four problems that might arise when a researcher attempts to synthesize the material collected and prepares a narrative account:

- Trying to infer causation from correlated events. Just because two events occurred together does not necessarily mean that one event was the cause of the other.
- Defining and interpreting key words so as to avoid ambiguity and to ensure that they have the correct connotation.

- Differentiating between evidence indicating how people should behave and how they in fact did behave.
- Maintaining a distinction between intent and consequences. In other words, educational historians must make sure that the consequences that were observed from some activity or policy were the intended consequences (Johnson & Christensen, 2005).

36.10 REPORTING OF HISTORICAL RESEARCH

In contrast to the reports of experimental or survey studies, which typically include generally accepted headings, reports of historical research often take the form of an unbroken narrative. For reporting historical research, it is often easier to enhance the continuity of ideas by not dividing the report. The research problem is usually identified early in the report, with a supporting context. Hypotheses or questions may be included, or a proposition (which is basically a hypothesis) may be presented that will be supported or refuted. Then the evidence is provided, synthesizing information from several sources. Finally, conclusions are presented, based on the evidence.

The past in the solution of present-day problems justifies the worthwhileness of historical research. The educational historian is not so much interested in the purely unique aspects of past experiences as in the elements which may serve as a basis for tentative generalization in analyzing current issues and problems.

36.11 COMMON ERRORS IN HISTORICAL RESEARCH

1. A research area is selected in which sufficient evidence is not available to conduct a worthwhile study or test the hypotheses adequately.
2. Excessive use of secondary sources of information is frequently found in studies not dealing with recent events.
3. Attempts to work on a broad and poorly defined problem.
4. Fails to evaluate adequately his historical data.
5. Allows personal bias to influence his research procedures.
6. The student's report recites facts but does not synthesize or integrate these facts into meaningful generalizations.

36.12 MERITS

(1) A knowledge of history of schools and other educational agencies is an important part of the professional training of social scientists/teachers or the school administrators;

(2) Much of the work of the school is traditional. The nature of work of the teacher and the school administrator is restrictive and tends to foster prejudices in favour of familiar methods. The history of education is the 'sovereign solvent' of educational prejudices;

(3) The history of education enables the educational worker to detect fads and frills whatever form they may appear and it serves as a necessary preliminary to educational reform;

(4) Only in the light of their origin and growth can the numerous educational problems of the present be viewed systematically and scientifically;

(5) The history of education how the socio-economic-cultural and political institutions influenced our educational system; and

(6) It 'inspires' respect for sound scholarship and reverence for great philosophers and teachers.

36.13 LIMITATIONS

(1) Oversimplification, i.e. failure to recognize that causes of events are more often multiple and complex, rather than single or simple;

(2) Overgeneralization on the basis of inadequate evidence and false reasoning by analogy, basing conclusions on superficial similarities;

(3) Failure to interpret words and expressions in light of their usage in earlier times;

(4) Failure to distinguish between significant and trivial facts in a situation; and

(5) Scholar own ideology sometimes contaminates the real interpretation of historical facts

REFERENCES

Borrowman, Merle L. (1960). History of Education. In Chester W. Harris (ed.), 3rd Edition. *Encyclopedia of Educational Research.* New York: Macmillan Co. pp. 661-66.

Festinger, L. and Katz, D. (1976) (eds.). *Research Methods in the Behavioural Sciences.* New Delhi: Amerind Publishing Co.

Good, Carter V. (1966). *Essentials of Educational Research: Methodology and Design.* New York: Applleton-Century Crofts.

Goode, W.J., and Hatt, P.K. (1990). *Methods in Social Research.* New Delhi: McGraw-Hill.

Howell, M. and Prevenier, W. (2001). *From Reliable Sources: An Introduction to Historical Methods.* Ithaca: Cornell University Press.

Kerlinger, F. (1986). *Foundations of Behavioural Research.* 5th edition, Orlando: Harcourt Brace.

Koul, L. (2009). *Methodology of Educational Research.* Vikas Publishing House, New Delhi.

McCullagh, C.B. (1984). *Justifying Historical Description*, New York (1984): Cambridge University Press.

Punch, K.F. (2009). *Introduction to Research Methods in Education*. New Delhi: Sage.

Shafer, R.J. (1974). *A Guide to Historical Method.* Illinois: The Dorsey Press.

Somekh, B., and Lewin, C. (2005). *Research Methods in the Social Sciences.* New Delhi. Vstaar Publications.

Sukhia, S.P., Mehrotra, P.V. and Mehrotra, R.N. (1974). *Elements of Educational Research.* New Delhi: Allied Publishers.

William Wiersma (1986). *Research Methods in Education: An Introduction*. Allyn and Bacon, Inc., London.

CHAPTER

37

Laboratory Experiments

37.0 LABORATORY EXPERIMENTS

A laboratory is any environment where variables can be well controlled. Laboratory experiments allow for precise control of variables in artificial environment. The purpose of control is to enable the experimenter to isolate the one key variable which has been selected (the independent variable), in order to observe its effect on some other variable (the dependent variable); control is intended to allow us to conclude that it is the independent variable, and nothing else, which is influencing the dependent variable. Lab experiments involve the deliberate manipulation of one variable, while trying to keep all other variables constant. Sometimes the independent variable is thought of as the cause and the dependent variable as the effect. Furthermore, experiments can usually be easily replicated. The experimental method consists of standardised procedures and measures which allow it to be easily repeated.

There are a number of means by which the researcher holds all of the variables constant other than the independent and dependent variables. These include: randomly assigning participants to the different conditions (which ensures equality in the long-run), carrying out the study in the controlled setting of a laboratory where hopefully other factors are constant, and making the conditions as similar as possible for all participants except as far as they are in the experimental or control condition.

37.1 PURPOSES OF LABORATORY EXPERIMENTS

- To test hypothesis derived from theory.
- To study the precise interrelations of variables and their operation.
- To makes prediction on the basis of the function i.e. the test of predictions derived from theory. Primary and other research series of tests are conducted to confirm the findings.
- To refine theories and hypotheses, to formulate hypothesis related to other experimentally or non-experimentally tested hypothesis to help build theoretical systems. Most of the lab-experiments are strongly theory-oriented.

37.2 PRINCIPLES OF LABORATORY EXPERIMENT DESIGN (FISHER, 1935)

37.2.1 Comparison

In many fields of study it is hard to reproduce measured results exactly. Comparisons between treatments are much more reproducible and are usually preferable. Often one compares against a standard, scientific control, or traditional treatment that acts as baseline.

37.2.2 Randomization

Random assignment is the process of assigning individuals at random to groups or to different groups in an experiment. The random assignment of individuals to groups (or conditions within a group) is a distinguished feature of lab experiment.

37.2.3 Replication

Measurements are usually subject to variation and uncertainty. Measurements are repeated and full experiments are replicated to help identify the sources of variation, to better estimate the true effects of treatments, to further strengthen the experiment's reliability and validity, and to add to the existing knowledge of about the topic.

37.2.4 Blocking

Blocking is the arrangement of experimental units into groups (blocks) consisting of units that are similar to one another. Blocking reduces known but irrelevant sources of variation between units and thus allows greater precision in the estimation of the source of variation under study.

37.3 FACTORIAL EXPERIMENTS

There is use of factorial experiments instead of the one-factor-at-a-time method. These are efficient at evaluating the effects and possible interactions of several factors (independent variables).

In the process of experimentation, the participants are normally split into two groups namely, control group and experimental group.

37.3.1 Control Group

The control group carries out a task in the controlled environment. Control group is often used in lab experiment. This is a group which does not receive the manipulation of the independent variable and can be used for comparison with the experimental group.

37.3.2 Experimental Group

The experimental group carries out the same task but one crucial variable has been changed—this is the independent variable. The researcher measures the outcome and because of the strict controls any difference between the control group and the experimental group *must* be down to the Independent Variable.

37.4 STEPS OF LABORATORY EXPERIMENT

1. Survey the literature relating to the problem.
2. Identify and define the problem.
3. Formulate a problem hypothesis, deducing the consequences, and defining basic terms and variables.
4. Construct an experimental plan:
   (a) Identify all non-experimental variables that might contaminate the experiment, and determine how to control them.
   (b) Select a research design.
   (c) Select a sample of subjects to represent a given population, assign subjects to groups, and assign experimental treatments to groups.
   (d) Select or construct and validate instruments to measure the outcome of the experiment.
   (e) Outline procedures for collecting the data, and possibly conduct a pilot or "trial run" test to perfect the instruments or design.
   (f) State the statistical or null hypothesis.
5. Conduct the experiments.
6. Reduce the raw data in a manner that will produce the best appraisal of the effect which is presumed to exist.
7. Apply an appropriate test of a significance to determine the confidence one can place on the results of the study.

37.5 MERITS OF LABORATORY EXPERIMENTS

- The laboratory experiment has a key role in psychological

research in that it allows the investigation of causal relationships between variables. In other words, it identifies whether one variable affects another in a cause and effect sequence.

- The classic "do basic research in the laboratory and then apply it" model of applying research to practice is context sensitive, while almost all educational interventions are context sensitive. This being the case, more research in practice is essential to understand which contextual factors are critical and which are not. (Burkhardt and Schoenfeld, 2003).
- Measurements are repeated and full experiments are replicated to help identify the sources of variation, to better estimate the true effects of treatments, to further strengthen the experiment's reliability and validity, and to add to the existing knowledge of about the topic.
- By changing one variable (the independent variable) while measuring another (the dependent variable) while we control all others, as far as possible, then the experimental method allows us to draw conclusions with far more certainty than any non-experimental method. If the independent variable is the only thing that is changed then it must be responsible for any change in the dependent variable.
- Lab-experiment can make prediction on the basis of the function as :

  $Y = f(x)$ tells us how good our prediction of the dependent variable is, with this set of independent variables.

  (a) It is important to know how good our prediction is, by knowing how much of the variance we can account for.

  (b) We also need to know how important each independent variable is in accounting for this variance.

37.6 LIMITATIONS

- However, laboratory experiments are not always typical of real life situations. These types of experiments are often conducted in strange and contrived environments in which people are asked to perform unusual or even bizarre tasks. The artificiality of the situation, together with the 'unnatural' things that the participants may be asked to do, jointly produces a distortion of behaviour. Therefore, it should be difficult to generalise findings from experiments because they are not always ecologically valid (true to real life).

- A further difficulty with the experimental method is demand characteristics. Demand characteristics are all the cues/hints which allow the participant guess the purpose of the experiment. If a participant knows they are in an experiment they may behave how they think they are expected to behave.
- Sometimes we may have a problem around ethics. For example, there are many areas of human life which cannot be studied using the experimental method because it would be simply unethical to do so.
- Furthermore, the number of variables that can be manipulated in a single experiment is limited which can be frustrating when one is studying a complex psychological process.
- Lack of perfect control even under laboratory condition, low effect size, lack of high degree of precision in procedure and instrument, difficulty in operationally defining the variable in case of 'construct' are some of other limitations of lab-experiments.
- Although lab-experiments have relative high internal validity, then they lack external validity.

References

Ackoff, R.L. (1962). *Scientific Method.* New York: John Wiley & Sons.

Best, J.W. and Kahn, J.V. (2008). *Research in Edcation.* Pearson, Prentice Hall, Inc. and Dorling Kindersley Publishing, Inc. (India).

Brodbeck, M. (1963). Logic and scientific method in research on teaching. In N.L. Gage (ed.), *Handbook of Research on Teaching* (pp. 44-93), Chicago: Rand McNally.

Burkhardt, H., and Schoenfeld, A.H. (2003). Improving Educational Research: Toward a More Useful, More Influential, and Better-Funded Enterprise. Educational Researcher, Vol. 32, No. 9, pp. 3-14.

Englehart, Max D. (1972). *Methods of Educational Research.* Chicago: Rand McNally.

Festinger, L. and Katz, D. (1976) (eds.), *Research Methods in the Behavioural Sciences.* New Delhi: Amerind Publishing Co.

Freedman, P. (1960). *The Principles of Scientific Research.* 2nd ed., New York: Pergamon Press.

Plutchik, R. (1968). *Foundations of Experimental Research.* New York: Harper and Row.

CHAPTER

38

The Report Writing and Presentation

Preparation and presentation of a research report is the most important part of research process. No matter how brilliant the hypotheses are formulated and how well research study is designed, they are of little value unless communicated effectively to others in the form of research report. Moreover, if the report is confusing or poorly written, the time spent on gathering and analyzing of data would be wasted. It is, therefore, essential to design, write and communicate the results in a logical way in a research report.

38.0 FORMAT OF RESEARCH REPORT

The format of a research report comprises three main sections: (1) the preliminary section, (2) the body of the report or text, and (3) the reference section. Each main section contains several sub-sections.

38.1 PRELIMINARY SECTION

1. Title page
2. Acknowledgement
3. Abstract
4. Table of contents
5. List of tables
6. List of figures, maps, or illustrations (if any).

38.2 BODY OF THE REPORT OR TEXT

Introduction

1. Need and importance of study
2. Review of literature specific to the problem
3. Statement of the problem
4. Operational definition of important terms
5. Statement of specific research objectives
6. Assumptions underlying research questions or hypotheses
7. Statement of research questions or hypotheses
8. Significance of the problem
9. Delimitations of the study

38.3 DESIGN OF THE STUDY OR METHODOLOGY

1. Method
2. Sampling techniques, sampling frame, and sample size
3. Sources of data
4. Data gathering instruments

38.4 ANALYSIS AND INTERPRETATION OF THE DATA

1. Text
2. Tables are usually included into the text
3. Figures are usually included into the text

38.5 SUMMARY AND CONCLUSIONS

1. Principal findings and conclusions
2. Implications of the study
3. Suggestions for further research
4. Brief statement of problem and procedures

38.6 REFERENCE SECTION

1. Bibliography
2. Appendix
3. Index (if any).

38.7 COVER PAGE OR TITLE PAGE

The title page contains the following information:

1. The title of the research
2. Department/faculty to which dissertation is submitted
3. Degree for which it is submitted
4. Name of the researcher
5. Name of the supervisor
6. University/organizational emblem

7. Name of the university/organization and its address
8. Month and year of submission

A SAMPLE COVER PAGE IS SHOWN IN EXHIBIT

A CRITICAL STUDY OF THE PERFORMANCE LEVEL IN MATHEMATICS OF 8TH CLASS STUDENTS IN JAMMU BLOCK

University Seal

A DISSERTATION SUBMITTED TO THE UNIVERSITY OF JAMMU IN PARTIAL FULFILLMENTOF THE REQUIREMENTS FOR THE AWARD OF THE DEGREE OF MASTER OF EDUCATION

SUPERVISOR

Dr. D. R. Kapoor
Associate Professor
University Roll No. 206

By

Ms. Manisha
University Roll No.206

POST – GRADUATE DEPARTMENT OF EDUCATION
MIER COLLEGE OF EDUCATION
B.C.ROAD, JAMMU-180001
AUGUST 2010

38.8 ACKNOWLEDGEMENTS

In the process of carrying out any research, the researcher would have received help from different persons and organizations. So, all those helps should be acknowledged under this heading. In an academic research, a sample list of people who are to be acknowledged is as follow:

- Research supervisor
- Organizational head
- Colleagues of the department who rendered their valuable suggestions and criticism during the research period
- Heads of different organizations who provided data and literature for the research
- The programmer, librarians, and computer personnel.

38.9 ABSTRACT

Abstract gives the overview of the research report outlining:

- the title of the research,
- research methodology—method, sample, tools,
- main findings of the study and its implications.

Abstract is usually a one page summary of the objectives of the research; the methodology used and the main findings of the work.

38.10 TABLE OF CONTENTS

Table of contents is the catalogue of the research report which summarizes every aspect of the report. Table of contents of a survey based research is shown in Exhibit.

38.11 LIST OF TABLES

In research reports, the data and results are presented in the form of tables for quick grasp. Each and every table must be numbered. The numbering should be such that it is internal to each chapter. For example, if the total number of tables in Chapter 7 is 6, then the numbering should be from Table 7.1 to Table 7.6.

38.12 LIST OF FIGURES

In research reports, the results are presented in the form of figures for better understanding and comparison. Each and every figure must be numbered. The number should be internal to each chapter. For example, if the total number of figures in chapter 7 is 4, then he numbering should be from Figure 7.1 to Figure 7.4. The geographic locations and conceptual foundations of the research are also presented in the form of figures.

Exhibit 1—Table of Contents

Exhibit 2—List of Tables

Exhibit 3—List of Figures

38.13 TEXT

As mentioned in Exhibit-1 , the different items under 'Text' are Chapters, Main Sections, Sub-sections, and Conclusion.

38.14 CHAPTERS

The text of the report should be divided into different chapters depending on the type of research. In the case of survey-based research, the different chapters are as listed below:

1. Introduction
2. Literature Review
3. Objectives and Hypotheses
4. Research Methodology
5. Data Analysis
6. Conclusion

38.15 INTRODUCTION

It is the place where you should–

- The chapter on introduction should begin with the background of the research and state of the present scenario in brief.
- The origin and the development of the research concept along with the most significant contributions in the past must be summarized in this chapter.
- Discuss the motivation for the work that is being reported.
- When writing the motivation for the research work that has been carried out, do not go into the details.
- Give a brief overview of the problem that you are tackling, and be specific about what the work is trying to achieve, and what you will be doing to meet these objectives.
- State and define the problem that the research is trying to address or solve.

38.16 LITERATURE REVIEW

Literature review is the crucial part of any research. This chapter focuses on the past literature in the field of research and its classification under different angles. The critique comparison of the past literature will narrow down the research topic and provide a base for further direction. The following tips should be considered:

38.16.1 Include only those Works that is Relevant to Your Research

You may have read dozens upon dozens of papers, but there will be some that do not contribute to the points that your are trying to make, or there will be papers that give identical information. Because of the time you spent trying to understand them, you may be tempted incorporate all that you have read. Attempting to do this will make what is already a difficult task impossible.

38.16.2 Make sure that you have read and understood cited work, otherwise you can get into hot water. Assessors like to ask questions like: "*So tell me what you understand about the proposal by Smith and Wesson, 1945*".

38.16.3 Organise your content according to ideas instead of individual publications. This helps ensure the smooth flow of contents and make the chapter more readable. It also shows that you have an appreciation of the subject area.

38.17 OBJECTIVES AND HYPOTHESES

Based on the direction of the literature review, the researcher should clearly spell out the objectives of the study and related hypotheses/research questions. The researcher should list a meaningful number of hypotheses which will be tested under chapter 'Data Analysis'.

38.18 RESEARCH METHODOLOGY

Research methodology aims to finalize the activities of research design and data collection procedures which are as listed below:

- Selection of research approach
- Design of sampling plan
- Sample size
- Sampling frame
- Determination of sample size
- Instruments of data collection
- Execution of survey

38.19 DATA ANALYSIS

The data analysis can be classified into preliminary analysis and hypotheses testing. This chapter deals with the application of statistical tools for the analysis of data and making inferences.

38.19.1 Types of Figures

In preliminary analysis, the data are presented in the form of figures to have insight into the research problem. Generally used figures in the report are line graphs, bar graphs, pie charts, organization charts, diagrams of apparatus and photographs. The researcher should ensure that:

- Figures, graphs, charts and diagrams should be presented in clearly, distinctly and meaningfully way.

- Lines or bars are to depict in different colours or by using different types of lines namely, solid, dotted, or alternate dots, and dashes.
- Figure should fit into the given margins from all sides.
- The co-ordinate axes should be made heavy enough to distinguish them from the other lines.
- Class interval on co-ordinate axles should be equidistance
- Use appropriate type of figure to convey the meaning.

Inferences can be drawn from the charts and graphs.

38.19.2 Content and Placement of Tables

The essential characteristics of a good table are simplicity and unity. There is no use in including too much data in a single table.

- It is advisable to concentrate on a limited number of ideas in a single table and to use several tables for making several comparisons of distinctly different kinds of data. A well constructed table integrates and presents several related facts in one main idea.
- Table should always be introduced by a suitable heading. Sub-headings should be clearly mentioned and indented.
- A single table should not be broken and displayed on another page.
- Significance of difference should be indicated by using single star (*) for 0.05 level, and two stars (**) for 0.01 level of statistical difference.

The second type of analysis is concerned with the testing of hypotheses. Inferences can be drawn and interpretation can be made. This chapter will have a major sub-section on results and discussions.

38.20 CONCLUSIONS AND RECOMMENDATIONS

Each section of the report should lead to number of conclusions. At the end of the section these are spelt out and the reasoning behind them explained. If there is a separate 'conclusions' section, these conclusions are pulled out and repeated as an ordered sequence, with reference back to the body of the report as necessary.

Not all reports present recommendations, some are merely required to present a set of information based on research. Where there are recommendations, these may be presented as a part of the report's conclusions, or in a separate section which may place towards the end of the report, after the conclusions, or immediately after the executive summary. Indeed, some writers prefer to make their recommendations part of the executive summary, since there are an important part of what the busy reader wants to know first.

38.21 APPENDICES

The value of placing certain lengthy detailed information in a series of appendices (sometimes called annexures) has already been mentioned. The type of information that may go in appendices includes:

- A detailed description of the research methods, including the questionnaire(s) (Manual providing details about administration, scoring sheet, scoring key, and interpretation of the results) used and how the sample was selected
- The research brief and members of the team producing the report
- Detailed research data
- Case studies
- Institutional Data in brief
- Description of different models/approaches/techniques
- It also contains those parts of dissertation that are either well known or does not contribute directly to the main text, but needs to be included for completeness.

38.22 BIBLIOGRAPHY

Bibliography is an alphabetical catalogue of different literatures which are used in the research. The references can be classified into books, journals, magazines, newspapers, research studies, and information retrieved from Internet, etc., these citation styles are illustrated below:

38.22.1 Citations Styles (American Psychological Corporation)

Book by one author

- Sheril, R. D. (1956). *The terrifying future: Contemplating color television*. San Diego, CA: Halstead.

Book by two authors

- Kurosawa, J. and Armistead, Q. (1972). *Hairball: An intensive peek behind the surface of an enigma*. Hamilton, Ontario, Canada: McMaster University Press.

Chapter in an edited book

- Mcdonalds, A. (1993). Practical methods for the apprehension and sustained containment of supernatural entities. In G.L. Yeager (Ed.), *Paranormal and occult studies: Case studies in application* (pp. 42–64). London, England: Other World Books.

Dissertation (Ph.D. or masters)

- Mcdonalds, A. (1991). *Practical dissertation title* (Unpublished doctoral dissertation). University of Florida, Gainesville, FL.

Article in a journal with continuous pagination (nearly all journals use continuous pagination)

- Rottweiler, F.T., & Beauchemin, J.L. (1987). Detroit and Narnia: Two foes on the brink of destruction. *Canadian/American Studies Journal, 54,* 66–146.
- Kling, K.C., Hyde, J.S., Showers, C.J. and Buswell, B.N. (1999). Gender differences in self-esteem: A meta-analysis. *Psychological Bulletin, 125,* 470-500. doi:10.1037/0033-2909.125.4.470.

Article in a journal paginated separately Journal Pagination

- Crackton, P. (1987). The Loonie: God's long-awaited gift to colourful pocket change? *Canadian Change, 64*(7), 34–38.

Article in a weekly magazine

- Henry, W.A., III (1990, April 9). Making the grade in today's schools. *Time, 135,* 28–31.

Article in a weekly magazine with DOI

- Hoff, K. (2010, March 19). Fairness in modern society. *Science, 327,* 1467–1468. doi:10.1126/science.1188537.

Article in a print newspaper

- Wrong, M. (2005, August 17). "Never gonna give you up," says mayor. *Toronto Sol,* p. 4.

Electronic sources

Online article based on a print source, with DOI (e.g., a PDF of a print source from a database)

- Krueger, R.F., Markon, K.E., Patrick, C.J., & Iacono, W.G. (2005). Externalizing psychopathology in adulthood: A dimensional-spectrum conceptualization and its implications for DSM-V. *Journal of Abnormal Psychology, 114,* 537-550. doi:10.1037/0021-843X.114.4.537

Online article based on a print source, without DOI (e.g., a PDF of a print source from a database)

- Marlowe, P., Spade, S. and Chan, C. (2001). Detective work and the benefits of colour versus black and white. *Journal of Pointless Research, 11,* 123–127.

Online article from a database, no DOI, available ONLY in that database (proprietary content—not things like Ovid, EBSCO, and PsycINFO)

- Liquor advertising on TV. (2002, January 18). Retrieved from http://factsonfile.infobasepublishing.com/

OR

- Liquor advertising on TV. (2002, January 18). Retrieved from *Issues and Controversies* database.

Article in an Internet-only journal

- McDonald, C., & Chenoweth, L. (2009). Leadership: A crucial ingredient in unstable times. *Social Work & Society, 7.* Retrieved from http://www.socwork.net/2009/1/articles/mcdonaldchenoweth

Article in an Internet-only newsletter (eight or more authors)

- Paradise, S., Moriarty, D., Marx, C., Lee, O.B., Hassel, E., Thyme, E.J., . . . Bradford, J. (1957, July). Portrayals of fictional characters in reality-based popular writing: Project update. *Off the Beaten Path, 7.* Retrieved from http://www.newsletter.offthebeatenpath.news/otr/complaints.html

Article with no author identified (the title moves to the "author" position)

- Britain launches new space agency. (2010, March 24). Retrieved from http://news.ninemsn.com.au/technology/1031221/britain-launches-new-space-agency

Article with no author and no date identified (e.g., wiki article)

- Harry Potter. (n.d.). In *Wikipedia*. Retrieved August 28, 2010, from http://en.wikipedia.org/w index.php?title=Harry_Potter&oldid=380786432

Entry in an online dictionary or reference work, no date and no author identified

- Verisimilitude. (n.d.). In *Merriam-Webster's online dictionary* (11th ed.). Retrieved from http://www.merriam-webster.com/dictionary/verisimilitude

E-mail or other personal communication (cite in text only)

- (A. Monterey, personal communication, September 28, 2001)

Book on CD

- Nix, G. (2002). *Lirael, Daughter of the Clayr* [CD]. New York, NY: Random House/Listening Library.

Book on tape

- Nix, G. (2002). *Lirael, Daughter of the Clayr* [Cassette Recording No. 1999-1999-1999]. New York, NY: Random

House/Listening Library.

Movie

- Gilby, A. (Producer), & Schlesinger, J. (Director). (1995). *Cold comfort farm* [Motion picture]. Universal City, CA: MCA Universal.

38.23 STYLE AND FORMAT OF RESEARCH REPORT

Language style is an unpretentious medium designed to convey content as quickly and clearly as possible. It should mean that what a scholar writes can be understood at first reading by a reasonably literate and well-intentioned person. Oxford Language Reference (Law, 2007) has given some guideline for effective style as mentioned below.

38.23.1 Control Sentence Length

There are five main ways of dealing with overlong sentences namely:

- Split and disconnect
- Split and connect
- Use a list
- Cut verbiage
- Dicard the sentence and start again

38.23.2 Use words your readers will understand

There are two ways of removing jargon:

- Use simpler alternatives
- Where necessary, reconstruct your sentences

38.23.3 Use only as many words as you really need

There are three main techniques to follow:

- Striking out useless words
- Pruning the dead wood and grafting on the vigorous
- Rewriting completely

38.23.4 Use strong lively verbs

Good verbs give your writing its power and passion and delicacy. It is simple truth that in most sentences you should express action through verbs. Three types of construction are considered:

- Nominalization linked to parts of *to be or to have*
- Nominalization linked to active verbs or infinitives
- Nominalization linked to passive verbs. For example,

An examination of the school records was carried out by Dr. Raina.

This becomes, by the same technique:
Dr. Raina examined the school records.

38.23.5 Use vertical lists

Vertical lists have become a common feature of many documents in this process, complicated text is broken up in manageable chunks. For example, instead of writing this:

Abstract gives the overview of the research report outlining the title of the research, research methodology, i.e. method, sample and tools and main findings of the study and its implications.

We could write this:

Abstract gives the overview of the research report outlining:

- the title of the research,
- research methodology—method, sample, tools,
- main findings of the study and its implications.

38.23.6 Put your points positively when you can.

When two, three or more negatives are gathered together in the same sentence, meaning may become obscure. Therefore, sentence containing more negatives should be replaced or to be reconstructed to make it more understandable and meaningful.

38.23.7 Avoid personal pronouns

I, we, you, my, our and us should not be used. For example, instead of saying "I administered achievement test in general science to both the groups of students" it should be "achievement test in general science was administered on both the groups of students".

38.23.8 Abbreviations

The use of abbreviations, except some acceptable ones such as I.Q., M.A., etc. should be avoided in the main text of the research report. In the footnotes, the table and the bibliography, some standard abbreviations are used to conserve space. Some standard abbreviations are given below:

Abbreviation	*Full form*	*Abbreviation*	*Full form*
bk., bks	book, books	chap., chaps	chapter, chapters
p., pp.	page, pages	anon	anonymous
cf.	compare	co., cols.	column, columns
e.g.	for example	edn., edns.	eddition editions
ed., eds.	editor, editors	et al.	and others
Ibid.	same reference	op. cit.	previously cited
Loc. cit.	the place cited	fig., figs.	figure, figures
Idem	same person	Illus.	illustration

l., li.	line, lines	f., ff.	the following page, the following pages
			note, notes
Mimeo	mimeograph	n., nn.	please note
MS., MSS.	manuscript, manuscripts		N.B.
n.d.	no date	N.S.	new series/new style
n.n.	no name	no., nos	number, numbers
n.p.	no place	pt., pts.	part, pasts
sec., secs.	section, sections	viz,	namely
vol., vols.	volume, volumes	vs.	verssus
Rev.	revised	passim	scattered
Sic.	thus	vide.	see

38.23.9 Quotations and References

Make sure that it is clear when you are quoting directly from another person. Short quotations can go into the body of your text, marked off by quotation marks. Longer quotations should be separated and indented.

38.23.10 Ellipsis

They are used to indicate omissions in quotations. It can occur at the beginning or at the end of a quotation. An ellipsis (...) is indicated by three full stops.

38.23.11 Footnotes

Footnotes are generally found at the foot of a page. The footnotes usually include the source of information-name of the author, the title of the source, exact page(s) of the source of reference, date of publication, and publisher and place of publication.

38.24 TYPING OF THE RESEARCH REPORT

General rules for typing the research report are:

- A white bond paper of 8.5 by 11 inches size of 13 to 16 pound weight should be used.
- Material should be typed on one side of the paper
- left margin: 40 mm, top, bottom and right margin: 25 mm
- text font: 12 point Times-Roman or Times-New-Roman
- line spacing: 1.5 lines
- dividing of words at the end of the line should be avoided as far as possible
- throughout the manuscript an indent of seven spaces should be used at the beginning of paragraph and quotations.

38.25 EDITING OF THE RESEARCH REPORT

The process of editing involves examining and correcting the typed materials of the report for its content, format and language.

- The purpose of editing is to critically and thoroughly examine the precision in the statement of the problem, it as objectives, hypotheses or research questions, methodology, analysis of data and their interpretation, drawing inferences and conclusions.
- There should be logical links between objectives, hypotheses, design of research, interpretations and conclusions. Make sure transitions are succinct, with one section naturally flowing into another.
- In case of any divergence between the established theories or findings, the report must provide substantial evidence to support the thesis.
- Structure of the report, presentation of figures and tables, writing of footnotes and references or bibliography should be thoroughly checked and rechecked to ensure good presentation.
- Ensure the proper use of language in the presentation of report. Guidelines for effective writing style should be followed.
- Correction in ink should not be done. In case of two or more mistakes, new corected typed paper should be inserted in its place.

It is necessary to go for proof reading twice or thrice to ensure error free presentation.

Student should submit a full first draft for comment by supervisor before the final draft is begun.

38.26 CRITICALITY A TOOL OF APPRAISAL/EVALUATION

Criticality is a key factor in assessment or evaluation of research work. Composition, reflection, context, transparency, enquiry, healthy scepticism, positiveness, and evolution in process are the basic elements of criticality. Research scholar should go through critically in order to develop a good thesis.

38.27 PRESENTATION

- Good quality presentation implies clarity, conciseness,

organization, structure, and coherence, cohesion, referencing and formatting.

- Presentation should preferably be through power point.
- Brief introduction which may include-Need and importance of the study, objectives, limitations and delimitations (two slides).
- Substantiate the validity of approaches from a position of detachment (one slide).
- Concise and precise explanation of methodology-research design, sample (size and selection procedures), tools used (reliability and validity), statistical methods used for analysis of data (three slides).
- Present the significant findings of the study. Appraise the research work in the light of current theory and accepted practice (two slides).
- Compare and contrast, support or not a particular argument or line of thinking.
- The researcher has to provide supporting evidence for all his assertions. This usually takes the form of reference to the research literature. One should not make unsubstantiated claims.
- Present briefly the implications of the study (one slide).
- Make things explicit and open to scrutiny.

References

Bazerman, C. (1988). *Shaping Written Knowledge: The Genre and Activity of the Experimental Article in Science.* Madisan: University of Wisconsin University Press.

Berger, A.A. (1993). *Improving Writing Skills: Memos, Letters, Reports and Proposals.* New Delhi: Sage.

Best, J., and Kahn, J. (2009). *Research in Education.* 10th edn. Needham Heights: Allyn and Bacon.

Burton, S., and Steane, P.(2004). *Saving Your Thesis.* London: Sage.

Hart, C. (2005). *Doing your Master Dissertation.* New Delhi: Vistaar Publications.

Koul, L. (2009). *Methodology of Educational Research.* New Delhi: Vikas Publishing House.

Leedy, P., and Ormod, J. (2010). *Practical Research: Planning and Designing.* 9th edn. Needham Heights: Allyn and Bacon.

Madsen, D. (1992). *Successful Dissertation and Thesis.* San Francisco: Jossey-Bass.

Montagnes, I. (1991). *Editing and Publication: Training Manual.* International Rice Research Institute, Manila.

Mounsey, C. (2005). *Essay and Dissertation.* New Delhi: Oxford Press.

Paneerselvam, R. (2004). *Research Methodology*. New Delhi: Prentice Hall of India.

Richardson, L. (1990). *Writing Strategies: Reaching Diverse Audiences.* New Delhi: Sage.

Shah, V.P. (1977). *Reporting Research.* Allahbad: Rachna Prakashan.

Strunk,W., and White, B.B. (2000). *The Elements of Style.* 4th edn. Needham Heights: Allyn and Bacon

Walliman, N. (2005). *Your Undergraduate Dissertation: The Essential Guide for Success*. London: Sage.

UNIT V

DATA ANALYSIS AND INFERENCES

CHAPTER

39

Classification of Data

In broader sense, data can be classified as: (i) qualitative data and (ii) quantitative data.

Qualitative data measures behaviour which is not computable by arithmetic relations and is represented by pictures, words, or images. Qualitative data is also called categorical data, as they can be classified into categories such as class, individual, object, or the process they fall in.

Quantitative data involves numerical process of measurement and on which basic mathematical operations can be done, i.e. addition, subtraction, multiplication and division. The data remains quantitative in nature. Quantitative data can be further classified into:

(1) *Non-metric data*: Data collected conforms to binary scales, nominal scales and ordinal scales. These scales do not possess a meter with which distance between scale values can be measured.

(2) *Metric data*: Data collected is in the form of interval scales and ratio scales. Thus, metric data defines distance between the scale values. Metric data can be further classified into two groups:

- *Discrete data*: Discrete data is countable data, for example, the number of students in the class.
- *Continuous data*: When the variables are measurable, they are expressed on a continuous scale, for example, measuring the height of a person.

39.1 DESCRIPTIVE STATISTICS

Descriptive statistics can be further classified into two categories and shown in Figure 39.1.

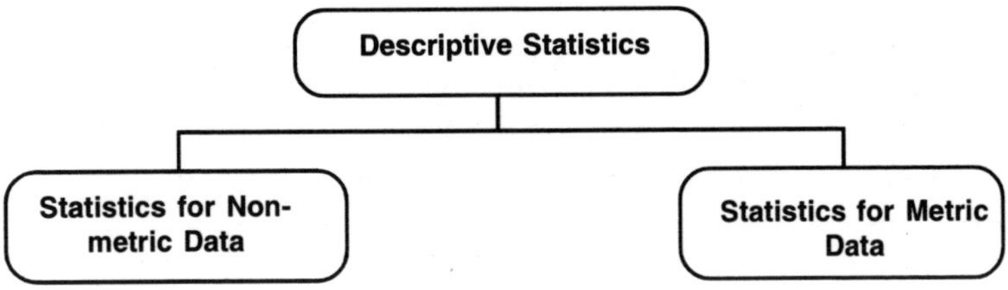

Figure 39.1 : Non-metric Data and Metric Data

Statistical methods can be classified into two categories: (i) descriptive statistics, and (ii) inferential statistics. Descriptive statistics are used to describe, summarize, or explain a given set of data. Inferential statistics are used to infer from measured value based upon samples (statistic) and population value (parameters) from which samples have been drawn. Figure 39.2 reveals analysis of descriptive statistics.

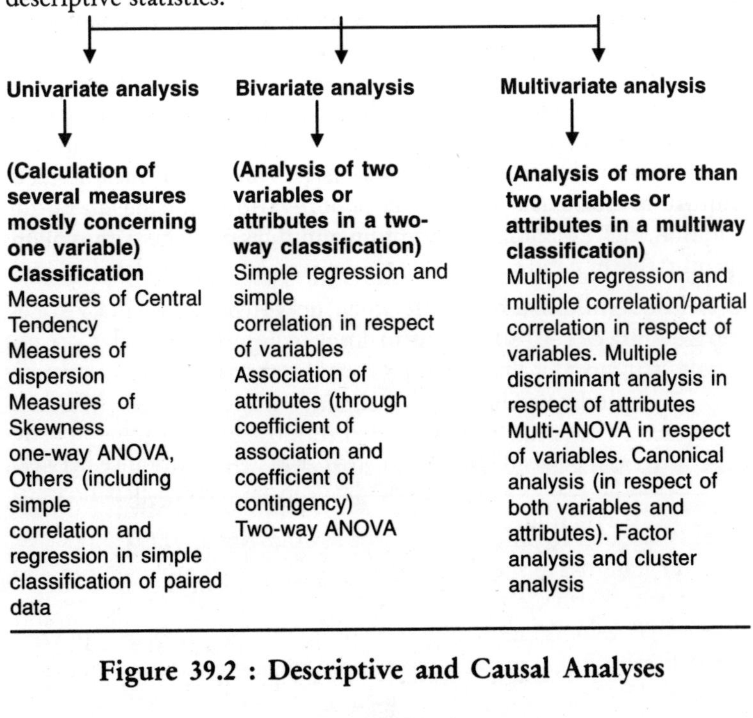

Figure 39.2 : Descriptive and Causal Analyses

39.2 UNIVARIATE ANALYSIS

Univariate is the simplest form of descriptive statistics. It describes a case in terms of a single variable. Univariate analysis provides analytical information about one variable. It could be metric or non-metric in nature.

39.2.1 Data Presentation

(a) Non-metric data (binary, nominal and ordinal) is best displayed in the form of tables or charts for further analysis. Frequency or one-way tables, depicting information in row or column is the simplest method of analyzing non-metric data. They are often used as one of the exploratory procedures to review how different categories of values are distributed in the sample.

In case of binary variables information is displayed in two categories, for example, the number of respondents saying 'yes' or 'no' to a question. Though, in case of nominal data, there may be three or more categories. Charts and graphs can also be used interchangeably. Charts for non-metric data are limited largely to line graph, bar chart, pie chart, polygon, ogive curve as well as other forms of presentation of data.

(b) Metric data: The most important technique in *metric univariate analysis* for metric data is measures of central tendency. It provides information about the central location of distribution.

39.3 MEASURES OF CENTRAL TENDENCY

The three most frequently used measures of central tendency are:

- *Mean* is an average of scores. In case of highly-skewed distribution, the arithmetic mean may get distorted on account of a few items with extreme values. Mean as a measure of central tendency, is a preferred indicator both as a descriptive of the data and as an estimate of the parameter. Other forms of mean are: geometric mean and harmonic mean. Mid-men, trimmed mean, Winsorized mean, and mid-range mean are used to minimize the effect of outliners.

39.4 MEASURES OF DISPERSION

The measure of central tendency does not capture the variability in distribution; hence measure of dispersion is also very essential. These measures of dispersion are:

Range, coefficient of range, inter-quartile range, percentiles, percentile rank, quartiles, average deviation, standard deviation, variance, coefficient of variance, skewness, kurtores, etc.

39.5 ONE-WAY ANALYSIS OF VARIANCE (ANOVA)

In this analysis we are comparing groups on some dependent variable. Imagine three comparison groups, with all people in them measured on some dependent variable of interest. The question is—do the groups differ on their scores? There are two possible sources of variance in our scores. There is variance within the groups, and variance of scores between the groups. Our problem is to decide whether the variance between the groups is larger than the variance within the groups. If it is, we can conclude that the groups differ, if not we can conclude the groups do not differ.

This is done by first finding the mean score for each group, then finding out how much individual scores within the group vary around the group means, then finding the overall mean for the whole sample irrespective of groups (grand mean), then finding out how much group means vary around the overall mean. This enables us to calculate two quantities, between-groups variance and within-groups variance. We then form a ratio, called F, to compare the two, such that:

$$\text{F-ratio} = \frac{\text{Mean square between-groups}}{\text{Mean square within-groups}}$$

F-ratio is used to judge whether the difference among several sample means (groups) is significant or just a matter of sampling fluctuations. For this purpose F-ratio thus derived for given degrees of freedom is compared to Table value to identify statistical significance at .01 level or .05 level.

39.6 SIMPLE CORRELATION AND SIMPLE REGRESSION

In simple correlation, correlation between two groups is identified on one variable. For example, correlation between boys and girls on the single variable of professional choices. Regression can only interpret what exists physically, i.e., there must be a physical way in which independent variable X can affect dependent variable Y. The basic relationship between X and Y is given by:

$$Y = a + bX$$

where the symbol Y denotes the estimated value of Y for a given value of X. This equation is known as the regression equation of Y on X which means that each unit change in X produces a change in Y, which is positive for direct and negative for inverse relationship.

39.7 BIVARIATE ANALYSIS

Bivariate is analysis of two variables or traits in two-way classification. Bivariate involves sub-group comparisons; describes a case in terms of two variables simultaneously. Focus is on the variables and the empirical relationships. Cases are divided into groups according to the attributes of the independent variable. Each sub-group is described in terms of attributes of the dependent variable. The table is read by comparing independent variable sub-groups in terms of an attribute of the dependent variable

The first-step in data analysis of non-metric data is construction of a bivariate cross-tabulation. It is also referred as contingency or two-way table. In a contingency table nominal frequencies are displayed in cells of cross tabulation. Each cell represents a unique combination of specific values. Thus, cross-tabulation allows examining frequencies of observations that belong to specific categories on more than one variable. Cross-tabulation is the easiest way of summarizing data and can be of any size in terms of rows and columns. Relationships between variable can be identified based on the cell values. Example of contingency Table is given blow:

TABLE 39.1

Contingency or Two-Way Table

	Adjusted	*Mal-adjusted*	*Total*
High	70	30	100
Low	45	55	100
Total	115	85	200

39.7.1 Coefficient for Nominal Variables

When data is collected on the basis of some attributes, purpose is to know whether attributes are associated with each other or not. For example, finding out whether association between variables of practice and performance exists. Association may be positive or negative. It can be put symbolically:

(i) If $(AB) > \frac{(A)}{N} \times \frac{(B)}{N} \times N$, then AB are positively related/associated.

(ii) If $(AB) < \frac{(A)}{N} \times \frac{(B)}{N} \times N$, then AB are negatively related/associated.

(iii) If $(AB) = \frac{(A)}{N} \times \frac{(B)}{N} \times N$, then AB are independent i.e., have no association.

In order to judge the significance of association between two attributes, chi-square test is used. The formula for the calculation of chi-square is :

$$X = \frac{\Sigma(\text{observed frequency} - \text{expected frequency})^2}{(\text{expected frequency})} \quad \text{or}$$

$$\chi^2 = \frac{(fo - fe)^2}{fe}$$

37.7.2 Coefficient of Ordinal/Ranked Variable

Ordinal measures are lay emphasis on ranking and pairs. For example, respondents are asked to indicate their interest in watching movie on four point scale: (1) always, (2) usually, (3) sometimes, and (4) never interested. Here the researchers desire relative coefficient from ranking pairs, based on assumption that rank order of one pair predict the rank order of the other pair. In such cases, Spearman's R is calculated as a measure of association between the ranked variables. Spearman's Rho is a very useful measure of association between two ordinal variables.

$$\text{Rho} = 1- \frac{6\Sigma D^2}{N(N^2-1)}$$

39.8 BIVARIATE ANALYSIS IN CASE OF METRIC DATA

Measures may include two or more variables. Selection of appropriate measures of association depend on several factors such as a type of distribution, that is, whether the variable follows a discrete distribution or a continuous distribution, data characteristics and measurement level of data.

Researcher has to ascertain whether an association exists, if so what is the direction of association, whether positive or negative. Moreover, it is imperative to ascertain whether association is statistically significant or large enough to be important.

39.8.1 Correlation

Pearson's Product-moment Correlation coefficient is a measure of linear association between two interval-ratio variables. The measure, represented by the letter r, varies from –1 to +1. A zero correlation indicates that there is no correlation between the variables. A correlation coefficient indicates both the types of correlation as well as the strength of the relationship. The statistical method whereby relationship is expressed on a quantitative scale is called the 'coefficient of correlation' and is designated by the letter 'r'. More accurately we can interpret coefficient of correlation (r) as follow:

r from .00 to ± .20	means almost negligible correlation
r from .20 to ± .40	means low positive or negative correlation depending upon +ve or –ve sign
r from .40 to ± .70	means substantial positive or negative correlation depending upon +ve or –ve sign
r from .70 to ± 1.00	means high to very high positive or negative correlation depending upon +ve or –ve sign

39.8.2 Correlation of Dichotomies

(1) *Bi-serial* (r_{bis}) correlation is a special case of correlation, which is used in the case of correlation between an interval variable and a dichotomous variable.

(2) *Widespread biserial correlation* (r_{wbis}) deals with widespread artificial dichotomy and continuous variables. It is used when one is especially interested in persons at the extremes on the dichotomized variable.

(3) *Point-biserial correlation* (r_{pbis}) deals true dichotomous and continuous variables. It yields lower correlation than r and r_{bis}.

(4) *Tetrachoric correlation* (r_t) deals with artificial dichotomous variables. It is used when both variables can be split at critical points.

(5) *Phi* correlation is a special case of association for dichotomous variables. Its value ranges from –1 to +1 and is the same as Pearson correalation.

(6) *Contingency coefficient* is a case of correlation between two or more categories. It is comparable to r_t under certain conditions and closely related to chi-square.

39.9 REGRESSION

Regression analysis attempts to establish the 'nature of the relationship' between variables—that is, to study the functional relationship between the variables and thereby provide a mechanism for predicting or forecasting. (Chou, 1994). It is used in estimating the values of the dependent variable from the values of the independent variable. It is also used to calculate the standard error of estimate. With the help of regression coefficients we can calculate the correlation coefficient. The square of correlation coefficient (r), called coefficient of determination, measures the degree of association of correlation that exists between the two variables.

The regression equation of Y on X is expressed as follows:

$$Y = a + bX$$

In this equation Y is a dependent variable, i.e., its value depends on X. X is independent variable, i.e., we can take a given value of X and compute the value of Y.

'a' is 'Y-intercept' because its value is the point at which the regression line crosses the Y-axis, that is, the vertical axis. 'b' is the 'slope' of line. It represents change in Y variable for a unit change in X variable.

'a' and 'b' in the equation are called numerical constants because for any given straight line, their values do not change.

39.10 TWO-WAY ANALYSIS OF VARIANCE (ANOVA)

Two-way ANOVA analyses the variance between dichotomous independent variables and a dependent variable. When the people can simultaneously be classified in two ways to form comparison groups, we move from one-way ANOVA to two-way ANOVA. For example, the dependent variable is educational achievement, and students are jointly classified by gender and by socio-economic status. There are possible differences between gender groups (main effect due to gender) and possible differences due to SES (the main effect due to SES). But there is another possibility called interaction between the two classifications. Example of Two-Way ANOVA is shown inTable 39.2.

TABLE 39.2

Two-way ANOVA: Gender × SES with Educational Achievement as Dependent Variable

	Boys	*Girls*
High SES	Average score for boys, high SES	Average score for girls, high SES
Medium SES	Average score for boys, medium	Average score for girls, medium SES
Low	SES Average score for boys, low SES	Average score for girls, low SES

39.11 MULTIVARIATE ANALYSIS

Multivariate is analysis of more than two variables or attributes simultaneously in a multi-way classification. Multivariate analyses make use of various statistical techniques for analyzing data in which a number of observations are available for each object. For example, teacher effectiveness is reflected in a variety of specific performance measures which may involve psycho-social-cognitive and personal variables or attributes. Most of the research studies involve more than two variables in which situational analysis is desired of the association between one (at times many) criterion variable and several independent variables, or we may be required to study the association between variables having no dependency relationships. Multivariate techniques are used to understand the relationships among variables more fully. Multivariate techniques have been found more appropriate because of:

- Multivariate methods decrease the probability of experiment-wise Type I errors; Multivariate tests can be "much more powerful" against Type II error than univariate tests of the same data.
- Multivariate methods honour the reality to which the researcher is purportedly trying to generalize because only (a) multivariate analyses simultaneously consider all relationships among the variables, and (b) all the variables coexist in reality. If the researcher is interested in making probability statements on the basis of sampled multiple measurements, then the best strategy of data analysis is to use some suitable multivariate statistical techniques (Takeuchi, Yanai, and Mukerji, 1982).
- Multivariate analyses are consistent with a worldwide evidence that (a) most effects are multiply caused (e.g., reading curricula may affect reading achievement but so may free-lunch programs) and conversly, (b) most interventions have multiple effects (e.g., successful reading interventions may affect more positive attitudes toward schooling).
- Multivariate analyses address different research questions and analyse different variables. MANOVAs enable researcher to investigate "group of subjects on several dependent variables simultaneously; focusing on cases where the variables are correlated and share a common conceptual meaning" (Stevens, 2002, p. 173). In contrast, ANOVAs allow groups to be investigated on only one outcome variable at a time.
- The two-way ANOVAs actually tests the differences of the means on the observed or measured variables, X and Y, whereas the MANOVA actually test the difference of the

mean of the DDA function scores of the women versus the mean of the DDA function scores of the men. Thus ANOVAs ask research questions about measured outcome variables, whereas MANOVAs ask questions about means on unobserved latent variables or constructs. In canonical analyses, sets of multiplicative weights are applied to the predictor variables to obtain scores on unobserved latent predictor variables, and sets of multiplicative weights are also applied to the criterian or outcome variable to obtain scores on unobserved latent outcome variables. "One would usually be well advised to follow-up a significant multivariate test with a discriminent function analyses in order to study the nature of the group differences more closely" (Tatsuoka, 1971, p. 50).

39.11.1 Multivariate Technique

Multivariate technique can be classified into two broad categories:

(1) When researchers know specifically about the dependent variables and the independent variables and try to assess the relationship between the dependent variables and the independent variables such as in the case of multiple regression, discriminate analysis, logistic regression and MANOVA, etc.,

(2) When researchers do not have any idea about the interdependency of the variables and have large set of data, they try to do factor analysis. Analysis of multivariate data is shown in Figure 39.3.

39.11.2 Multiple Correlation and Regression

Multiple correlation and regression has more than one independent variable, and one dependent variable. We wish to study factors affecting the dependent variable. Like the simple correlation coefficient, the squared multiple correlation coefficient (R^2) also tells us how good our prediction of the dependent variable is with this set of independent variables.

- It is important to know how good our prediction is, by knowing how much of the variance we can account for, and
- We also need to know how important each independent variable is in accounting for this variance.

Therefore, regression weights in our regression equation give a direct estimate predictor variable. The computations produce two

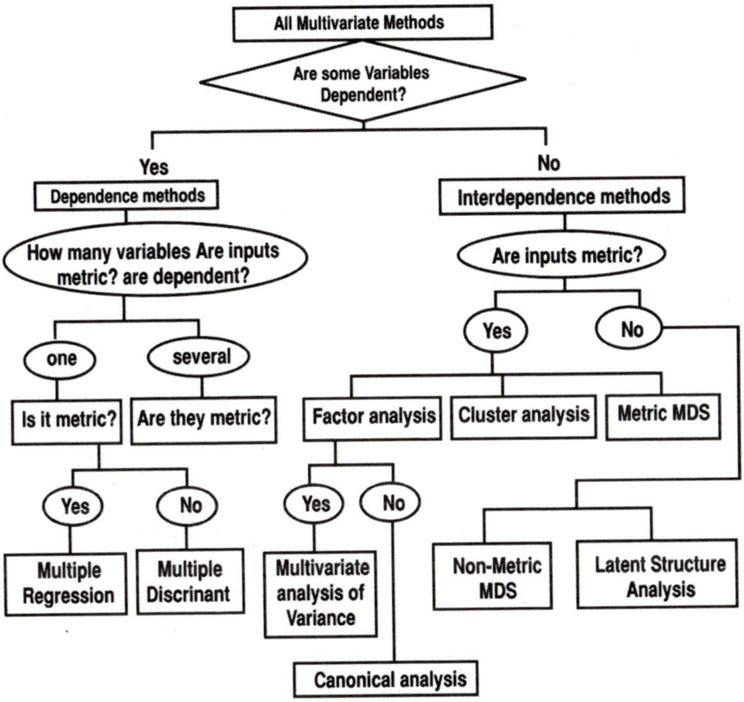

Figure 39.3 : Analysis of Multivariate Data (Kothari, 2007)

types of weights—raw weights, suitable for use with the raw scores as input to the analysis, and standardized weights, for use with standardized scores. Latter is usually named as beta (β) weights. Their technical interpretation is important. The β weight for independent variable X_1 tells us how much of a change we would make in the dependent variable by making a one unit change in the variable $X_{1,}$ while keeping all other variables constant.

Multiple regression, a straightforward generalization of simple regression, is the most commonly used multivariate technique. In simple regression, there is one dependent variable and one independent variable, whereas in multiple regression, there is one dependent variable and many independent variables. It examines the relationship between a single metric dependent variable and two or more metric independent variables. The technique relies upon the linear relationship with lowest sum of squared variance and, therefore, assumption of normality, linearity and equal variance should be checked before using multiple regressions.

Multiple linear regressions take the following form:

$$Y = a + b_1x_1 + b_2x_2 + \text{———} + b_kx_k$$

where Y is a dependent variable and x_1, x_2, ———x_k are independent variables and a, b_1, b_2———b_k are the parameters/regression coefficient.

There are three major types of multiple regression: standard multiple regression, hierarchical or sequential regression and stepwise or statistical regression. In standard multiple regression, all the independent variables are entered into the equation together. In hierarchical regression, independent variables are entered in a pre-specific manner by the researcher, which is driven by theoretical considerations. In stepwise regression, order of entry of variables is solely based on statistical criteria.

39.12 MULTIPLE DISCRIMINANT ANALYSIS

Multiple discriminant analysis is considered an appropriate technique when the single dependent variable happens to be non-metric and is to be classified into two or more groups, depending upon its relationship with several independent variables which all happens to be metric. The objective in discriminant analysis happens to be to predict an object's likelihood of belonging to a particular group based on several independent variables. In case we classify the dependent variable in more than two groups, then we use the name multiple discriminant analysis; but in case only two groups are to be formed, we simply use the term discriminant analysis.

39.13 CANONICAL CORRELATION ANALYSIS

This technique was first developed by Hotelling wherein an effort is to made to simultaneously predict a set of criterion variables from their joint co-variance with a set of explanatory variables. Both metric and non-metric data can be used in the context of this multivariate technique. The procedure followed is to obtain a set of weights for the dependent and independent variables in such a way that linear composite of the criterion variables has a maximum correlation with the linear composite of the explanatory variables. For example, if we want to relate grade school adjustment to health and physical maturity of a child, we can then use canonical correlation analysis, provided we have for each child a number of adjustment scores (such as tests, teacher's ratings, parent's ratings and so on) and also we have for each child a number of health and physical maturity scores (such as heart rate, height, weight, index of intensity of illness and so on). The main objective of canonical correlation analysis is to discover factors separately in the two sets of variables such that the multiple correlation between sets of factors will be the maximum possible.

39.14 FACTORIAL MANOVA

Factorial Manova analyses the variance between multiple nominal independent variable and multiple dependent variables. Factorial MANOVA can be further classified into three categories based on the subject design:

- *Factorial between subject design*: In this case, the researchers want to compare a single variable for multiple groups.
- *Factorial within subject design*: In this case, each respondent is measured on several variables. This is widely used in time series-studies.
- *Mixed between subject and within subject design*: In some situations, both between subject and within subject designs are important and thus both designs are used.

The idea behind factor analysis is based on the correlation between variables.

39.15 DATA REDUCTION AND SCALE RELIABILITY : FACTOR ANALYSIS

Having many variables often makes it difficult to understand the data. This difficulty has led to the development of technique to reduce the number of variables, but without loosing the information the original variables provide. Variables that have a high correlation between them, and are largely independent of other subsets of variables, are combined into factors.

Basic Concepts

39.15.1 Factors and Components

Factors are produced by Factor Analysis (FA), while components are produced by Principal Components Analysis (PCA). Both FA and PCA essentially are data reduction techniques. In PCA, all the variance in the observed variables is analysed whereas in FA, only shared variance is analysed.

39.15.2 Factor Loadings

Factor Loadings help in identifying which variables are associated with the particular factors.

39.15.3 Rotation

Rotation helps in arriving at simple pattern of factor loadings maximizing high correlations and minimizing low ones.

39.15.4 Communalities

Communality gives the variance accounted for a particular variable by all factors.

39.15.5 Eigenvalue

Looking at the eigenvalue, one can determine if the factor explains sufficient amount of variance to be considered as a meaningful factor.

39.15.6 Scale Reliability

After identifying the dimensions underlying a factor, a researcher may prepare a scale of those dimensions to measure the factor. Such a scale has to be tested for validity and reliability.

39.15.7 Sample Size Considerations

A Sample size of less than 100 is not very suitable for conducting factor analysis. A sample size of above 500 is considered to be excellent.

Respondents (N=56) were asked to rank teachers on five point scale on 14 variables of namely, attractive, classy, beautiful, elegant, sexy, dependable, honest, reliable, trustworthy, sincere, expert, experienced, knowledgeable, qualified. SPSS was used to factor analysis. Output obtained was given in Table 39.3.

There are only three factors with eigenvalues greater than 1 suggesting a three-factor solution. Sometimes we may find eigenvalues of some of the factors dropping below 1 after rotation. A judgement has to be made in such cases about the number of factors to be extracted.

Extraction method: Principal Axis Factoring and Rotation Method: Varimax with Kaiser Normalization were used . Table 39.4 reveals pattern of factor loadings—maximizing high correlations and minimizing low ones.

Once we obtain the variables corresponding to particular factors, we may give suitable names to the factors. For example, in this case factor-1 comprises five variables—Honest, Trustworthy, Reliable, Sincere and Dependable; factor-2 comprises four variables—Knowledgeable, Qualified, Experienced and expert; factor-3 comprises five variables—Beautiful, Attractive, Classy, Elegant and Sexy. These three factors can be clubbed together and termed "Trustworthiness, Expertise and Attractiveness.

TABLET 39.3

Total Variance Explained

Factor	*Initial Eigenvalues*			*Extractions sum of squared loadings*			*Rotation sums of squared loadings*		
	Total	*% of variance*	*Commulative %*	*Total*	*% of variance*	*Commulative %*	*Total*	*% of variance*	*Commulative %*
(1)	*(2)*	*(3)*	*(4)*	*(5)*	*(6)*	*(7)*			
1	6.201	41.337	41.337	5.952	39.683	39.683	4.490	29.934	29.934
2	2.398	15.984	57.321	1.977	13.183	52.866	3.197	21.314	51.247
3	2.064	13.76	71.081	1.800	12.001	64.867	2.043	13.620	64.867
4	0.985	6.564	77.646						
5	0.796	5.305	82.95						
6	0.604	4.024	86.975						
7	0.445	2.969	89.944						
8	0.402	2.677	92.621						
9	0.277	1.846	94.467						
10	0.245	1.633	96.100						
11	0.225	1.502	97.602						
12	0.153	1.023	98.625						
13	0.094	0.628	99.253						
14	0.065	0.436	99.688						
15	0.047	0.312	100.00						

TABLE 39.4
Rotated Factor Matrix

	Factor		
	1	*2*	*3*
Honest	0.925	0.207	0.091
Trustworthy	0.889	0.22	0.024
Reliable	0.87	0.256	0.032
Dependable	0.865	0.233	0.022
Sincere	0.857	0.207	-0.02
Knowledgeable	0.208	0.88	-0.022
Qualified	0.234	0.878	0.078
Experienced	0.096	0.762	0.061
Expert	0.28	0.73	0.035
Skilled	0.462	0.501	0.065
Beautiful	0.001	0.044	0.952
Attractive	-0.036	0.016	0.655
Classy	0.335	0.174	0.493
Elegant	0.274	-0.025	0.477
Sexy	-0.132	0.015	0.460

REFERENCES

Auerbach, C.F., and Silverstein, L.B. (2003): *Qualitative Data: An Introduction to Coding and Analysis.* New York: New York University Press.

Bagozzi, R.P., Fornell, C., and Larcker, D.F. (1981): Canonical Correlation Analysis as a Special Case of a Structural Relations Model. *Multivariate Behavioural Research, 16, 437-54.*

Bray, J.H., and Maxwell, S.E. (1985): *Multivariance Analysis of Variance.* Thousand Oaks, CA: Sage.

Cohen, J. (1968): Multiple Regression as a General Data-analytic System. *Psychological Bulletin, 70, 426-33.*

Cudeck, R. (1989). Analysis of Correlation Matrices Using Covariance Structure Models. *Psychological Bulletin, 105, 317-27.*

Edgington, E.S. (1964): A Tabulation of Inferential Statistics Used in Psychological Journals. *American Psychologist, 19, 202-03.*

Gorsuch, R.L. (1983): *Factor Analysis* (2nd ed.) Hillsdale, NJ: Lawrence Erlbaum.

Graham, J.M. (2008): The General Linear Model as Structural Equation Modeling. *Journal of Educational and Behavioural Statistics, 33, 485-506.*

Kothari, C.R. (2011): *Research Methodology: Methods and Techinques.* New Delhi: New Age International Publications.

Thompson, B. (2006b). Research Synthesis: Effect Sizes. In J. Green, G. Camilli, and P.B. Elmore (Eds.). *Handbook of Complementary Methods in Education Research* (pp. 583-603). Washington, DC: American Educational Research Association.

Takeuchi, K., Yanai, H., and Mukherjee, B.N. (1982): *The Foundations of Multivariate Analysis*. New Delhi: Wiley Eastern Ltd.

Thompson, B. (2008): Standards in Conducing and Publishing Research in Education. *Mid-western Educational Researcher, 21*(1), 10-16. Available at http:// www.coe.tamu.edu/ ~ bthompson/mwera.htm

CHAPTER

40

Inferential Statistics

40.0 INTRODUCTION

Inferential statistics cover all the techniques which allow us to explore relationships between variables. They provide a very powerful way of asking questions of numerical data. There are three main approaches: (i) *to explore differences;* (ii) *to explore the nature and extent of relationships; and* (iii) *to classify and make predictions*. The focus is to explain the most commonly used procedures in exploring differences and relationships.

Inferential statistical procedures are divided into two main types: *parametric and non-parametric*. Parametric statistics are based on the principles of the normal curve. Therefore, in order to be able to use parametric statistics, the data must be normally distributed and interval level data (some form of counting rather than categorical or a ranked response). Suggested sample sizes vary according to the kind of statistical test; a general rule of thumb is to have a minimum sample of above thirty.

When sample is less than 30 it is often better to use non-parametric statistics—or statistics which are distribution-free (that is, not based on the principles of the normal curve). Category variables, either nominal or ordinal are analyzed using non-parametric techniques because the mean and standard deviation cannot be calculated.

40.1 SELECTION OF APPROPRIATE STATISTICAL TECHNIQUE

One of the most difficult tasks in analysing data is to select the most appropriate statistical technique that both addresses the research question and fits the data you have collected. An appropriate technique should consider:

- the type of data (categorical, ordinal, interval);
- whether testing for differences or relationships;
- number of groups of participants (two or more);
- whether the groups are *dependent or related* (a single group exposed to different conditions or tested at different points in time) or *independent* (two or more unrelated groups of participants); and
- whether the test should be parametric or non-parametric.

40.2 EVALUATING STATISTICAL RESULTS

Carrying out a statistical procedure is a two-stage process. First, we carry out the appropriate statistical test; second, we use the appropriate test of significance to see true difference. The test of statistical significance enables us to say how confident we are that the result achieved from the analysis of the data from the sample is a 'real' result or if it is as a result of 'chance'. Probability theory allows us to ask what are the chances of achieving a similar result from another sample drawn from the same population? This process validates our results.

Two important assumptions of significance testing are: (1) random selection of sample from a well-defined population, and (2) reliability and validity of instruments of measurement.

Significance testing uses 'degrees of freedom', or 'df'—as it is commonly written. For example, in a classroom with 30 desks, the first student to arrive can choose where to sit, as can each of the following 28 students although from a decreasing number of possibilities each time. But the last student to arrive will have no choice because there will only be one empty desk left. So the degrees of freedom in this case will be the number of desks minus one: 29. In simplistic terms the degrees of freedom figure approximates to the sample size and so provides helpful information when reading quantitative research reports.

Every statistical procedure will have a formula for calculating the degrees of freedom. Often it is:

n –1 (if there is only 1 group of people,
n = number in group)

or:

$n_1 + n_2 - 2$ (if there are 2 groups, n_1 = number in group 1, n_2 = number in group 2).

The results of statistical tests are written in conventional notation, which typically include four pieces of information: the statistical test used, the actual result, the degrees of freedom and the probability that the result is a real or chance result. (Coolidge, 2000; Freedman *et al.*, 1998; Salkind, 2000).

To evaluate the significance of results researchers present their findings in terms of different probability levels. The level of 0.05 ($p < 0.05$ — 'p' stands for probability value) is that the probability of a difference or relationship has been detected in error is less than 5 in 100. The probability values which we tend to use in the social sciences ($p<0.05$, $p<0.01$, $p<0.001$) are based on the shape of the normal distribution curve.

There are a number of cautions about the interpretation of statistical results and their associated probabilities.

- The 0.05 and 0.01 levels of significance used throughout the research world are arbitrary. Their use is now common convention and that is the only reason they- continue to be used. It actually makes more sense to state the actual probability value (p-value) rather than $p < 0.05$—most statistical packages do now report the actual probability value.
- The p-value depends on sample size. The larger the sample the smaller the difference needed to reach statistical significance.
- Researchers should always summarize their data using descriptive statistics so that readers can draw their own conclusions about the importance of any statistically significant p-values. For example, it would be important to state the mean values for each group.
- p-values are only relevant for samples as they are based on probability or chance models. When you have data from a whole population it is irrelevant to do a significance test as you would only be comparing the population with itself.
- Tests of significance do not check for design errors. So if a researcher has chosen the sample incorrectly or used invalid or unreliable measures, or used an inappropriate test, there is no way to identify this statistically. (Freedman *et al.*, 1998)

One aspect of significance testing that is often difficult for new researchers is the idea of one- or two-tail tests of significance. In the normal curve there are two 'tails' one in either direction that stretch to infinity. If you have a research question that is very specific about the result you are testing (that is, looking for a greater mean value of a variable in one group in comparison to a second group) then you can use a one-tailed test of significance and only look for the specific result. For example, to answer the question 'Do boys complete more sit-ups in 5 minutes than girls?' is quite specific and we can look only to see if boys do complete more sit-ups than girls. However, if we phrase this question as 'Is there a difference in the number of sit-ups boys and girls complete in 5 minutes?' it suggests that we could have either group completing more sit-ups and here a two-tailed test is more appropriate. In this case, we cannot predict the direction of change so we consider both possibilities (boys may do more sit-ups than girls or girls may do more than boys).

40.3 THE GENERAL LINEAR MODEL

The vast majority of parametric statistical procedures in common use are part of a single analytic family called the General Linear Model (GLM), including t-test, analysis of variance (ANOVA), multiple regression, descriptive discriminant analysis (DDA), multivariate analysis of variance (MANOVA), canonical correlation analysis (CCA), and structural equation modeling (SEM). (Graham, 2008). This is depicted in Figure 40.1.

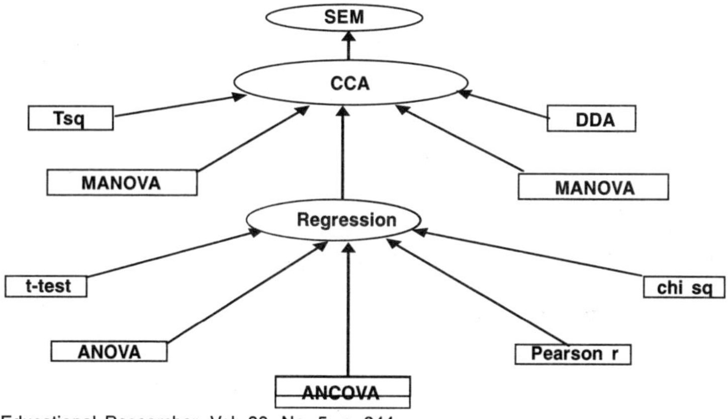

*Educational Researcher, Vol. 38, No. 5, p. 344.

Figure 40.1 : Conceptual Map of General Linear Model*

40.4 T-TESTS

For interval or ratio data, the main parametric techniques are the t-test (when we have only two groups) and the analysis of variance or ANOVA when we have more than two groups.

t-tests are similar to commonly used z-tests in many ways. But t-tests and z-tests use different assumptions. For z-tests, the population mean and population standard deviation should be known exactly. In many real life problems, while population mean is known, the exact population standard deviation cannot be calculated. In such cases, t-tests should be used. Besides, the t-test does not require a big sample size. Many statisticians feel that with a sample size of 30-40, results of the t-test are very close to those obtained from the z-test.

We use the t-test when we wish to test if there is a significant difference between two sample means. In other words, we are using this test to see if two samples can be thought of as coming from the same, or two different population(s). Our null hypothesis is that there is no difference between the two sample means. Our alternative hypothesis is that there is a statistically significant difference between the means.

Various options for different types of t-tests can be found in the *Compare Means* option when using SPSS under the *Analyze menu.* These options are (1) One Sample t-test, (2) Independent Samples t-test, and (3) Dependent (Paired) Samples t-test.

There are two t-test formulas to consider when you have independent samples, that is two groups of people which are totally unrelated (for example, males/females; doctors/patients; 10-year-olds/12-year-olds). The *separate model t-test* is used when each group has the same number of participants. The t-test formula is to be used when you have unequal sample sizes and is called the *pooled variance model t-test.* The difference in the two formulas comes in the way that the variance (distribution of data around the mean) of each sample is calculated. In case of dependent (paired) samples t-test, one can compare these cases with previous ones to observe the difference. The subjects in all these cases are the same and observations are taken at two different times.

One assumption of the t-test is that the variances of the two groups are the same. SPSS also conducts a separate kind of test automatically to look for equality of variances or that the spread of values around the mean of each group being compared is similar. SPSS reports the Levene's test (so called because Levene invented it) based on the null hypothesis that the two variances are equal. If the result of Levene's test is significant at $p < 0.05$ then the null hypothesis is rejected and the alternative hypothesis is accepted; the variances are not equal. If the results of Levene's test are not significant then the null hypothesis is accepted; the variances are assumed to be equal. SPSS generates two different t-test results according to whether the variances are equal or not and provides the results for both of them, clearly labeled.

There is a third t-test formula used when there is only one group of people when data are collected about the same participants under two different conditions (known as a *dependent or related* design). This is called the paired sample t-test and is most commonly used in pre-test/post-test designs. Teachers often give a class a test at the beginning of term to assess pupils' knowledge of a subject. At the end of the term the pupils are tested again. Obviously teachers hope that pupils will have performed better in the end of term test than the initial test and that there is a significant difference in the means suggesting great improvement.

40.5 ANOVA (ONE-WAY)

When testing for differences between three or more groups, analysis of variance (ANOVA) is used instead of a t-test. An ANOVA will identify whether or not there is a significant difference in the means across a number of different groups on a given dependent variable. The null hypothesis for this test is that there is no difference in the means for the different groups. For example, an ANOVA would be required to test for any variation between three exam markers, each marking 100 exam scripts. Here the dependent variable being tested would be the exam mark given to each student and the grouping variable (Independent) would be the exam marker. In this case, we would hope not to find a difference (i.e. that the test result is non-significant) demonstrating that the exam markers are consistent with each other.

In the ANOVA we are looking to see if the difference between the groups is greater than the difference within the groups. The result of the ANOVA test is called the F-ratio (after the creator of the statistics, Fisher). This ratio compares the variability (variance or sum of squares) between groups (the differences you might expect because of the grouping factor) to the variability within the groups (the differences that arise due to chance factors, irrespective of the group they are in). The larger the variability between groups and the smaller the variability within groups, the larger the F-ratio will be and the more likely that the difference between the groups will be a real one.

For ANOVA two different degrees of freedom (df) calculations are required. The degrees of freedom for the between groups measure is the number of groups minus one. The degrees of freedom for the within groups measure is the total number in the sample minus the degrees of freedom for the between groups measure. For example, results of the ANOVA are shown in Table 40.1.

TABLE 40.1

Example of ANOVA Results

	df	*Sum of squares*	*Mean squares*	*F*
Between Groups	3	270	270/3=90	90/55.67=1.617
Within Groups	12	668	668/12=55.67	
Total	15			

Degree of freedom (df): 4x4 table;
Between Groups (a–1) = (4–1=3)
Within Group (N–a) = (16–4=12)
Total (N-1) = (16–1=15)

In Table 38.1 the value of the calculated F-ratio is 1.61, the value of F-ratio from statistical table for a significance level of 0.05 and degree of freedom (3, 12) is 3.49. i.e.

$$F_{calculated}^{[1.61]} < F\alpha = {}_{0.05 \text{ and } df=(3,12)}^{[3.49]}$$

Hence, the null hypothesis (H_o) should be accepted.

Inference: This means that there is no significant difference in terms of any variation between the exam markers.

40.6 ANOVA (TWO–WAY)

ANOVA two-way is used when we have two independent variables and one dependent variable. For example, we have two independent variables namely, educational background and work experience, and one dependent variable salary, the output derived from the analysis of data using SPSS is given below in Table 40.2 and Figure 40.2.

TABLE 40.2

Relationship between Capacity Building, Organizational Environment (Independent) and Managerial Skills (dependent)—ANOVA

Dependent Variable : Managerial Effectiveness

Source	*Sum of Squares*	*df*	*Mean Squares*	*F*	*Sig.*	*Partial Eta Squared*
Model	97.689(a)	5	19.538	8.467	.000	.250
Intercept	23689.146	1	23689.146	10265.898	.000	.988

Level of Capacity Building	78.973	1	78.973	34.223	.000	.212
Open, Moderate, Close Org. Environment	9.190	2	4.595	1.991	.141	.030

40.6.1 Output: Descriptive Statistics

Infernece

Statistically significant associations has been found between organizational environment and capacity building (independent variables) and managerial skills (dependent variable) at 0.01 levels. Impact of capacity building on developing managerial skills is to the extent of 21 percentage.

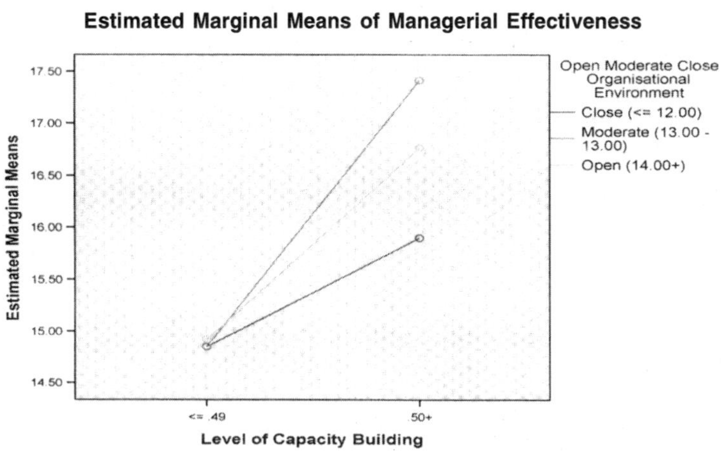

Figure 40.2 : Interaction between Capacity Building, Organizational Environment and Managerial Effectiveness

40.6.2 Inference

Managerial skills namel, planning, decision-making, resourcefulness and time management have been found more in moderate organizational environment with high level of participation of professionals in capacity building programmes as compared to open or close organizational environment. Impact of organization environment and capacity building programmes on the development of managerial skills among professionals has been found the lowest in close organization environment.

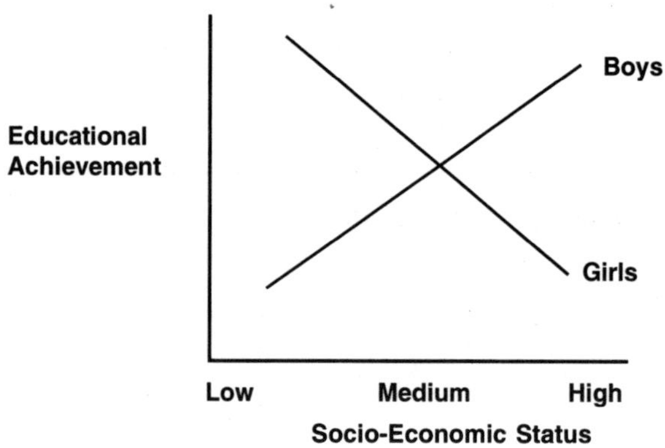

Figure 40.3 : Interaction between Variables

40.6.3 ANOVA is also used to see interaction between variables. Figure above shows interaction between variables (hypothetical).

Interpretation

- Do boys score higher than girls in the results shown in diagram? The answer is that it depends on SES.
- Do students from the high SES backgrounds perform better than those from middle-class SES backgrounds? Again it depends on whether we are talking about boys or girls with high SES scored more than medium boys. Hence, we are dealing with two independent variables namely, different SES levels and the gender and educational achievement as dependent variable.

It is not surprising that interaction is described as 'ubiquitous'. An important consequence of interaction is that it invalidates our

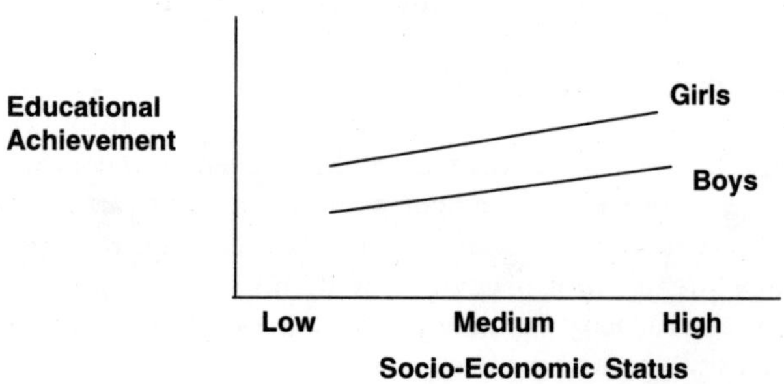

Figure 40.4 : No Interaction between Variables (hypothetical)

attempts to make simple and sweeping generalizations. With the results above we can not generalize about gender differences in achievement, that is, we can not say that boys achieve better than girls, or *vice versa*. Nor can we generalize about social class differences.

If there is no interaction, we talk about main effects due to gender and due to socio-economic. It validates our attempts to make generalizations.

40.6.4 Duncan's Range Test

Output obtained from ANOVA is shown in Table 40.3.

TABLE 40.3

Significance of Difference between Mean Scores of Groups

Source of variation	*Degree of Freedom*	*Sum of squares*	*Mean sum of squares (MSS)*	*F-Ratio*
Between Treatments	3	3570.0	3570/3 = 1190	1190/112.43 = 10.58
Within Treatments	16	1798.8	1798.8/16 = 112.43	
Total	19	5368.8		

The value of the calculated *F*-ratio is 10.58. The value of *F*-ratio from the statistical table for a significance level of 0.05 and degrees of freedom (3,16) is 3.24. Then

$F_{\text{calculated}}\,[10.58] > F\acute{a}_{\,= 0.05 \text{ and df} = (3,16)}\,[3.24]$

Hence, the null hypothesis (H_0) should be rejected.

Since, the null hypothesis is rejected, for further interpretation on the difference between different treatments means, Results of Duncan's multiple range test are shown in Table 40.4.

TABLE 40.4

Summary of Comparison of Duncan's Multiple Range Test

Treatment pair	*Actual difference between means*	*Least significant range*	*Remarks*
3 and 4	34.2	15.31	Significant
2 and 4	15.8	14.93	Significant
1 and 4	3.6	14.22	Not significant
3 and 1	30.6	14.93	Significant
2 and 1	12.2	14.22	Not significant
3 and 2	18.4	14.22	Significant

The comparison of differences between different pairs of treatment means with the corresponding least significant ranges are summarized in Table 40.4. It is cleared that the actual difference between the means of the treatment pairs (3, 4), (2, 4), (3, 1) and (3, 2) are significant. For the remaining pairs of treatment [(1, 4) and (2, 1)], the actual differences between their means are not significant.

40.6.5 Factorial Design

The results of Factorial Design (ANOVA) are summarized in Table 40.5. It is cleared that the components A, AB, C, AC and ABC are significant. This means that these components have significant effect on the scores. The remaining components (B and BC) are not significant.

TABLE 40.7

Results in Factorial Design

Source of variation	*Degree of freedom*	*Sum of squares*	*Mean sum of squares (MSS)*	*F-Ratio (calculated)*	*F-Ratio (at α = 0.05)*	*Comment*
SS_A	2	243.584	121.79	41.71	3.89	Significant
SS_B	1	13.500	13.50	4.62	4.75	Not significant
SS_{AB}	2	60.750	30.38	10.40	3.89	Significant
SS_C	1	139.166	139.17	48.00	4.75	Significant
SS_{AC}	2	80.584	39.29	13.80	3.89	Significant
SS_{BC}	1	13.500	13.50	4.62	4.75	Not significant
SS_{ABC}	2	22.750	11.38	3.90	3.89	Significant
SS_{error}	12	35.000	2.92			
Total	23	609.834				

40.7 CORRELATION : LOOKING FOR RELATIONSHIPS

When we explore the relationships between variables we are using a process called correlation. In social science research correlation procedures are very popular. Coefficient of correlation is calculated to compare groups of individuals on different tasks. The correlation coefficient (r) tells us the degree of linear association between the two variables or the strength of the relationship. By linear we mean how straight a line they form when plotted on a graph showing their relationship. One of the implications of exploring linear relationships is that the things being measured must be continuous (i.e., interval or ratio) so they could theoretically form a straight line. Only interval and ratio numbers where means and standard deviations can be calculated can be used to explore linearity. The correlation coefficient (r) will be somewhere between -1.0 and + 1.0. When r = 1 or – 1 it tells us the data fall in a perfect straight line. When r is positive then the correlation is positive meaning that scores on both variables increase together. When r is negative then the correlation is negative meaning that as the value of one variable increases the value of the other variable decreases. When r = 0 it tells us that there is no association between the two variables. Values of r between 0 and 1 show the different strength of the relationship between the two variables. Generally speaking, if r is below 0.33 it is considered to be a weak relationship; if r is between 0.34 and 0.66 it indicates a medium strength relationship; and if r is between 0.67 and 0.99 it indicates a strong relationship.

One way to understand what we mean by linear relationships is to draw a scatterplot of the two variables. The more 'line' or cigar shaped a scatterplot looks the greater the linear relationship. If the scatterplot is a straight line that is a perfect correlation.

Example

The scatterplots in Figure 40.5 shows relationship between variable X and Variable Y.

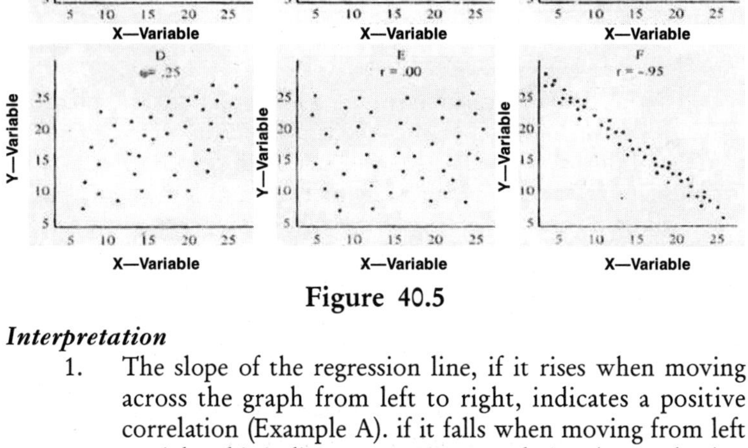

Figure 40.5

Interpretation

1. The slope of the regression line, if it rises when moving across the graph from left to right, indicates a positive correlation (Example A). if it falls when moving from left to right, this indicates, negative correlation (Example F).

2. When all the dots appear to be very close to the regression line (Example A) the correlation is very high, ranging between 0 .95 to 1.00.
3. When all dots appear to be close to the regression line (Example B), the correlation is high, ranging from moderate to high.
4. When the dots scatter around the regression line forming an ellipse midway between straight line and a full circle (Example C), the correlation is moderate approaching 0.50.
5. When the dots scatter around the entire graph more or less equally disperse in all directions, and resembling full circle (Example E), the correlation is very low, approaching zero.

Table 40.6 Shows correlation between course work and overall marks.

TABLE 40.6

Pearson Correlations between Course Work and Overall Marks

		Course work	*Overall mark*
Course work	Pearson Correlation	1	.908**
	Sig. (2-tailed)		0
	N	193	193
Overall mark	Pearson Correlation	.908**	1
	Sig. (2-tailed)	0	
	N	193	193

**Correlation is significant at the 0.01 level (t-ailed).

Example of SPSS output from correlation.

To interpret a correlation we use a minimum of three pieces of information: r (the correlation coefficient indicating the strength of the relationship, described above); the statistical significance of r (the probability value); and the size of the sample. To interpret correlations all these factors can be taken into account. Clearly, statistical significance is relevant but so is the strength of the relationship. Correlation is greatly affected by sample size. With very large samples weak correlation coefficients may be statistically significant; with small samples only very strong correlations will reach statistical significance.

As with other tests, we first decide if we are hypothesizing a result in a particular direction or not-so do we use a one- or two-tailed level of significance? We then decide what is the minimum level of significance we are prepared to accept - 0.05, 0.01, 0.001 or whatever? The choice about what level of significance to use as the standard for a particular study depends on the reliability and validity of the data being analysed as well as the original research question being addressed. Always, your reasons for the decisions taken will need to be explained when reporting the outcomes.

40.8 PARTIAL CORRELATION

In partial correlation, the extent of the specific correlationship between two variables is established, factoring out the effect of one or more other variables. For example, we can obtain the correlation between interest in learning and marks while controlling the effect of the IQ level. The output produced using SPSS is shown in Table 40.7.

TABLE 40.7
Results of Partial Correlation

Control Variable	*Correlational Variables*		*Scores on Interest*	*Marks%*
I.Q.	Scores on Interest Inventory	Correlation	1	0.333
		Significance (2-tailed)	—	0.112
		df	0	2
	Marks (in percentage)	Correlation	0.333	1
		Significance (2-tasiled)	0.112	—
		df	22	0

Inference

If we control I.Q. level of the students, the scores on interest inventory will not be significantly related to the academic performance of the students.

Step-wise Regression

It means dropping out variables from the regression equation, usually one at a time, or step-wise, to see what difference it makes. In other way we can assess how important an independent variable is. First we use all the independent variables in regression equation, to see how much of the dependent variable variance we can account for. That is measured by R^2, then we drop out an independent variable, re-compute the regression equation, and see what change there has been in, or how much variance we can account for, a second R^2, comparing the two R^2s tells us how important the variable was that we dropped out, in accounting for variance in the dependent variable.

40.9 ANALYSIS OF COVARIANCE

When two variables are related, positively or negatively, they vary together. This means they share common variance, or co-vary. This points to an important property of the correlation coefficient. If we square it, we get numerical estimate of the proportion of variance in one variable which is held in common with, or accounted for by, the other. Thus the correlation of +0.50 between two variables tells us that approximately 25% of the variance is held in common between them. Similarly, if $r=-0.70$, r^2 = nearly 0.49, that is 50%.

40.10 PREDICTION AND CAUSATION—A CAUTION

One of the most common mistakes researchers make when using correlations is to talk about cause and effect. If there is an association between two variables that does not necessarily mean that one causes the other. There are three conditions, which must be satisfied in order to prove cause and effect relationships:

- There must be a significant correlation between the 'cause' and 'effect' variables.
- The correlation must be 'real', not due to some other factor (we call this spurious).
- The cause variable must precede the effect variable in real time.

A significant correlation, on its own, does not provide any evidence for causality. For example, there is a positive association between height and weight-taller people tend to weigh more than shorter people or people who weigh less tend to be shorter than people who weigh more. We cannot say that tall people weigh more because they eat more because it is equally possible that they weigh more because they grow taller and need to eat more. Association does not mean causation.

Also, the significant correlation between the variables must be seen to be 'real'. Freedman and Pisani (1998) use the example of searching for the cause of polio back in the 1950s where there was a worldwide epidemic. Researchers gathered massive amounts of information from polio victims and their families and discovered two very significant correlations:

- an increase in the incidence of polio and an increase of drinking soft drinks; and

- an increase in the incidence of polio and an increase in temperature.

Only one of these is a 'real' relationship. The other is 'spurious'. The polio virus spreads as the temperature rises and so that is a real relationship. However, as the temperature rises we tend to drink more liquids and so the connection between polio and soft drinks is spurious because it is connected to temperature and doesn't exist on its own.

The final condition which must be met to examine prediction and causality is that the cause variables must precede the effect variable. For example, an intervention to improve the teaching of reading must take place before the test measuring reading ability is undertaken. However, sometimes in the social sciences the cause and effect is harder to unravel. Think about the relationship between job satisfaction and productivity. Which comes first?

Factor Analysis

In factor analysis we are aiming to reduce the number of variables by finding the common factors among them. For example, we have six educational tests one in each arithmetic, algebra and geometry, and one each in Hindi, English and Punjabi. If we measure a sample of students with these six tests, we would find two clusters of correlations among the tests. The first cluster would show the overlap between arithmetic, algebra and geometry and another cluster Hindi, Punjabi and English.

Figure 40.6 shows the levels of abstraction as given below.

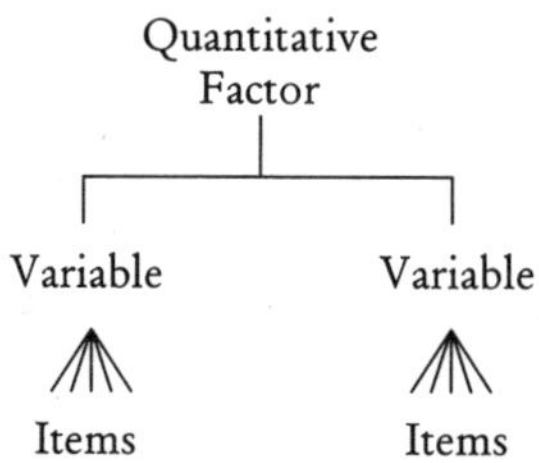

Figure 40.6 : Levels of Abstraction

40.11 SIGNIFICANCE OF DIFFERENCE: NON-PARAMETRIC TECHNIQUES

For nominal or ordinal data there are many non-parametric tests of difference. Each technique has a specific purpose and each has specific requirements about level of measurement (that is nominal or ordinal data), number of categories, number of groups and type of difference explored. It is crucial to know what kinds of differences are being explored using what types of data in order to select the most appropriate technique.

These techniques can also be used with interval data when you have very small samples or when there are violations of the assumptions which underlie parametric tests (for example, when data cannot be described as having a normal distribution) non-parametric tests typically use ranking of data to compare groups and are based on fewer assumptions. For example, they are distribution free, that is the data is not assumed to be normally distributed. The Mann-Whitney U test is the non-parametric equivalent of the independent sample t-test. The Wilcoxon signed-rank test is the non-parametric equivalent of the paired sample t-test.

40.11.1 Chi-square

Chi-square is one of the most used techniques to explore relationships using nominal and/or ordinal data. It does two things in one test. It is a test of independence and also a test of association. In chi-square we formally are testing the null hypothesis that two things are independent. If we reject the null hypothesis because we have significant results we can do further analysis to look at the kind of relationship that exists between two variables and the strength of that relationship.

The first step in interpreting a significant chi-square, is to look carefully at the values and/or percentages in the frequency table as a way of understanding the association between different variables. The frequency table indicates how many cases (people for example) exhibit each of the possible combinations of the two nominal variables being tested. The example in Table 40.4 shows how many boys and how many girls use computers outside school and how many do not. By using the 'Cross tab' procedure in SPSS it is possible to produce this two-way contingency table.

However, by also using SPSS to display the percentages in each column and row as in Table 40.8 it is easier to interpret the relationship between gender and out-of school use of computers in this sample.

The percentages help us to take into account that there are many more pupils reporting use of computers out of school than not, and slightly more boys than girls in this sample. SPSS chi-square output produces the results of many tests. The most commonly used chi-square statistic is the Pearson chi-square (χ^2) SPSS output for chi-square test is given in Table 40.9.

TABLE 40.8

GENDER* Usage of Computer Outside School

			Use a computer outside school		*Total*
			No	*Yes*	
Gender	Male	count	322	2963	3285
		% with GENDER	9.80%	90.20%	100.00%
		% within Use a computer outside school	52.80%	53.60%	53.50%
Gender	Female	count	288	2566	2854
		% with GENDER	10.10%	89.90%	100.00%
		% within Use a computer outside school	47.20%	46.40%	46.50%
Total		count	610	5529	6139
		% with GENDER	9.90%	90.10%	100.00%
		% within Use a computer outside school	100.00%	100.00%	100.00%

Example of cross-tabulation with row and column percentages.

TABLE 40.9

Chi-Square Tests

	Value	*df*	*Asymp. Sig. (2-sided)*	*Exact sig. (2-sided)*	*Exact sig. (1-sided)*
Pearson Chi-Square	.142˜	1	0.706		
Continuity Correlation**	0.112	1	0.738		
Likelihood Ratio	0.142	1	0.706		
Fisher's Exact Test				0.732	0.369
Linear-by-Linear Association	0.142	1	0.706		
N of Valid Cases	6139				

*Computed for 2 × 2 table.

˜0 Cells (.0%) have expected countless than 5. The minimum expected count is 283.59.

SPSS output for Chi-Square test.

χ^2=0.142, df=1, p=0706

The df for chi-square is (number of rows -1) multiplied by (number of columns -1). For a table with two rows and two columns (a 2 × 2 table) the df = 1. It also tells us that the probability of achieving a $\chi^2 = 0.142$ is totally by chance because $p > 0.05$ (p =

TABLE 40.10

Rank Correlation between Students and their Parents on Vocational Preferences

Correlation (N =300)	*Rank of P1*	*Rank of P2*	*Rank of P3*	*Rank of P4*	*Rank of P5*	*Rank of P6*	*Rank of P7*	*Rank of P8*	*Rank of P9*	*Rank of P10*
(1)	*(2)*	*(3)*	*(4)*	*(5)*	*(6)*	*(7)*	*(8)*	*(9)*	*(10)*	*(11)*
Rank of S1	-.099									
Rank of S2		.179(**)								
Rank of S3			-.003							
Rank of S4				.095						
Rank of S5					.062					
Rank of S6						-.063				
Rank of S7							-.016			
Rank of S8								-.041		
Rank of S9									-.060	
Rank of S10										.149(**)

**Significant at .01 level.

0.706). Therefore, there is no relationship between gender and reported use of computers outside of school.

The chi-square statistic is the most used and most abused statistic in social science research. The abuse comes from researchers making interpretations about the association between variables beyond what the result indicates. In and of itself chi-square only tells us if there is an association between two things or if there is independence. To explore the strength of relationship requires using one of the post-hoc analyses in measures of association such as phi or Cramer's V (Field, 2000: 67). Similarly to correlation coefficients, these give a measure of strength between 0.0 and 1.0; the closer to 1.0 this statistic is, the stronger the association.

Rank Correlation

Example of rank correlation indicating students and parents vocational preferences is given in Table 40.10.

Inference

- There is a significant correlation between students and parents for second preference. (i.e., .179 at .01 level).
- There was statistically significant correlation between students and parents at .01 levels with regard to 10th preference given by them.
- No significant correlation was found in other preferences for vocations.

Selection of appropriate statistical tests for the analysis of data depends on the nature of data. A summary of statistical tests for the analysis of data is shown in Table 40.11.

TABLE 40.11

Statistical Tests for the Analysis of Data

Univariate	*Bi/multivariate*		
	Normal	*Ordinal*	*Interval/Ratio (Assumption of normality—if not normal use ordinal tests)*
(1)	*(2)*	*(3)*	*(4)*
Nominal 2-point scale: gender-	Compare 2 or more Groups: Chi-Square	Compare 2 goups: Mann-Whitney 3 or more groups: Kruskal-Wallis	Compare 2 or more groups: ANOVA followed by t-test.

(*Contd.*)

TABLE 40.11 (*Contd.*)

(1)	*(2)*	*(3)*	*(4)*
1 = female, 2 = male 3-point scale: religion – 1 = Catholic, 2 = Protestant and 3 = Jewish Central tendency: Mode Dispersion: NSA Compare sample to population: Chi-squared Univariate Bi/multivariate Normal Ordinal Interval / Ratio (Assumption of normality – if not normal use ordinal tests) INTERVAL/ RATIO Interval – IQ score ratio—real numbers, age, height, weight Central tendency: Mean	Compare within same group over times: 2 pts: McNemar test 3+ pts: Cochran's Q Relationship with other variables: Yes/ no: Chi-squared Strength 2 pts: Phi Strength 3+ pts: Lambda	Compare within same group over times: 2 pts: Wilcoxon signed rank test Relationship with other variables: yes/ no: Chi-squared Strength 2+ pts: Lambda Relationship with other variables: Small < 10: Kendall's Tau Larger Sample: Spearman's Rho with 1 variable as dependent: Somer's d Small sample < 10: Kendall's Tau Larger sample: Sperman's Rho With 1 variable as dependent: Somer's d	Compare within same group over time (2+pts): ANOVA followed by t-test Relationship with other variables: yes/no: Pearson's product moment correlation Strength: f-test With 2 or more independent and 1 dependent variable: MANOVA 2+ dependent variable and 3+ groups: Multiple regression or path analysis. Relationship with other variables Jaspen's coefficient of multiserial correlation With the interval/ ratio variable as dependent : ANOVA Relationship with other variables – no dependent/ independent distinction: Pearson's product moment correlation. With 1 independent and 1 dependent

Dispersion: Standard deviation		variable: Pearson's linear correlation.
Compare sample to population: t-test.		With 2 or more independent and 1 dependent variable: Multiple regression.
		With 2 or more independent and 2 or more dependent variablesm Canonical correlation.

References

Aiken, I.S.,West, S.G. and Millsap, R.E. (2008). Doctoral Training in Statistics, Measurement, and Methodology in Psychology: Replication and Extension of Aiken, West, Sechrest, and Reno's (1990) Survey of Ph.D. Programs in North America. *American Psychologist,* 63, 32-50.

American Statistical Association (2007). *Using Statistics Effectively in Mathematics Education Research.* Alexandria,VA: Author.

Bray, J.H. and Maxwell, S.E. (1985). Multivariate Analysis of Variance. Thousand Oaks,CA: Sage.

Campbell, K.T. and Taylor, D.L. (1996): Canonical Correlation Analysis as a General Linear Model: A Heuristic Lesson for Teachers and Students. *Journal of Experiment Education.* 64, 157-71.

Elmore (Eds.): Handbook of Complementary Methods in Educational Research. (pp. 583-603) Washington, DC: American Educational Research Association.

Graham, J.M. (2008): The General Linear Mmodel as Structural Equation Modeling. *Journal of Educational and Behavioural Statistics.* 33, 485-506.

Keith, F. Punch (2009): *Introduction to Research Methods in Education*. New Delhi, Sage Publications.

Sally Barnes and Cathy Lewin (2008): An Introduction to Inferential Statistics: Testing for Differences and Relationships. *Education and Social Research Institute*, Manchester Metropolitan University, UK.

Thompson, B. (2006 b): Research Synthesis: Effect Sizes. In J. Green, G. Camill and P.B. Zientek, L.R. and Thompson, B. (2006). Commonality Analysis: Partitioning Variance to Facilitate Better Understanding of Data. *Journal of Early Intervention,* 28, 299-307.

Zientek, L.R., and Thompson, B. (2009): Matrix Summaries Improves Research Reports: Secondary Analyses Using Published Literature. *Educational Researcher.* Vol. 38, No. 5, pp. 343-52.

CHAPTER

41

Analysis of Qualitative Data

41.0 INTRODUCTION

The difficulty faced in the researches in the use of qualitative data is that the methods of analysis are not well formulated. For quantitative data, there are conventions the researchers can follow. But the analyst faced with a bank of qualitative data has very few guidelines for protection against self-delusion, biases and subjectivity. Lack of substantial evidence makes it difficult for the policy planners to formulate action plan.

41.1 ELEMENTS OF QUALITATIVE RESEARCH

A summary of the recurrent elements in qualitative research is given by Miles and Huberman (1994):

- Qualitative research is conducted through an intense and/ or prolonged contact with a 'field' or life situation. These situations are typically 'banal' or normal ones, reflective of the everyday life of individuals, groups, services or organizations.
- The researcher's role is to gain a 'holistic' overview of the context under study: its logic, its arrangements, its explicit and implicit rules.
- The researcher attempts to capture data on the perceptions of local actors 'from the inside' through a process of deep attentiveness, of empathetic understanding, and of

suspending or 'bracketing' preconceptions about the topic under discussion.

- Reading through these materials, the researcher may isolate certain themes and expressions that can be reviewed with informants, but that should be maintained in their original forms throughout the study.
- The main task is to explicate the ways people in particular settings come to understand, account for, take action, and otherwise manage their day-to-day situations.
- Many interpretations of this material are possible, but some are more compelling for theoretical reasons or on grounds of internal consistency.
- Relatively little standardized instrumentation is used at the outset. The researcher is essentially the main 'instrument' in the study.
- Most analysis is done with words. The words can be assembled, sub-clustered, broken into semiotic segments. They can be organized to permit the researcher to contrast, compare, analyze, and bestow patterns upon them.

Qualitative research in education concentrates on the study of human behaviour and social life in natural settings. Its richness and complexity mean that there are different ways of analyzing social life, and therefore, multiple perspectives and practices in the analysis of qualitative data are to be considered.

41.2 ANALYSIS OF QUALITATIVE DATA

- A repertoire of analytic techniques thus characterizes qualitative research, and different techniques can be applied to the same body of qualitative data, illuminating different aspects of it.
- Methods for the analysis of data need to be systematic, disciplined, and transparent.
- The concept of 'audit trail' through the data analysis is now realistic for much qualitative research.
- Induction is central to analysis of qualitative data for generation of theory. But deduction is also needed for the verification of the theory. This sort of data analysis is a series of alternating inductive and deductive steps, whereby data-driven inductive hypothesis generation is followed by deductive hypothesis examination for the purpose of verification.

41.3 INTERACTIVE MODEL OF DATA ANALYSIS

The main components of data analysis are :

- *Data reduction*: the objective of data reduction is to reduce the data without significant loss of information.
- *Data display*: organize, compress and assemble information. There are many different ways of displaying data-graphs, charts, networks, diagrams of different types (Venn diagram, causal models, etc.)
- *Drawing and verifying conclusions*: conclusions will be in the form of propositions, and once they have been drawn, they need to be verified.

41.3.1 Coding

Codes are tags, names, labels against the pieces of the data. There are two types of codes—descriptive codes and inferential (pattern) codes. Descriptive codes are very useful in summarizing the segments of data, and which provide the basis for inferential codes. Inferential codes are more interpretive, and focus on pattern codes. A pattern code is more inferential, a sort of 'meta-code'. Pattern codes pull together material into smaller and more meaningful units. A good way to understand pattern codes is by analogy with factor analysis in quantitative research.

41.3.2 Memoing

Memoing is the second basic operation of qualitative data analysis. Memoing begins at the start of the analysis along with coding. Memoing is recording of ideas whatsoever may be. These memos can cover many things. They may be substantive, theoretical, methodological or even personal. Ideas may lead to new patterns and higher level of pattern coding. They may also elaborate a concept or relate different concepts to each other. This last type of memo produces propositions.

41.3.3 Abstracting

Like factor analysis in quantitative research, numerous ideas or indicators are reduced to first order concept, and then second order concept. Or it is proceeding from first level abstraction to second level abstraction. It is continuum from concrete- to- abstract and specific-to-general which is remarkably similar in both approaches.

41.3.4 Comparing

Comparison is fundamental to systemic inquiry, whether data are qualitative or quantitative. Comparison is the intellectual activity in the analysis of qualitative data. Comparing is essential to conceptual development. Comparison helps in going from the first level of abstraction to higher level of abstraction.

41.4 GROUNDED THEORY ANALYSIS

Three steps are involved in the analysis of grounded theory:

(1) First step is to find conceptual categories in the data,
(2) The second is to find relationships between these categories, and
(3) The third is to conceptualize and account for these relationships at a higher level of abstraction. Therefore, there are three general types of codes:
    (a) Substantive codes (produced by open coding), which are the initial conceptual categories in the data,
    (b) Theoretical codes (produced by axial coding), which connect these categories, and
    (c) The core code (produced by selective coding), which is higher order conceptualization of the theoretical coding around which theory is built.

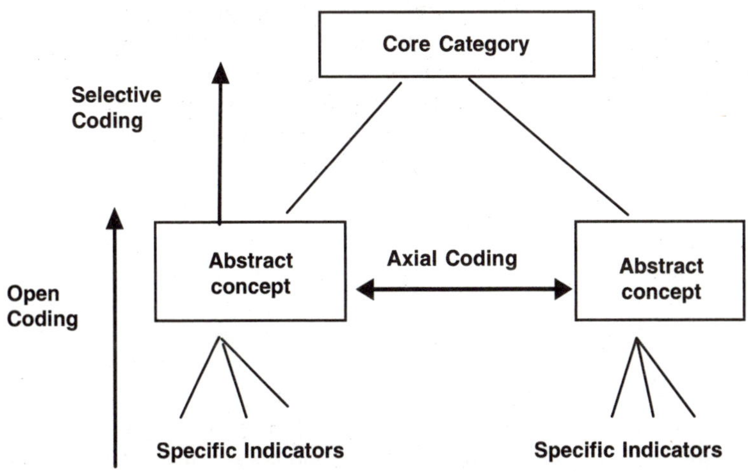

Figure 41.1 : Diagrammatic Representation of Grounded Theory Analysis (Mites & Huberman, 2001)

41.5 OTHER ANALYTIC APPROACHES IN QUALITATIVE ANALYSIS

41.5.1 Narrative Analysis

In narrative analysis, form and content can be studied together and a concern with narrative can illuminate how informants use language to convey particular meanings and experiences. For example, Connelly and Clendenin (1999) present stories from both teachers and administrators. The authors analyze and reflect upon these stories to make links between knowledge, context and identity for both teachers and administrators. Cortazzi (1991) examined important aspects of 123 primary teachers' experience and through their stories a clear picture is built up of how teachers are teaching.

41.5.2 Ethnomethodology

The primary focus is on how central features of a culture, its shared meanings and social norms, are developed, maintained and changed rather than on the content of those meanings and norms. (Feldman, 1995). With so much of social life mediated through written and especially spoken communication, the study of language is at the heart of ethnomethodology.

41.5.3 Discourse Analysis

Discourse encompasses ideas, statements, knowledge that are dominant at a particular time among particular sets of people... and which are held in relation to other sets of individuals.... Implicit in the use of such knowledge is the application of power. However, it is not restricted exclusively to verbalized propositions, but can include ways of seeing, categorizing and reacting to the social world in everyday practices. (Jupp, 1996). Coulthard (1985) has many examples of micro-level discourse analysis in the language teaching context.

41.5.4 Semiotics

Semiotics, or a science of signs, lays out assumptions, concepts and methods for the analysis of sign systems. There are many sign systems (for example, mathematics, music, etiquette, symbolic rites, and secret signs) to which semiotic can be applied. Semioticians identify mechanisms by which meaning is produced (the most common ones are metaphor, metonymy and opposition), and have devised techniques using these mechanisms for interpreting qualitative data. Mavers (2007) conceptualizes writing as a process of design to study how meaning is made by a 6-year old child who uses semiotic resourcefulness in email exchanges with her uncle.

41.5.5 Documentary and Textual Analysis

All documentary sources are the result of human activity, produced on the basis of certain ideas, theories or commonly accepted, taken-for granted principles, and these are always located within the constraints of particular social, historical or administrative conditions and structures (Finnegan, 1997). Words and their meanings depend on where they are used, by whom and to whom. Woods (1979) analyses school reports, and shows the concepts and categories teachers use to make normative judgments about pupils.

41.6 ANALYSIS OF QUALITATIVE DATA SOFTWARE

41.6.1 Weft QDA

Weft QDA is originally written out of curiosity whilst completing a Masters in Social Research Methods at the University of Surrey in 2004. The software is tied up and documented, and then first released in 2005. *Weft QDA* is an easy-to-use, free and open-source tool for the analysis of textual data such as interview transcripts, field-notes and other documents. The software isn't being maintained or updated, but the current version is available and includes some standard CAQDAS features. These are :

- Import documents from plain text or PDF
- Character-level coding using categories organised in a tree structure
- Category and document memos
- Retrieval of coded text and "coding-on"
- Simple coding statistics
- Fast free-text search
- Combine coding and searches using boolean queries: AND, OR, AND NOT
- "Code Review" to compare the coding of multiple categories.

Version 2.0 provides support for multilingual text, photos, audio and video documents, along with other new features and interface improvements, and has been found going to work well on OS X and modern Linux distros..

41.6.2 ATLAS.ti

ATLAS.ti Software is used for analysis of qualitative data such as interviews, field notes, textual sources, graph and all audio and video, image, and geo-data.

ATLAS.ti in its *welcome wizard* offers four options on beginning a session an already existing Hermeneutic Unit (HU), on at project, create a new one, or just continue with the programme. Hermeneutic Unit is researcher's project and documents, codes, memos, and other files associated with it. The Hermeneutic Unit Editor is main workpace area and main menu provides access to different components of the Hermeneutic Unit (HU). The researcher can view the documents through Primary Document Pane. Main Tool Bar provides easy access to primary documents, quotations, codes, memos.

- First of all the researcher has to ensure that data must be in text-based, electronic format.
- Next step is assign or import the files you plan to analyze
- Open textual primary documents and assign codes to them. Researcher can select one of four types of coding techniques namely, open coding, code-by-list, in-Vivo coding, quick coding. Researcher can assign multiple codes to the selected text.
- Quotations in ATLAS.ti are segments of primary documents. Researcher can choose to code these segments.
- Store different kinds of objects in Families. (i.e. Male or Female). All procedures for displaying, editing, and creating families are found in the menu of their object types.
- Use different search options for Simple search, Category search and GREP search(i.e. search for all years between 2000 and 2011).
- Retrieve coded texts, graphic or audio segments that match your specified criteria and Interpret the data accordingly.

Researcher can export and import qualitative data for analysis to other software (for example, SPSS). In addition to textual documents, researcher can work with graphic files and other audio and video formats (like WAV, MP3, WMA, SND, AVI, MPG, WMV, MDV, etc.).

41.6.3 NVIVO 9

NVIVO 9 helps researcher to easily organize and analyze data in documents, pictures. Surveys audio and video, so one can deliver robust findings quickly. NVIVO delivers simpler, flexible analysis with greater insight. Themes as 'nodes' are stored in containers. Nodes that represent anything at all like people, places and organizations and assign any demographic data can be created. Researcher can assign his or her colours to nodes sources, attribute values and can see themes in coding strips, charts and models. Sub-nodes can be rolled up into the parent node.

Researcher can identify the most frequently materials (sources) or nodes and display results in a word tree. Connections between items can be explored and displayed visually with 'connection map' which help researcher to see pattern and convert the graph to a model.

Cluster analysis can be conducted to visualize the similarities and differences. Researcher can conduct Framework analysis using NVIVO's new Framework matrices.

References

Feldman, N. (2001): *Strategies for Interpreting Qualitative Data.* Thousand Oaks: CA: Sage.

Huberman, A.M. and, Miles, M.B. (1994): Data Management and Analysis Methods. In N.K. Denzin and Y.S. Lincoln (eds). *Handbook of Qualitative Research.* Thousand Oaks, CA: Sage.

Marshall, C. and Rossman, G.B. (1989): Designing Qualitative Research. Newbury Park, CA: Sage.

Miles, M.B., and Huberman (1994): Qualitative Data Analysis. 2nd edn. Thousand Oaks, CA: Sage.

APPENDIX

TABLE 1
Areas under a Normal Curve

This table shows the area between zero (the mean of the standard normal variable) and z. For example, if z = 1.61, look at the row titled 1.6 and then move over to the column titled .01 to get the result .4463.

S	*.00*	*.01*	*.02*	*.03*	*.04*	*.05*	*.06*	*.07*	*.08*	*.09*
(1)	*(2)*	*(3)*	*(4)*	*(5)*	*(6)*	*(7)*	*(8)*	*(9)*	*(10)*	*(11)*
0.0	.0000	.0040	.0080	.0120	.0150	.0199	.0239	.0279	.0319	.0359
0.1	.0398	.0438	.0478	.0517	.0557	.0596	.0636	.0675	.0714	.0754
0.2	.0793	.0832	.0871	.0910	.0948	.0987	.1026	.1064	.1103	.1141
0.3	.1179	.1217	.1253	.1293	.1331	.1368	.1406	.1443	.1480	.1517
0.4	.1554	.1591	.1628	.1664	.1700	.1736	.1772	.1808	.1844	.1879
0.5	.1915	.1950	.1985	.2019	.2054	.2088	.2123	.2157	.2190	.2224
0.6	.2258	.2291	.2324	.2357	.2389	.2422	.2454	.2486	.2518	.2549
0.7	.2580	.2612	.2642	.2673	.2704	.2734	.2764	.2794	.2823	.2852
0.8	.2881	.2910	.2939	.2967	.2996	.3023	.3051	.3078	.3106	.3133
0.9	.3159	.3186	.3212	.3288	.3264	.3289	.3315	.3340	.3365	.3389
1.0	.3413	.3438	.3461	.3485	.3508	.3531	.3554	.3557	.3559	.3621
1.1	.3642	.3665	.3686	.3708	.3729	.3749	.3770	.3790	.3810	.3830
1.2	.3849	.3869	.3888	.3907	.3925	.3944	.3962	.3980	.3997	.4015
1.3	.4032	.4049	.4066	.4082	.4099	.4115	.4131	.4147	.4162	.4177
1.4	.4192	.4207	.4222	.4236	.4251	.4265	.4279	.4292	.4306	.4319

1.5	.4332	.4345	.4357	.4370	.4382	.4394	.4406	.4418	.4429	.4441
1.6	.4452	.4463	.4474	.4484	.4495	.4505	.4515	.4525	.4535	.4545
7	.4554	.4564	.4573	.4582	.4591	.4599	.4608	.4616	.4625	.4633
1.8	.4641	.4649	.4656	.4664	.4671	.4678	.4686	.4693	.4699	.4706
1.9	.4713	.4719	.4726	.4732	.4738	.4744	.4750	.4756	.4761	.4767
2.0	.4772	.4778	.4783	.4788	.4793	.4798	.4803	.4808	.4812	.4817
2.1	.4821	.4826	.4830	.4834	.4838	.4842	.4846	.4850	.4854	.4857
2.2	.4861	.4864	.4868	.4871	.4875	.4878	.4881	.4884	.4887	.4890
2.3	.4893	.4896	.4898	.4901	.4904	.4906	.4909	.4911	.4913	.4916
2.4	.4918	.4920	.4922	.4925	.4927	.4929	.4931	.4932	.4934	.4936
2.5	.4938	.4940	.4941	.4943	.4945	.4946	.4948	.4949	.4951	.4952
2.6	.4953	.4955	.4956	.4957	.4959	.4960	.4961	.4962	.4963	.4964
2.7	.4965	.4966	.4967	.4968	.4969	.4970	.4971	.4972	.4973	.4974
2.8	.4974	.4975	.4976	.4977	.4977	.4978	.4979	.4979	.4980	.4981
2.9	.4981	.4982	.4982	.4983	.4984	.4984	.4985	.4985	.4986	.4986
3.0	.4987	.4987	.4987	.4988	.4988	.4989	.4989	.4989	.4990	.4990

TABLE 2

Values of the t-distribution (two-tailed)

DF	*AP* 0.80 0.20	0.90 0.10	0.95 0.05	0.98 0.02	0.99 0.01	0.995 0.005	0.998 0.002	0.999 0.001
(1)	(2)	(3)	(4)	(5)	(6)	(7)	(8)	(9)
1	3.078	6.314	12.706	31.820	63.657	127.321	318.309	636.619
2	1.886	2.920	4.303	6.965	9.925	14.089	22.327	31.599
3	1.638	2.353	3.182	4.541	5.841	7.453	10.215	12.924
4	1.533	2.132	2.776	3.747	4.604	5.598	7.173	8.610
5	1.476	2.015	2.571	3.365	4.032	4.773	5.893	6.869
6	1.440	1.943	2.447	3.143	3.707	4.317	5.208	5.959
7	1.415	1.895	2.365	2.998	3.499	4.029	4.785	5.408
8	1.397	1.860	2.306	2.897	3.355	3.833	4.501	5.041
9	1.383	1.833	2.262	2.821	3.250	3.690	4.297	4.781
10	1.372	1.812	2.228	2.764	3.169	3.581	4.144	4.587
11	1.363	1.796	2.201	2.718	3.106	3.497	4.025	4.437
12	1.356	1.782	2.179	2.681	3.055	3.428	3.930	4.318
13	1.350	1.771	2.160	2.650	3.012	3.372	3.852	4.221
4	1.345	1.761	2.145	2.625	2.977	3.326	3.787	4.140
15	1.341	1.753	2.131	2.602	2.947	3.286	3.733	4.073
16	1.337	1.746	2.120	2.584	2.921	3.252	3.686	4.015
17	1.333	1.740	2.110	2.567	2.898	3.222	3.646	3.965
18	1.330	1.734	2.101	2.552	2.878	3.197	3.610	3.922

19	1.328	1.729	2.093	2.539	2.861	3.174	3.579	3.883
20	1.325	1.725	2.086	2.528	2.845	3.153	3.552	3.850
21	1.323	1.721	2.080	2.518	2.831	3.135	3.527	3.819
22	1.321	1.717	2.074	2.508	2.819	3.119	3.505	3.792
23	1.319	1.714	2.069	2.500	2.807	3.104	3.485	3.768
24	1.318	1.711	2.064	2.492	2.797	3.090	3.467	3.745
25	1.316	1.708	2.060	2.485	2.787	3.078	3.450	3.725
26	1.315	1.706	2.056	2.479	2.779	3.067	3.435	3.707
27	1.314	1.703	2.052	2.473	2.771	3.057	3.421	3.690
28	1.313	1.701	2.048	2.467	2.763	3.047	3.408	3.674
29	1.311	1.699	2.045	2.462	2.756	3.038	3.396	3.659
30	1.310	1.697	2.042	2.457	2.750	3.030	3.385	3.646
31	1.309	1.695	2.040	2.453	2.744	3.022	3.375	3.633
32	1.309	1.694	2.037	2.449	2.738	3.015	3.365	3.622
33	1.308	1.692	2.035	2.445	2.733	3.008	3.356	3.611
34	1.307	1.691	2.032	2.441	2.728	3.002	3.348	3.601
35	1.306	1.690	2.030	2.438	2.724	2.996	3.340	3.591
36	1.306	1.688	2.028	2.434	2.719	2.991	3.333	3.582
37	1.305	1.687	2.026	2.431	2.715	2.985	3.326	3.574
38	1.304	1.686	2.024	2.429	2.712	2.980	3.319	3.566
39	1.304	1.685	2.023	2.426	2.708	2.976	3.313	3.558
40	1.303	1.684	2.021	2.423	2.704	2.971	3.307	3.551
42	1.302	1.682	2.018	2.418	2.698	2.963	3.296	3.538

(Contd.)

TABLE 2 (*Contd.*)

(1)	(2)	(3)	(4)	(5)	(6)	(7)	(8)	(9)
44	1.301	1.680	2.015	2.414	2.692	2.956	3.286	3.526
46	1.300	1.679	2.013	2.410	2.687	2.949	3.277	3.515
48	1.299	1.677	2.011	2.407	2.682	2.943	3.269	3.505
50	1.299	1.676	2.009	2.403	2.678	2.937	3.261	3.496
60	1.296	1.671	2.000	2.390	2.660	2.915	3.232	3.460
70	1.294	1.667	1.994	2.381	2.648	2.899	3.211	3.435
80	1.292	1.664	1.990	2.374	2.639	2.887	3.195	3.416
90	1.291	1.662	1.987	2.369	2.632	2.878	3.183	3.402
100	1.290	1.660	1.984	2.364	2.626	2.871	3.174	3.391
120	1.289	1.658	1.980	2.358	2.617	2.860	3.160	3.373
150	1.287	1.655	1.976	2.351	2.609	2.849	3.145	3.357
200	1.286	1.652	1.972	2.345	2.601	2.839	3.131	3.340
300	1.284	1.650	1.968	2.339	2.592	2.828	3.118	3.323
500	1.283	1.648	1.965	2.334	2.586	2.820	3.107	3.310
∞	1.282	1.645	1.960	2.326	2.576	2.807	3.090	3.291

TABLE 3
F Distribution Critical Values for P = 0.05

Denominator DF	*Numerator DF*													
	1	*2*	*3*	*4*	*5*	*7*	*10*	*15*	*20*	*30*	*60*	*120*	*500*	*1000*
(1)	*(2)*	*(3)*	*(4)*	*(5)*	*(6)*	*(7)*	*(8)*	*(9)*	*(10)*	*(11)*	*(12)*	*(13)*	*(14)*	*(15)*
1	161.45	199.50	215.71	224.58	230.16	236.77	241.88	245.95	248.01	250.10	252.20	253.25	254.06	254.19
2	18.513	19.000	19.164	19.247	19.296	19.353	19.396	19.429	19.446	19.462	19.479	19.487	19.494	19.495
3	10.128	9.5522	9.2766	9.1172	9.0135	8.8867	8.7855	8.7028	8.6602	8.6165	8.5720	8.5493	8.5320	8.5292
4	7.7086	6.9443	6.5915	6.3882	6.2560	6.0942	5.9644	5.8579	5.8026	5.7458	5.6877	5.6580	5.6352	5.6317
5	6.6078	5.7862	5.4095	5.1922	5.0504	4.8759	4.7351	4.6187	4.5582	4.4958	4.4314	4.3985	4.3731	4.3691
7	5.5914	4.7375	4.3469	4.1202	3.9715	3.7871	3.6366	3.5108	3.4445	3.3758	3.3043	3.2675	3.2388	3.2344
10	4.9645	4.1028	3.7082	3.4780	3.3259	3.1354	2.9782	2.8450	2.7741	2.6996	2.6210	2.5801	2.5482	2.5430
15	4.5431	3.6823	3.2874	3.0556	2.9013	2.7066	2.5437	2.4035	2.3275	2.2467	2.1601	2.1141	2.0776	2.0718
20	4.3512	3.4928	3.0983	2.8660	2.7109	2.5140	2.3479	2.2032	2.1241	2.0391	1.9463	1.8962	1.8563	1.8498
30	4.1709	3.3159	2.9223	2.6896	2.5336	2.3343	2.1646	2.0149	1.9317	1.8408	1.7396	1.6835	1.6376	1.6300
60	4.0012	3.1505	2.7581	2.5252	2.3683	2.1666	1.9927	1.8365	1.7480	1.6492	1.5343	1.4672	1.4093	1.3994
120	3.9201	3.0718	2.6802	2.4473	2.2898	2.0868	1.9104	1.7505	1.6587	1.5544	1.4289	1.3519	1.2804	1.2674
500	3.8601	3.0137	2.6227	2.3898	2.2320	2.0278	1.8496	1.6864	1.5917	1.4820	1.3455	1.2552	1.1586	1.1378
1000	3.8508	3.0047	2.6137	2.3808	2.2230	2.0187	1.8402	1.6765	1.5811	1.4705	1.3318	1.2385	1.1342	1.1096

TABLE 4
F Distribution Critical Values for P = 0.01

Denominator DF	*Numerator DF*													
	1	*2*	*3*	*4*	*5*	*7*	*10*	*15*	*20*	*30*	*60*	*120*	*500*	*1000*
(1)	*(2)*	*(3)*	*(4)*	*(5)*	*(6)*	*(7)*	*(8)*	*(9)*	*(10)*	*(11)*	*(12)*	*(13)*	*(14)*	*(15)*
1	4052.2	4999.5	5403.4	5624.6	5763.6	5928.4	6055.8	6157.3	6208.7	6260.6	6313.0	6339.4	6359.5	6362.7
2	98.503	99.000	99.166	99.249	99.299	99.356	99.399	99.433	99.449	99.466	99.482	99.491	99.497	99.498
3	34.116	30.817	29.457	28.710	28.237	27.672	27.229	26.872	26.690	26.504	26.316	26.221	26.148	26.137
4	21.198	18.000	16.694	15.977	15.522	14.976	14.546	14.198	14.020	13.838	13.652	13.558	13.486	13.474
5	16.258	13.274	12.060	11.392	10.967	10.455	10.051	9.7222	9.5526	9.3793	9.2020	9.1118	9.0424	9.0314
7	12.246	9.5467	8.4513	7.8466	7.4605	6.9929	6.6201	6.3143	6.1554	5.9920	5.8236	5.7373	5.6707	5.6601
10	10.044	7.5594	6.5523	5.9944	5.6363	5.2001	4.8492	4.5582	4.4055	4.2469	4.0818	3.9964	3.9303	3.9195
15	8.6831	6.3588	5.4169	4.8932	4.5557	4.1416	3.8049	3.5223	3.3719	3.2141	3.0471	2.9594	2.8906	2.8796
20	8.0960	5.8489	4.9382	4.4306	4.1027	3.6987	3.3682	3.0880	2.9377	2.7785	2.6078	2.5167	2.4446	2.4330
30	7.5624	5.3903	4.5098	4.0179	3.6990	3.3046	2.9791	2.7002	2.5486	2.3859	2.2078	2.1108	2.0321	2.0192
60	7.0771	4.9774	4.1259	3.6491	3.3388	2.9530	2.6318	2.3522	2.1978	2.0284	1.8362	1.7264	1.6328	1.6169
120	6.8509	4.7865	3.9490	3.4795	3.1736	2.7918	2.4720	2.1914	2.0345	1.8600	1.6557	1.5330	1.4215	1.4015
500	6.6858	4.6479	3.8210	3.3569	3.0539	2.6751	2.3564	2.0746	1.9152	1.7353	1.5175	1.3774	1.2317	1.2007
1000	6.6603	4.6264	3.8012	3.3379	3.0356	2.6571	2.3387	2.0564	1.8967	1.7158	1.4953	1.3513	1.1947	1.1586

TABLE 5

Critical Values of the Pearson Product-Moment Correlation Coefficient

df = *n* -2

Level of Significance (p) for Two-Tailed Test *df*	*.1*	*.05*	*.02*	*.01*
(1)	(2)	(3)	(4)	(5)
1	.988	.997	.9995	.9999
2	.900	.950	.980	.990
3	.805	.878	.934	.959
4	.729	.811	.882	.917
5	.669	.754	.833	.874
6	.622	.707	.789	.834
7	.582	.666	.750	.798
8	.549	.632	.716	.765
9	.521	.602	.685	.735
10	.497	.576	.658	.708
11	.476	.553	.634	.684
12	.458	.532	.612	.661
13	.441	.514	.592	.641
14	.426	.497	.574	.623
15	.412	.482	.558	.606
16	.400	.468	.542	.590
17	.389	.456	.528	.575
18	.378	.444	.516	.561
19	.369	.433	.503	.549
20	.360	.423	.492	.537
21	.352	.413	.482	.526
22	.344	.404	.472	.515
23	.337	.396	.462	.505
24	.330	.388	.453	.496

(*Contd.*)

TABLE 5 (*Contd.*)

(1)	(2)	(3)	(4)	(5)
25	.323	.381	.445	.487
26	.317	.374	.437	.479
27	.311	.367	.430	.471
28	.306	.361	.423	.463
29	.301	.355	.416	.456
30	.296	.349	.409	.449
35	.275	.325	.381	.418
40	.257	.304	.358	.393
45	.243	.288	.338	.372
50	.231	.273	.322	.354
60	.211	.250	.295	.325
70	.195	.232	.274	.303
80	.183	.217	.256	.283
90	.173	.205	.242	.267
100	.164	.195	.230	.254

Table 6
Chi-Square (÷^{2}) Critical Values

DF						*P*					
	0.995	0.975	0.20	0.10	0.05	0.025	0.02	0.01	0.005	0.002	0.001
(1)	*(2)*	*(3)*	*(4)*	*(5)*	*(6)*	*(7)*	*(8)*	*(9)*	*(10)*	*(11)*	*(12)*
1	0.0000393	0.000982	1.642	2.706	3.841	5.024	5.412	6.635	7.879	9.550	10.828
2	0.0100	0.0506	3.219	4.605	5.991	7.378	7.824	9.210	10.597	12.429	13.816
3	0.0717	0.216	4.642	6.251	7.815	9.348	9.837	11.345	12.838	14.796	16.266
4	0.207	0.484	5.989	7.779	9.488	11.143	11.668	13.277	14.860	16.924	18.467
5	0.412	0.831	7.289	9.236	11.070	12.833	13.388	15.086	16.750	18.907	20.515
6	0.676	1.237	8.558	10.645	12.592	14.449	15.033	16.812	18.548	20.791	22.458
7	0.989	1.690	9.803	12.017	14.067	16.013	16.622	18.475	20.278	22.601	24.322
8	1.344	2.180	11.030	13.362	15.507	17.535	18.168	20.090	21.955	24.352	26.124

(Contd.)

TABLE 6 (*Contd.*)

(1)	(2)	(3)	(4)	(5)	(6)	(7)	(8)	(9)	(10)	(11)	(12)
9	1.735	2.700	12.242	14.684	16.919	19.023	19.679	21.666	23.589	26.056	27.877
10	2.156	3.247	13.442	15.987	18.307	20.483	21.161	23.209	25.188	27.722	29.588
11	2.603	3.816	14.631	17.275	19.675	21.920	22.618	24.725	26.757	29.354	31.264
12	3.074	4.404	15.812	18.549	21.026	23.337	24.054	26.217	28.300	30.957	32.909
13	3.565	5.009	16.985	19.812	22.362	24.736	25.472	27.688	29.819	32.535	34.528
14	4.075	5.629	18.151	21.064	23.685	26.119	26.873	29.141	31.319	34.091	36.123
15	4.601	6.262	19.311	22.307	24.996	27.488	28.259	30.578	32.801	35.628	37.697
16	5.142	6.908	20.465	23.542	26.296	28.845	29.633	32.000	34.267	37.146	39.252
17	5.697	7.564	21.615	24.769	27.587	30.191	30.995	33.409	35.718	38.648	40.790
18	6.265	8.231	22.760	25.989	28.869	31.526	32.346	34.805	37.156	40.136	42.312
19	6.844	8.907	23.900	27.204	30.144	32.852	33.687	36.191	38.582	41.610	43.820
20	7.434	9.591	25.038	28.412	31.410	34.170	35.020	37.566	39.997	43.072	45.315
21	8.034	10.283	26.171	29.615	32.671	35.479	36.343	38.932	41.401	44.522	46.797
22	8.643	10.982	27.301	30.813	33.924	36.781	37.659	40.289	42.796	45.962	48.268
23	9.260	11.689	28.429	32.007	35.172	38.076	38.968	41.638	44.181	47.391	49.728
24	9.886	12.401	29.553	33.196	36.415	39.364	40.270	42.980	45.559	48.812	51.179
25	10.520	13.120	30.675	34.382	37.652	40.646	41.566	44.314	46.928	50.223	52.620
26	11.160	13.844	31.795	35.563	38.885	41.923	42.856	45.642	48.290	51.627	54.052
27	11.808	14.573	32.912	36.741	40.113	43.195	44.140	46.963	49.645	53.023	55.476
28	12.461	15.308	34.027	37.916	41.337	44.461	45.419	48.278	50.993	54.411	56.892
29	13.121	16.047	35.139	39.087	42.557	45.722	46.693	49.588	52.336	55.792	58.301
30	13.787	16.791	36.250	40.256	43.773	46.979	47.962	50.892	53.672	57.167	59.703

TABLE 7
ρ Critical Values for Spearman's Rank Correlation Coefficient
(Critical values for one-tailed tests using ρ)

N	*5%*	*1%*	*n*	*5%*	*1%*
4	1.000	*	18	.401	.550
5	.900	1.000	19	.391	.535
6	.829	.943	20	.380	.522
7	.714	.893	21	.370	.509
8	.643	.833	22	.361	.497
9	.600	.783	23	.353	.486
10	.564	.745	24	.344	.476
11	.536	.709	25	.337	.466
12	.503	.678	26	.331	.457
13	.484	.648	27	.324	.449
14	.464	.626	28	.318	.441
15	.446	.604	29	.312	.433
16	.429	.582	30	.306	.425
17	.414	.566	40	.264	.368

TABLE 8
Significance Value of Coefficient of Correlation*

Df	*.10*	*.05*	*.02*	*.01%*
4	.729	.811	.882	.917
6	.622	.707	.789	.834
8	.549	.632	.716	.765
10	.497	.576	.658	.708
12	.458	.532	.612	.661
14	.426	.497	.574	.623
16	.400	.468	.542	.590
18	.378	.444	.516	.561
20	.360	.423	.492	.537
25	.323	.381	.445	.487
30	.295	.349	.409	.449
35	.275	.325	.381	.418
40	.257	.304	.358	.393
45	.243	.288	.338	.372
50	.231	.273	.322	.354
60	.211	.250	.295	.325
70	.195	.232	.274	.302
80	.183	.217	.256	.283
90	.173	.205	.242	.267
100	.164	.195	.230	.254
200	.116	.138	.164	.181

The 90%, 95%, 98% and 99% two-tailed significance levels of the correlation coefficient are listed in the table below (assuming normally distributed datasets).

TABLE 9

Kolmogorov-Smirnov Test

(If calculated ratio is greater than value shown, then reject the null hypothesis at the chosen level of confidence.)

Sample Size (n)	*Level of Significance for D = Maximum $[F_o(x) - S_n(x)]$*				
	.20	*.15*	*.10*	*.05*	*.01*
1	.900	.925	.950	.975	.995
2	.684	.726	.776	.842	.929
3	.565	.597	.642	.708	.828
4	.494	.525	.564	.624	.733
5	.446	.474	.510	.565	.669
6	.410	.436	.470	.521	.618
7	.381	.405	.438	.486	.577
8	.358	.381	.411	.457	.543
9	.339	.360	.388	.432	.514
10	.322	.342	.368	.410	.490
11	.307	.326	.352	.391	.468
12	.295	.313	.338	.375	.450
13	.284	.302	.325	.361	.433
14	.274	.292	.314	.349	.418
15	.266	.283	.304	.338	.404
16	.258	.274	.295	.328	.392
17	.250	.266	.286	.318	.381
18	.244	.259	.278	.309	.371
19	.237	.252	.272	.301	.363
20	.231	.246	.264	.294	.356
25	.210	.220	.240	.270	.320
30	.190	.200	.220	.240	.290
35	.180	.190	.210	.230	.270
Overs 35	$\frac{1.07}{\sqrt{N}}$	$\frac{1.14}{\sqrt{N}}$	$\frac{1.22}{\sqrt{N}}$	$\frac{1.36}{\sqrt{N}}$	$\frac{1.63}{\sqrt{N}}$

TABLE 10
Critical Values of T in the Wilcoxon Matched Pairs Test

N	*Level of Significance*	*For One tailed test*	
	.025	.01	.05
	Level of Significance	*For two=tailed test*	
	.05	-02	.01
6	0	—	—
7	2	0	—
8	4	2	0
9	6	3	2
10	8	5	3
11	11	7	5
12	14	10	7
13	17	13	10
14	21	16	13
15	25	20	16
16	30	24	20
17	35	28	23
18	40	33	28
19	46	38	32
20	52	43	38
21	59	49	43
22	66	56	49
23	73	62	55
24	81	69	61
25	89	77	68

Index